T0214268

Lecture Notes of the Institute for Computer Sciences, Social Informatics and Telecommunications Engineering   310

More information about this series at http://www.springer.com/series/8197

Ana Lúcia Martins · Joao Carlos Ferreira ·
Alexander Kocian (Eds.)

Intelligent Transport Systems

From Research and Development to the Market Uptake

Third EAI International Conference, INTSYS 2019
Braga, Portugal, December 4–6, 2019

 Springer

Editors
Ana Lúcia Martins ⓘ
ISCTE-IUL
Lisbon, Portugal

Joao Carlos Ferreira ⓘ
ISCTE-IUL
Lisbon, Portugal

Alexander Kocian ⓘ
University of Pisa
Pisa, Italy

ISSN 1867-8211 ISSN 1867-822X (electronic)
Lecture Notes of the Institute for Computer Sciences, Social Informatics
and Telecommunications Engineering
ISBN 978-3-030-38821-8 ISBN 978-3-030-38822-5 (eBook)
https://doi.org/10.1007/978-3-030-38822-5

This Springer imprint is published by the registered company Springer Nature Switzerland AG
The registered company address is: Gewerbestrasse 11, 6330 Cham, Switzerland

Preface

We are delighted to introduce the proceedings of the second edition of the International Conference on Intelligent Transport Systems (INTSYS 2019) from the European Alliance for Innovation (EAI). This conference brought together researchers, developers, and practitioners from around the world who are leveraging and developing Intelligent Transportation Systems (ITS) to increase efficiency, safety, mobility, and tackle Europe's growing emission and congestion problems. The theme of INTSYS 2019 was "Intelligent Transport Systems (ITS) has the Edge on Innovation."

The technical program of INTSYS 2019 consisted of 20 full papers, presented in oral sessions at the main conference tracks, and selected out of 35 submission received. All of the accepted papers were subjected to a blind peer-review process with a minimum of four reviews for each paper. Concerning the committees, it was a great pleasure to work with the excellent organizing team of the EAI, which was absolutely essential for the success of the INTSYS 2019 conference. In particular, we would like to express our gratitude to Kristina Lappyova and Marek Kaleta for all the support they provided in all subjects. We would like also to express our gratitude to all the members of the Technical Program Committee, who have helped in the peer-review process of the technical papers, as well as ensured a high-quality technical program. We would like to thank the extensive list of external reviewers from several areas of expertise and from numerous countries around the world.

A special acknowledgement has to be addressed to all the authors for their effort producing such good quality papers and also for the extremely rich and positive feedback shared at the conference.

We strongly believe that the INTSYS conference provides a good forum for all researcher, developers, and practitioners to discuss all science and technology aspects that are relevant to ITS. We also expect that the future INTSYS conferences will be as successful and stimulating, as indicated by the contributions presented in this volume.

January 2020

Ana Lúcia Martins
Joao Carlos Ferreira
Alexander Kocian

Organization

Steering Committee

Imrich Chlamtac   Bruno Kessler Professor, University of Trento, Italy

Organizing Committee

General Chairs

Ana Lúcia Martins   Instituto Universitário de Lisboa (ISCTE-IUL), Portugal
Joao Ferreira   Instituto Universitário de Lisboa, Portugal

TPC Chair and Co-chair

Alexander Kocian   Pisa University, Italy

Sponsorship and Exhibit Chair

José Crespo de   Instituto Universitário de Lisboa, Portugal
  Carvalho

Local Chair

Vitor Monteiro   University of Minho, Portugal

Workshops Chair

Elsa Cardoso   Instituto Universitário de Lisboa, Portugal

Publicity and Social Media Chair

Carlos M. P. Sousa   Molde University College, Norway

Publications Chair

Vera Costa   Universidade do Porto, Portugal

Web Chairs

Marcia Baptista   INOV – Inesc Inovação, Portugal
Rui Maia   INOV – Inesc Inovação, Portugal

Posters and PhD Track Chair

Rossella Arcucci   Imperial College London, UK

Panels Chair

Rubén Pereira   Instituto Universitário de Lisboa, Portugal

Demos Chair

Frederica Gonçalves   University of Madeira, Portugal

Tutorials Chairs

Alberto Silva   Instituto Superior Técnico, Portugal

Conference Manager

Karolina Marcinova   EAI - European Alliance for Innovation, n.o., Belgium

Technical Program Committee

Ana Lúcia Martins   ISCTE-IUL, Portugal
Dagmar Caganova   Slovak University of Technology in Bratislava, Slovakia
Ghadir Pourhashem   Slovak University of Technology in Bratislava, Slovakia
Giuseppe Lugano   University of Žilina, Slovakia
Joao C. Ferreira   ISCTE-IUL, Portugal
Lorna Uden   Staffordshire University, UK
Lubos Buzna   University of Žilina, Slovakia
Marek Kvet   University of Žilina, Slovakia
Michal Kohani   University of Žilina, Slovakia
Michal Kvet   University of Žilina, Slovakia
Miroslav Svitek   Czech Technical University in Prague, Czech Republic
Peter Brida   University of Žilina, Slovakia
Peter Holečko   University of Žilina, Slovakia
Peter Jankovic   University of Zilina, Slovakia
Peter Pocta   University of Zilina, Slovakia
Porfirio Filipe   ISEL, Portugal
Teresa Grilo   ISCTE-IUL, Portugal
Sofia Kalakou   ISCTE-IUL, Portugal
Tatiana Kováčiková   University of Žilina, Slovakia
Veronika Sramova   University of Žilina, Slovakia
Vitor Monteiro   University of Minho, Portugal

Contents

Modelling

Design of a Route-Planner for Urban Public Transport, Promoting Social Inclusion

Rafael Dias[1], Tânia Fontes[2(✉)], and Teresa Galvão[1,2]

[1] Faculty of Engineering, University of Porto, Rua Dr. Roberto Frias,
4200-465 Porto, Portugal
[2] INESC TEC, Rua Dr. Roberto Frias, 4200-465 Porto, Portugal
tania.d.fontes@inesctec.pt

Abstract. People that do not have access to the transport system and therefore, a facilitated access to goods and services essential to daily life, can be regarded as transport-related social excluded. This is a big issue, namely for groups of people that have physical, sensorial and/or cognitive limitations. This paper provides guidelines to design route planners for socially excluded groups, by promoting social inclusion in public transportation. For this purpose, a set of mock-up user-interfaces of an inclusive inter-modal route planning application were developed. These interfaces will deliver ready availability of information about infrastructures and other journey related data.

Keywords: Information · Public transport · Social exclusion

1 Introduction

Public transport play a big role in today's society, especially because it facilitates the access to goods and services as health and education. As a result, transport-related social exclusion is part of our reality, since individuals that do not have access to the transport system can be regarded as excluded.

The term social exclusion was initially introduced in the European policy domain during the 1990s [1] and it was perceived as some sort of happening that stroke the poor exclusively. In the literature, the terms social exclusion, poverty and deprivation have often been used interchangeably [2]. These terms have been exhaustively discussed throughout these last decades, and, in its essence, they can be understood as the process whereby and individual becomes deprived, and not the actual deprivation itself, and in fact, poverty and deprivation can be argued as the outcomes of that process [2]. This means that the socially excluded are the ones who are not only poor, but also those who lost their ability to get a job or proceed education. Mackett et al. [3] explain that the exclusion process covers various circumstances where individuals or groups of people are unable to participate in activities or to access certain goods (e.g. services, work, school, etc.) that are available to others as a fundamental part of belonging to society [3]. Additionally, Kenyon et al. [4] state that mobility-related exclusion is the process by which people are prevented from participating in the economic, political and social life of the community because of reduced accessibility to opportunities, services and social networks, due in whole or in part to insufficient mobility in a society and

A. L. Martins et al. (Eds.): INTSYS 2019, LNICST 310, pp. 3–17, 2020.
https://doi.org/10.1007/978-3-030-38822-5_1

environment built around the assumption of high mobility. Thus, social exclusion is directly related to social disadvantage, transport poverty and transport disadvantage [5].

In Europe, especially in Hungary, Bulgaria and Romania, 90% of the citizens perceive poverty to be a widespread phenomenon, this value being considered the highest registered. In Denmark, Cyprus and Sweden mark the lowest values as 38%, 38% and 33% respectively [6]. According with the Eurobarometer [6], elderly, disabled and long term ill person, children and young people, and women are some of the groups most risk of social exclusion.

For social excluded groups that have physical, sensorial or/and cognitive limitations, the level of quality of information provision is quite important since strongly restrict its mobility. Park and Chowdhury [18] explain that the main barriers for physically impaired people are related to the urban environment, terminals and stops, services, and quality of footpaths, while the main barriers for visually impaired users are the poor presentation of information and obstructions on footpaths. Also, the common barrier for both groups is the bus driver's attitude and unawareness of their needs. Similar findings were found for other social groups with disadvantages [10, 14]. However, these barriers can be minimized if relevant, simple and reliable information is provided in order to allow passengers to travel as fast, comfortable, safe and cheap as they possibly can, while at the same time being able to easily access certain core information about the trip [7].

A trip planner can be considered a smart travel assistance tool, which can provide certain information to the passenger for a given origin and destination stops [9], minimizing thus, its social exclusion. However, sometimes such information needs to be provided contextualized, taken into consideration the needs and limitations of each travel profile. Houghton et al. [8] explain that advanced technologies can be used to collect more and better data, and the process of analysis can be also enhanced to create an end result that is more efficient, effective and targets services for passengers.

Cheung and Sengupta [11] assessed 20 popular route planners considering its features, usability and popularity. Bearing in mind a high level feature evaluation, Google Maps, TripGo, Here WeGo, Citymapper and TfGM have the best score. Concerning the usability evaluation, three main features have been considered: effectiveness, efficiency and satisfaction. The top five apps in usability are Citymapper, Traveline GB, TripGO, London Journey Planner and Transit, while the highest popular applications are Google Maps, MAPS-ME and HERE WeGo.

Note that not all the applications analysed support all public transport modes. For instance, 'MAPS.ME', 'Voyager' and 'Maps, Navigation & Directions' do not own information regarding trains, trams, buses and others. Meanwhile, 'Transit: Real-Time Transit App', 'Journey Planner (TFI)', 'Offi - Journey Planner' and 'London Journey Planner' are able to provide information about trains, trams and buses, but they do not support information about car, walking or bicycle trips. Among all the applications analysed, only 'Maps' by Google, 'My TfGM', 'TripGo' and 'HEREWeGo' are the only ones that, in addition to being considered multi-modal, also manage to create viable travel routes using car, walk, bicycle, train, tram, bus and other modes of transport available (i.e. scooter, boat). However, information regarding accessibility is not provided by these applications.

Besides these general and popular applications, few mobility applications have been developed taking in mind social excluded groups of people. HKeMobility [19] is a route planner for Hong Kong. This is an all-in-one mobile application integrating three previous mobile applications ("Hong Kong eTransport", "Hong Kong eRouting" and "eTraffic News") that offers an elderly friendly user interface. HKeMobility displays concession fares for the elderly and has simple user interface with high colour contrast. Also, Wu et al. [20] build a barrier-free and friendly environment for the disabled people, by using information and communication technology (ICT) based on past experience. These authors design a customer-centric transportation service platform. The platform enables customers to access diversified services, such as Rehabuses, LTC-buses, barrier-free taxis, Welcabs, and general taxis, through mobile applications, phones, websites, and convenience stores.

The literature review allowed to conclude that a substantial amount of groups of people are excluded in today society since they having particular needs and limitations that restrict its mobility. At this level, the main factor of social exclusion is the limitation to information access. Several applications for route planning of public transport were accessed; however, few barriers that limit the mobility of several groups of people are addressed by these applications. In order to promote social inclusion, this work aims to define a set of guidelines to design route planners of public transport for socially excluded groups with physical, sensorial and/or cognitive limitations. For this purpose, several interfaces that can allow for improving the experience in public transportation use for these groups will be designed and evaluated. Thus, the main questions of this research are:

(i)   What are the main current social excluded groups with physical, sensorial and/or cognitive limitations and why?
(ii) Which necessities and limitations do those groups have?
(iii) What kind of information regarding mobility do they need the most?
(iv) In what way should the information be organized and delivered?

The paper is organized as follow. Section 2 presents the data collection and the methods applied to conduct the study. Results and discussion are presented in Sect. 3 and the main conclusions are outlined in Sect. 4.

2   Material and Methods

This section presents a three-step methodology to define a set of guidelines to design route planners of public transport for socially excluded groups.

2.1   Scope

This work is focused on excluded groups with physical, sensorial and/or cognitive disabilities, henceforth, elderly, disable and people with reduced mobility (i.e. pregnant women, cane or crutches users, or people with physical or mental disability as blind and handicapped). This selection was based on four main criteria:

(i) *Some diseases can provoke mobility restrictions in particular groups of population:* Several diseases can provoke severe damage in the humans basic organs and lead to defectiveness such as: hearing loss (presbycusis), decrease of visual acuity (presbyopia), muscle loss, lower walking speed, mobility disability, cognitive aging, dementia and depression [15]. This means that physical obstructions as be steps, edges, steep lopes or simple obstructions on the pavement take a role on stopping the mobility reduced people from accessing public transport.

(ii) *The elderly population is growing fast:* The world's population aged 60 and older were numbered 962 million in 2017. This population increased more than twice in less than three decades and is expected to double again by 2050 [21]. In Europe, the elderly people (65 and older) will almost double from 87.5 million in 2010 to 152.6 million in 2060, growing from 19% in 2017 to 29.5% in 2060 [22, 23]. With life expectancy increasing in the coming decades the age structure of the European population will change significantly with the demographic old-age dependency ratio (people aged 65 or above relative to those aged 15–64) increasing from about 25% in 2010 to 51.2% in 2070 [22].

(iii) *The elderly can acquired with age more than one limitation:* Accessibility is rather affected as functional limitations become more common with age, and many older people will have acquired more than one such limitation [13]. The elderly social exclusion is related to long-term illness or disability, social isolation and lack of independence [12]. Other factors of elderly social exclusion are related with the loss of mobility due to the onset of partner illness or death, severe senescence or inability to drive [14].

(iv) *Some particular social excluded groups has particular needs of mobility:* Follmer et al. [16] found that shopping and leisure are the two most prominent motives for people above the age of 60 to travel. Many facilities such as food shops, libraries and town centres are believed significant for this group to have easy access to, being the healthcare services considered extremely important in this matter [10]. In addition, physical excluded people as pregnant and disabled records high access to health services.

2.2 Methods

The ISO 9241-210 was followed to ensure that the design created for an interface is user-centered. This allows to develop interfaces that address the user limitations and needs and therefore enhances efficiency as well as effectiveness of the interface and promotes well-being, satisfaction, accessibility and sustainability to the users [28]. This standard is supported in six main principles [29]:

(i) The design is based upon an explicit understanding of users, tasks and environments;
(ii) Users are involved throughout design and development;
(iii) The design is driven and refined by users;
(iv) The process is iterative;
(v) The design addresses the whole user experience;
(vi) The design team includes multidisciplinary skills and perspectives.

Based on these principles, a three-step methodology was defined: (i) requirements elicitation, (ii) interfaces development, and (iii) usability evaluation. Next sections presents a description of each of these steps.

2.2.1   Requirement Elicitation

Requirements elicitation were defined based on the identification of limitations and needs of physical disability people. Such analysis was supported by the results of: (i) literature review and (ii) data collected in the field.

In a first step, the literature review allowed to conclude that, people with sight problems might have a hard time seeing the letters or numbers and also colours, so the information has to be provided in a simple and intuitive way, utilizing icons and distinct colours to improve contrast [25]. Hounsell et al. [10] state that a wide range of information may be needed to attend the people needs, namely:

(i)   Bus and subway networks and routes;
(ii) Stop locations, like bus stops, in order to promote a better overall intermodal experience;
(iii) Schedule timetable of all the public transport services;
(iv) Ticket price for each trip;
(v)   Pavement conditions;
(vi) Overall accessibility in vehicles and stations.

The list of information stated by Hounsell et al. [10] is significant to any individual who uses public transport. For groups of people social excluded, the route planner should not, for example, merely describe a bus network or the fastest route. In this case, the application should provide the traveller information about routes that meet the individual capabilities, needs, preferences and restrictions of the users addressed [26]. In the case of elderly, these ranges from avoiding overcrowded buses to the inability of stair usage or simply having trouble understanding complex subway, bus or train stops.

In a second step, interviews and a survey were used to collect data in the field and to understand if the findings obtained from the literature review were in line with the observed in the field. Data was collected from users of a public transport network from a medium-sized metropolitan area (Porto, Portugal). This network is distributed along 1,575 km^2 and split into 26 zones, it serves 1.75 million inhabitants. The network is based on an intermodal system that includes: 126 buses lines (urban and regional), six subway lines, one cable line, three tram lines and three train lines [17].

The interviews were conducted in order to identify what features of a route planner for public transport would matter the most, what information they would seek and how they would like the information to be presented (i.e. icons or sentences). The questions ranged from the individuals personal use of public transport to the experience of using a route planning application. Appendix I shows the script followed. To easy conduct of interviews, three scenarios were defined in order to place the respondent in different situations:

(i)   a trip to go to a shopping mall just opened: extract information about which applications the person will use to find the route towards the mall. It will also inform us of which transport is preferable to the individual;

(ii)   a trip to go to the beach in a hot summer day: identify which transport would be more suitable for trips in a heat climate;

(iii) a trip to go work: identify what transport people use the most, and what bothered them while in that trip (i.e. overcrowd, loudness, heat, etc.).

The participants were selected considering three main requirements: (i) being the use of public transport, (ii) being the use of a smartphone and (iii) have more than 60 years. All participants in the interviews received information about the purpose and aims of the study and signed an informed consent form.

Interviews were conducted in presence and individually (N = 10) and each one had from 10 to 20 min long. Notes were taken during the interviews. Participants in the survey reveal that usually travel 35 min daily (90%) on buses (40%) or buses and subway (30%).

The survey was conducted to understand why or why not people use applications for route planning, in particular, to collect the feedback on what features and information would be important to implement in these apps so that it would make the person start using them. Four sections were defined, namely: (i) General approach and basic requirements; (ii) Route planning usage; (iii) Application disusage; and (iv) Application improvement. Appendix II displays the survey applied. The participants were selected considering two main requirements: (i) being the use of public transport, and (ii) being the use of a smartphone.

The survey was distributed by email to students and workers from the university as well as for several non-profit associations related with social inclusion of people with reduced mobility (e.g. Associação Salvador). Data was collected (N = 30) from people that travel daily, between 10 to 30 min each trip (50%), by bus. Data from people from different age ranges were collected ($N_{[18;30[} = 7\%$, $N_{[30;40[} = 27\%$, $N_{[40;50[} = 33\%$, $N_{[50;60[} = 17\%$, $N_{[60;100[} = 17\%$). From these, 36.7% have physical, sensory or cognitive limitations.

Data collected from interviews and from the survey have allowed to obtain valuable insights on what people consider useful and useless information in a route planner. The results from interviews and the survey are in line with each other.

In general, people seek an intuitive and reliable route planning application, which needs to be able to: (i) define in real-time the estimated time arrival of vehicles; (ii) state information about routes and schedules; (iii) maintain coherent schedules depending on traffic; (iv) alerts/notifications in case of traffic suspension, route or schedule changes; and the (v) indication of the existence or nonexistence of accessibility for wheelchair users or baby carriages. People that use route planning applications (80% and 60% of the participants in the interviews and survey respectively) mostly use it to gain information about estimated travel arrival, bus schedules (in particular during vacations and on holidays) and sometimes route planning. Information about malfunctions in the vehicles and other equipment, overcrowded transport, crosswalks near each stop and station, pinpointing ramps and elevators with the hypothesis of them having to use a wheelchair or a baby carriage, and detailed information about their location and how to reach a destination was also identified as information important to be included in route planning applications.

About 80% of the interviewed want to be notified mostly about whether the bus is going to miss or not and whether the vehicle is overcrowded or not. Prices are not considered as valuable information to obtain, but an online payment method should be integrated. Only 10% of the interviewed did not feel the need to use an application to help either create a route or check schedules and 40% of the survey respondents of the survey do not use any app to check schedules or plan routes. Most of the people do not feel the need to use while some use the website of the transport company, or simply do not believe in the information provided by the applications. Few point out that apps do not inform people about the accessibility of the vehicles and so they have no use for it. No differences were found between answers between people who or who do not use apps.

The data collected both from literature review and data collected in the field, allowed to identify what kind of information is lacking in route planners towards socially excluded groups selected in this study, particularly elderly. Based on that, some requirements to define the interfaces were defined:

(i) *Vehicle:* information about the type of vehicles that are touring through a route should be provided (e.g. the vehicle has or has not equipment to access a wheelchair).

(ii) *Stop/station:* information that help people locate themselves in subway stations or other locations that are part of the journey, for example, in which side of the street is the stop or how to get to a certain station should by delivered.

(iii) *Pavement:* while trying to access a station or moving inside it, information such as the location of crosswalks with light and sound signals, traffic lights, automatic stair cases, elevators, bathrooms, ramps and steps need to be considered.

(iv) *Schedule:* when travellers are on a station/stop waiting or a public transport or already in a vehicle they should be warned about multiple events that are happening or will happen in a near future, for example when to leave the vehicle, which stop comes next, how much time until the connecting vehicle arrives and which vehicle to enter and when.

(v) *Ticket price and purchase:* if a person is able to purchase a ticket in an app, it will reduce moving.

2.2.2 Interface Design

A web app called Figma was used to create the mock-up interfaces. This is an app that it is possible to run it in a browser and therefore on most operating systems. Figma provides all the tools needed for the design phase of a project, including vector tools which are capable of fully-fledged illustration, as well as prototyping capabilities and code generation for hand-off [24]. Figma also promotes team collaboration. Since it is browser-based, teams can collaborate as they would in Google Docs.

To design the application, first, a visual terminology to define equipment as stairs, elevators and crosswalks, and warnings as overcrowd places was established. Figure 1 show this terminology. Additionally, a crowdsourcing concept, that aims to improve the experience of people with reduced mobility in the use of public transport was defined. The interfaces cover multi-modal public transport information, in particular, information regarding the use of subway and bus. Information provision also includes information of how to arrive or leave a station or stop.

Symbol	Terminology
♿	Accessible space
👥	Overcrowd
👤	Low population
🚶	Crosswalk
🚦	Traffic light signal
◀))	Sound signal
🚌	Bus stop
🚆	Subway stop
🚶	Walk

Symbol	Terminology
📍	Destination
🔊	Audio speaker
🛗	Elevator
⚠	Warning/report situation
↰	Turn left
↱	Turn right
☆	Favourite
◺	Ramp

Fig. 1. Main elements terminology.

2.2.3   Usability Evaluation

The usability of an interface is closely associated with how easy it is for a user use it and it can be considered a quality attribute. Usability can be defined by five quality components [27]: learnability, efficiency, memorability, errors and satisfaction. To identify and understand what needs improvement regarding the interfaces developed previously, and if what has been done is viable or not, in this work, the effectiveness of the user interface of the low-level prototype, was assessed following the recommendations of Nielsen and Budiu [27]. Two stages were followed:

(i) *A session with experts:* a one-hour session was conducted with software developers experts for route planning of public transport. The session was organized in three steps: (i) an introduction to what had been done; (ii) a free exploration through the interfaces by the experts; and (iii) a discussion about the design and the information provided by the interfaces. Four experts participated in the tests.

(ii) *A survey:* the survey had the main objective to grasp how easy it was for the population to understand the information contained in the various interfaces. This survey contained most of the interfaces that were developed. For each interfaces responders were asked to access if the interfaces were easily perceived or not. For this purpose the Likert scale was used, ranging from 1 to 5, where 1 represented very easy and 5 represented very difficult. People that participated in the requirements elicitations was invited to participate in this survey. We collect N = 30 answers (one of the samples was disregarded due was incomplete). People from different age ranges ($N_{[18;30[} = 7\%$, $N_{[30;40[} = 17\%$, $N_{[40;50[} = 21\%$, $N_{[50;60[} = 28\%$ and $N_{>60} = 28\%$) and mobility experience was considered. Close to a third of the participants refer to had physical, sensory or cognitive limitations.

3   Results

The results of this work consisted in developing the interfaces for the inclusive and intermodal route planner and then evaluate their usability with experts in applications for public transport as well as a survey towards the population. Next sections present the main results obtained.

3.1 Interfaces

In Figs. 2, 3, 4 and 5, it is possible to see some of the interfaces that were developed and assessed on the usability survey. The symbol terminology previously defined is now clearly visible as an integral part of these interfaces. This allows for an intuitive and easy understand of the information that is being provided, as well as it helps develop a more interesting appeal.

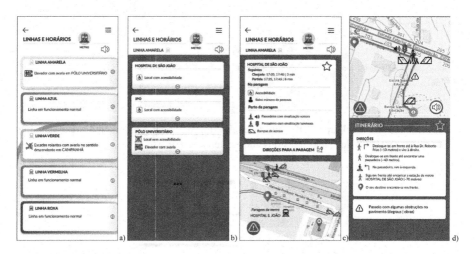

Fig. 2. Main screen mock-ups of the interfaces developed for subway.

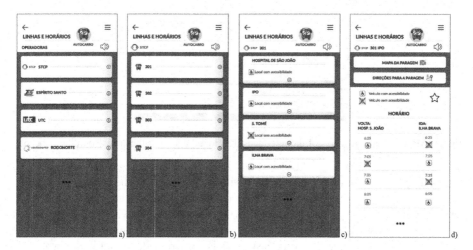

Fig. 3. Main screen mock-ups of the interfaces developed for buses.

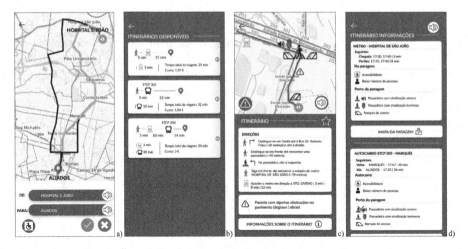

Fig. 4. Main screen mock-ups of the interfaces developed showing intermodal route-planning and several accessibility levels to the stops and vehicles.

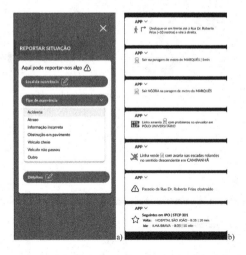

Fig. 5. Main screen mock-ups of the interfaces developed applying the crowdsourcing concept.

The results of usability evaluation, both with experts and with the general population through the survey conducted, allow to conclude that the interfaces are very intuitive and easy to interact with. Table 1 outlines the main results obtained with the survey.

The responders of the survey scored the interfaces around 1 and 2, that means that interaction with users is easy or very easy. This is extremely important in this work, as it has the objective to create simple and intuitive mock-up interfaces that contained a substantial amount of information towards mobility reduced people and people in general. Overall, most people considered the design appealing and intuitive. Only the interfaces with a bigger amount of information had a score of 2 or higher (i.e. easy, medium, difficult or very difficult). The survey had an open question after each interface, but barely anyone wrote any comments besides the good choice in colours and clean design.

Experts highlighted that users want information fast. Some interfaces, as the used to check schedules, demands too many button clicks. To solve this, they suggest add in the main page map a near the user location (also suggested by two responders of the survey). This way, the user could press the desired stop and instantly see the lines passing there, and with a second click check the schedules.

Table 1. Results of survey for the usability evaluation.

Variables		Screenshot	Average score
Terminology		Figure 1	2.0
Subway lines interfaces	List of lines	Figure 2a	1.1
	List of stations of a line	Figure 2b	1.1
	Station information	Figure 2c	1.8
	Route creation	Figure 2d	1.7
Bus interface	Operators	Figure 3a	1.9
	Lines	Figure 3b	1.2
	Stops of a line	Figure 3c	1.4
	Stop information	Figure 3d	2.0
Route planner interface	Map	Figure 4a	2.0
	Itinerary options	Figure 4b	2.1
	Itinerary to walk to a public transport stop	Figure 4c	2.4
	Itinerary in a public transport	Figure 4d	2.5

3.2 Guidelines

During the various research phases, including literature review, user observation, mock-ups design and usability tests, a number of usage patterns, themes and recommendations started to arise. The compilation of these findings resulted in a set of guidelines for designing mobile applications that may be used as guidelines for software developers and policymakers to support information exchange in public transport. Such guidelines can be described as follows:

(i) *Incentivise user participation:* user participation is crucial in developing interfaces both for the requirements elicitation as for the usability evaluation phase. Without the interviews and the survey conducted, the requirements specifications would only be dictated by the literature review, and there is a need to know people's opinions and compare them to the bibliography. For the usability evaluation, the best way to improve the design and identify what information is lacking is to promote feedback within the users. This will help future iterations to be more successful.

(ii) *Contextualization motivates the participation of users:* different environmental and/or personal conditions (e.g. sunny day vs. rainy day, working day vs.

holidays) may influence the use of different mobility ways. Nevertheless, during data collection people is mostly caught off guard and usually can't define quickly the influence of some of these factors on its daily mobility. In order to help participants in this process, mobility scenarios could be defined to help people to imagine different mobility situations.

(iii) *Information complementarity:* the requirements elicitation must be based on different data sources and using distinct data collection methods in order to be robust and complementary;

(iv) *Weight the data:* a wide variety of information can be initially thought and discussed, but it is essential to keep in mind what information are the users most interested in. This means that it is important to not overboard the interfaces with unnecessary data.

(v) *Ensure an intuitive design:* despite the age range that an app is oriented to, it should always be intuitive to provide high usability. Information must be clear and the icons should be carefully chosen;

(vi) *Information sharing:* The participation of passengers with their own knowledge about the transportation network is central to the success and usefulness of a mobility information-sharing platform. In this way a certain level of participation of users is required for the application to be useful and appealing as a source of public transport information. In order to leverage the vast crowd of consumers as providers, some gamification must be included.

4   Conclusions

A user-centered design was followed to define a set of guidelines to design route planners of public transport for socially excluded groups. To achieve this goal, a three-step methodology was defined: (i) Requirements elicitation; (ii) Interfaces development; (iii) and Usability evaluation.

In the first phase, a literature review and data collected in the field, through interviews and a survey, in a medium-sized European Metropolitan Area, was conducted. This allowed to identify the main social excluded groups, its main limitations and needs, and the information that is lacking in route planners of public transport. Based on the information collected, a set of requirements to design the user interfaces were defined. Then, the mock-ups were designed following these requirements. Lastly, the usability evaluation was accomplished by promoting a session with experts in software development for public transport and by conducting a survey to the population. In this process, the difficulty in perceiving the information was evaluated.

The social excluded group selected to study in this work were the people with physical, sensorial and/or cognitive limitations. This group was selected based on four main criteria: (i) Particular groups of population are affected by some diseases that can limit the perception and their mobility when physical obstructions as steps or edges are present on the path; (ii) The elderly population is growing at a fast rate; (iii) The elderly can acquired with age more than one limitation; and (iv) Some social excluded groups has particular needs of mobility, sometimes limited by their inability to drive.

The results achieved demonstrate that the methodology defined in this work was coherent and robust. The overall results demonstrate that the information provided to the users, especially to mobility reduce ones, was well handled and extremely accurate. Most people considered the design appealing and intuitive. This work covered most of the information needed to improve social excluded people public transport usage experience. Based on the findings, some guidelines for software developers and policymakers were defined.

Acknowledgement. This work is financed by the ERDF - European Regional Development Fund through the Operational Programme for Competitiveness and Internationalisation - COMPETE 2020 Programme and by National Funds through the Portuguese funding agency, FCT-Fundação para a Ciência e a Tecnologia within project PTDC/ECI-TRA/32053/2017 - POCI-01-0145-FEDER-032053. Tânia Fontes also thanks FCT for the Post-Doctoral scholarship SFRH/BPD/109426/2015.

Appendix

Appendix I: Interviews script

  (i)   Which modes of public transportation do you utilize and how often?
  (ii) What is the average time of each trip?
 (iii) How do you get information about the schedule?
 (iv) Name one positive and one negative factor about public transport.
  (v) Do you utilize a route planning app?

- If the individual said no to question 5, then:
  - For any specific reason?
  - What information would you like to receive in order to make use of a journey planner?
- If the individual said yes to question 5, then:
  - Which application do you use?
  - Which information do you retain as most important?
  - What attracts you the most about the design?
  - Which features do you consider very important in the app?
  - Which features would you like to see included in the app?

Appendix II - Survey script (requirements elicitation phase)
Part 1 - General approach

  (i)   Which age range do you belong to? ([18;30[, [30;40[, [40;50[, [50;60[and [60;100[years old)
  (ii) Do you use a smartphone? (Yes or No)
 (iii) With what frequency do you use public transport? (Daily, Sometimes per week, Sometimes per month or I do not use public transport)
 (iv) Which transport do you utilize? (Bus, Train, Subway, Private vehicle or Others)

(v)   Do you have any kind of physical, sensory or cognitive deficiency? (Yes or No)
(vi) Average time per trip? (<10 min, 10 < 30 min, 30 < 60 min or >60 min)
(vii) How do you obtain information about schedules? (Mobile app, Website, Bus stops, I do not need to know or Others)
(viii) Indicate 1 positive and negative factor about public transport. (Open answer)

Part 2 - Application usage or disusage

(i)   Do you use any app to route plan or check schedules? (Yes or No)

Part 3 - Application disusage (if answer No on Part 2)

(i)   What is the reason for the disuse of an app related with public transport? (Open answer)
(ii) Indicate 2 features that would make you use the an app. (Open answer)

Part 4 - Application usage (if answer Yes on Part 2)

(i)   Which application related to public transport do you utilize? (Open answer)
(ii) Which information do you consider most important in the app? (Schedules, Prices, Routes, Delays or Estimated time of arrival)
(iii) What other information do you consider important? (Open answer)
(iv) What attracts you the most in the design of the app? (Open answer)
(v)   What do you dislike the most about the design of the app? (Open answer)
(vi) Which features do you consider the most important in the app? (Open answer).

References

1. Shortall, S.: Are rural development programmes socially inclusive? Social inclusion, civic engagement, participation, and social capital: exploring the differences. J. Rural Stud. **24**(4), 450–457 (2008)
2. Kamruzzaman, M., Yigitcanlar, T., Yang, J., Mohamed, M.A.: Measures of transport-related social exclusion: a critical review of the literature. Sustainability **8**(7), 6–11 (2016)
3. Mackett, R.L., Thoreau, R.: Transport, social exclusion and health. J. Transp. Health **2**(4), 610–617 (2015)
4. Kenyon, S., Lyons, G., Rafferty, J.: Transport and social exclusion: investigating the possibility of promoting inclusion through virtual mobility. J. Transp. Geogr. **10**(3), 207–219 (2002)
5. Lucas, K.: Transport and social exclusion: where are we now? Transp. Policy **20**, 105–113 (2012)
6. Eurobarometer, TNS Opinion & Social, Opportunities Directorate General for Employment Social Affairs and Equal Opportunities, and Opportunities Directorate General for Employment Social Affairs and Equal Opportunities, "Poverty and Social Exclusion Report", p. 428 (2010)
7. Ștefănescu, P., Mocan, M., Ștefănescu, W., Neculai, P.V.: Trip planners used in public transportation. Case Study on the city of Timișoara. Proc. - Soc. Behav. Sci. **124**, 142–148 (2014)

8. Houghton, J., Reiners, J., Lim, C.: Intelligent transport: how cities can improve mobility. IBM, New York (Ref. GBE03232-USEN-00) (2009). https://pdfs.semanticscholar.org/90b8/ 4d9ca30a98a20a60f27af866cb0e7949f687.pdf
9. Rout, D., Borole, N., Vedagiri, P., Mathew, T.V., Goel, N.: Multimodal public transit trip planner with real-time transit data. Proc. - Soc. Behav. Sci. **104**, 775–784 (2013)
10. Hounsell, N.B., Shrestha, B.P., McDonald, M., Wong, A.: Open data and the needs of older people for public transport information. Transp. Res. Proc. **14**, 4334–4343 (2016)
11. Cheung, E., Sengupta, U.: Analysis of Journey Planner Apps and Best Practice Features. Manchester School of Architecture, MMU, Manchester (2016). http://e-space.mmu.ac.uk/ 618521/
12. Lodovici, M.S., Torchio, N.: Social Inclusion in EU Public Transport, European Parliament, Directorate-General for Internal Policies, Brussels (Ref. IP/B/TRAN/IC/2014-093) (2015)
13. Sundling, C., Berglund, B., Nilsson, M.E., Emardson, R., Pendrill, L.R.: Overall accessibility to traveling by rail for the elderly with and without functional limitations: the whole-trip perspective. Int. J. Environ. Res. Public Health **11**(12), 12938–12968 (2014)
14. Aguiar, B., Macário, R.: The need for an elderly centred mobility policy. Transp. Res. Proc. **25**, 4355–4369 (2017)
15. Barron, J., Jaul, E.: Age-related diseases and clinical and public health implications for the 85 years old and over population (2017). https://www.ncbi.nlm.nih.gov/pmc/articles/ PMC5732407/
16. Follmer, R., Lenz, B., Jesske, B., Quandt, S.: Ergebnisbericht - Mobilität in Deutschland 2008. Tempo, 214 (2008). http://www.mobilitaet-in-deutschland.de/pdf/ MiD2008_Tabellenband.pdf
17. TIP: Relatório e contas (2015). https://www.linhandante.com/uploadFiles/RC_TIP_2015-20160329.pdf
18. Park, J., Chowdhury, S.: Investigating the barriers in a typical journey by public transport users with disabilities. J. Transp. Health **10**, 361–368 (2018)
19. HKeMobility: Transport Department, HKSAR Government (2019). https://apps.apple.com/ us/app/id426108163
20. Wu, Y.J., Yuan, C.-H., Yuan, C.H.: A mobile-based barrier-free service transportation platform for people with disabilities. Comput. Hum. Behav. (2018, in press)
21. UN: World Population Ageing, Department of Economic and Social Affairs of United Nations, New York, Ref. ST/ESA/SER.A/397 (2017)
22. EU: Population ageing in Europe: facts, implications and policies. Publications Office of the European Union, Luxembourg (2014)
23. EU: The 2018 Ageing Report: Underlying Assumptions & Projection Methodologies, Publications Office of the European Union, Luxembourg (2017)
24. Kezz, B.: What is Figma? (2018). https://webdesign.tutsplus.com/articles/what-is-figma–cms-32272
25. Evett, L., Brown, D.: Text formats and web design for visually impaired and dyslexic readers-ClearTextforAll. Interact. Comput. **17**(4), 453–472 (2005)
26. Schlingensiepen, J., Naroska, E., Bolten, T., Christen, O., Schmitz, S., Ressel, C.: Empowering people with disabilities using urban public transport. Proc. Manuf. **3**, 2349–2356 (2015)
27. Nielsen, J., Budui, R.: Mobile Usability, 1st edn. New Riders, Indianapolis (2012)
28. Saito, S., Ogawa, K.: Ergonomics of human-system interaction. Jpn. J. Ergon. **30**(1), 1–1 (1994)
29. Travis, D.: ISO 13407 is dead. long live ISO 9241-210! (2011). https://www.userfocus.co. uk/articles/iso-13407-is-dead.html

Simulating a Three-Lane Roundabout Using SUMO

Bernardo Leite⑩, Pedro Azevedo$^{(\boxtimes)}$⑩, Rui Leixo⑩,
and Rosaldo J. F. Rossetti⑩

Artificial Intelligence and Computer Science Lab (LIACC),
Department of Informatics Engineering (DEI), Faculty of Engineering,
University of Porto (FEUP), Rua Dr. Roberto Frias, s/n, 4200-465 Porto, Portugal
{bernardo.leite,pedro.jazevedo,rui.leixo,rossetti}@fe.up.pt

Abstract. Transportation issues have imposed major challenges in many countries around the world, especially in large urban areas. A great deal of such challenges is related to factors such as: speed limits of particular sites, minimum safe distance between two vehicles, and the uncertainty inherent to drivers' behaviour. These apply to urban and inter-urban roads, to traffic flow models, and to traffic control at intersection points. Nowadays, there are several problems that lead to traffic congestion. Just to mention a few of them: waiting queues, drivers' increased reaction time after an accident, traffic shock waves, not abiding by intersections rules, and many others. Roundabouts are an example of spots where congestion represents a huge problem in need of a careful analysis in order to be solved. In this paper we will examine the effect of speed and acceleration reduction/increase within a roundabout, as well as the reduction of the minimum distance between vehicles, drawing conclusions about their flow throughout the roundabout. We use a method that combines several factors inherent to SUMO default car-following model (i.e. Krauss' model) in order to understand which configuration gives us higher performance in terms of throughput. Calibration was also a very important aspect to achieve good and realistic values. Future research will be needed to further study speed reduction relative to roundabouts. In addition, it will be necessary to calibrate the model, according to driver behavioural aspects of the studied region.

Keywords: Three-lane roundabouts · Simulation · Traffic ·
Car-following model · Speed · Gap acceptance · Acceleration · Krauss'
model · SUMO · Shock wave

1 Introduction

Roundabouts are widely accepted for their safety as they are better in this aspect than traditional signal-controlled or stop-signed intersections for car drivers, as argued by Hels and Orozova-Bekkevold [10], also implying capacity and environmental advantages. They have caused fewer injury accidents for both motor car drivers and pedestrians, as reported elsewhere [11,15].

© ICST Institute for Computer Sciences, Social Informatics and Telecommunications Engineering 2020
Published by Springer Nature Switzerland AG 2020. All Rights Reserved
A. L. Martins et al. (Eds.): INTSYS 2019, LNICST 310, pp. 18–31, 2020.
https://doi.org/10.1007/978-3-030-38822-5_2

The problem at hand is traffic congestion in roundabouts, assessing through a computer simulation whether a change in speed, acceleration and minimum distance (min gap) can result in better throughput and diminished waiting time. Congestion in roundabouts is a daily problem affecting many people, with higher incidence in the morning and late afternoon in urban centres. Moreover, the fact that many drivers do not know is that their contour rules make the circulation even more difficult. With the rush of not arriving late at work and with the worry to get home to rest after an exhausting day, drivers tend to create more traffic, even without knowing it. This happens because drivers usually change quickly to other lanes causing the so-called shock-wave effect, leading to a slowdown of all cars behind in a chain reaction. Besides all these problems, there are also an increasing number of accidents within rush hours creating even more problems by blocking an entire lane [3]. In order to improve the use of roundabouts we decided to analyze some changes relatively to speed, acceleration and minimum distance (min Gap) so as to understand the ultimate impact of doing so. We consider our approach well indicated, taking into account that there are several roundabouts recommendations regarding speed, acceleration and minimum distance [22]. It is important to determine which of them are the most effective for a better traffic circulation. From our point of view it is necessary to solve/improve this problem because it has a direct impact on people's daily lives. Thus, if we draw relevant conclusions about our Simulations, we will be able to indicate which factors are the most important and suitable for a better traffic flow in certain scenarios.

The remainder of this paper is as follows. In Sect. 2 we make an analysis on the available literature to gain a solid basis of the studies that have already been done in this area of research, from the various types of roundabouts to their inherent problems. We also look at speed and acceleration reduction approaches in order to achieve better roundabout performance. In Sect. 3 we will show our methodological approach clarifying which are our Data Requirements (input and output) as well our reference and what-if Scenarios. Specific details about each of the experiments will also be here explained. In Sect. 4 we will show the results obtained in each of our scenarios, and make a comparative analysis of them as well. In Sect. 5 we explain in detail the implementation we have done, particularly regarding the use of SUMO. Finally, Sect. 6 concludes with some discussion and notes about future development.

2   Literature Review

Shaaban and Hamad [17] present a method to analyze driver behaviour and estimate the critical gap for three-lane roundabouts. The operations of multilane roundabouts, especially three-lane roundabouts, are unique and more complicated than any other type of roundabouts. Data was collected at two roundabouts in the city of Doha, Qatar. Analysis showed that the vast majority of the vehicles accept the gap in groups and the critical gap was estimated accordingly. The overall critical gap value was 2.40 s. The critical gap for passenger vehicles was the lowest (2.39 s) compared to average (2.53 s). The study provides a new explanation for the operation of multilane roundabouts.

Guo, Liu and Wang [7] try to analyse the capacity of a roundabout based on the gap acceptance. Incoming vehicles can enter the roundabout when there is a time gap larger than the critical gap; otherwise, the vehicles need to wait until there is a large enough gap. The gap acceptance theory was used to analyze the entrance capacity of roundabouts, which can be derived from queuing theory involving two vehicle streams. They conclude, when the critical gap is constant, the deviation of the capacity model is conveniently used to obtain the equations and calculate the accurate capacity values.

Wang and Ruskin [20] propose a multi-stream minimum acceptable space (MMAS) approach based on cellular automata (CA) models to study non-signalised multi-lane (two- or three-lane) urban roundabouts. The method is able to reproduce many features of urban traffic, for which gap-acceptance models are not robust. The operations of two- and three-lane roundabouts are compared in terms of throughput. They conclude that the performance of tree-lane roundabouts is almost the same as two-lane roundabouts where left-turning (LT) vehicles use left lane only, right-turn (RT) vehicles using right lane only, and straight-through (ST) vehicles can use both lanes. The main advantage of three-lane roundabouts is not obvious for situations where LT vehicles are filtered out directly.

Silva and Vasconcelos [18] listed the roundabout types and their inherent problems in Portugal. This provided some background story to contextualize the current situation of our country concerning the problematic. They have shown that single-lane roundabouts are scarce, normally located on rural residential areas. The authors concluded that the main problems are: typical behaviours when some driver circulates inappropriately, geometrical design problems such as large roundabouts, lack of entry deflection, lack of channelisation and traffic signals, and obstructions in the central island. This work provides some useful information relatively to headway distribution models and estimation of critical headways.

Ziolkowski [23] points the fact that the high number of accidents occurring in roundabouts deserves a deeper study. This article concludes that the influence of roundabouts on drivers behaviour expressed by their speed in approach arms as well as by the manoeuvres they perform, vary depending on the geometric parameters of roundabouts, though this dependency is not uniform and so there is no direct relationship.

Al-Saleha and Bendakb [2] highlight the number of deaths and injuries due to roundabouts in Saudi Arabia over 15 years (1994–2008). For these authors it is clear from the results that many drivers do not follow traffic regulations on roundabouts and this explains the high number of accidents.

Leksono and Andriyana try to improve the traffic issues on Idrottsparken roundabout in Norrköping, Sweeden by providing an alternative model to reduce queue and travel time. They use two different simulations models: the first one adds an extra lane for right turn from East leg to North and from North leg to West; the second scenario restricts the heavy goods vehicles from passing Kungsgatan which is located in the Northern leg of Idrottsparken roundabout, during peak hours. This thesis concludes that the parameters which give more effects to calibration process in a SUMO project are the driver imperfection (σ) and the driver's reaction time (τ).

Figure 1 summarizes the contributions from the referenced authors in this section. For instance, data collection and gap acceptance to calibrate our model while SUMO gives us some insight into how microscopic roundabout simulations are done. For a further discussion on other microscopic simulation models, the interested reader is referred to [14] for an additional appraisal.

Authors/ Features	Roundabout types	Roundabout inherent problems	Gap Acceptance	Headway distribution models	Estimation of critical headways	Driver's behaviour	Data Collection	SUMO
K. Shaaban and H. Hamad	x		x	x		x	x	
Ruijun Guo, Leilei Liu and Wanxiang Wang			x	x	x	x	x	
Ruili Wang and Heather Ruskin	x	x	x			x	x	
A.Silva and L. Vasconcelos	x	x		x	x			
R. Ziolkowski						x		
K. Al-Saleha and S. Bendakb	x					x	x	
Catur Yudo Leksono and Tina Andriyana	x						x	x

Fig. 1. Related work gap analysis

3   Methodological Approach

In this section we begin by elucidating the way we develop the research presented in this paper. We present the starting point and then by describing our simulation scenarios as well as our setups for Car following-model calibrations.

3.1   Fundamentals of Roundabouts - Process Model

First of all, we start by clarifying that, by definition, a roundabout is a circular intersection (or junction) in which road traffic is permitted to flow in one direction around a central island, and priority is typically given to traffic already in the junction. Some relevant aspects are that vehicles circulate around the central island in one direction at speeds in a range of 25–40 km/h and multi-lane roundabouts are typically less than 75 m in diameter [4].

The flowchart below, Fig. 2, modelled using Business Process Model Notation, is a detailed description of a roundabout operation. This was the starting point of our research.

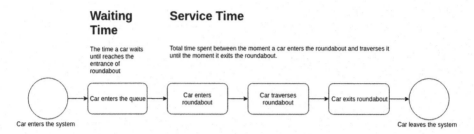

Fig. 2. Roundabout operation flowchart in Business Process Modelling Notation (BPMN)

The gap acceptance is based on the velocity of the vehicle moving in the front, and the maximum speed that can be attained by the vehicle that tries to overtake it. The entrance capacity, delay and queue length can be calculated by using the gap acceptance theory. In Germany, gap acceptance theory was well developed [21]. The base theory was proposed by Major, Buckley and Tanner [6,9]. The capacity model had been developed based on different signal timing, different lane numbers, and different vehicle traffic characteristics. After enormous amount of research, countries developed their own capacity methods for their own traffic conditions including Highway Capacity Manual in USA, Swedish CAPCAL, SETRA method, aaSIDRA, AUSTROADS and NAASRA in Australia, and CETUR method in Germany. This is very important to understand so we could achieve a gap acceptance that simulated the real case.

To understand the congestion problem, bottleneck's occurrence and to formulate solutions for it, a thorough study of vehicle-to-vehicle interactions is necessary [12]. These interactions are able to achieve with a car-following model. This brings to a common problem in traffic congestion called shock waves [13]. This are a chain reaction phenomenon which leads to traffic congestion well after the first car, the on who started the congestion, has departed [16]. Due to its perpetuation after the front car's leave it is akin to a ghost like occurrence. Shock waves happen fewer times by reducing the maximum velocity imposition within the lanes [8]. With this in mind, our main goal, is to prevent shock waves to happen so the throughput is higher by reducing the speed in case of congestion on a three-lane roundabout.

3.2   Experimental Scenario

Taking into consideration the previous subsection, now we are going to describe our particular case. It was decided to choose a roundabout that we knew well. This one is located in Ermesinde, Valongo, Porto, Portugal next to the Santa

Rita's church. To set peak hours for the roundabout saturation we decided to use traffic information made available by Google Maps. Through this information, presented in Fig. 3 we know the most critical times for congestion. Based on the color scale defined in Fig. 3 we can conclude that the critical moments (orange color) are at the end of the afternoon as predicted based on our experience and knowledge of this place.

Fig. 3. Santa Rita roundabout - color scale congestion by Google Maps (Color figure online)

These are our simulation Scenarios:

- Standard Roundabout: Base scenario which will serve as a control model in our simulation environment. It will be used to achieve the main values and the calibration setup as well as a base comparison to the other scenario;
- Standard Roundabout with maximum permissible speed variations: Similar to the standard roundabout, now with decreases in maximum speeds. This is the system we used to avoid shock waves having a better traffic flow.

3.3   Car Following-Model Calibration Setup

In this subsection we explain how was achieved, in the better way possible, the traffic situation shown in Fig. 3 by calibrating the car-following model. In traffic flow theory, car-following model is a method used to determine how vehicles follow one another on a roadway. These models describe how cars are spaced between each other and how many drivers react to changes caused by road events. Some well known models are: Krauss, Gipps and Wiedemann. Well will

Table 1. Default Krauss following-model parameters

Name	accel	decel	maxSpeed	minGap
Krauss	$2.6\,\mathrm{m\,s^{-2}}$	$4.5\,\mathrm{m\,s^{-2}}$	$55.5\,\mathrm{m/s}$	$2.5\,\mathrm{m}$

use the default modified version of Krauss Model used in SUMO as our reference. The default input parameters are defined in the Table 1.

We will focus on the following to achieve the best traffic scenario:

– Maximum Speed Imposition in indoor lanes: we evaluate the car flow of the outdoor lane and, at the same time, the effect of the overall throughput.
– Varying minGap: Here we study the effect of varying the minimum distance between two cars in terms of speeds and throughput;
– Varying minGap and accelaration: Here we study the conjugation of two of the attributes that characterise Krauss car-following model. The goal is also to understand the results in terms of speeds and throughput.

For our simulation plan we have perform around 10–12 runs per experiment. Each run lasts 2000 ms and is repeated if any of its output values is biased or unrealistic. If the warm ups prove to be long, we will use batches to only pay the warm-up price once, saving the state of the model after reaching a congested state, where the vehicles will have reached saturation speed. We end this simulation project when a satisfactory outcome is achieved or failing to fulfill it if the proposed number of runs is surpassed.

4 Implementation

The first step to implement the simulation was to export Santa Rita's Roundabout to the OSM format using Open Street Maps. From here we made the necessary changes in NETEDIT [1] so that the rules of the roundabout correspond to the existing one. Let's observe the final result obtained through NETEDIT in Fig. 4.

There are in total 28 detectors responsible for recording the velocities and the time that each vehicle pass by them. There are two detectors per entrance, one for each lane, same for the exits. Inside the roundabout there are 4 for each lane that covers the main junctions so we could collect data.

Every detector gives information about the moment each vehicle, enters, stays on and exists. Therefor, the entrance velocity can be defined as the velocity at the moment the vehicle exits the detector and the exit velocity as the given velocity when entering the detector.

RandomTrips.py, a script created by German Aerospace Center (DLR), that allowed us to populate the scenario with trips. We changed it to fit our needs, so it was possible to have a saturation point and to force every vehicle to pass through the roundabout. Also, we created a parser to collect all the data and

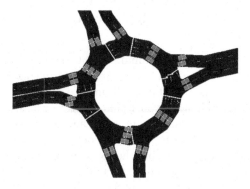

Fig. 4. NETEDIT final roundabout after subtle changes to match the real one.

manage to better understand the output information from each run and their detectors. Figure 5 represents an example of an experiment using SUMO-GUI. The roundabout is already in a state of saturation.

Fig. 5. Roundabout experiment, state of Saturation.

5   Results and Discussion

In this section we will explain in detail the results of our 3 experiments. The first experiment focuses on the imposition of maximum speed limits within the interior lanes of a roundabout. The second is about the krauss-following-model calibration relative to the minGap parameter. Finally the third one that combines the minGap and acceleration parameters to calibrate the same model. The discussion of experiences essentially addresses the possibilities and challenges that we find based on the results.

5.1   Experiment 1 - Speed Analysis According to Maximum Speed Impositions

No driver is perfect. Having that in mind, one of the main car traffic issues are shock waves. This happens due to a driver's reduction in speed leading to a chain reaction, where all the vehicles behind will have to stop originating congestion. In an ideal scenario, this phenomenon would not take place.

To prevent this event from happening we believe that if the vehicles circumventing a roundabout travel with a lower velocity, reaction time will increase and consequently, the vehicles entering the roundabout will be able to do it with greater ease and in a safer way. This will nullify the shock waves or at least minimise its impact in the eventuality of its occurrence.

In a three lane roundabout, in which each entrance has two lanes, generally speaking, the right most lane will always be the occupied by vehicles which will exit on the first exit. Due to this, after diminishing the maximum speed imposition in the right most lane, we observed that there were no significant results. Thus we consider that would not be relevant to reduce the maximum speed imposed on this lane.

Considering the above mentioned, we started to reduce the speed only for the middle and left most lanes. The average speed detected by the sensors at the entrances, middle and the exits of the roundabout are shown in Fig. 6 whereas in Fig. 7 the throughput results are shown.

Even after reducing the maximum speeds imposed on the innermost lanes, both entrance and exit velocities remain unchanged when compared to our base configuration. In spite of the fact, the roundabouts throughput increases, indicating that this is a promising experiment.

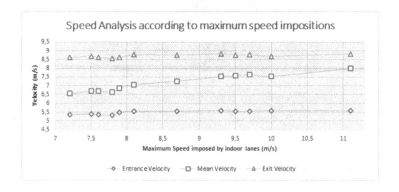

Fig. 6. Speed analysis according to maximum speed impositions.

After reducing the roundabout's maximum speed circulation following the criteria explained above, it's noticeable a higher number of cars traversing a roundabout. This way we can observe that reducing maximum speed of circulation is effective in a three lane congested roundabout.

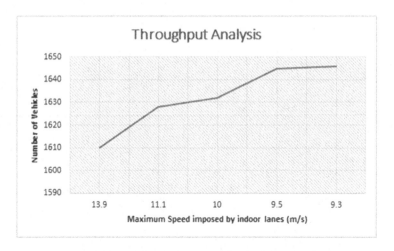

Fig. 7. Throughput analysis according to maximum speed impositions.

5.2   Experiment 2 - Calibration of the Krauss Model by Varying MinGap Parameter

The minimum safety distance between two vehicles is a very important topic in the context of car traffic. By definition we are talking about sufficient distance to avoid an accident if the front vehicle stops or reduces speed. This parameter proved to be very important in order to conclude about the impact on the roundabout throughput when its value is modified.

SUMO tracks gaps between vehicles that are on the same edge. By default, whenever these gaps are greatly reduced there is a possibility of collision between cars. Our goal was to prevent any kind of situations because this would invalidate our simulations. This way, we started by using SUMO default value (2.5 m) and from there, we added or subtracted small plots.

Comparing the graphic on Fig. 8 with the experience 1 presented on Fig. 6 we noticed that there are some similarities relative to entrance and exit mean velocities. However, there is now a significant difference, mean velocity for circulation has increased as the minGap decreases. This result is justified by the allowability of the short distances for drivers within the same lane. This gives them the possibility to maintain higher velocity values.

Concerning Fig. 9 we can observe significantly positive results regarding the throughput by decreasing the minGap between vehicles. These results were already expected but now it is necessary to discern and to decide what should be the minimum distance we could establish to maintain safety. We believe that a variation between 2.5 and 1.5 m inside a roundabout is safe but this is a debatable subject and requires more research.

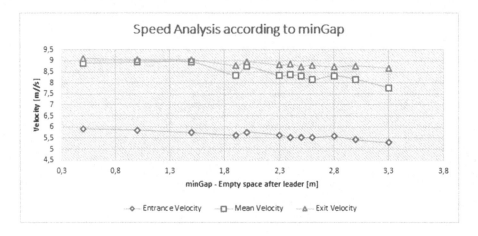

Fig. 8. Speed analysis by varying minGap.

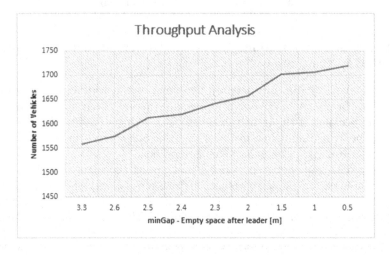

Fig. 9. Throughput analysis by varying minGap.

5.3 Experiment 3 - Calibration of the Krauss Model by Varying Acceleration and MinGap Parameters

In this experiment we try to go further in the studies of the parameters that characterise krauss car-following-model. In this case we add the acceleration to our analysis. We expect, as the acceleration is increased, the throughput will be improved. The same situation occurs for the diminution of minGap. Here we intend to find a balance between acceleration and minGap in order to find realistic and reasonable values.

If we observe the first table below we conclude that the best conjugation of values would be with minGap $= 2.4$ m and accel $= 3.2\,\mathrm{m\,s^{-2}}$, giving us a value of 1688 vehicles that concluded the simulation with a saturated roundabout. If we look at Table 2 these values are reinforced because they allow a minimum time of circulation equal to 11.23 s.

Although these values are the best we want, as we said before, we want to find values that are more realistic and that provide equally good results. This way, we suggest using the minGap = 2.8 m and accel = 2.9 m s^{-2} configuration, since it has a result in terms of throughput equal to 1684 (less four compared to the previous one) and a circulation time of 11.84 (more 0.61) (Table 3).

For this last proposed configuration the results are very close to the previous ones with two differences to highlight. The acceleration is lower and the minGap is larger providing greater safety to the driver and all the surroundings.

Table 2. Throughput according to acceleration and minGap parameters

minGap/accel	2.4	2.6	2.9	3.2
3.3	1545	1558	1596	1643
2.8	1603	1628	1684	1681
2.4	1614	1620	1677	1688

Table 3. Recorded average times [s] of circulation according to acceleration and min-Gap parameters

minGap/accel	2.4	2.6	2.9	3.2
3.3	15.08	16.14	13.80	11.97
2.8	14.32	12.94	11.84	11.11
2.4	13.13	13.18	13.61	11.23

6 Conclusions

From our experiments we are able to draw some interesting inferences. Firstly, by imposing a maximum speed reduction on the two innermost routes within the roundabout, we conclude that it is possible to significantly improve throughput. In order to obtain such reduction in vehicle speed we suggest the use of speed bumps or a more rugged pavement, because solely decreasing the allowed maximum speed for the entire roundabout is not enough to enforce it. On the other hand, by studying the impact of the minimum safety distance between vehicles we also observed significant improvements in the flow of cars at the roundabout. It is important to note that safety distances must be met in the context of a particular roundabout, taking into account its characteristics. The Krauss' car-following model calibration for acceleration and minGap parameters allowed us to find a balance between minimum safe distance and adequate acceleration.

The main lesson that we draw is that some results obtained through simulation in a traffic context may not be linear. We are aware of this because there are many factors to take into account when, for example, a parameter such as the maximum speed (or acceleration) is changed. A change in one of these parameters causes a particular trip to perform in a different way and when coupled with thousands of trips the result may not be what was expected. In spite of this we believe that our efforts to make a correct calibration of the default SUMO model helped leading us to quite satisfactory conclusions.

As final remarks we would like to mention that there are several paths in order to continue this study. As future work, the procedures used in the Krauss' car-following model could be improved with more iterations and also varying other parameters such as reaction time, and driver imperfection factor. In addition, it has the potential of being extensible with other car-following models. It is also possible to continue this work by creating new geometries for such roundabouts and analyse how the new designs affect results. We also intend to enrich the behaviour of vehicles using the agent-based models through the combination of SUMO and TraSMAPI [5,19].

References

1. NETEDIT, graphical network editor for SUMO. https://sumo.dlr.de/docs/NETEDIT.html. Accessed 30 Sept 2019
2. Al-Saleh, K., Bendak, S.: Drivers' behavior at roundabouts in Riyadh. Int. J. Inj. Control Saf. Promot. **19**, 19–25 (2011). https://doi.org/10.1080/17457300.2011.581378
3. Silva, A.B., Vasconcelos, L.: Roundabouts in Portugal state of the art (2011)
4. Ashley, C.A.: Traffic and Highway Engineering for Developments. Blackwell Scientific Publications, Hoboken (1994)
5. Azevedo, T., de Araújo, P.J.M., Rossetti, R.J.F., Rocha, A.P.C.: JADE, TraSMAPI and SUMO: a tool-chain for simulating traffic light control. CoRR abs/1601.08154 (2016). http://arxiv.org/abs/1601.08154
6. Daganzo, C.F.: Traffic delay at unsignalized intersections: clarification of some issues. Transp. Sci. **11**(2), 180–189 (1977). https://doi.org/10.1287/trsc.11.2.180
7. Guo, R., Liu, L., Wang, W.: Review of roundabout capacity based on gap acceptance. J. Adv. Transp. **2019**, 1–11 (2019). https://doi.org/10.1155/2019/4971479
8. Hegyi, A., De Schutter, B., Hellendoorn, J.: Optimal coordination of variable speed limits to suppress shock waves. IEEE Trans. Intell. Transp. Syst. **6**(1), 102–112 (2005). https://doi.org/10.1109/TITS.2004.842408
9. Heidemann, D., Wegmann, H.: Queueing at unsignalized intersections. Transp. Res. Part B: Methodol. **31**(3), 239–263 (1997). https://doi.org/10.1016/S0191-2615(96)00021-5
10. Hels, T., Orozova-Bekkevold, I.: The effect of roundabout design features on cyclist accident rate. Accid. Anal. Prev. **39**, 300–307 (2007). https://doi.org/10.1016/j.aap.2006.07.008
11. Hydén, C., Varhelyi, A.: The effects on safety, time consumption and environment of large scale use of roundabouts in an urban area: a case study. Accid. Anal. Prev. **32**, 11–23 (2000)

12. Kanagaraj, V., Asaithambi, G., Kumar, C.N., Srinivasan, K.K., Sivanandan, R.: Evaluation of different vehicle following models under mixed traffic conditions. Procedia - Soc. Behav. Sci. **104**, 390–401 (2013). https://doi.org/10.1016/j.sbspro. 2013.11.132. 2nd Conference of Transportation Research Group of India (2nd CTRG)

13. Leksono, C.Y., Andriyana, T.: Roundabout microsimulation using SUMO: a case study in Idrottsparken Roundabout Norrkping, Sweden. Master's thesis, Linköping University (2012)

14. Passos, L.S., Rossetti, R.J.F., Kokkinogenis, Z.: Towards the next-generation traffic simulation tools: a first appraisal. In: 6th Iberian Conference on Information Systems and Technologies (CISTI 2011), pp. 1–6, June 2011

15. Retting, R., Persaud, B., Gårder, P., Lord, D.: Crash and injury reduction following installation of roundabouts in the united states. Am. J. Public Health **91**, 628–31 (2001). https://doi.org/10.2105/AJPH.91.4.628

16. Richards, P.I.: Shock waves on the highway. Oper. Res. **4**(1), 42–51 (1956). https://doi.org/10.1287/opre.4.1.42

17. Shaaban, K., Hamad, H.: Group gap acceptance: a new method to analyze driver behavior and estimate the critical gap at multilane roundabouts. J. Adv. Transp. **2018**, 1–9 (2018). https://doi.org/10.1155/2018/1350679

18. Silva, A.B., Santos, S., Vasconcelos, L., Seco, Á., Silva, J.P.: Driver behavior characterization in roundabout crossings. Transp. Res. Procedia **3**, 80–89 (2014). 17th Meeting of the EURO Working Group on Transportation, EWGT 2014, 2–4 July 2014, Sevilla, Spain

19. Timóteo, I.J.P.M., Araújo, M.R., Rossetti, R.J.F., Oliveira, E.C.: TraSMAPI: an API oriented towards multi-agent systems real-time interaction with multiple traffic simulators. In: 13th International IEEE Conference on Intelligent Transportation Systems, pp. 1183–1188, September 2010. https://doi.org/10.1109/ITSC.2010. 5625238

20. Wang, R., Ruskin, H.: Modelling traffic flow at multi-lane urban roundabouts. Int. J. Mod. Phys. C **19**, 693–710 (2006). https://doi.org/10.1142/S0129183106008777

21. Wu, N.: A universal procedure for capacity determination at unsignalized (priority-controlled) intersections. Transp. Res. Part B: Methodol. **35**(6), 593–623 (2001). https://doi.org/10.1016/S0191-2615(00)00012-6

22. Zhao, M., Käthner, D., Söffker, D., Meike, J., Lemmer, K.: Modeling driving behavior at roundabouts: impact of roundabout layout and surrounding traffic on driving behavior, January 2017

23. Ziolkowski, R.: The influence of roundabouts on drivers' speed and behaviour, vol. 1020, June 2014. https://doi.org/10.4028/www.scientific.net/AMR.1020.674

Directional Grid-Based Search for Simulation Metamodeling Using Active Learning

Francisco Antunes[1]([✉]), Francisco Pereira[2], and Bernardete Ribeiro[1]

[1] University of Coimbra, Rua Sílvio Lima - Polo II, 3030-790 Coimbra, Portugal
fnibau@uc.pt
[2] Technical University of Denmark, Bygningstorvet, 2800 Kongens Lyngby, Denmark

Abstract. Within dense urban environments, real-world transportation systems are often associated with extraordinary modeling complexity. Where standard analytic methods tend to fail, simulation tools emerge as reliable approaches to study such systems. Despite their versatility, simulation models can prove to be computational burdens, exhibiting prohibitive simulation runtimes. To address this shortcoming, metamodels are used to aid in the simulation modeling process.

In this paper, we propose a directional training scheme, combining both active learning and simulation metamodeling, to address the challenge of exploring the input space, within the context of computationally expensive simulation models. Using a Gaussian Process (GP) as a simulation metamodel, we guide the exploration process towards the identification of specific regions of the input space that trigger a particular simulation output search value of interest defined a priori by the user, saving a significant amount of simulation time in the process.

The results obtained from applying our methodology to an Emergency Medical Service (EMS) simulator, show that it is capable of identifying such important input regions while minimizing the number of simulation runs at the same time, thus making the simulation input space exploration process more efficient.

Keywords: Machine learning · Active learning · Simulation metamodeling · Gaussian Processes

1 Introduction

Real-world urban transportation environments are systems often exhibiting overwhelming complexity and multidimensional dynamism. These intrinsic properties traditionally pose effective and practical constraints when it comes to the modeling process. Simulation tools are usually regarded as the only reliable approach to study such complex systems [22]. However, despite their obvious advantages, simulation models are not exempted from its drawbacks.

© ICST Institute for Computer Sciences, Social Informatics and Telecommunications Engineering 2020
Published by Springer Nature Switzerland AG 2020. All Rights Reserved
A. L. Martins et al. (Eds.): INTSYS 2019, LNICST 310, pp. 32–46, 2020.
https://doi.org/10.1007/978-3-030-38822-5_3

Perhaps the most evident and persistent disadvantage is that when designed with sufficiently high resolution and realism, simulation methods tend to exhibit prohibitive runtimes and massive computational workloads, even considering today's standards. A straightforward solution to this problem is to consider the use of simulation metamodels [11], which are specially conceived to approximate the simulation results and, consequently, the underlying function inevitably defined by the simulation model itself.

Within similar experimental setups, characterized by the lack or expensiveness of data, active learning emerges as a dominant modeling paradigm that tries to address this problem, being particularly popular among the machine learning community. Similarly to the simulation metamodels, the primary goal of active learning is to reduce the computational burden during the learning stage of a given machine learning model. It provides any model the ability to choose the most informative data points from which it learns, making it perform better with less training points and in a more efficient manner [28].

In this work, we propose a directional training scheme that combines the best of both worlds, active learning and simulation metamodeling, to address the challenge of exploring the input space, within the context of computationally expensive simulation models. A Gaussian Process (GP) is employed as a simulation metamodel, guiding the exploration process towards the identification of specific regions of the input space that trigger a particular simulation output search value of interest defined a priori by the user.

Using an Emergency Medical Service simulation model, the results show that the proposed approach can identify such important input regions while minimizing the number of required simulation runs at the same time, thus effectively making the exploration process of the simulation input space computationally more efficient.

2   Background

Simulation metamodeling [12, 16, 17, 21] is quite an old topic among the simulation literature [5]. Its main purpose is to develop and provide approximation models for the simulation results, allowing for a systematic exploration of the functional behavior of complex and time-consuming simulation models in a rather less expensive way.

Simulation models are usually associated with computationally fast and structurally simple functions that map the same input/output domains of the original simulator. Hence, metamodels should reflect both the problem entity under study (e.g., some real-world system) and the simulation model itself. However, the validation degree is closely related to the accuracy requirements, which eventually depend on the metamodeling goals. In [19], four possible primary goals are identified, namely, problem entity understanding, simulation output prediction, optimization, and verification/validation. In this work, however, we are mostly concerned with understanding the real underlying system and with assessing the prediction performance of the metamodel. We assume that the simulation model of interest is ideally validated, verified, optimized, and thus calibrated concerning the real problem under study.

The simplest applications of simulation metamodeling involved queuing systems with linear models as approximation functions [16]. Due to their simplicity and easy interpretation, GPs are also quite popular as simulation metamodels [6,8,10,18]. Although their application essentially started as deterministic simulation approximators, it was later extended to stochastic ones [3,7,20,29].

Similarly, as simulation metamodels are designed to reduce the computational burden of systematic and exhaustive computer experiments, active learning aims to increase the predictive performance of a given model with a few training points as possible. It does so by providing the model with the ability to actively choose the most informative data points that should be included in the training set, which iteratively expands as the fitting stage evolves.

As seen in [30], any active learning scheme is traditionally comprised of five key players, summarily presented in

$$(\mathcal{L}, \mathcal{U}, \mathcal{M}, \mathcal{O}, \mathcal{Q}).$$

The first two elements represent the labeled and unlabeled data sets, respectively. As active learning is often associated with modeling scenarios where labeled data is scarce or expensive to obtain, the size of $\mathcal{U}$ is oftentimes massively greater than that of $\mathcal{L}$. Next, we have $\mathcal{M}$, which denotes the machine learning model or any other kind of predictive algorithm, followed by $\mathcal{O}$, which represents the labeled instance provider, commonly known as the oracle. The only role of the latter is to provide labeled instances from the ground truth function underlying the process of the system under study. A human annotator traditionally played the role of the oracle. However, it can take several forms, as long as it constitutes a label provider, which trivially includes simulators, among others. Finally, $\mathcal{Q}$ is the query function, which essentially defines how the new data points should be selected from $\mathcal{L}$ to be labeled by $\mathcal{O}$. It commonly encompasses not only search strategies but also criteria to evaluate which are the most informative instances that best increase the performance of $\mathcal{M}$.

Closely associated with the query function is the definition of the stopping criteria. Being an iterative sampling method, active learning must be stopped at some point in time. As pointed out in [28], this point can be identified in two decisive situations: (a) when the cost of obtaining a new labeled point is higher than the model's errors and (b) when the model has reached a performance threshold, from which the addition of new training points will have no or almost no effect.

Due to its Bayesian properties, a GP can be easily implemented to follow an active learning scheme. As its predictions come in the form of fully-defined probability distributions, rather than single point-wise estimates, it accounts for data uncertainty in a quite intuitive way. Assuming that the predictive variance can be considered a proxy for informativeness, the GPs can be used to explore the most informative points within a given simulation input space. These approaches are commonly associated with exploration-exploitation strategies in Bayesian Optimization problems [15,23].

3 Approach

Our approach is based on an active learning scheme built on the top of a simulation metamodeling approach, and it is specially designed to extract relevant information regarding the underlying simulation model under study with as few simulation runs as possible. First, we introduce the GP modeling framework, acting as our simulation metamodel, and then move to the presentation of the proposed approach.

3.1 Gaussian Process

According to [27], a GP is a stochastic process in which any finite set of variables follows a multivariate Gaussian distribution. This collection of random variables is fully characterized by a pair of functions, namely, a mean and a covariance (or kernel) function, respectively represented and defined by $m_f(\mathbf{x}) = \mathbb{E}[f(\mathbf{x})]$ and $k_f(\mathbf{x}, \mathbf{x}') = \mathbb{E}[(f(\mathbf{x}) - m_f(\mathbf{x}))(f(\mathbf{x}') - m_f(\mathbf{x}'))]$, with x and x' being two different D-dimensional input data points. Consequently, a GP is often denoted by $\mathcal{GP}(m_f(\mathbf{x}), k_f(\mathbf{x}, \mathbf{x}'))$. When applied to regression problems, the GP framework is known as Kriging [9]. Such denomination has its origins in the geostatistics field.

The GP framework places a prior over functions. Within a regression setup, this means that the functional relationship between the dependent variable $\mathbf{x}$ and the independent variable y is assumed to follow a GP. Formally put, we have $y = f(\mathbf{x}) + \epsilon$, where $f(\mathbf{x}) \sim \mathcal{GP}(m_f(\mathbf{x}), k_f(\mathbf{x}, \mathbf{x}'))$ and $\epsilon \sim \mathcal{N}(0, \sigma^2)$. Thus, the values of the signal function f are represented by the random variables comprising the GP and defined over an high-dimensional feature space, for example, $\mathbb{R}^D$.

For prediction purposes, the conditional distribution of a new test point $\mathbf{x}_*$ is given by

$$f_* | X, \mathbf{y}, \mathbf{x}_* \sim \mathcal{N}(\bar{\mathbf{f}}_*, cov(\mathbf{f}_*)),$$

with

$$\bar{\mathbf{f}}_* \triangleq \mathbb{E}[f_* | X, \mathbf{y}, \mathbf{x}_*] = k_{f*}^\top [K_y]^{-1} \mathbf{y},$$
$$cov(\mathbf{f}_*) = \mathbb{V}[f_*] = k_{f**} - k_{f*}^\top [K_y]^{-1} k_{f*},$$

where $k_{f*} = k_f(X, \mathbf{x}_*)$, $k_{f**} = k_f(\mathbf{x}_*, \mathbf{x}_*)$, and $(X, \mathbf{y})$ representing the training data set. Here, notice that instead of a point-wise prediction, each GP prediction is associated with a completely defined Gaussian distribution, allowing it for a effective Bayesian treatment of the uncertainty not only present in the training data but also regarding its the predictions themselves.

Most of the functions used to define GPs have a set of free parameters (also called hyper-parameters), allowing for their optimization with respect to the training data, commonly via maximum likelihood estimation. However, mainly for simplicity reasons, the mean function can be set to zero for the majority of the applications. On the contrary, the covariance function plays a vital role in the modeling performance of the GP.

In this work, we use the Squared-Exponential with Automatic Relevance Determination (SE-ARD) function as the GP's kernel, generally defined as

$$k(\mathbf{x}, \mathbf{x}') = \sigma_f^2 \exp\left(-\frac{1}{2}(\mathbf{x} - \mathbf{x}')^\top M(\mathbf{x} - \mathbf{x}')\right),$$

where σ_f^2 corresponds to the variance of the underlying signal function f, $M = diag(\boldsymbol{\sigma})^{-2}$ and $\boldsymbol{\sigma} = [\sigma_1, \sigma_2, \ldots, \sigma_D]^\top$ is a positive real-valued vector. Each diagonal element of M represents the characteristic length-scale for each of the D input dimensions. These length-scales weight the importance of the each dimension during the inference process. The standard version of the SE version with isotropic distance measure can be obtained by setting $\sigma_1 = \sigma_2 = \ldots = \sigma_D$. This function is one of the most widely used kernel functions, not only for GPs but also for other well-known kernel-based machines, such as the Support Vector Machines (SVMs).

3.2   Directional Grid-Based Search

The modeling approach developed in this work is summarized in Algorithm 1, combining elements of both active learning and simulation metamodelling strategies.

Before running the algorithm, three entities must be defined a priori, namely, the search value (sV), the initial training grid ($trGrid$), and the search grid ($sGrid$). Whereas sV and $sGrid$ are fixed, $trGrid$ evolves over time. The basic idea of the presented methodology is to use a GP to guide the expansion process of $trGrid$ towards the identification of simulation input regions that trigger simulation output values close to sV. In other words, this methodology allows the user to search for sets of input values whose simulation results are close to a pre-specified output of interest, by conducting sequential predictions over $sGrid$. For the sake of simplicity, we focus on the two-dimensional case. An illustration of the grid-based training unit used in this work is depicted in Fig. 1(a).

We call it directional since it steers the simulation requests (or runs) exclusively in the direction of those input values that are more likely to assume output values similar to sV. On the other hand, it is grid-based as it comprises a series of iterative training grids used to locally approximate the simulation results within the neighborhoods of the search value. By proceeding in such a directional way, we can minimize the number of required simulation runs, therefore making the input space exploration process faster and computationally more efficient. This is particularly useful for those simulation models that exhibit prohibitive simulation runtimes and workloads.

After sV, $trGrid$ and $sGrid$ are set, the algorithm is ready to start. It does so by obtaining, via simulation requests, the simulation output results ($simR$) corresponding to the input values comprised in $trGrid$. Note that in this firstiteration, $trGrid$ matches the established training grid-based unit exactly,

---

Algorithm 1. Directional Grid-based Active Learning pseudo-algorithm.

1: **Inputs**: sV, $trGrid$, $sGrid$
2: **Repeat**
3: Obtain $simR$ corresponding to the input values in $trGrid$
4: Fit a GP to the training data set $(trGrid, simR)$
5: Use the fitted GP to make predictions over $sGrid$
6: Define training sub-grids according to the predicted values closest to sV
7: Expand $trGrid$ with the newly defined grids
8: Compute AAD between predictions and sV
9: **Until** AAD stabilizes
10: **Output**: $trGrid$

---

which in turn is defined over the simulation input space in which we believe that sV is triggered. Then, a GP is fitted to the training set $(trGrid, simR)$. The prediction stage follows this initial step. Here, the obtained GP is used to make predictions over $sGrid$. Remember that the latter does not contain any simulation result, only unlabeled instances.

Additionally, $sGrid$ should be sufficiently dense so that the GP can populate it with the associated predictions with enough detail. This does not constitute a computational hindrance since the GP, after training, is rather fast when making predictions. This is often the case for most machine learning frameworks. Afterward, the predictions obtained from the previous step are used to explore the simulation input space, especially to locate those that are value-wise closer to sV. At this point, new grids are defined, and $sGrid$ is expanded. Note that these newly defined grids are essentially sub-grids within the initial one with the same structure, as previously seen in Fig. 1(a). Lastly, we compute the Average Absolute Difference (AAD) between the GP predictions and sV.

The process is repeated until AAD shows no significant variation from iteration to iteration. We are not interested if the GP approximation is below or above the search value, but rather how close it is in absolute terms. We compute the average so that we have an indicator of the GP's overall fitting performance. As we expand the training set with data points whose simulation output values are successively closer to sV, it is expected that AAD decreases over time, eventually reaching a certain threshold. This threshold represents the point from which the GP can no longer improve its predictions, by merely adding more data points to the training set. Ultimately, the main goal of the algorithm is to provide a final mesh grid that delimits the input space region of interest that triggers explicitly the value we are searching for. In Fig. 1(b), a graphical depiction of the proposed approach is shown.

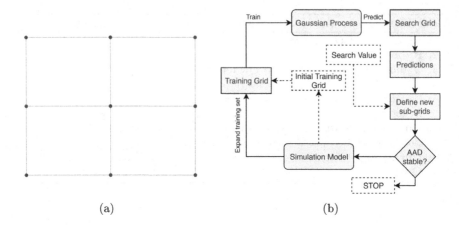

(a)   (b)

Fig. 1. (a) Grid-based training unit and (b) flow diagram of the proposed active learning metamodeling methodology.

4   Experiments

In this section, we illustrate the proposed approach using an Emergency Medical Service simulator. As for the software used, we implemented our approach using the free and open-source Matlab toolbox Gaussian Processes for Machine Learning (GPML), developed and maintained by [27]. As mentioned earlier, we choose the SE-ARD function as the GP kernel and set the GP mean as the average of the simulation output values within the training set.

4.1   EMS Simulation Model

According to a publication released by the United Nations, more than half of the world's population in 2016 lived in urbanized areas. By the year 2030, it is expected that around 60% will globally live within urban settlements, and 33% will live in cities with at least half a million inhabitants [25]. This migration from the countryside places unprecedented pressure on the existing urban infrastructures, consequently leading to further and unpredictable urban transformations. The impact of these transformations, and thus the future of our cities, are mostly dependent on decisions that are taken in the present day to prepare and plan for this inevitable urban growth [24].

Emergency Medical Services (EMS) play a particularly vital role within the exponential growth of today's cities. This kind of service ensures the safety and well-being of its citizens by promptly dispatching emergency vehicles to the locations of the life-threatening events, generally relying on public emergency phone lines. The quality of service is highly dependent on the information that the service operator obtains from the caller, the severity of the case and the accuracy of its medical needs assessment, as well as, obviously, on the final decision taken and the corresponding actual response. Especially within high-density urban areas, EMSs are forcibly constrained by the city dynamics. Daily traffic and population changes are two fundamental forces that directly affect the outcome performance of medical services [2]. Hence, the planning of EMS is of utmost importance. Simulation modeling is a standard tool to design and explore the response of EMS since the evaluation of policy decisions or operational solutions are often deemed unfeasible in the real-world [4].

In this work, we used the agent-based EMS simulator developed by [1]. The underlying simulation model implements the vehicles' allocation and dispatching according to the closest dispatching rule [13, 14, 31], i.e., the emergency event is assigned by the closest idle vehicle. Moreover, the simulator encompasses three fundamental input dimensions, namely, location change probability, traffic error, and vehicle station locations. The latter also includes the number of vehicles per station. Whereas the latter is easy to interpret, the former two might not be so obvious. The location change probability is designed to induce a certain level of randomness to the emergency call's spatial distribution so that it differs significantly from the available historical data. On the other hand, the traffic error encompasses the uncertainty present in the difference between the predicted and the real traffic conditions.

Two main outputs are provided by this simulator, covering both the EMS vehicles' response times and the victims' survivability, which serve as performance metrics of the EMS. These are respectively represented by the average survival rate and the average response time. Whereas the latter trivially encodes the outcome of the emergency event, the former is defined by the time difference between the emergency call and the medical team's arrival.

The simulation model is configured to emulate an emergency system with real data from the city of Porto, Portugal, with 90 emergency vehicle locations. Furthermore, to present our methodology, we only consider the location change probability and the traffic error as inputs, and the average response time as a system performance metric. The first two assume real values in the interval $[0, 1]$. As for the response times, these can assume any positive value. The emergency station locations and their corresponding number of vehicles were maintained constant.

4.2   Results

Following the observations made in [26], which discusses the recommended guideline of a maximum response time of 8 min (480 s), we apply our methodology in order to search for the set of input simulation points that explicitly trigger this threshold within the mentioned EMS simulation model.

As previously seen in Sect. 3.2, several inputs for the proposed algorithm must be defined a priori. This led us to define 480 as our search value. Thus we have $sV = 480$. Next, we fixed $sGrid$ as a mesh grid of 10000 (unlabeled) points scattered uniformly in $[0,1] \times [0,1]$, as this is the domain of the simulation input space under study. Lastly, the initial training grid, $trGrid$, corresponds to the first nine-point training unit, as depicted in Fig. 1(a), whose vertices exactly match those of the input domain. Recovering the notation associated to active learning presented in Sect. 2, we now have that $\mathcal{L} = trGrid$ and $\mathcal{U} = sGrid$. The GP is the oracle $\mathcal{O}$, and the query function $\mathcal{Q}$ is essentially represented by the way we select the new training grids that are added to the expanding training set.

The results are presented in Figs. 2, 3, 4 and 5. As mentioned earlier, the algorithm starts by requesting the simulation model to label the instances present in $sGrid$. Then, a GP is fitted to these simulation points. In Fig. 2(a), we can see the first GP approximation, here depicted by a three-dimensional surface defined over the two-dimensional simulation input space $[0,1]^2$ using the unlabeled observations present in $sGrid$. After, the algorithm searches for the best candidate sub-grids within the initial grid. Such grids contain the GP predictions that are most similar to the search vale sV. This can observed in Fig. 3(b) and (c). The algorithm has detected that the most likely simulation input region to trigger sV is contained somewhere within $[0,1] \times [0,0.5]$. The AAD is then computed, and the algorithm proceeds.

The GP fitting, as well as the expansion of the training set, continues sequentially by sub-dividing the previous' iteration training grid into smaller and finer replicas of itself. In Fig. 3, we can clearly see the sequence of these grids. Due to paper space constraints, we only present part of the results, skipping iterations 7 to 13. Eventually, the process stops when the simple addition of new points does not alter AAD. Figure 5(a) shows that the algorithm took 15 iterations to stop. As a result of the continuous expansion of the training set, it is expected that the predictive variance associated with the data points lying near the input space region of interest tends to decrease. This decrease is depicted in Fig. 5. More than expected, this is the ultimate goal of the proposed methodology. Observe that the latter mentioned region, roughly approximated by the proposed grid-based training structure, gets narrower as the active learning process advances. Figure 4 clearly shows this evolution. Here, we depict the absolute difference between the GP predictions and the search value. Darker tones imply small differences. In the end, and by combining Figs. 3(h) and 4(h), we can observe that the points that are more likely to trigger the search value of interest, are concentrated in the input simulation region roughly by the grid contained in $[0,1] \times [0.625, 0.750]$.

Note that we showed little concern regarding the prediction performance of the final GP approximation. Its main goal, more than being a reasonably good approximation of the underlying function defined by the simulation model itself, is to guide the active learning towards the most informative data points concerning the given output search value. As a consequent, this GP-based metamodeling approach ultimately leads us to the discovery of relevant input regions within the simulation space in a rather expeditious manner.

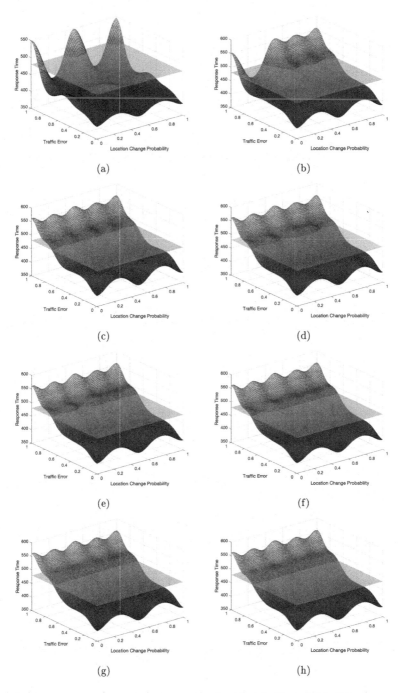

Fig. 2. Iterative GP surface approximations. Panels (a)–(f) and (g)–(h) correspond to iterations 1–6 and 14–15, respectively. The flat horizontal surface is located at z = 480.

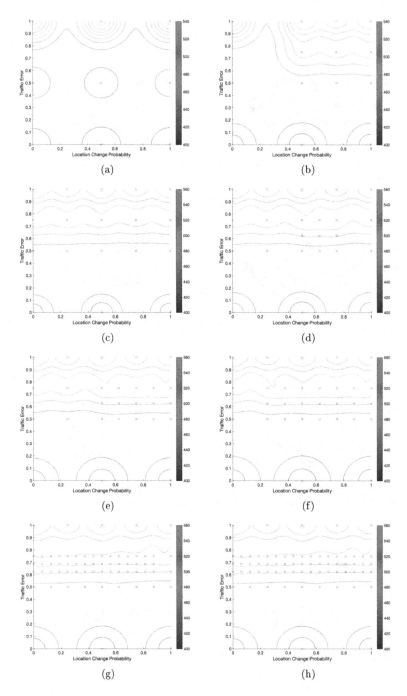

Fig. 3. Iterative training grids and associated GP surface approximation contours. Panels (a)–(f) and (g)–(h) correspond to iterations 1–6 and 14–15, respectively. The flat horizontal surface is located at z = 480.

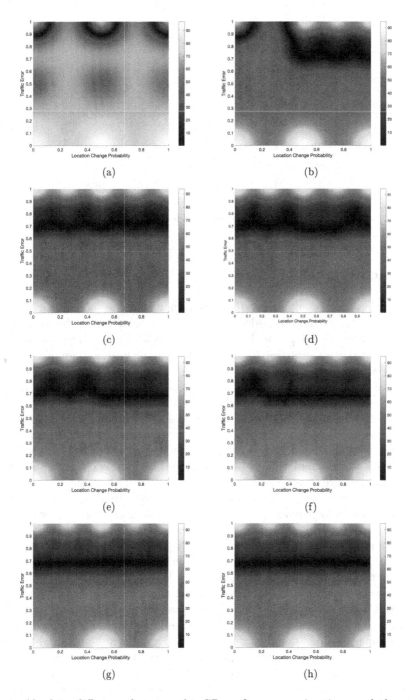

Fig. 4. Absolute difference between the GP surface approximations and the given search value (480). Panels (a)–(f) and (g)–(h) correspond to iterations 1–6 and 14–15, respectively. The flat horizontal surface is located at z = 480.

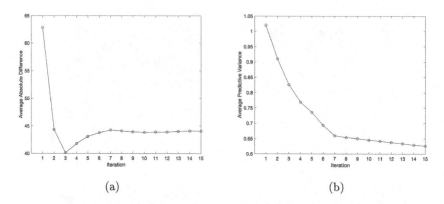

Fig. 5. Evolution of (a) Average Absolute Difference and (b) Average Predictive Variance

5   Conclusion and Future Work

In this paper, we presented a methodology that combines active learning and simulation metamodeling to address the challenge of exploring the input space of any simulation model, particularly those that exhibit great runtimes and computational workloads. Starting from a simple training grid, and guided by a GP acting as a simulation metamodel, the proposed approach uses active learning to build an increasing mesh grid of training points iteratively. This mesh grid comprises a set of sequential subgrids that are steered towards specific regions of the simulation input space that trigger a specific simulation output value, defined a priori by the user. This directional scheme used to train the associated GP-based metamodel makes the exploration process more efficient, as only those input values whose simulation results are more likely to be closer to the search value of interest are considered to be included in the training set.

This work can be improved within several research directions. A straightforward expansion is to generalize our approach from a single search value to multiple search values or even sets of intervals. Additionally, it would be interesting to consider a multi-output approach, where multiple output performance measures could be explored simultaneously. This will not bring a significant challenge from the computational point-of-view, as, in principle, the output variables and associated metrics are always available throughout the entire simulation experiment workflow. Closely related to this, multiple output regression should be embraced in the future so that possible correlations among the output variables can be captured.

Increasing the dimensionality of the proposed approach should also be considered. Along with it, further numerical experiments and graphical representation challenges will emerge. The key contribution of our work is the identification of important regions within the simulation input space, which inherently implies graphical elements. Therefore, new ways of presenting the results, especially for hyper-dimensional spaces, must be explored and developed.

The grid-based unit used to train the simulation metamodel should be revised in the future. Maintaining the concept of grid, more appropriate geometric forms, rather than square-based ones, should be taken into account in accordance with the characteristics of the simulation input space. As this training unit represents how we run the simulation experiments, new sampling strategies should be adopted in order to achieve improved fitting performance. For example, we plan to combine the current approach with statistical designs for computer experiments, such as the widely known Latin hypercube. This kind of scheme provides a systematic sampling framework that ensures the statistical significance as well as the prediction performance of the obtained simulation metamodels.

In our particular case of application, the simulation model did not exhibit very complex output behavior. Nevertheless, the results show the potential of this type of active learning metamodeling approach when searching for specific input regions. Hence, an important step is to apply our approach against new simulation models with an increased degree of complexity, especially with regards to the model's output behavior. This would not only provide further validation for the current work, but it would also stimulate more discussion on the topic.

Acknowledgments. The support of FCT (Portuguese national funding agency for science, research, and technology) under grant No. PD/BD/128047/2016 is greatly acknowledged. This work has additionally received funding from the People Programme (Marie Curie Actions) of the European Union's Horizon 2020 research and innovation programme under the Marie Sklodowska-Curie Individual Fellowship H2020-MSCA-IF-2016, ID number 745673.

References

1. Amorim, M., Ferreira, S., Couto, A.: Emergency medical service response: analyzing vehicle dispatching rules. Trans. Res. Rec.: J. Transp. Res. Board **2672**(32), 10–21 (2018). https://journals.sagepub.com/doi/abs/10.1177/0361198118781645. https://journals.sagepub.com/toc/trra/2672/32
2. Amorim, M., Ferreira, S., Couto, A.: Corrigendum to how do traffic and demand daily changes define urban emergency medical service (uEMS) strategic decisions?: A multi-period survival approach. J. Transp. Health **12**, 60–74 (2019). p. 100570
3. Ankenman, B., Nelson, B.L., Staum, J.: Stochastic kriging for simulation metamodeling. Oper. Res. **58**(2), 371–382 (2010)
4. Antunes, F., Amorim, M., Pereira, F., Ribeiro, B.: Active learning metamodeling for policy analysis: application to an emergency medical service simulator. Simul. Model. Pract. Theory **97**, 101947 (2019)
5. Barton, R.R.: Simulation metamodels. In: Simulation Conference Proceedings, Winter, vol. 1, pp. 167–174. IEEE (1998)
6. Boukouvalas, A.: Emulation of random output simulators. Ph.D. thesis, Aston University (2010)
7. Boukouvalas, A., Cornford, D., Singer, A.: Managing uncertainty in complex stochastic models: design and emulation of a rabies model. In: 6th St. Petersburg Workshop on Simulation, pp. 839–841 (2009)
8. Chen, T., Hadinoto, K., Yan, W., Ma, Y.: Efficient meta-modelling of complex process simulations with time-space-dependent outputs. Comput. Chem. Eng. **35**(3), 502–509 (2011)
9. Chilès, J.-P., Desassis, N.: Fifty years of Kriging. In: Daya Sagar, B.S., Cheng, Q., Agterberg, F. (eds.) Handbook of Mathematical Geosciences, pp. 589–612. Springer, Cham (2018). https://doi.org/10.1007/978-3-319-78999-6_29

10. Conti, S., O'Hagan, A.: Bayesian emulation of complex multi-output and dynamic computer models. J. Stat. Plan. Infer. **140**(3), 640–651 (2010)
11. Friedman, L.W.: The Simulation Metamodel. Springer, Heidelberg (2012)
12. Friedman, L.W., Pressman, I.: The metamodel in simulation analysis: can it be trusted? J. Oper. Res. Soc. **39**(10), 939–948 (1988)
13. Haghani, A., Yang, S.: Real-time emergency response fleet deployment: concepts, systems, simulation & case studies. In: Zeimpekis, V., Tarantilis, C.D., Giaglis, G.M., Minis, I. (eds.) Dynamic Fleet Management. Operations Research/Computer Science Interfaces Series, vol. 38, pp. 133–162. Springer, Boston (2007). https://doi.org/10.1007/978-0-387-71722-7_7
14. Jagtenberg, C., van den Berg, P., van der Mei, R.: Benchmarking online dispatch algorithms for emergency medical services. Eur. J. Oper. Res. **258**(2), 715–725 (2017)
15. Jones, D.R., Schonlau, M., Welch, W.J.: Efficient global optimization of expensive black-box functions. J. Global Optim. **13**(4), 455–492 (1998)
16. Kleijnen, J.P.: A comment on blanning's "metamodel for sensitivity analysis: the regression metamodel in simulation". Interfaces **5**(3), 21–23 (1975)
17. Kleijnen, J.P.: Regression metamodels for generalizing simulation results. IEEE Trans. Syst. Man Cybern. **9**, 93–96 (1979)
18. Kleijnen, J.P.: Kriging metamodeling in simulation: a review. Eur. J. Oper. Res. **192**(3), 707–716 (2009)
19. Kleijnen, J.P., Van Beers, W.C.: Application-driven sequential designs for simulation experiments: Kriging metamodelling. J. Oper. Res. Soc. **55**(8), 876–883 (2004)
20. Kleijnen, J.P., Van Beers, W.C.: Robustness of Kriging when interpolating in random simulation with heterogeneous variances: some experiments. Eur. J. Oper. Res. **165**(3), 826–834 (2005)
21. Kleijnen, J.: Model behaviour: regression metamodel summarization. Encycl. Syst. Control **5**, 3024–3030 (1987)
22. Law, A.M.: Simulation Modeling and Analysis, 5th edn. McGraw-Hill Higher Education, New York City (2015)
23. Ling, C.K., Low, K.H., Jaillet, P.: Gaussian process planning with Lipschitz continuous reward functions: towards unifying Bayesian optimization, active learning, and beyond. In: AAAI, pp. 1860–1866 (2016)
24. Martine, G., Marshall, A., et al.: State of world population 2007: unleashing the potential of urban growth. In: State of World Population 2007: Unleashing the Potential of Urban Growth. UNFPA (2007)
25. United Nations: The World's Cities in 2016, Data Booklet, ST/ESA/SER.A/392. Department of Economic and Social Affairs, Population Division (2016)
26. Pons, P.T., Markovchick, V.J.: Eight minutes or less: does the ambulance response time guideline impact trauma patient outcome? J. Emerg. Med. **23**(1), 43–48 (2002)
27. Rasmussen, C.E., Williams, C.: Gaussian Processes for Machine Learning (Adaptive Computation and Machine Learning). The MIT Press, Cambridge (2006)
28. Settles, B.: Active Learning: Synthesis Lectures on Artificial Intelligence and Machine Learning. Morgan & Clay Pool, Long Island (2012)
29. Van Beers, W.C., Kleijnen, J.P.C.: Kriging for interpolation in random simulation. J. Oper. Res. Soc. **54**(3), 255–262 (2003)
30. Wang, X., Zhai, J.: Learning from Uncertainty. CRC Press, Boca Raton (2016)
31. Yang, S., Hamedi, M., Haghani, A.: Online dispatching and routing model for emergency vehicles with area coverage constraints. Transp. Res. Rec. **1923**(1), 1–8 (2005)

A Generic Predictive Model for On-Street Parking Availability

Eren Unlu(✉), Jean-Baptiste Delfau, Bich Nguyen, Eric Chau,
and Mehdi Chouiten

Datategy, 1 Parvis de la Defense, 92800 Puteaux, France
eren.unlu@datategy.net

Abstract. Despite the previously demonstrated considerable negative effects of on-street parking availability on a city's traffic flux, the developed literature on this issue is far from being voluminous. It is shown that, the duration for finding a vacant parking space consume a sizeable portion of a driver's time. Especially, for huge megacities, even small, local traffic disturbances can generate chaotic results due to their complex, inter-connected nature. Hence, being able to predict the probability of finding a vacant on-street parking place on a spot at a given time up to a reasonable degree shall be at paramount of interest for future smart-city oriented conurbations. In this paperwork, we present a generic framework supported by a machine learning model, which predicts the spatio-temporal on-street parking availability, where spots are characterized according to amenities in their vicinity.

Keywords: On-street parking · Machine learning · Smart city

1 Introduction

High price index and lack of available vacant areas make it difficult to build new off-street parking sites in contemporary metropolitan cities. Hence, most of the time, drivers have to rely on limited on-street parking. The impact of drivers searching for a parking space on urban traffic congestion ranges from around 14% [6] to 30% [19,23], highlighting the importance of this issue. A recent study shows that the average parking space search per driver per day is approximately 9 min and that one third of all drivers gave up on searching for a vacant on-street parking place at least once during the past year [11]; the average driver looses roughly 17, 41 and 44 h per year while searching for parking spot in the US, UK and Germany respectively; finally, 72.7 billion US dollars, 23.3 billion UK pounds and 40.4 billion euros are wasted every year due to traffic disturbances [11]. Taking into account the hundreds of millions of drivers in large cities around the globe, even few minutes of blockage may result in sizeable environmental hazard due to extra carbon emission and economic loss due to wasted time and fuel.

© ICST Institute for Computer Sciences, Social Informatics and Telecommunications Engineering 2020
Published by Springer Nature Switzerland AG 2020. All Rights Reserved
A. L. Martins et al. (Eds.): INTSYS 2019, LNICST 310, pp. 47–60, 2020.
https://doi.org/10.1007/978-3-030-38822-5_4

The academic literature and industrial attempts on optimizing vehicle parking are relatively scarce compared to its potential impact. Existing literature generally focuses on parking price optimization [15, 16, 25] or calculates the required parking space of an area based on the maximum demand [5, 13], targeting decision makers. On the other hand, studies on real-time parking availability for drivers are quite rare. The tracking of vacant on-street parking spots is generally coined with the term *smart parking* under the smart city concept. For instance, a private entrepreneurship [1] offers its clients real time vacancy predictions of parking spots in various cities using the cellular and GPS data acquired from their partners. Due to industrial copyright, they do not provide any details of their algorithm.

On the academic side, there were various attempts to solve the parking place occupancy prediction problem with different approaches. Generally, researchers apply time-series regression methods, where they estimate the future states of parking slots based on the historical data. [22] uses a Long-Short Term Memory (LSTM) Recurrent Neural Network (RNN) to predict the future occupancy rates of a parking location. In [7], authors propose a Bayesian regularized neural network using parking spot's historical data, current weather and traffic flow conditions. On the other hand, [21] develops a spatio-temporal auto-regressive model to predict the occupancy rates of parking slots in San Francisco and Los Angeles. In addition to these, there are various other similar approaches in the literature such as [10, 24, 26].

As it can be noticed, all of these approaches propose local models that rely on a single parking spot's historical data to predict its future state. In the best case, a spatial or spatio-temporal auto-correlation model is employed, which means the locality of information is constrained by the city. This approach thus requires previous data of an existing parking location in order to make predictions. This is a very strong limitation as parking occupancy data is not available in most of the cities in the world. Moreover even if it exists, the data are generally dispersed and confidential. Therefore, a unified, generic framework capable of making predictions for parking occupancy in various cities in the world is essential.

Considering this, we propose a predictive model for on-street parking occupancy rates, based on the hypothesis that cities, especially large metropolitan areas in our current global world shall have similar spatio-temporal characteristics. Our idea is to represent a location in a city by its surrounding amenities, where amenity is synonymous to any social and/or commercial point of interest, such as a restaurant or grocery shop. At the end of the day, it would be a reasonable assumption to consider that on-street parking demand is mostly generated by the nearby amenities. The information about the amenities of a city is taken from the well known, open source geolocation initiative OpenStreetMap [14]. *Volunteered Geographic Information (VGI)* has huge potential for any kind of smart city oriented application and is not only limited to parking. However it is quite rare to find studies which exploit these rich data sources for urbanism.

We present a global on-street parking occupancy level prediction framework, which is trained by the historical parking information of a few cities with the aim of projection on other cities without data. To the best of our knowledge, this is the first such global attempt in the literature for on-street parking. As mentioned previously, there exists various non-global approaches for on and off-street parking vacancy regression. Due to locality, it can be expected that these models may give more precise prediction compared to a global one. Nevertheless, considering the limited accessibility of parking data on most of the cities in the world, study of a global predictive framework is highly influential using the amenity content of urban locations. Therefore, we desire to construct a pioneering data scientific scheme addressing the issue and evaluate the future potential with extended datasets.

2   Training Dataset

The principal aim of the study is to be able to predict the parking occupancy ratio in various areas of any kind of metropolitan city in the world at a given time, as mentioned previously. For this purpose, one needs to choose certain common spatial characteristics of cities, which are universally correlated to temporal parking demands. As mentioned previously, we propose to use numerous types of social and/or commercial points of interest, which are tagged as *amenities* in OpenStreetMap.

OpenDataParis initiative provides all on-street parking transactions for the city center of Paris in 2014, across its 7800 parking meters [2]. It consists of a list of parking transactions records. Each transaction has a parking meter id along with its latitude and longitude (where the purchase is validated). Note that, we wish to create a global predictive structure, where we are interested in the ratio of occupancy of parking spots. Compared to off-street parking, the ratio of occupancy can only be defined loosely for on-street parking. Indeed, the maximum capacity is usually not well defined for parking meters. A driver parks to an available curbside spot in a permitted area and validates its purchase at the closest parking meter. In addition to this, there can be multiple parking meters in the same area so that one can validate his/her purchase at several locations, which makes the notion of capacity arbitrary. First, we convert the transactions to temporal statistics per parking meter indicating the instantaneous number of cars registered at a given time. For this study, we have chosen to follow hourly statistics. The capacity of a parking meter will be estimated by looking at the distribution of transactions for a given parking meter.

In Paris, on-street parking is charged only during weekdays and saturday, between 8 a.m. and 7 p.m.. Even if there are variations across cities in the world, the on-street parking is generally free of charge during night-time and weekends. For the sake of generality, we have excluded the transactions of Saturday. And in a global sense, without loss of generality, it is more convenient to assume that there shall be no significant variations for on-street parking demand within weekdays. Thus, the only temporal feature we have considered in this work is the hour of the day, which is treated as a categorical variable.

2.1   On-Street Parking Occupancy Indicator

When it comes to on-street parking, finding a universal indicator for the parking place availability on a global scale is non-trivial. First of all, on-street parking regulations are highly diverse from city to city, but also within a city. On-street parking can be prohibited, free of charge during different hours within different parts of a city. While certain streets may be available for on-street parking on both sides, others may only allow it on one side of the road.

In addition to regulations, there exists also the issue of on-street parking capacity due to street geometry. Defining a capacity as for off-street parking is not evident. Even, we may able to predict the number of parking demands, defining the occupancy level from this, is problematic. At this scale of diversity and obscurity, it is challenging to reach a common indicator for parking space availability. In order to develop a global scale prediction framework as accurate as possible, a normalized indicator for on-street parking load shall be calculated. After evaluating the number of cars assigned to each parking meter for every hour of the dataset, we have calculated the means (μ) and standard deviations (σ) of each parking meter. Then, we have defined a virtual parking meter capacity as $\mu + 1.5\sigma$ for each parking meter separately. This value is attained by empirical analysis of the parking transactions record. Next, we calculate hourly occupancy ratio of each parking meter by dividing the instantaneous number cars to the virtual capacity of the parking meter. In the case where the number of cars is larger than this value, the ratio is set to 1.0. At the end of the day, the idea is to represent a normalized universal spatio-temporal on-street parking availability metric.

3   Amenities

Each parking meter is characterized by the number of major amenity types contained in a rectangle of 150, 200, and 300 m centered on it. We assume that the on-street parking demand will depend on the points of interest within these range limits. Indeed, the distribution of amenities within these ranges shall represent the type of neighbourhood as a residential, business, touristic, leisure, dense or sparse sector; which at the end, is related to the temporal on-street parking demand. Rather than using a circular periphery, we have defined range limits in squares as in Fig. 1, where we believe it is more convenient with the rigid street geometry of most of the major cities.

In OpenStreetMap, there are hundreds of amenity types which are mostly tagged by voluntary contributors, including rare definitions which are specific to certain countries (e.g. *biergarten* in germany) or no definition at all (empty amenity type). Hence, in order to construct a universal framework, we should focus on amenities which are common to all cities, such as pharmacies or grocery shops. In addition to this, we should group amenities together into major amenity types which shall have similar temporal parking occupancy characteristics. For instance, it would be logical to claim that restaurants and cafes attract customers in similar days and hours. The categorization of amenities into four main types

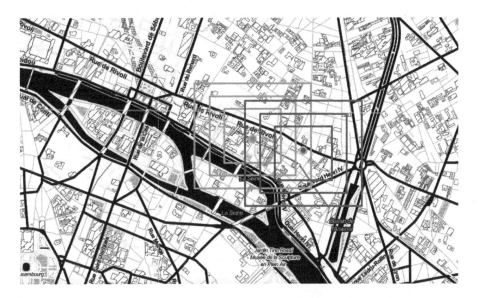

Fig. 1. Each parking meter or point in a city is represented by the number of 4 major amenity types in 150, 200 and 300 m.

is shown in Table 1. Note that it is important to consider amenity types which are expected to show high similarities in all cities. For instance, a university or an administrative amenity can be highly variant in terms of size and impact, hence also for the parking demand. However, ATM machines, banks or cafes are much more similar across the world with respect to these criteria.

Let us describe the four amenity types we chose: first, a *financial amenity* is defined, which is composed of ATM machines, banks and money transfer offices. In addition to generating parking demands directly, the density of these financial of points interest is highly correlated with the human activity around them. For example, a location with a high number of ATM machines is expected to be a more central node compared to others. Second, a *social food amenity* type is considered, including restaurants, cafes, bars etc. These are points of interest expected to have similar correlations with on-street parking occupancy within their peripheries. Another considered amenity type is the *commercial amenities* such as grocery shops, supermarkets, bakeries etc. And finally, all the rest of tagged amenities are grouped in *other amenities* general type, for which central locations tend to be more densely tagged in OpenStreetMap.

The correlation coefficients of counts of these 4 major amenity types in 3 radii of interest of 150, 200, 300 m with the normalized on-street parking occupancy for the training dataset parking meters are given in Table 2. Note that, we have also considered correlation coefficients while choosing the major amenity types and interested radii. As it can be seen, for all ranges and amenity type combinations, there exists a positive correlation with occupancy ratio up to a degree.

Table 1. 4 major amenity types defined to reflect on-street parking demand corresponding to amenities in OpenStreetMap.

Major amenity type	
Financial	Bank, ATM, Money Transfer Office
Commercial	Grocery, Supermarket, Florist, Bakery, Butcher, Rotisserie, Chocolate, Cosmetics, Pet, Dry Cleaning, Dairy, Health Food, Internet Cafe, Copyshop, Tabacco, E-Cigarette, Laundry, News Agent, Real Estate, Hair Dresser, Electronics, Clothes, Pharmacy
Social food	Cafe, Restaurant, Bar, Pub, Fast-Food
Other	–

Table 2. Correlation Coefficients of 4 major amenity types and 3 ranges for training dataset parking meters' hourly occupancy rates.

Major amenity type/range (meters)	150	200	300
Financial	0.032	0.026	0.054
Commercial	0.065	0.069	0.073
Social food	0.020	0.028	0.041
Other	0.046	0.047	0.049

4   Predictive Machine Learning Model

4.1   CatBoost

For each parking meter, we have 12 static physical features due to the number of 4 major amenity types in 150, 200 and 300 m periphery. As a temporal feature, we use the hour of the day, which we treat as a categorical variable. Before feeding these features to a machine learning algorithm, we shall convert hour category to a numerical feature. For this purpose, we have used *categorical boosting (CatBoost) encoding* algorithm [12]. Even though, this encoding scheme has been introduced recently, it has gained a significant reputation in the research community, thanks to its reported performances [4,27]. Each hour category is converted to a single numerical values between 0 and 1 after encoding, and combined with 12 physical features of each parking meter, thus producing a final feature vector with length of 13.

4.2   Random Forest Regression

We have chosen random forest regression [18], which is known for producing plausible results for voluminous datasets while avoiding overfitting. After shuffling our OpenDataParis dataset, we divided it into 80% training and 20% test datasets for evaluation. Note that category encoding and numerical scalings are only used on the training dataset. Following detailed experimentation, the optimal number of estimators for Random Forest algorithm is found to be 150, with a maximum depth of 30. Mean absolute error for the test dataset is found to be approximately 0.19, which can be considered as an acceptable deviation for our amenity related model.

Another main advantage of the Random Forest algorithm is its high level of interpretability, similarly to other tree based approaches [8,17]. It is indeed crucial to be able to evaluate the relative importance of the features used in our model for understanding the impact of major amenity types on on-street parking demand. A well established metric of features relevance is the Mean Decrease Gini or more generally the Mean Decrease of Impurity (MDI) [20]. The MDI can be computed as follows: a decision tree is built by splitting the data in a way which minimizes a measure of impurity i (such as the Gini, Shannon entropy or Renyi entropy for example). For each node t of tree T, we thus want to find the split s_t that maximizes the impurity decrease given by,

$$\Delta i(s,t) = i(t) - p_L i(t_L) - p_R i(t_R) \tag{1}$$

where, $i(t_L)$ and $i(t_R)$ refer to impurity measures of the left and right portions of the dataset split by this node. And p_L, p_R are the proportions of samples in left and right parts of the node respectively, so that $p_L = N_{tL}/N_t$ and $p_R = N_{tR}/N_t$.

The MDI of a feature X_m is given by: [9,20]:

$$Imp(X_m) = \frac{1}{N_t} \sum_{T} \sum_{t \in T; v(s_t) = X_m} p(t) i(s_t, t) \tag{2}$$

where, N_T is the total number of trees of the forest, p_t is the proportion of samples reaching node t so that $p_t = N_T/N$, N being total number of samples on tree T and $v(s_t)$ is the feature used in split s_t [9,20]. Intuitively speaking, MDI thus measure how many times a feature was used for a split, highlighting its importance.

After training our model, we have reached the weighted normalized importance of 13 features as in Table 3. As expected, hour feature has by far the most significant effect, constituting more than half of the total impact. We observe that up to 300 m range, the effect of major amenity types do not vary significantly, whereas all contribute to the prediction process.

5   Hourly Predictions for the Streets of Various Cities

Unfortunately, there are only a very limited number of tagged on-street parking meters in OpenStreetMap. For most of the cities, tagged parking meters do not even exist. Due to this fact, in order to have a more universal model, we

Table 3. Mean impurity decrease based normalized feature importance of the trained random forest model for 13 features.

Mean impurity decrease			
Normalized feature importance	*150*	*200*	*300*
Category/Range (meters)			
Financial	0.013	0.017	0.034
Commercial	0.036	0.037	0.050
Social food	0.040	0.043	0.062
Other	0.045	0.043	0.051
Hour	0.51		

estimate the hourly occupancy levels of streets over world. Without loss of generality, we only consider roads which are tagged as *residential* or *living street* in OpenStreetMap. Note that, major avenues and roads may not be eligible for parking with greater probability. We do not make any assumptions about the parking regulations of streets which is obscure and we make predictions for all the considered streets. The geometrical center of the street is considered as the location for our predictive model.

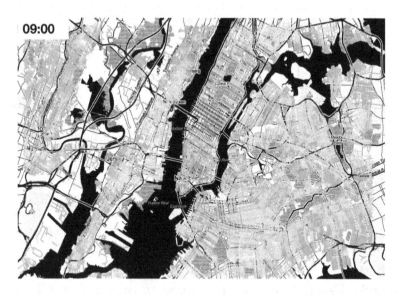

Fig. 2. Predicted on-street parking occupancies in New York, USA for 9 a.m. in weekdays. Higher occupancy levels are represented with redder hue and lower occupancy levels are represented with greener hue. (Color figure online)

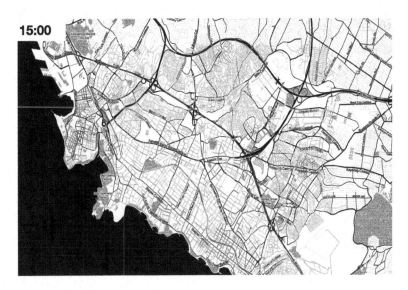

Fig. 3. Predicted on-street parking occupancies in Istanbul, Turkey for 3 p.m. in week-days. Higher occupancy levels are represented with redder hue and lower occupancy levels are represented with greener hue. (Color figure online)

Due to limited space, we only demonstrate the results for 6 cities around globe as in Figs. 2, 3, 4, 5, 6 and 7 for three different periods of a weekday. One can observe the higher parking demands are generally centered around important hot spots as expected, especially in early morning and afternoon. Also, we can notice the medium to high occupancy levels around residential suburban areas in the morning and evening times.

In order to present a better validation, we have compared our predictions with the municipality of Seattle's parking data [3]. The dataset contains the instantaneous number of cars and capacity of each parkmeter in the city, for 2017. As we are developing a model which considers the hours between 8 a.m. and 7 p.m., we have taken the overall mean of each parkmeter for each weekday in the dataset for each hour. Then, we have calculated the amenity based static features of each parkmeter and performed our predictions. Figure 8 shows the means of real data and our predictions in a weekday at 6 p.m.

As it can be observed from Fig. 8, our model is capable of capturing the parking hot-spot regions highly accurately. For all hours considered, the mean difference (error) between real data and our predicitions is approximately 6%.

Fig. 4. Predicted on-street parking occupancies in Rennes, France for 7 p.m. in weekdays. Higher occupancy levels are represented with redder hue and lower occupancy levels are represented with greener hue. (Color figure online)

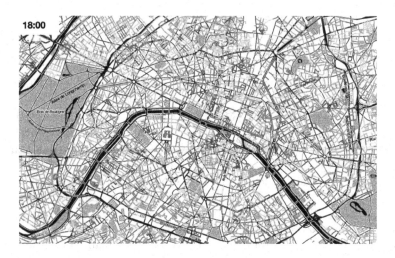

Fig. 5. Predicted on-street parking occupancies in Paris, France for 6 p.m. in weekdays. Higher occupancy levels are represented with redder hue and lower occupancy levels are represented with greener hue. (Color figure online)

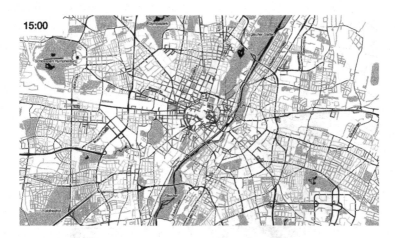

Fig. 6. Predicted on-street parking occupancies in Munich, Germany for 12 a.m. in weekdays. Higher occupancy levels are represented with redder hue and lower occupancy levels are represented with greener hue. (Color figure online)

Fig. 7. Predicted on-street parking occupancies in Lyon, France for 12 a.m. in weekdays. Higher occupancy levels are represented with redder hue and lower occupancy levels are represented with greener hue. (Color figure online)

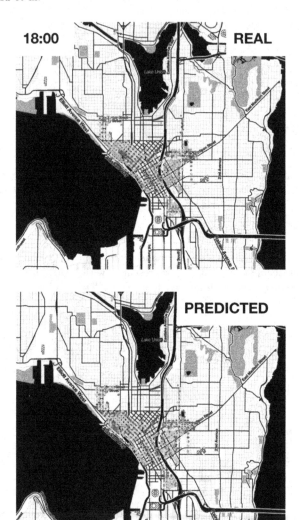

Fig. 8. Predicted on-street parking occupancies in Rennes, France for 7 p.m. in week-days. Higher occupancy levels are represented with redder hue and lower occupancy levels are represented with greener hue. (Color figure online)

6   Conclusion and Future Work

Expecting similarities in terms of parking dynamics in contemporary global cities is a reasonable approach. Especially, if proper common points of interests (i.e. amenities) are chosen as a reference, one can estimate the on-street parking slot vacancy probabilities up to a certain extent. Even though on-street parking is a highly important subject considering the proven negative economic impact, a universal predictive model for occupancy levels had not been proposed to the best of our knowledge. In this study, we have presented a generic framework for this purpose, where locations in cities are characterized by the number of various types of points of interests within three different radii. Constructing a unified, accurate model is quite complex due to highly variant dynamics, geometries and regulations in different cities. However, we believe this issue of a global regressive model is required to be investigated in detail due to aforementioned motivations and reasons. Therefore, we have introduced a pioneering study addressing this challenge by employing state-of-the-art machine learning algorithms. As it can be observed from the presented results in this paper, we can attain justifiable results for different cities. Unfortunately, we believe the most important bottleneck is the scarcity of open datasets about on-street parking. One can expect more and more accurate predictions with more available data sources. As a next step, we also would like to consider additional urban features such as bus stops, traffic lights, individual buildings and street geometry.

References

1. eParkomat, city smart parking s.r.o. http://eparkomat.com. Accessed 12 May 2019
2. opendataParis, 2014 on-street parking transactions. https://opendata.paris.fr/explore/dataset/horodateurs-transactions-de-paiement/information/. Accessed 31 May 2019
3. AlAwadhi, S., Scholl, H.J.: Aspirations and realizations: the smart city of Seattle. In: 2013 46th Hawaii International Conference on System Sciences, pp. 1695–1703. IEEE (2013)
4. Anghel, A., Papandreou, N., Parnell, T., de Palma, A., Pozidis, H.: Benchmarking and optimization of gradient boosting decision tree algorithms
5. Arnott, R., Inci, E., Rowse, J.: Downtown curbside parking capacity. J. Urban Econ. **86**, 83–97 (2015)
6. Arnott, R., Rowse, J.: Downtown parking in auto city. Reg. Sci. Urban Econ. **39**(1), 1–14 (2009)
7. Badii, C., Nesi, P., Paoli, I.: Predicting available parking slots on critical and regular services by exploiting a range of open data. IEEE Access **6**, 44059–44071 (2018)
8. Boulesteix, A.L., Janitza, S., Kruppa, J., König, I.R.: Overview of random forest methodology and practical guidance with emphasis on computational biology and bioinformatics. Wiley Interdisc. Rev.: Data Min. Knowl. Discov. **2**(6), 493–507 (2012)
9. Breiman, L.: Manual on setting up, using, and understanding random forests v3. 1. Statistics Department University of California Berkeley, CA, USA 1 (2002)
10. Chen, X.: Parking occupancy prediction and pattern analysis. Department Computer Science, Stanford University, Stanford, CA, USA, Technical Report CS229-2014 (2014)
11. Cookson, G., Pishue, B.: The impact of parking pain in the us, UK and Germany. Hg. v. INRIX Research (2017). Online verfügbar unter http://inrix.com/research/parking-pain/. zuletzt geprüft am 21, 2018
12. Dorogush, A.V., Ershov, V., Gulin, A.: CatBoost: gradient boosting with categorical features support. arXiv preprint arXiv:1810.11363 (2018)

13. Franco, S.F.: Downtown parking supply, work-trip mode choice and urban spatial structure. Transp. Res. Part B: Methodol. **101**, 107–122 (2017)
14. Haklay, M., Weber, P.: OpenStreetMap: user-generated street maps. IEEE Pervasive Comput. **7**(4), 12–18 (2008)
15. Inci, E.: A review of the economics of parking. Econ. Transp. **4**(1–2), 50–63 (2015)
16. Kobus, M.B., Gutiérrez-i Puigarnau, E., Rietveld, P., Van Ommeren, J.N.: The on-street parking premium and car drivers' choice between street and garage parking. Reg. Sci. Urban Econ. **43**(2), 395–403 (2013)
17. Kursa, M.B., Rudnicki, W.R., et al.: Feature selection with the Boruta package. J. Stat. Softw. **36**(11), 1–13 (2010)
18. Liaw, A., Wiener, M., et al.: Classification and regression by randomforest. R News **2**(3), 18–22 (2002)
19. Lin, T.S.: Smart parking: network, infrastructure and urban service. Ph.D. thesis, Lyon, INSA (2015)
20. Louppe, G., Wehenkel, L., Sutera, A., Geurts, P.: Understanding variable importances in forests of randomized trees. In: Advances in Neural Information Processing Systems, pp. 431–439 (2013)
21. Rajabioun, T., Ioannou, P.A.: On-street and off-street parking availability prediction using multivariate spatiotemporal models. IEEE Trans. Intell. Transp. Syst. **16**(5), 2913–2924 (2015)
22. Shao, W., Zhang, Y., Guo, B., Qin, K., Chan, J., Salim, F.D.: Parking availability prediction with long short term memory model. In: Li, S. (ed.) GPC 2018. LNCS, vol. 11204, pp. 124–137. Springer, Cham (2019). https://doi.org/10.1007/978-3-030-15093-8_9
23. Shoup, D.C.: Cruising for parking. Transp. Policy **13**(6), 479–486 (2006)
24. Tiedemann, T., Vögele, T., Krell, M.M., Metzen, J.H., Kirchner, F.: Concept of a data thread based parking space occupancy prediction in a Berlin pilot region. In: Workshops at the Twenty-Ninth AAAI Conference on Artificial Intelligence (2015)
25. Van Ommeren, J., Russo, G.: Time-varying parking prices. Econ. Transp. **3**(2), 166–174 (2014)
26. Vlahogianni, E.I., Kepaptsoglou, K., Tsetsos, V., Karlaftis, M.G.: A real-time parking prediction system for smart cities. J. Intell. Transp. Syst. **20**(2), 192–204 (2016)
27. Zhang, F., Fleyeh, H.: Short term electricity price forecasting using CatBoost and bidirectional long short term memory neural network (2018)

Optimization

Identifying Relevant Transfer-Connections from Entry-Only Automatic Fare Collection Data: The Case Study of Porto

Joana Hora[1,2](✉)[iD], Teresa Galvão[1,2][iD], and Ana Camanho[1,2][iD]

[1] Faculdade de Engenharia da Universidade do Porto, Porto, Portugal
[2] INESC TEC, Porto, Portugal
joana.hora@gmail.com,
{acamanho,tgalvao}@fe.up.pt

Abstract. The synchronization of Public Transportation (PT) systems usually considers a simplified network to optimize the flows of passengers at the principal axes of the network. This work aims to identify the most relevant transfer-connections in a PT network. This goal is pursued with the development of a methodology to identify relevant transfer-connections from entry-only Automatic Fare Collection (AFC) data. The methodology has three main steps: the implementation of the Trip-Chaining-Method (TCM) to estimate the alighting stops of each AFC record, the identification of transfers, and finally, the selection of relevant transfer-connections. The adequacy of the methodology was demonstrated with its implementation to the case study of Porto. This methodology can also be applied to PT systems using entry-exit AFC data, and in that case, the TCM would not be required.

Keywords: Public Transportation · Transfers · Automatic Fare Collection

1 Introduction

The decisions made at the Transit Planning Process (TPP) are grounded on passengers' behavior assumptions, such as the expected demand of passengers. These assumptions are mainly drawn from the analysis of historical records or surveys. In its turn, the implementation of TPP decisions impacts the Public Transportation (PT) service delivered to passengers, e.g., with changes in routes' design, frequencies or schedules. Finally, changes in the PT service will impact the behavior of passengers, which is not deterministic and often does not evolve as expected (e.g., choosing to commute with private car or PT, or choosing between alternative PT routes when several options are available for the same Origin-Destination (OD)). Figure 1 shows this causal cycle interrelating the TPP, the PT service, and the behavior of passengers.

© ICST Institute for Computer Sciences, Social Informatics and Telecommunications Engineering 2020
Published by Springer Nature Switzerland AG 2020. All Rights Reserved
A. L. Martins et al. (Eds.): INTSYS 2019, LNICST 310, pp. 63–76, 2020.
https://doi.org/10.1007/978-3-030-38822-5_5

Several sequential stages integrate the TPP. The Network Design (ND) stage returns the set of routes composing the PT network, designed to provide the best possible transportation service by meeting the passenger demand. The Frequencies Setting (FS) stage assigns frequencies for all daily Uniform Demand Period (UDP) on each route (e.g., assign one vehicle every 15 min during a morning peak). The Timetabling (TT) stage returns the timetables with the departure and arrival times of all daily trips on each route, typically at the level of Time Control Point (TCP)s or stops. Follows the Vehicle Scheduling (VS), the Driver Scheduling (DS) and the Driver Rostering (DR) stages. Although aspects such as passenger demand can never really be known or accurately described by its historical observations, the adoption of assumptions related to them is needed to sustain decision-making at any TPP stage.

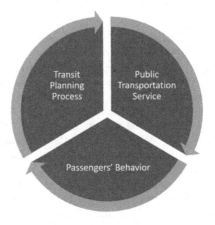

Fig. 1. Cycle 'Transit Planning Process - PT service - Passengers behavior'.

The technological advent of the last decades had endowed planners and decision-makers with access to a higher volume of accurate data, such as Automated Fare Collection (AFC) records, fostering its application into research and development activities. At the same time, improved computational tools have increasingly been applied to solve TPP problems.

There are different techniques used for TT, depending on the experience and resources of planners and companies [1]. One popular approach is the implementation of the Synchronization Timetabling Problem (STP) [2–4]. The STP builds timetables pursuing the reduction of the overall inconvenience for passengers. The idea is to obtain coordinated timetables that enable smooth interchanges through the minimization of passengers' waiting-time and bunching of vehicles.

The STP is usually applied to simplified, yet realistic networks. This simplification is considered not only due to the complexity of the STP (i.e., NP-hard [2]) but also because increasing the size of the network significantly reduces the flexibility of the solutions obtained, which is critical for finding compatible solutions in the TPP downstream stages, especially at the VS.

This work aims to identify the most relevant transfer-connections within a PT network, which can be further used to build a *simplified yet realistic* representation of the routes that should be coordinated to provide a quality service to passengers.

A methodology is proposed to identify relevant transfer-connections from entry-only AFC records. The methodology has three main steps: the implementation of the Trip-Chaining Method (TCM) to estimate the alighting stops of each AFC record, the identification of transfers, and finally, the selection of relevant transfer-connections. Relevant transfer-connections are selected considering four main assumptions: (1) identification by experts, (2) in case of shared paths, favor the selection of connections positioned at strategic stops such as merging or crossing routes, (3) compliance with a maximum walkable distance threshold, and (4) compliance with a specified threshold of demand.

The TCM estimates the alighting stops of entry-only AFC records. It considers the sequence of trips made by each passenger in each day, connecting trip-legs of each smart-card. The literature on TCM counts with several implementations at different PT systems worldwide, differing mainly in the set of assumptions implemented [5–9]. The majority of these works keep the two grounding assumptions proposed in the seminal work of [5]: (1) most passengers will start the next trip of the day at or near the alighting stop of their previous trip, and (2) most passengers end the last trip of the day at or near the boarding stop of their first trip of the day.

The identification of transfers as also been addressed in literature considering assumptions of transfer walking distance [6,8,10], transfer time thresholds [8,10, 11] and transfer network feasibility conditions [10].

2   Concepts: Transfer-Node, Transfer-Connection and Transfer-Event

This work distinguishes the concepts of transfer-connection and transfer-node. A transfer-node is the geographic area where two or more routes meet, cross, or merge. A transfer-connection refers to the possible interchange of passengers between two specific directed-routes, possibly separated by a walkable path. A transfer-event is the observation of passengers transferring through a transfer-connection, with specific detail on the vehicles involved and on time.

2.1   Transfer-Event

Figure 2 schematizes a transfer-event. A transfer-event has four main moments: (1) a Feeding Vehicle (FV) from the Feeding-route (FR) arrives and passengers alighting; (2) passengers walk between the alighting-stop and the boarding-stop when a walkable path exists; (3) passengers wait at the boarding-stop; (4) a Receiving Vehicle (RV) from the Receiving-route (RR) arrives and passengers board.

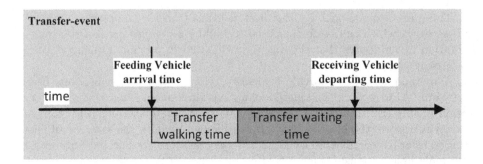

Fig. 2. Scheme of a transfer-event.

Several runs serve each directed-route over a day. A transfer-event addresses the interchanging process between two specific trips, operated by specific runs of each directed-route. A transfer-event encompasses knowledge on the specific time for the FV arrival and the RV departure.

In the case when the FV arrives earlier than scheduled and the RV is on-time, passengers are unlikely to miss the RV. Passengers willing to perform this transfer-event will have extra transfer waiting-time, or in some cases, they might be able to board a prior run of that receiving-directed-route.

In the case when the FV arrives later than scheduled and the RV is on-time, passengers are likely to lose the transfer-event and wait for the next run of that receiving-directed-route, or they might board the RV with almost zero transfer waiting-time.

Many other transfer-event scenarios can be studied considering different FV and RV arrival and departing-time. The study of transfers is of utmost importance to enhance as much as possible successful transfer-events, reducing transfer waiting-time that is inconvenient for passengers, and improve overall passenger flow within the PT network.

2.2 Transfer-Connections and Transfer-Nodes

The simplest case of a transfer-node is the case where two route-terminus meet, as illustrated in Fig. 3. The last stop of one route is at the same geographic area of the first stop of another route. This type of transfer-node is commonly found in peripheral areas of cities, aiming to connect PT service from the suburbs to strategic PT routes traveling into cities. In this particular case, the transfer-node encompasses only two possible transfer-connections, as identified in Fig. 3.

Another common type of transfer-node occurs when two routes cross or merge, as illustrated in Fig. 4. In both situations, the resulting transfer-node always includes eight transfer-connections, as identified in Fig. 4. This analysis deliberately excludes any interchanging of passengers between trips of the same route, regardless of route direction. The main reasoning is that passengers would only board into the same route at a consecutive trip in case of (i) a mistake, or

Fig. 3. Possible transfer-connections in the case when the terminus of two routes meet.

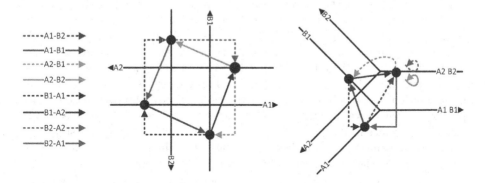

Fig. 4. Possible transfer-connections in the crossing and merging of two routes.

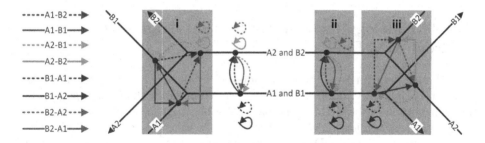

Fig. 5. Merging and splitting of two routes, sharing a segment path.

Table 1. Possible transfer-connections when four routes cross each-other at a common transfer-node.

	A1	A2	B1	B2	C1	C2	D1	D2
A1	Na	Na	•	•	•	•	•	•
A2	Na	Na	•	•	•	•	•	•
B1	•	•	Na	Na	•	•	•	•
B2	•	•	Na	Na	•	•	•	•
C1	•	•	•	•	Na	Na	•	•
C2	•	•	•	•	Na	Na	•	•
D1	•	•	•	•	•	•	Na	Na
D2	•	•	•	•	•	•	Na	Na

(ii) the start of a new journey which takes place after an activity (even when the two consecutive trips occur within a short duration). Either way, they do not reflect an interchange and therefore are not included in this analysis.

Figure 5 represents the case of two routes sharing a segment path, with their merging and splitting transfer-nodes. Possible transfer-connections at the merging/splitting transfer-nodes are represented at boxes (i) and (iii), while possible transfer-connections at the shared path are represented at the box (ii).

Considering the case of Fig. 5, although passengers can interchange over the shared path represented in box (ii), the methodology followed in this work considers that the transfer-connections positioned at the merging and splitting transfer-nodes (boxes i and iii) should be given priority with respect to any stop positioned at the shared path (box ii). This concept is further included as an assumption to identify relevant transfer-connections. The overall goal is to optimize passenger waiting-time and vehicle congestion, which is achieved more efficiently by concentrating transfers in a reduced number of strategic stops.

Finally, the analysis of transfer-connections when three or more routes intersect or merge at the same geographic area is easily understood with a matrix approach, as the one exemplified in Table 1. For example, a transfer-node crossed by three routes has 24 possible transfer-connections, and a transfer-node crossed by four routes has 48 possible transfer-connections.

3   Methodology to Identify Relevant Transfer-Links from AFC Data

This section details the methodology adopted to identify relevant transfer-links from entry-only AFC data. This methodology embodies three main steps: (1) implementation of the TCM to estimate alighting stops for all AFC records, (2) the subsequent application of criteria to identify transfers, which also allows to link trip-legs and reveal OD, (3) the identification of transfer-links of improved relevance regarding further consideration for further optimization techniques, particularly the synchronization.

The data-set of AFC records is sorted by smart-card Unique IDentifier (UID) and then chronologically. The following two steps consider AFC records sequentially in this order. These steps are schematized in Fig. 6, and detailed in Sects. 3.1 and 3.2.

The third step is performed independently of the first two steps. After the estimation of alighting stops and transfer-connections for all AFC records, the identification of relevant transfers will be carried out in a new algorithmic procedure detailed in Sect. 3.3. Figure 7 schematizes this procedure.

3.1   TCM Implementation

The TCM allows to estimate the alighting stops for each AFC record. The TCM implementation adopted in this work follows all details provided in [12]. The main assumptions adopted for this implementation are detailed in Table 2.

When there are two or more AFC records for the same smart-card, the algorithm proceeds to estimate their alighting locations, applying the TCM. When there is only one AFC record, the TCM cannot be applied, and the algorithm cannot estimate the Destination of that trip. In that case, the algorithm proceeds to the next smart-card UID in the data-set.

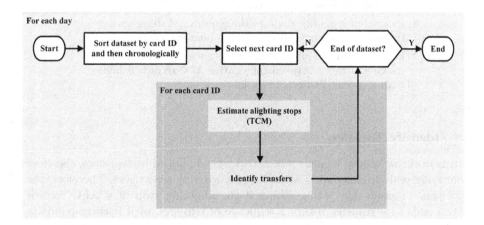

Fig. 6. Methodology followed to estimate alighting stops and identify transfers from entry-only AFC data.

When there are two or more AFC records for the same smart-card, the algorithm continues by selecting the next record. Knowing the boarding stop, route, and direction, the algorithm specifies as possible alighting stops all of the stops that were not yet traveled in that path. If the current AFC record is not the last of the day, the TCM estimates that the passenger alights, from the set of possible alighting, at the stop with the shortest walking distance regarding the boarding stop of the subsequent record. If the AFC record is the last of the day, the same approach is adopted but regarding the boarding stop of the first AFC record of the day (assuming the passenger would travel back home at the end of the day).

When the walking distance between the current alighting stop and the subsequent boarding stop is higher than the threshold of 3 km, we assume that the passenger traveled off the transportation system between these two AFC records. For example, picking up a ride or using another transportation mode. In that case, the estimation made regarding its alighting location is discarded. Similarly, for the case of the last AFC record of the day, if the walking distance between the current alighting stop and the first boarding stop of the day is higher than 3 km, we assume that the passenger traveled off the transportation system on its return home and that estimation is discarded as well.

Table 2. Assumptions adopted to implement the TCM using entry-only AFC data.

	Assumption
1	Passengers start the next journey stage at or near the alighting location of their previous trip
2	Passengers end the last trip of the day at the boarding location of the first trip of the day
3	Passengers can only alight in the sequence of stops not yet traveled by the route direction they boarded
4	Passengers travel off the transportation system when the walking distance between consecutive AFC records is higher than a specified threshold (in km)

3.2 Identify Transfers

In this work, we aim to identify which trip-legs are linked by transfers, therefore identifying real Origins and Destinations incurred by passengers. Therefore, the algorithm proceeds by distinguishing if the alighting stop of a AFC records corresponds to a transfer within a sequence of trip-legs, or if it corresponds to the Destination of a trip. The main assumptions adopted to identify transfers from AFC records, regarding the behavior adopted by passengers in their daily travel patterns, are detailed next.

Table 3. Assumptions to distinguish transfer-events from trip-ends.

	Assumption
1	Passengers will not transfer to another vehicle of the same route in which they are traveling, regardless of its direction
2	Passengers are not willing to walk more than a specified threshold to transfer to another route (in meters)
3	Passengers are not willing to wait for more than a specified threshold to transfer to another route (in minutes)
4	The boarding stop of the first AFC record of the day is the Origin of a trip
5	The alighting stop of the last AFC record of the day is the Destination of a trip
6	When passengers travel out of the system, the next AFC record is the beginning of a trip

Assumption 1 implies that passengers will only perform two consecutive AFC records on the same route when executing two different trips. That is, a passenger does not perform a transfer to board the same route he was already traveling, even if in the opposite direction, unless by mistake. This way, if a passenger boards the same route in the consecutive AFC record traveling in the opposite direction, we consider that the passenger is performing a new trip and not a transfer. For example: (a) a passenger travels from home to bank, and then from bank to home using the same route, in less than 30 min; (b) a passenger travels from home to school, pick up the kids, and go back home using the same route, in less than 30 min. The main reasoning of this assumption is that it helps to distinguish transfers from trip ends. In these examples, there was an activity that took less than 30 min, and the walking distance between the two AFC records is lower than 200 m. Assumptions 2 and 3 are aligned with the literature on the topic.

Assumptions 4, 5, and 6 establish basic rules that identify trips' start and end. Assumption 4 considers that the boarding station of the first daily trip of each smart-card will always be the beginning of a trip. Analogously, Assumption 5 states that the landing station of the last daily trip of each smart-card will be a Destination of a trip. Finally, assumption 6 addresses situations in which passengers travel by alternatives to the PT system (e.g., by private cars or bicycles). When the estimation of the landing stop of a AFC record is discarded (the passenger traveled off the transport system), the following AFC record is always considered as the beginning of a new trip.

From the successful estimations of alighting stops other than the last trip of the day, the algorithm will distinguish between transfers and trip ends. To perform this distinction, we implemented three criteria, aligned with the assumptions previously defined.

For each pair of consecutive AFC records, the algorithm will assess: (1) if both records are from the same route, in that case, both records are considered to belong to different journeys. (2) if the walking distance is within the specified threshold; (3) if the time elapsed is within the specified threshold; The algorithm identifies a transfer when all three criteria are met. If at least one of these criteria do not meet, the first AFC record of the pair classifies as a trip end (its alighting stop is the trip Destination), and the boarding stop of the next AFC record is the Origin of a new trip.

3.3   Selecting Relevant Transfer-Connection

The methodology for the identification of relevant transfer-connections is grounded on four main assumptions. These assumptions are not perceived as rigid criteria, but instead as a framework to support the selection process. A description of the four assumptions is provided in Table 4.

Assumption 1 considers that the expertise and knowledge of distinguished stakeholders must be accounted in to identify relevant connections, even without meeting any quantitative criteria. This includes cases such as providing transportation service in areas with lower population density, maintain a transfer-connection that has existed for a long time and therefore is awaited by passengers, or to ensure the connection between the last trips of specific routes (allowing passengers that travel late to reach home).

Table 4. Assumptions for the selection of relevant transfer-connections.

	Assumptions
1	A transfer-connection is relevant when identified as such by experts, considering social, historical, and service quality aspects
2	When two routes have shared path segments, favor the selection of transfer-connections at their merging and splitting transfer-nodes
3	A transfer-connection is relevant if it links stops within a specified threshold of walking-distance (in meters)
4	A transfer-connection is relevant if it complies with a specified threshold of demand (frequency of passengers)

Assumption 2 considers situations where two or more routes share a portion of the path. In these cases, the algorithm prioritizes transfer-connections positioned at strategic stops such as route meeting, merging, or crossing. This assumption translates into a binary variable called *Network strategic value*.

Assumption 3 ensures the geographic vicinity of transfer-connections, mainly to ensure it is walkable. Although a similar criterion was applied in step 2, any connection proposed by experts must also comply with this condition.

Assumption 4 considers that the importance of transfer-connections relates to the number of passengers using them. The implementation of this assumption

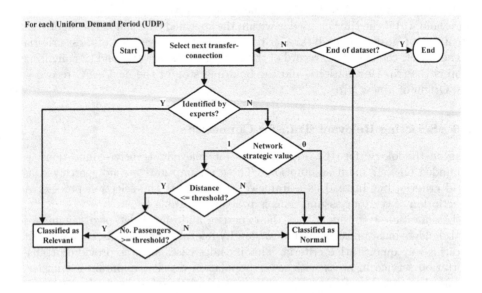

Fig. 7. Algorithm to identify relevant transfer-connections.

consists of selecting all transfer-connections with a frequency of transfer-events higher than a specified threshold.

Figure 7 schematizes the application of the assumptions described in this section into an algorithm. This algorithm runs after the completion of the previous two steps of the methodology.

In contrast to the previous two steps, this algorithm does not use the AFC data-set. The data for this algorithm includes the following features for each transfer-connection in the system: (i) experts identified the connection as relevant (y/n), (ii) the network strategic value (binary), (iii) the walkable distance between the two stops, (iv) the passenger daily frequency. The algorithm performs the sequential validation of all assumptions, as shown in Fig. 7.

4   Results

The database software PostgreSQL was used to select and sort data. The TCM algorithm was implemented in C++, using a 3.4 GHz Intel Core i7 processor and 16 GB of Random Access Memory (RAM). The computational effort of solving the TCM in this particular application is considerably low, less than 10 seconds. The performance of this algorithm in more significant instances was reported in [12]. The methodology described in Sect. 3 was applied to the case study of Porto considering a sample of 4000 randomly selected smart-cards. All smart-cards were analyzed over the entire year of 2013.

This implementation considered the following thresholds: 3 km in assumption 1 of Table 2, 200 m in assumption 2 of Table 3 and in assumption 3 of Table 4, 30 min in assumption 3 of Table 3 and 80 annual transfer-events in assumption 4 of Table 4.

Table 5. Overview of results.

Month	1	2	3	4	5	6	7	8	9	10	11	12	Total
Original data-set													
AFC-records	16783	15080	15965	17160	18460	15088	16349	12891	15232	17851	16360	14719	191938
Alighting not estimated - single daily AFC-record													
AFC-records	1458	1243	1452	1481	1607	1434	1465	1091	1327	1449	1363	1311	16681
%	8.69	8.24	9.09	8.63	8.71	9.50	8.96	8.46	8.71	8.12	8.33	8.91	8.69
Alighting not estimated - distance $\geq$3 km													
AFC-records	447	417	409	475	494	428	404	357	381	464	450	458	5184
%	2.66	2.77	2.56	2.77	2.68	2.84	2.47	2.77	2.50	2.60	2.75	3.11	2.70
Pairs of consecutive AFC-records identified as transfer-connections													
Pairs	1830	1632	1664	1866	2076	1668	1864	1479	1677	1912	1587	1337	20592
%	10.90	10.82	10.42	10.87	11.25	11.06	11.40	11.47	11.01	10.71	9.70	9.08	10.73

Table 5 shows the summary of the results obtained for the first two steps of the methodology as described in Sects. 3.1 and 3.2. The results are detailed by month, and the last column provides the aggregate value for the entire year. The first row provides information on the total number of AFC records analyzed. The number and percentage of AFC records to which the TCM could not estimate alighting stops are detailed in two groups. The first group includes the cases where there was only one daily record - and therefore, the assumption of returning home could not be applied. The second group refers to the cases where the distance of the estimated alighting stop was higher than 3 km - those estimations were discarded since the passenger is assumed to travel out of the system.

Finally, from the AFC records with successful estimations of alighting stops, Table 5 shows the number of transfer-events that were identified, and its proportion regarding the original AFC data-set. For a yearly aggregate perspective, transfer-events accounted for around 11% of total AFC records. Note that a transfer-event is identified amid two AFC records, but its accounting is not duplicated. Therefore, each transfer-event is accounted for just once - making them comparable to the total number of AFC records.

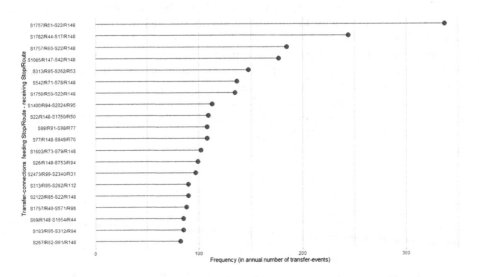

Fig. 8. Selected relevant transfer-connections.

The last step of the methodology proposed in this work was implemented as described in Sect. 3.3. It returned the identification of 20 relevant transfer-connections. Figure 8 shows the selected connections regarding their annual passenger frequency. The selected transfer-connections accounted for 36.40% of all transfer-events under analysis.

5   Conclusions

The main goal of this work was to develop and implement a methodology able to retrieve the most relevant transfer-connections of a PT system. The need to identify the relevant transfer-connections within a PT context arises as a preliminary stage to the implementation of the STP algorithm, usually applied to a simplified network of the PT system which reflects its main demand flows. The identification of such a simplified network is not an easy task, especially in PT systems using entry-only AFC ticketing systems, such as the case study of this work, the city of Porto.

Following this goal, a methodology was developed encompassing three main steps. Step 1 addressed the estimation of the alighting stop of each AFC record using the TCM, step 2 the identification of transfer-events considering all pairs of consecutive AFC records, and step 3 the identification of the most relevant transfer-connections in the PT system following a set of criteria.

This methodology was applied to the case study of Porto, considering a sample of 4000 randomly selected smart-cards over the entire year of 2013. This analysis served as a proof of concept of the methodology. The results obtained are promising and call for the replication of this methodology to larger data-sets, and to perform statistic analysis regarding the type of passengers (frequent passenger and occasional passengers), as well as to compare the set of relevant transfer-connections in different UDP, such as peak and off-peak hours of the day. Future work also includes using this methodology to build PT networks of relevant transfer-connections and feed them as inputs to STP algorithms.

Acknowledgements. Funding: This work was supported by (a) the Foundation for Science and Technology (FCT), [grant number PD/BD/113761/2015]; and (b) by the European Regional Development Fund (ERDF) through the Operational Programme for Competitiveness and Internationalisation - COMPETE 2020 Programme and by National Funds through the FCT within project POCI-010145-FEDER-032053 - PTDC/ECI-TRA/32053/2017.

References

1. Ceder, A.: Public Transit Planning and Operation: Theory, Modeling and Practice. Elsevier, Butterworth-Heinemann (2007). ISBN 978-0-7506-6166-9
2. Ibarra-Rojas, O.J., Rios-Solis, Y.A.: Synchronization of bus timetabling. Transp. Res. Part B: Methodol. **46**(5), 599–614 (2012). https://doi.org/10.1016/j.trb.2012.01.006
3. Fouilhoux, P., et al.: Valid inequalities for the synchronization bus timetabling problem. Eur. J. Oper. Res. **251**(2), 442–450 (2016). https://doi.org/10.1016/j.ejor.2015.12.006
4. Cao, Z., et al.: Optimal synchronization and coordination of actual passengerrail timetables. J. Intell. Transp. Syst. **23**(3), 231–249 (2019). https://doi.org/10.1080/15472450.2018.1488132
5. Barry, J., et al.: Origin and destination estimation in New York City with automated fare system data. Transp. Res. Rec.: J. Transp. Res. Board **1817** (2002). https://doi.org/10.3141/1817-24

6. Trépanier, M., Tranchant, N., Chapleau, R.: Individual trip destination estimation in a transit smart card automated fare collection system. J. Intell. Transp. Syst.: Technol. Plan. Oper. **11**(1), 1–14 (2007). https://doi.org/10.1080/15472450601122256

7. Barry, J., Freimer, R., Slavin, H.: Use of entry-only automatic fare collection data to estimate linked transit trips in New York City. Transp. Res. Rec.: J. Transp. Res. Board **2112**, 53–61 (2009). https://doi.org/10.3141/2112-07

8. Alsger, A., et al.: Use of smart card fare data to estimate public transport origin-destination matrix. Transp. Res. Rec.: J. Transp. Res. Board **2535**, 88–96 (2015). https://doi.org/10.3141/2535-10

9. Nunes, A.A., Galvão, T., Cunha, J.F.: Passenger journey destination estimation from automated fare collection system data using spatial validation. IEEE Trans. Intell. Transp. Syst. **17**(1), 133–142 (2016). https://doi.org/10.1109/TITS.2015.2464335

10. Munizaga, M., Palma, C.: Estimation of a disaggregate multimodal public transport Origin-Destination matrix from passive smartcard data from Santiago, Chile. Transp. Res. Part C: Emerg. Techn. **24**, 9–18 (2012). https://doi.org/10.1016/j.trc.2012.01.007

11. Nassir, N., et al.: Transit stop-level origin-destination estimation through use of transit schedule and automated data collection system. Transp. Res. Rec.: J. Transp. Res. Board **2263**(1), 140–150 (2011). https://doi.org/10.3141/2263-16

12. Hora, J., et al.: Estimation of Origin-Destination matrices under Automatic Fare Collection: the case study of Porto transportation system. Transp. Res. Procedia **27**, 664–671 (2017). https://doi.org/10.1016/j.trpro.2017.12.103

Optimising Supply Chain Logistics System Using Data Analytics Techniques

Eleni Mangina[1,2]([✉]) [ID], Pranav Kashyap Narasimhan[1], Mohammad Saffari[2,3] [ID],
and Ilias Vlachos[4] [ID]

[1] School of Computer Science, University College Dublin, Dublin, Ireland
{eleni.mangina,mohammad.saffari}@ucd.ie
[2] UCD Energy Institute, University College Dublin, Dublin, Ireland
[3] School of Mechanical and Materials Engineering, University College Dublin,
Dublin, Ireland
pranavkashyap2006@gmail.com
[4] La Rochelle Business School, Excelia Group, La Rochelle, France
ivlachos@gmail.com

Abstract. The transport sector's share of global energy-related carbon emissions is about 23%. Transportation and logistics can improve the economic growth of nations and profitability in businesses, and if efficiently designed and managed their carbon footprints will be reduced. Important progresses have been made to enhance the efficiency of logistics supply chain using mathematical optimisation techniques. However, recent needs in collaborative supply chain on one hand, and advancements in data science have heightened the need for optimisation techniques based on big data analytics. This paper studies and evaluates models for European freight transport logistics actions utilising advanced data analytics solutions. Three new supply chain algorithms of horizontal collaboration, pooling, and physical internet have been developed using historical data of European road freight transport. Then, two indicators of sustainability and efficiency were used to evaluate each developed strategy. The results have shown that there is substantial potential in pursuing these strategies and encourages future research into logistic supply chain and data analytic methods for designing sustainable transport systems.

Keywords: Supply chain strategies · Transport optimisation · Carbon emissions reduction

1 Introduction

The European Union (EU) road freight industry is one of the largest consumers of energy [1]. Since 2014, GHG emissions from the EU-28 transport sector have been increasing. Road transport and aviation caused 3% rise in greenhouse gas emissions in 2016, compared to its levels in 2015. In 2016, transport contributed

---

Supported by University College Dublin and University of Leeds.

A. L. Martins et al. (Eds.): INTSYS 2019, LNICST 310, pp. 77–91, 2020.
https://doi.org/10.1007/978-3-030-38822-5_6

27% of total GHG emissions in the EU-28, of which road transport was responsible for almost 72% of total greenhouse gas emissions from transport (including international aviation and international shipping) [2]. For this reason, the EU countries adopted the objective to cut down emissions by 80–95% by the year 2050 in comparison to the 1990 levels [3].

Figure 1 shows CO_2 emissions per mode of transport in Europe [4] from 2000 to 2014. It can be observed that the amount of carbon emissions in maritime and road transport had been the highest among other modes of transport, and since 2013 onward road freight transport had the highest rate of CO_2 emissions.

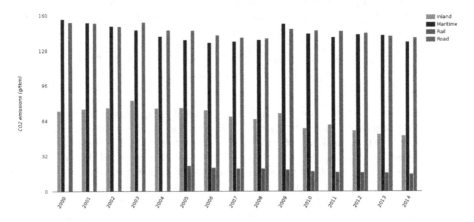

Fig. 1. Specific CO_2 emissions per tonne-km by freight transport mode in Europe [4]

Logistics network design and sustainable logistics management policies are two essential aspects for developing a low-carbon regional logistics system [5]. There has been an increasing emphasis on the necessity for efficient supply chains worldwide. There are several factors which influence the efficiency and effectiveness of transport systems such as traffic congestion problems, carbon emissions, road user charges, regulatory directives and skill shortages [6]. These inefficiencies lead to poor asset utilisation, unnecessary administration, excessive waiting time and inventory management, increased emissions and more importantly an increase in costs [7].

A large and growing body of literature has investigated the supply change efficiency improvement [8], as well as simulation and optimisation methods [9]. For example, in a recent study, Muñoz-Villamizar et al. [10] proposed a new methodology for assessing the environmental performance of logistics systems to improve the sustainability of urban freight transport systems. In another study, Andrés and Padilla [11] evaluated the most influential factors that have affected the energy consumption and carbon emissions trends of road freight transport in Spain from 1996 to 2012. Additionally, Mrazovik et al. [12] presented a routing optimisation method based on data analytics to improve the circulation of vehicles and utilisation of urban parking spaces.

Recent developments in data analytics have heightened the need for methods and tools to make data-driven supply change management [13]. Recent evidence shows that significant progresses have taken place in the field of logistics for reducing carbon emissions and improving the supply chain efficiency, such as Horizontal Collaboration [14], Pooling [15], and Physical Internet [16]. This is an important multidisciplinary and interdisciplinary research topic, nevertheless, there has been little quantitative analysis of data-driven techniques for sustainable supply chain [17] which makes this field of study an excellent opportunity for the development of new techniques and methods.

The main objective of this study is to develop data-driven optimisation algorithms for three popular supply chain methods of Pooling, Horizontal Collaboration, and Physical Internet and performing data analysis on the European road freight transport operations to improve the vehicle usage efficiency, and decrease carbon dioxide emissions per journey.

2   Background Study

2.1   The Sustainable Global Supply Chain

The world economy is likely to grow rapidly and a feature of this growth would be increased demand for transport and logistics. Correspondingly, this requires governments and other stakeholders to plan carefully to cope with the environmental, social and economic needs of a rapidly-growing supply chain network [18]. It is essential to invest further in infrastructure of logistics operations and intelligent transport systems for empowering efficient planning and better coordination of logistics operations [19].

There have been several studies to demonstrate the link between an increase in demand for transport operations and the rise in economic indicators [20]. Governments have realised the impact of free and easy trade and have responded by deregulating transport which has helped in removing unnecessary barriers to competition and has helped in making markets more competitive and ensured that prices come down and the services improve. However, as the supply chains are fast growing, it is essential that they are sustainable [21].

For this, previous studies have investigated the use of optimisation based on heuristic methods for logistics supply chain. For example, Wei and Dong [22] proposed a new multi-objective optimisation solution using adaptive-weight Genetic Algorithm method to optimise freight costs and transport time in new dry-port-based cross-border logistics networks in Chinese inland regions. In another recent study, Liu et al. [23] proposed a real-time information-driven dynamic optimisation method for smart vehicles and logistics operations to achieve green logistics. They showed that, by using internet-of-things (IoT) technology, vehicles utilisation rate can be improved, and by providing the optimal routing with ensured efficiency of logistics services, fuel consumption, number of vehicles used, and costs can be reduced. In addition, and in lines with previous researches reviewed in this paragraph, Abbbassi et al. [24] and Masson et al. [25] used different mathematical optimisation methodologies to improve the logistics transportation system.

However, the use of big data and data analytics for supply chain management and logistics has recently gained prominence [26,27]. The recent trends in supply chain logistics and data analytics suggest that there is a need to shift from heuristics methods to data-driven decision making techniques [28]. This is a step change towards more sustainable logistics supply chain which is addressed in current study. Three important supply chain logistics strategies are horizontal collaborations, pooling, and physical internet which are explained further in next sections.

2.2   Horizontal Collaborations

Horizontal collaborations are characterised by companies sharing supply chain services for common interests which can increase the efficiency and competitiveness of the participating companies [29]. Nevertheless, in the field of supply chain and logistics, more research is required to be done in the domain of horizontal collaboration or swap operations. Several benefits are associated with horizontal collaboration. For example, costs could be shared between participating organisations. Moreover, better production flexibility can be attained. Also, the involved businesses can use the capability of their partners to access new customers and markets. However, the cost of establishing coordination among the different partners is quite high and it requires significant capital investments which is a drawback. The quality of offered products could also be reversely affected by choosing the wrong partner, where losing reputation among customers could be a threat for the company and project.

2.3   Pooling

In supply chain logistics pooling means grouping of shipments that are bound to the same region and are centralised onto trailers for the entire or part of the journey. Pooling, in order to be successful needs that the demands to be met are similar and compatible. When third party logistics (3PL) provider is used for pooling, there is a higher security risk since customers require their products to be always detectable and prefer routine updates about the condition of their product. Moreover, combining hazardous products with inflammable products as they may affect the safety of the journey could be a risk [30].

2.4   Physical Internet

Internet has strongly influenced and changed the manner of information exchange and flows globally. Today, the internet is not about data and information anymore but there is a strong tie between internet and physical world. In other words, the physical internet is using the basics of the internet to logistics. The physical internet encases physical goods into green and modular containers which are usually made from environment friendly materials. This needs minimum packaging in which the so-called smart packets are tagged with sensors to facilitate proper routing and maintenance. This has been brought through progresses in the 'Internet of Things' technology and the application of sensors and radio-frequency identification (RFID) [31].

Based on the literature review, there is a great potential for improving the efficiency of logistics systems and shifting from traditional to integrated logistics systems such as collaborative logistics [32]. The important advantages of such collaborative logistics are: lower prices due to aggregated purchasing quantities, reduction of supply risk and administration cost due to centralised purchasing activities, reduction of inventory and transportation costs, logistics facilities through a rationalisation of equipment and improved sharing of data and manpower [33]. The basis of these methods is 'coopetition' or 'collaborative competition' where direct rivals collaborate on those parts of the supply chain where they do not have a specific advantage, instead of competing [34].

The current literature on big data analytics for supply chain logistics up to now has been descriptive with recent examples of applying data analytics into practice for improving the supply chain [35]. In addition, no research has been found that developed horizontal collaboration, pooling, and physical internet optimisation algorithms based on big data analytics, which is the main scope of this study.

3 Methodology

3.1 Overview

The data used in this study was obtained from the European Road Freight Transport (ERFT) survey, which consisted of road freight operations information of 27 European nations and European Free Trade Association (EFTA) countries between 2011 and 2014. The dataset contained over 11 million journeys with vehicle-related variables, journey-related variables, and goods-related variables. IBM SPSS Modeller [36] and Python [37] data analysis and programming software were used to develop pooling, horizontal collaboration, and physical internet supply chain logistics algorithms.

Anomaly detection and data preparation models of IBM were used. Then outliers were removed and the data was normalised. The data used in the survey did not include details about the efficiency of each journey neither the carbon emissions per journey which are the two indicators utilised to analyse journeys. The dataset did not include data on return journey and the distance covered on empty load, neither handling costs. So that, it was not possible to perform reverse logistics. The journeys of dataset were mainly categorised in 3 distinct classes; 1. intra-regional journeys, 2. inter-regional journeys belonging to the same country, and 3. international journeys between two different countries. The formula and steps used to calculate these variables are explained herein. The efficiency of the journeys can be calculated using Eq. 1, which also could be called the ratio of load factor [38].

$$\eta = (\phi/\chi) \times 100 \tag{1}$$

where η stands for Efficiency in percentage, ϕ for Load, and χ for Capacity. To calculate the total emissions, a simplified formula proposed by the European Association for Forwarding, Transport, Logistics and Customs Services (CLECAT) [39] was used. Then, the overall greenhouse gas emissions per tonne kilometre is calculated using Eqs. 2 and 3:

$$G_T = T_{cap} \times g_t \qquad (2)$$

$$T_{cap} = \frac{(W_g - \phi + \chi) \times d}{1000} \qquad (3)$$

where G_t is the total greenhouse gas emissions per tonne kilometres (g CO_2/t-km), T_{cap} is transport capacity, g_t is emissions factor depending on the vehicle weighting, W_g is gross weight, and d is distance.

Analysing the influence of the supply chain strategies on the efficiency and sustainability of Journeys was the most important step in this study.

To do this, the concepts available in literature on logistics in supply chain management had to be converted to executable code. These algorithms were written and developed in Python v2.7. The Python scripts were developed to read in journeys from a .csv or .sav file and save them as objects and modify them based on the supply chain strategy.

3.2 Supply Chain Logistics Strategies

Horizontal Collaboration. The main aim of Horizontal Collaboration algorithm was to find a similar journey with same destination and type of goods but with shorter distance travels to approach the destination and swap these journeys. Then, to enhance the analysis efficiency of the algorithm, a nested dictionary which was of the form: journeys ["*year*"] ["*quarter*"] ["*destination*"] was used in Python environment. This was utilised to decrease the computational complexity of the algorithm and decrease the number of comparisons. Nevertheless, there is a restriction placed on the relevant period which needs to be taken into account for the swap actions and by default, for this analysis, this period was set to 4 quarters (including the current quarter). It should be noted that this algorithm only swaps the categories of goods but it can be improve further by considering the product's name or type. Figure 2 represents the flowchart for horizontal collaboration algorithm developed in this study.

In this method the execution time is linear, and browse the candidate list to find the first journey which meets the condition for swapping, which is another journey that covers a shorter distance to the same destination when compared to the original journey. The candidate list is classified in increasing order of time (year and quarter) so priority is given to the first journey which meets this condition and not certainly the best journey. There is a method switch as a part of the Journey class which takes in two arguments, the journey to be swapped and the original journey. Afterwards, the algorithm builds a new journey with

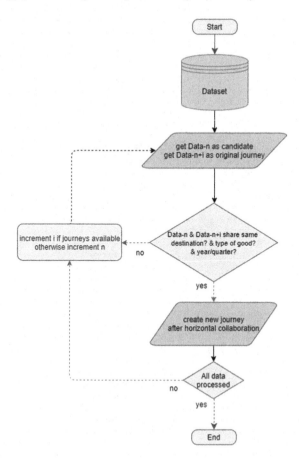

Fig. 2. Flowchart for Horizontal Collaboration algorithm

the same vehicle variables and origin as the journey for swapping and the load and the item weights from the original journey.

Pooling. Pooling means uniting two journeys which are less than complete capacity to enhance the total efficiency and decrease the total hazardous emissions.

Pooling, in order to take place successfully, requires the two journeys to take place in the same time frame, and follow the same route. Additionally, the objects contained in these journeys have to be compatible with each other. The algorithm developed for the analysis only considered journeys which had the same origin and destination, but, it is possible that this can be improved to allow for pooling of partial journeys and the creation of hubs along the way which would also serve as co-ordination centres. The nested dictionary utilised for the Pooling algorithm is similar to the dictionary utilised for Horizontal Collaboration, however the origin of each journey was also considered: journeys ["year"]

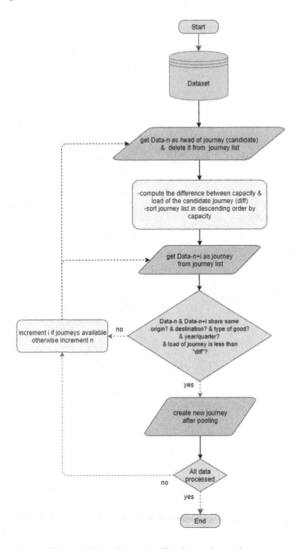

Fig. 3. Flowchart for Pooling algorithm

["*quarter*"] ["*origin*"] ["*destination*"]. Figure 3 demonstrates the flowchart of Pooling algorithm developed in this study.

In this method, the journey list is taken as an input and returns a list of result with the final journeys after pooling has taken place. The first element of the journey list is initialised as head and removed from the list and the difference between the capacity and the load is calculated. The journeys in the journey list are then placed in descending order according to their capacity and the head is then compared with all the other journeys in the journey list and two conditions need to be fulfilled before the journeys can be pooled; first, the items present in the head and the journey being compared do not violate the blacklist, and second, the load of the journey being compared is less than the difference between the head capacity and the load. This method is iterated until all journeys are pooled.

Physical Internet. The algorithm for the Physical Internet only took into account 'port to port' logistics and optimising of partial journeys because of the lack of clear information on exact locations in the data was not taken into account. This algorithm was an extension of the Pooling Algorithm with some design changes including the creation of a new class named PI-Container which contained information about the individual Physical Internet container, type, origin, and destination of goods, vehicle registration number, and weight of each container. The Journey Class was also modified to store the information about all the Containers in that journey and a dictionary was used to store all the containers in circulation for easy searching and tracking. There containers were created dynamically at run time based on a user-selected set of weights for the Physical Internet containers which only contained one type of goods. A Greedy Approach was followed with respect to creating these containers with the preference being given to the bigger weighted containers first. This algorithm only performs pooling based on the Physical Internet containers, nevertheless, the Physical Internet is more than just a horizontal collaboration strategy since it aims to change the way physical objects are handled in the supply chain.

3.3 Data Visualisation

Since the study involved geographic data, it was important that a GIS tool be used to visualise the routes taken during the period. The journey visualisation was carried out using ArcGIS [40] which is a popular GIS developed by ESRI and widely used in several research projects. The advantage of using ArcGIS over several other JavaScript libraries which can visualise GIS data is that ArcGIS has greater support for regions outside the US and was easy to embed into a website or view online. Another advantage was that ArcGIS supported Python 2.7 so it could be easily adapted to build a Spatial Decision Support System in the future using some of the algorithms developed in this project in the future. Apart from ArcGIS, Tableau [41] was also used to visualise the routes and provide other information such as the efficiency of regions or the volume of goods. Tableau is a popular Business Intelligence software that can be used to build interactive dashboards to allow decision makers to quickly analyse the data and make decisions. It should be mentioned that, it was not possible to do a simulation of the journeys using agent-based software or other open source libraries due to the high degree of generality in the data.

4 Results

4.1 Assessment of Supply Chain Logistic Strategies

Horizontal Collaboration. The results of efficiency improvement in percentage, emissions reduction in $g\,CO_2/t.km$, and distance reduction in km after applying Horizontal Collaboration strategy are presented in this section. The optimisation algorithm developed for Horizontal Collaboration used big dataset of European road freight transportation. Table 1 shows the results after applying Horizontal Collaboration by different Journey IDs. It can be observed that distance reductions from 9 to 160 km achieved. In addition, a maximum CO_2 reduction of 0.282 $g\,CO_2/t.km$ was observed. Because the covered distance is short, the overall carbon emissions are negligible. Also, it can be seen that in some cases negative efficiencies are achieved when swapping was used with a high-capacity vehicle.

Furthermore, 42.29% of efficiency improvement was achieved only in case of Journey C. From the analyses performed on five randomly chosen journeys (Journeys A to E), Horizontal Collaboration has demonstrated to be a suitable strategy to decrease carbon emissions. This could be a good strategy for small-size manufacturers since the reduction in the distance covered can also lead to reduction in overall costs and offer better profitability.

Table 1. Comparison of efficiency, distance, and emissions after Horizontal Collaboration

Journey ID	Efficiency improvement	Distance reduction	Emissions reduction (g CO_2/t-km)
A	−0.08%	9 km	0.282
B	−4.91%	29 km	0.039
C	42.29%	8 km	0.013
D	0.00%	95 km	0.157
E	−66.19%	160 km	0.163

Pooling. From data analyses and optimisation performed, it was shown that Pooling can improve both the efficiency and reduce the carbon emissions in road fright transport. Figures 4 and 5 compare emissions reduction and efficiency improvement by using Pooling strategy in different years in some selected EU countries including Germany, France, Spain, Netherlands, Austria, United Kingdom, and Ireland, respectively. It can be seen that in the selected EU countries freight transport efficiency improved substantially, and the CO_2 emissions decreased in all years. For greenhouse gas emissions a maximum reduction of 12% (350000 $g\,CO_2/t - km$) was recorded from 2011 to 2014 (see Fig. 4), and in terms of overall efficiency an improvement of 23% was observed considering all countries (see Fig. 5).

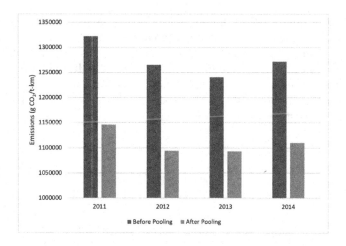

Fig. 4. Comparison of total emissions before and after Pooling by year

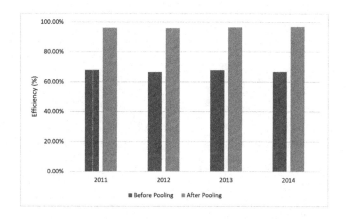

Fig. 5. Comparison of efficiency before and after Pooling by year

4.2 Data Visualisation

The last phase of the Analysis was Data Visualisation is a very important phase of the Knowledge Discovery Process as it helps to convey the findings of the Analysis and good analysis would be incomplete without good visualisation to convey the story or message from the results. Since the study involved Geographic data, it was important that a GIS tool be used to visualise the routes taken during the period. A brief description is given on how the visualisations were created.

Tableau is probably the most popular Business Intelligence software and is widely used by data analysts in industry to create interactive dashboards which can be used to represent a wide variety of information quickly. The interactive nature of Tableau makes it a popular choice for managers and decision makers. For example, in the interactive dashboard created for this study shown in Fig. 6, clicking on a country will display the emissions per year as well as the most popular goods in that country. For example, in case of Ireland it can be seen that the efficiency before Pooling was 52.50%, the trend of carbon emissions from 2011 to 2014 can be seen, and also it shows which products and goods were transported the most.

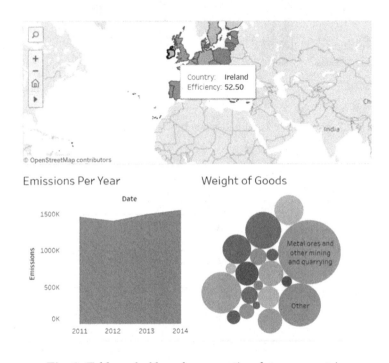

Fig. 6. Tableau dashboard representing data on countries

5   Conclusions

The main objective of this study was to develop three supply chain algorithms of Horizontal Collaboration, Pooling, and Physical Internet. Then, data from the European Road Freight Transport survey was used to assess the effectiveness of these three supply chain strategies to improve the efficiency and the sustainability of European road freight operations. The results were very impressive and there was as much as a 12% reductions in road freight transport emissions and a 23% increase in the overall efficiency, using Pooling strategy. The results of the present study would vary depending on the dataset used and the approach, however, the study has demonstrated that there are benefits to coopetition and horizontal collaboration in Logistics and this can be an area for future work and research in the field of supply chain management. The future work would also involve combining Horizontal Collaboration and Pooling and allow for pooling of swapped goods from different suppliers, in which more information about the location and the types of products involved will be required.

Acknowledgements. This publication has emanated from research conducted between School of Computer Science (UCD) and Business School (University of Leeds) as part of the collaborative/network project "Big Data Analytics for Sustainable Global Supply Chains" and data provided by the Commission (Eurostat) in the framework of the above mentioned collaborative/network project (Research entity identification number:2014/219/UK).

References

1. Nowakowska-Grunt, J., Strzelczyk, M.: The current situation and the directions of changes in road freight transport in the European Union. Transp. Res. Procedia **39**, 350–359 (2019)
2. European Environment Agency: Progress of EU transport sector towards its environment and climate objectives, pp. 1–13 (2017)
3. European Commission: EU Reference Scenario 2016 energy, transport and GHG emissions Trends to 2050, pp. 1–220 (2016)
4. European Environment Agency. https://www.eea.europa.eu/data-and-maps/figures/specific-co2-emissions-per-tonne-2. Accessed 12 June 2019
5. Jie, L., Chunhui, Y., Muhammad, H., Qiuyan, Y.: The relationship between environment and logistics performance: evidence from Asian countries. J. Clean. Prod. **204**, 282–291 (2018)
6. Marufuzzaman, M., Ekşioğlu, S.D.: Managing congestion in supply chains via dynamic freight routing: an application in the biomass supply chain. Transp. Res. Part E: Logist. Transp. Rev. **99**, 54–76 (2017)
7. Managan, J., Lalwani, C., Jadavpur, R., Butcher, T.: Global Logistics and Supply Chain Management. Wiley, Hoboken (2012)
8. Nikfarjam, H., Rostamy-Malkhalifeh, M., Mamizadeh-Chatghayeh, S.: Measuring supply chain efficiency based on a hybrid approach. Transp. Res. Part D: Transp. Environ. **39**, 141–150 (2015)
9. Hajian Heidary, M., Aghaie, A.: Risk averse sourcing in a stochastic supply chain: a simulation-optimization approach. Comput. Ind. Eng. **130**, 62–74 (2019)
10. Muñoz-Villamizar, A., Santos, J., Montoya-Torres, J., Velázquez-Martínez, J.: Measuring environmental performance of urban freight transport systems: a case study. Sustain. Cities Soc. **52**, 101844 (2020)
11. Andrés, L., Padilla, E.: Energy intensity in road freight transport of heavy goods vehicles in Spain. Energy Policy **85**, 101844 (2015)
12. Mrazovic, P., Eser, E., Ferhatosmanoglu, H., Larriba-Pey, J.L., Matskin, M.: Multi-vehicle route planning for efficient urban freight transport. In: 2018 International Conference on Intelligent Systems (IS), pp. 744–753 (2018)
13. Zhong, R.Y., Newman, S.T., Huang, G.Q., Lan, S.: Big Data for supply chain management in the service and manufacturing sectors: challenges, opportunities, and future perspectives. Comput. Ind. Eng. **101**, 572–591 (2016)

14. Cruijssen, F., Cools, M., Dullaert, W.: Horizontal cooperation in logistics: opportunities and impediments. Transp. Res. Part E: Logist. Transp. Rev. **43**, 129–142 (2007)
15. Pan, S., Ballot, E., Fontane, F.: The reduction of greenhouse gas emissions from freight transport by pooling supply chains. Int. J. Prod. Econ. **143**, 86–94 (2013)
16. Yang, Y., Pan, S., Ballot, E.: Freight transportation resilience enabled by physical internet. IFAC-PapersOnLine **50**, 2278–2283 (2017)
17. Govindan, K., Cheng, T.C.E., Mishra, N., Shukla, N.: Big data analytics and application for logistics and supply chain management. Transp. Res. Part E: Logist. Transp. Rev. **114**, 343–349 (2018)
18. Sdoukopoulos, A., Pitsiava-Latinopoulou, M., Basbas, S., Papaioannou, P.: Measuring progress towards transport sustainability through indicators: analysis and metrics of the main indicator initiatives. Transp. Res. Part D: Transp. Environ. **67**, 316–333 (2019)
19. Sun, S.C., Duan, Z.Y., Chen, C.: Energy overview for globalized world economy: source, supply chain and sink. Renew. Sustain. Energy Rev. **69**, 735–749 (2017)
20. Koberg, E., Longoni, A.: Freight transport impacts from the economic crisis in Greece. Transp. Policy **57**, 51–58 (2017)
21. Koberg, E., Longoni, A.: A systematic review of sustainable supply chain management in global supply chains. J. Clean. Prod. **207**, 1084–1098 (2019)
22. Wei, H., Dong, M.: Import-export freight organization and optimization in the dry-port-based cross-border logistics network under the Belt and Road Initiative. Comput. Ind. Eng. **130**, 472–484 (2019)
23. Liu, S., Zhang, Y., Liu, Y., Wang, L., Wang, X.V.: An 'Internet of Things' enabled dynamic optimization method for smart vehicles and logistics tasks. J. Clean. Prod. **215**, 806–820 (2019)
24. Abbassi, A., El hilali Alaoui, A., Boukachour, J.: Robust optimisation of the intermodal freight transport problem: modeling and solving with an efficient hybrid approach. J. Comput. Sci. **30**, 127–142 (2019)
25. Masson, R., Trentini, A., Lehuédé, F., Malhéné, N., Péton, O., Tlahig, H.: Optimization of a city logistics transportation system with mixed passengers and goods. EURO J. Transp. Logist. **6**, 81–109 (2017)
26. Wang, G., Gunasekaran, A., Ngai, E.W.T., Papadopoulos, T.: Big data analytics in logistics and supply chain management: certain investigations for research and applications. Int. J. Prod. Econ. **176**, 98–110 (2016)
27. Kamble, S.S., Gunasekaran, A., Gawankar, S.A.: Achieving sustainable performance in a data-driven agriculture supply chain: a review for research and applications. Int. J. Prod. Econ. **219**, 179–194 (2020)
28. Arunachalam, D., Kumar, N., Kawalek, J.P.: Understanding big data analytics capabilities in supply chain management: unravelling the issues, challenges and implications for practice. Transp. Res. Part E: Logist. Transp. Rev. **114**, 416–436 (2018)
29. Soysal, M., Bloemhof-Ruwaard, J.M., Haijema, R., van der Vorst, J.G.A.J.: Modeling a green inventory routing problem for perishable products with horizontal collaboration. Comput. Oper. Res. **89**, 168–182 (2018)
30. Bachmann, F., Hanimann, A., Artho, J., Jonas, K.: What drives people to carpool? Explaining carpooling intention from the perspectives of carpooling passengers and drivers. Transp. Res. Part F: Traffic Psychol. Behav. **59**, 260–268 (2018)
31. Lee, C.C., Chen, S.D., Li, C.T., Cheng, C.L., Lai, Y.M.: Security enhancement on an RFID ownership transfer protocol based on cloud. Future Gener. Comput. Syst. **93**, 266–277 (2019)

32. Moutaoukil, A., Derrouiche, R., Neubert, G.: Pooling supply chain: literature review of collaborative strategies. In: Camarinha-Matos, L.M., Xu, L., Afsarmanesh, H. (eds.) PRO-VE 2012. IAICT, vol. 380, pp. 513–525. Springer, Heidelberg (2012). https://doi.org/10.1007/978-3-642-32775-9_52
33. Bahinipati, B.K., Kanda, A., Deshmukh, S.G.: Horizontal collaboration in semiconductor manufacturing industry supply chain: an evaluation of collaboration intensity index. Comput. Ind. Eng. **57**, 880–895 (2009)
34. Li, X.: Operations management of logistics and supply chain: issues and directions. Discrete Dyn. Nat. Soc. **2014**, 7 (2014)
35. Mujica Mota, M., El Makhloufi, A., Scala, P.: On the logistics of cocoa supply chain in Côte d'Ivoire: simulation-based analysis. Comput. Ind. Eng. **137**, 106034 (2019)
36. SPSS Modeler. https://www.ibm.com/products/spss-modeler. Accessed 30 Jan 2019
37. Python. https://www.python.org. Accessed 30 Jan 2019
38. Load factors for freight transport, European Environment Agency. https://www.eea.europa.eu/downloads/064091f718cd81fb2042d01de9965765/1492593883/load-factors-for-freight-transport.pdf. Accessed 25 Sept 2019
39. Schmied, M., Knörr, K.: Calculating GHG emissions for freight forwarding and logistics services in accordance with EN 16258 Calculating GHG emissions for freight forwarding and logistics services. European Association for Forwarding, Transport, Logistics and Customs Services (CLECAT), Brussels (2012)
40. LNCS Homepage. https://www.arcgis.com/index.html. Accessed 30 Jan 2019
41. Tableau. https://www.tableau.com. Accessed 30 Jan 2019

Analyzing a Fleet Solution Using Scenarios

Ana Lúcia Martins[1,2(✉)], Ana Catarina Nunes[1,3],
and Bernardo Carvalho[1]

[1] Instituto Universitário de Lisboa (ISCTE-IUL), Lisbon, Portugal
alhm@iscte-iul.pt
[2] Business Research Unit (BRU-ISCTE), Lisbon, Portugal
[3] Centro de Matemática, Aplicações Fundamentais e Investigação Operacional
(CMAFcIO), Universidade de Lisboa, Lisbon, Portugal

Abstract. Transportation is one of the most important logistics activities, accounting for a significant part of the logistics costs and with high level of impact in terms of the service level provided to the customer. To counteract the upward trend in costs, it is fundamental to identify a transport strategy that can reduce costs and, at the same time, does not adversely affect the service levels agreed with customers. The main objective of this research is to propose a methodology for companies to identify, from a set of scenarios proposed and through a comparative analysis of scenarios, a new fleet solution, allowing the Company under study to reduce its transport costs without harming the current service level agreements with its customers. This research is grounded on a case study methodology. The case study used is of a small Portuguese company that produces, imports and distributes a wide range of products. The distribution is conducted based on both its own fleet and subcontracted transportation. The comparative analysis of scenarios allowed identifying the current transportation solution as the most advantageous one for the company. A roadmap to address fleet solution is provided.

Keywords: Transportation fleet · Costumer service · Case study

1 Introduction

The economic crisis that emerged in the beginning of the century is still producing effects. The price of fuel is at one of its highest values ever and transportation companies struggle to remain competitive.

Transportation is one of the logistical activities that absorb more costs and the transportation solution adopted influences the value proposal a company to the market [1]. Although intercontinental movements are mostly fulfilled with road transportation [2], the rising of its costs is leading companies to grasp for more effective solutions and there is no solution that best fits all companies. The transportation strategy can include different fleet options, outsourcing or a full reassessment of route solutions [2], but it should always reflect the goals of the company [3]. Although literature provides many topics for reflection in terms of the benefits and limitation of outsourcing versus insourcing, or even the use of a solution that considers a mix of both the approaches [2], each case and economical context needs to be analyzed individually. Approaching

© ICST Institute for Computer Sciences, Social Informatics and Telecommunications Engineering 2020
Published by Springer Nature Switzerland AG 2020. All Rights Reserved
A. L. Martins et al. (Eds.): INTSYS 2019, LNICST 310, pp. 92–107, 2020.
https://doi.org/10.1007/978-3-030-38822-5_7

this issue goes beyond the traditional minimization of cost and distance and needs to also address service quality in a decision roadmap that is not yet stable in literature.

A Portuguese company that produces, imports and distributes household products for large retail players is facing the challenge of having to reduce its costs but at the same time must maintain or eventually increase the service level it provides to its customer. The Company can: (1) absorb the increase of the cost of fuel and therefore reduce its margins; (2) pass these increased costs to the costs of the products it sells, with the risk of becoming less competitive; or (3) search for more efficient transportation alternatives that do not impact negatively on its service level. The only option the company wants to consider is the third one. Under this scope, the purpose of this research is to develop a roadmap, based on scenarios, that can help the company overcome the challenge of adjusting its transportation solution into a more efficient one while not disregarding service quality.

Accordingly, the goal of this research is twofold: propose a methodology to help companies deciding between the most appropriate transportation scenarios for their specific situation, by unfolding the most suitable transportation modes and their limitations, and compare the solutions in terms of cost the service level.

Due to its nature, this research will follow a case study methodology and Yin's [4] recommendations will be followed. After a conceptual approach to the topic, the methodological framework will be detailed and the Company and its constraints will be explored, scenarios will be developed based not only on its current operation but also on alternative solutions, and scenario comparison will regard cost, truck occupancy, and service level.

2   Literature Review

2.1   Transportation and the Relevance of Customer Service

Although transportation was not considered a much relevant topic some decades ago, nowadays it is recognized as one of the most impacting logistical activities, being responsible for a large proportion of the logistical costs [5]. Being able to influence de competitive position of a company [3], it needs to be carefully managed.

Transportation influences the value of the product as it can only deliver value once available for the customer [1]. It generates value through its utility of place and time [1, 6]. Being able to reach the required locations in due time is paramount, and service level agreements are increasingly demanding and impact heavily on the competitive level of a company [7]. Customer service can be influenced by many aspects such as frequency of deliveries, deliveries according to the request, inventory level, processing time, on-time deliveries, dependability, communication, flexibility [2, 6].

2.2   Factors Influencing Transportation Costs

Transportation costs can generically be divided in fixed costs (those the company has to support regardless of the use of the equipment, such as financial duties, wages, insurance, taxes, depreciation) and variable costs (those that results from the level of activity of the company and only occur if the equipment is being used, such as cost tires, fuel, maintenance, repair) [6]. Outsourcing, by its nature, dependent on the request of the organization, is considered a variable cost. Whatever factors that result in fluctuation in demand lead to variation in variable costs but not in fixed cost.

Economy in transportation can be influenced by several factors such as distance, volume, cargo density, stowability, handling, response, and market factors and empty return [6, 8].

Distance is the variable that influences the most transportation costs from a negative perspective as it impacts variable costs directly; as distance increases the fixed costs are diluted in the number of kilometers but the variable costs will increase proportionally [8].

Volume or weight also influence the transportation costs as the cost the unit of weight transported is affected by the total weight, leading to lighter cargo to be more expensive to move, if weight is considered [8]. The capacity of the equipment will limit the volume that is carried and therefore the cost per weight unit. As such, cargo with different weights should be grouped so that volume and weight limits are reached as simultaneously as possible.

Density is a variable that considers volume and weight simultaneously; the lower the density of the cargo, the higher the price per kilo [8].

Stowability of a product, or ability to be stored, influences greatly transportation costs as products that are out of format or with odd shapes lead to loss of cubic capacity in the equipment, which could be used for other products, leading to higher transportation costs [8].

Handling is also relevant in terms of transportation costs. Products that can be moved using standard equipment lead to less expensive handling as there is no need to use special equipment [8].

The market itself greatly influence transportation costs as due to location issues, routing, cargo aggregation of other factors, a delivery may lead to an empty return, which also have to be considered [8].

It is the reasoning between these factors that dictates the transportation costs for each situation, which often cannot be influenced by the companies but dictated by the nature of the cargo itself and the requests of the customer.

2.3   On-Road Transportation

Road transportation is usually linked to intra continental movements and is the most used one [2]. The flexibility and high adaptability of the road transportation, along with the low investment when compared to other transportation modes and low fixed and high variable costs, makes it very popular mainly to small cargo and shorter distances; nonetheless it is very dependent from external conditions, such as weather and existing infrastructures, limited in terms of cargo volume and more expensive and time-consuming for longer distances [8]. Road transportation has clear advantages within a specific geographical area, and although more sophisticated transportation modes are emerging, it is still the number one transportation option for traditional distribution.

2.4   Route Planning

One way of reducing transportation costs is by reducing distance and transit time, i.e. by identifying the most efficient routes. The longer a truck is in transit, the fewer deliveries are possible to complete in a specific period and the higher the transportation cost will be [9]. Under this scope, companies should strive for reducing transit time by adopting metrics that lead to new, shorter, and faster routes.

The Vehicle Routing Problem (VRP) combines a mathematical and a computer science perspective to servicing customers using vehicles [10]. Usually, when using this methodology, products are located at a central warehouse or at a starting point, and requests emerge from various customers. Generally, the main goal is the minimization of the total distance vehicles must travel or its associated time or cost [11]. Due to many variables involved in these mathematical models, heuristics have been developed to address them.

The Clarke and Wright [12] heuristic is still one of the most popular heuristics for the VRP due to its simplicity. It is based on the concept of savings, i.e., the reduction of costs by merging customers into the same route instead of considering a single route for each one of them. The development of computer technology and mathematical knowledge allowed the design and implementations of more sophisticated heuristics, able to improve initial routs in a reasonable amount of time. The Vehicle Routing Problem Heuristic (VRPH), by [13], is one such example and its authors made it available [14] by means of an open-source software library of several local search heuristics for some routing problems that are variations of the classical VRP. This local search heuristics are characterized by the search of new solutions in the neighborhood of previous ones, using initial solutions derived from Clarke and Wright's heuristic, and by diversifying solutions, returning the best solution.

2.5   Insourcing Versus Outsourcing

Outsourcing is the act of contracting from others parts of the activity of the company. Using outsourcing is a way companies use to become more agile, reduce infrastructure, equipment, and personnel. There are many reasons why outsourcing is used and it is not always an option but a necessity instead. A company may have the ability to perform the activity and decide not to do it for some reason, may need to use it as it required additional capacity, or may simply not have the skills required to complete the activity [15].

One of the main advantages that lead companies to contract service providers is that they can focus on their own activity, relying on others, specialists, the activities that are not considered critical, leading to cost reduction, but the reduction of complexity of the operations is also worth mentioning, as well as the reduction of fixed costs, which are transformed into variable ones; at the same time, and among other disadvantages, it makes them lose control over part of the logistical pipeline and limits their contact with the customer [2]. Additionally, outsourcing services should not operate without control; therefore, additional costs will emerge from this activity, and they also need to be considered in the decision of making or buying [15].

When demand is volatile, many companies aiming for better use of the capacity installed use solutions that are a mix of insourcing and outsourcing. This solution allows them the benefits of both insourcing and outsourcing while minimizing the disadvantages of outsourcing. This is a flexible solution and the volume of outsourced service can change over time according to the best scenario for the company at any given moment. This justifies why outsourcing is a solution that so many companies adopt to fulfill their transportation needs.

2.6   Final Remarks

Road transportation is a very flexible transportation mode and very popular among traditional distribution. To improve their customer service levels while maintaining competitive positions, companies continuously search for the best solutions in terms of fleet management and routing. Although having their own fleet presents advantages for the companies, it also involves challenges as transportation and delivery might not be the core of their business. Regardless these arguments, the choice of the best scenario of insourcing versus outsourcing or an eventual balance between the two requires the balance between efficiency in the use of the resources available but at the same time the need to fulfill service level agreements. A roadmap to properly address such challenge is not yet stable.

3   Methodological Framework

Building on [4] and [16], the research framework proposed and the collection techniques to be used in each research phase are shown in Fig. 1.

Although the phases of this roadmap are generic, for each particular case, adaptations may have to be introduced after exploring the nature of the company and its specificities. Interviews should be conducted throughout the process to assure the suitability of the scenarios and understand the company's perspective.

Phase 1 concerns the characterization of the company and its constraints: facilities, current owned fleet, employees, outsourcing delivery services, service level agreements with customers, customer delivery points, among other aspects. Such information is generally provided by company records, as well as interviews and direct observation.

Demand level and profile, in terms of number of pallets or other unit that expresses the volume do cargo of the company, correspond to Phase 2. Predictions and statistical analyses may have to be conducted, based on the data collected from the company records and interviews. In some cases there might be the need to conduct direct observations to collect additional data regarding weight or other relevant characteristics of pallets. For instance, incompatibility of certain items is relevant as it will influence cargo aggregation.

Identification of fixed and variable transportation costs, extracted from company records, are included in Phase 3. In some cases data regarding for instance fuel or toll costs might need confirmation from sources outside the company, but the remaining costs should be extracted from the company's system and records as to truly reflect its reality. The company perspective and the fleet challenges it wants to analyze is represented by different scenarios identified in Phase 4, mainly based on interviews. Some scenarios emerge from literature but are only worth pursuing if the company considers them as alternatives.

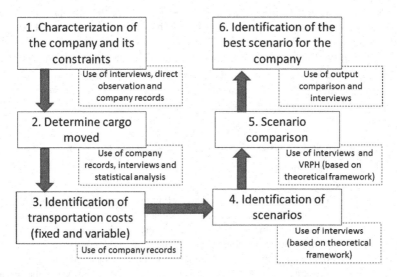

Fig. 1. Methodological framework of the research and data collection and analysis used in each research phase.

Scenarios' comparison and discussion are conducted on Phase 5. Comparison is both quantitative and qualitative, respectively for transportation costs and service levels. Optimization framework, as is the case of routing heuristics like VRPH, may have to be run for cost determination, while discussion reflects the company policies, with response time and logistics service quality having to be analyzed against cost reduction.

Finally, the best scenario for the company is identified in Phase 6, based on the output comparison and again supported by the company's perspective collected from interviews. As the fleet solution is a decision that involves some investment and impacts the company's competitive position, the choice of scenario should not be restricted to the near future of the company.

This roadmap of analysis will be tested based on a use case of a company in the need to assess its current fleet solution in comparison to alternatives that suit its reality. This is a case of a company who wants to optimize its costs but not at expense of it service levels and its competitive position in the market.

4   The Use Case

4.1   The Company

The Company is an average size one with an annual sales volume of about 5.5 million euros. It produces, imports and distributes a wide range of household products. Many of these products are not of regular shape, requiring additional care in handling and transportation efforts, such as ironing boards. The Company produces and sells under its own brand but also for its customers, with its own brand.

The Company operates out of a large facility located about 40 km west of Lisbon. The warehouse has about 8000 m^2 and uses a straight-through layout. Inbound movements are usually received in containers. This cargo can be stored for future customer needs or integrate cross-docking flows.

According to the Company's data, from its 238 customers, 7 of them represent 70% of the volume of sales. These are the main retailers and wholesalers in Portugal. The Company aggregates its customers in three different classes, as shown in Table 1. These classes are the basis for the selection of transportation solutions.

Table 1. Classes of customers and their characterization.

Classes of customers	Description
Class I	Class composed by the two main Portuguese retail chains. They represent about 50% of the sales of the Company. Service Level agreements are extremely demanding. Orders are received twice a day (at 7:00 and at 18:00) and also delivered twice a day (at 14:00 and 8:30). Orders are delivered at the central warehouse of the customers but are already prepared by store. The Company has to support a penalty if the service agreed is not fulfilled
Class II	Customers with delivery points located less than 100 km from the Company's facility. Service levels depend on the volume ordered and the delivery dates are defined when the order is received: (i) orders of full truckloads: service levels are at least 95% and deliveries are usually completed on the same day but can also be completed the day after; (ii) less than full truckloads: service levels agreed for each order
Class III	All other customers (i.e. more than 100 km away). There is no predefined service level as it is agreed for each order. The Company has a lower investment in service for this class of customers. These customers usually order less than full truck load

The Company currently uses both its own fleet and a logistics service provider to transport its cargo. The Company only uses one service provider and does not wish to add more providers or switch to another as the service levels are fulfilled and prices are considered competitive. This service provider has the particularity of charging by the weight of the cargo instead of the volume as the remaining players in the market do. The Company's products have an overall low-density level, i.e., comparatively have more volume than weight.

Over the years, with service providers becoming more popular, the Company reduced its own fleet and currently only has two trucks and two truck drivers. The truck drivers also perform other activities: 65% of their time is dedicated to driving the trucks and 35% to handling activities at the Company's facility.

The use of outsourcing or its own fleet depends on the Class of the customer and the quantity ordered. Class I has priority over Class II in using the Company's fleet. Deliveries for Class III customers are exclusively completed using outsourcing.

Delivery points for Class I customers are both located 66 km from the Company's facility. Unloading arrangement for one of the customers requires about 50 min, while for the other one involves about 2 h. For other customers, unloading times are always lower than 2 h. At the Company's facility, loading a truck requires about 45 min. The Company estimates that trucks travel at an average velocity of 80 km per hour.

Each driver works 8 h per day, 40 h per week. It is possible to use extra time, up to 2 h per day. Each of the trucks of the company has capacity to 10 pallets per journey.

Deliveries to the islands (Madeira and Azores) are transported to the Lisbon seaport (less than 100 km). Thus these customers belong to Class II, and selection of fleet follows the previously described criteria.

4.2   Demand and Costs

The information system of the Company does not allow identifying the number of pallets delivered, only the level of demand in euros. One full reference year was considered. For this year, 3346 deliveries were completed.

The number of units in each order was transformed into pallets based on information from the Company and from the suppliers regarding the number of units in a full mono-product pallet. From here, and for each order, the number of pallets was computed and rounded up. To assure that stowability issues did not affect the estimative for the number of pallets, samples were collected, and statistical analysis was conducted.

A sample of 46 real orders was considered. A very experienced employee was asked to estimate the real number of pallets each of those orders would generate. Then, using statistical analysis, this number was compared with the computed number of pallets for each of the orders. The distribution of the two samples did not show a normal distribution leading to the use of non-parametric tests. The Wilcoxon test for paired samples showed p-value = 0.366, allowing to conclude that the difference between the two distributions is not statistically relevant. This way, our method to estimate the number of pallets was considered reliable.

As the quantity ordered has an impact on the transportation option (own fleet or outsourcing), it was needed to classify orders into Groups (A, B and C). Group A orders include all orders from Class I customers, exclusively, even if they are not full truckload orders. Orders from Class III customers were all considered in Group C orders, even if full truckloads are involved. Regarding Class II customers, their orders were classified into Group B or Group C depending on the size of the order. Within this Class, orders were divided in multiples of 10 pallets (maximum capacity of the Company's trucks): (i) all orders with less than 10 pallets were included in Group C as the company does not consider delivering them with their own trucks; (ii) the parts of these orders that are lower than 10 pallets were also included in Group C as the policy of the Company is to not even consider them for their own trucks; and (iii) the parts of the orders with exactly a multiple of 10 pallets were included in Group B orders. Table 2 summarizes these Groups.

Table 2. Groups of orders and their characterization.

Groups of orders	Description
Group A	Orders from Class I customers
Group B	Orders or parts or orders from Class II customers that are of 10 full pallets
Group C	All orders from Class III customers plus the orders or parts of the orders from Class II customers that are less than 10 full pallets

Based on [1], transportation fixed costs for the Company were considered as all the costs with the two employees (wages, taxes, insurance, other costs), but only at 65% as they perform other tasks at the Company, added by the insurance and national taxes of the trucks, in a total of €14,487.23 for the considered year. Amortization was not considered as both trucks already have 12 years.

Variable transportation costs came from both the owned fleet and outsourcing. As for the owned fleet variable costs, it was considered fuel, maintenance, tolls and additional costs for meals of the truck drivers that occur when the deliveries take longer. It was estimated a variable cost of fuel of €0.1651 per km and a total volume of other insource variable costs per year of €9,471.31 (maintenance, tolls, and meals), already with national taxes included.

All outsourcing costs are considered variable costs as they only occur if and when the Company requests the service. The Company uses these services for deliveries of orders in Group C, and for orders from Groups A and B when there is not enough capacity available at the Company. This way, the priority is for the use of the Company's fleet.

The transportation service supplier charges based on the weight of the cargo moved. In order to assure that the amount charged by the service supplier is correct, all cargo is weighted before leaving the Company.

As the information system of the Company does not register the weight of the cargo per pallet, only its total, the average weight of a pallet was estimated. To be able to identify a reliable result, a random sample of 99 orders expedited using the outsourcer was used. This sample considered a total of 156 pallets, and the average weight computed was of 71.8 kilos.

4.3   Scenario Development

Based on the current situation of the Company, using a mix of insourcing (with two trucks, each of 10 pallets, used with priority for Group 1 orders but also used for Group B orders when there is capacity available) and outsourcing (for order from Group C and some of Group B when the owned fleet is not available), several scenarios can be considered. Whatever scenario is considered, the policy of the Company has to be respected: aim for the lowest cost possible as long as the service level agreements are fulfilled.

A natural scenario (Scenario 1) is to keep the current situation of the Company, with two trucks and the use of outsourcing. This is a conservative solution but one that needs to be addressed at least as a comparison point for the remaining ones. This scenario allows the company to keep control of one of its critical activities (transportation) but using outsourcing when there is not enough capacity available.

With the growth of the tendency to outsource, one inevitable scenario is the single use of outsourcing (Scenario 2). This involves selling the two trucks the Company currently owns and depend fully on a transportation service provider. As the Company does not consider the use of other transportation provider but the one it currently used, only this one and its costs will be considered.

The Company has two customers, representing together about 50% of its sales, with which service level agreements are very demanding. Simultaneously, the level of demand from these customers is quite variable and lead times are of less than half a day. As the outsourcing companies have difficulties fulfilling such demanding lead times, the Company could consider keeping one of its trucks, to assure the service level agreements, but increase the use of outsourcing as the tendency of these services are to be least expensive than insourcing. This option will be considered as a third scenario (Scenario 3).

The considered scenarios are shortly described in Table 3.

Table 3. Short description of each of the scenarios considered in the research

Scenario	Description
1	Current situation: two 10 pallet trucks plus outsourcing
2	Full outsourcing
3	Keeping one 10 pallet truck plus outsourcing

4.4 Scenario Comparison and Discussion

The number of pallets is a key element to compare the three scenarios. For each order, the corresponding number of pallets was thus computed using the procedure described in Sect. 4.2.

Orders allocation to the Company's fleet follows a similar procedure for Scenarios 1 and 3. The difference is the insource daily capacity: two trucks are available in Scenario 1, while a single one is available in Scenario 3.

For a given day, the route of a truck may consist of several trips: each trip is the way from the Company's facility to the discharge location and its return to the facility. The capacity of a truck for each trip is 10 pallets, while the total duration of the route is limited to 10 h (8 plus 2 h a day per driver). The traveled distance of a trip is twice the known distance between the Company's facility and the delivery location. Concerning the trip duration, it includes the obvious traveling time (based on 80 km/hour estimated average velocity), plus the loading time at the Company's facility and the unloading time at the customer. The resting and meal times required by legislation are also added up whenever they cannot occur simultaneously with unloading operations.

To simultaneously deal with the capacity and duration limitations, the VRPH was used for each day of the considered year, as described next.

Calculations for Scenario 1 started by running VRPH for Group A orders. Two 10 pallets trucks are available, each limited to 10 h per day. Two situations may occur in a given day: (i) the owned fleet was not enough to accommodate all Group A orders: the remaining Group A orders were outsourced, as well as all Group B and Group C ones; (ii) the owned fleet was enough to accommodate all Group A orders: if there is still capacity left from the owned fleet, VRPH was run for Group B orders, and the remaining Group B orders were outsourced, if any, as well as Group C ones. Distances and durations were recorded, as well as the number of outsourced pallets. Table 4 summarizes the information for Scenario 1.

Table 4. Relevant information for Scenario 1

Fixed costs (insourcing)		Employees	€12,730.21			
		Trucks	€1,757.02			
		Total fixed costs			€14,487.23	
Variable costs	Insourcing (variable)	Fuel	€12,663.50			(5245 pallets)
		Maintenance	€1,627.90			(76,702 km)
		Tolls	€6,302.31			(645 routes)
		Extra meals	€1,551.16			
		Insourcing (variable)		€22,144.87		
	Outsourcing	Outsourcing	€24,388.77			
		Outsourcing		€24,388.77		(2443 pallets)
	Total variable costs				€46,533.64	(7688 pallets)
Total cost scenario 1					€61,020.87	

Scenario 1 shows dominance from variable costs, nonetheless fixed costs count for about ¼ of the total costs. Considering that amortization was not taken into consideration as vehicles are quite old, the possible future adoption of new(er) vehicles may heavily increase fixed costs and lead to a total cost for the scenario that is much higher than the one identified here.

Regarding Scenario 2 (full outsourcing), pallets of the orders were gathered by day, their weights were added up (based on an average weight of 71.8 kilos per pallet) and the outsourcing cost calculated (supplier charges by weight). Information is presented in Table 5. This scenario is clearly more expensive for the Company than scenario 1, but if the Company decides to use new(er) vehicles the increase in cost from amortization could lead to invert the relative position of the Scenarios if only cost is considered.

Table 5. Relevant information for Scenario 2

Variable costs	**Outsourcing**	€77,753.17		(7688 pallets)
	Total variable costs		€77,753.17	(7688 pallets)
	Total cost scenario 2		€77,753.17	

For Scenario 3 the procedure is similar to the one described for Scenario 1, but only one 10 pallets truck limited to 10 h a day is available. As trucks reduce from two to one, fixed costs with employees and trucks reduce by half when compared to Scenario 1. Maintenance costs will reduce as well. However, that value will not be half as it is expected that the occupancy rate increases and thus the traveled distances. Hence, Maintenance costs were calculated proportionally based on the maintenance cost per kilometer of Scenario 1 (€0.0212/km), as well as fuel costs (€0.1651/km). Toll and meal costs were calculated proportionally from Scenario 1 (respectively €9.7710 and €2.4049, per route). This data is shown in Table 6. A summary of the total cost per scenario is provided in Table 7.

Table 6. Relevant information for Scenario 3

Fixed costs (insourcing)		Employees	€6,365.11			
		Trucks	€878.51			
		Total fixed costs			**€7,243.62**	
Variable costs	**Insourcing (variable)**	fuel	€8,041.69			(3419 pallets)
		maintenance	€1,032.61			(48,708 km)
		tolls	€3,605.51			(369 routes)
		extra meals	€887.41			
		Insourcing (variable)		**€13,567.22**		
	Outsourcing	outsourcing	€24,388.77			
		Outsourcing		**€43,024.32**		(4269 pallets)
	Total variable costs				**€56,591.54**	(7688 pallets)
Total cost scenario 3					**€63,835.15**	

Table 7. Summary of the cost per Scenario

	Scenario 1	Scenario 2	Scenario 3
Insourcing	36,632.10 €	–	20,810.83 €
Outsourcing	24,388.77 €	77,753.17 €	43,024.32 €
Total	61,020.87 €	77,753.17 €	63,835.15 €

Scenario 1 shows that it is not possible to use exclusively the fleet of the Company to serve customers, therefore outsourcing will always be required to fulfill the agreed service levels. It should be noted that, according to the current situation of the Company, i.e. the use of vehicles that no longer involve amortization, a pallet transported using the fleet of the Company costs about 30% less than a pallet transported using the outsourcing company, which corroborates the decision of the Company to prioritize insourcing. It is also interesting to observe in this scenario that the occupancy rates of the vehicles are not very high (see Table 8). It shows that there is capacity slack to be used if the customers increase their level of demand, which can be relevant in a market with such demand volatility as the one of the analyzed Company. Simultaneously, the occupancy rate might be considered lower than desired. Considering that (1) priority is given to Class A customers; (2) the service level agreed for Class A customers is very demanding; (3) orders for these customers often involve less than full pallets, are very variable in volume, and often result in less than full truckloads; the flexibility that this low occupancy rate provides can be advantageous to the Company in its competitive position in the market. The fact that insourcing is quite less expensive than outsourcing, adds to the strength of this Scenario.

Table 8. Occupancy rate of the trucks, per Scenario

	Scenario 1	Scenario 2	Scenario 3
Truck 1	73.61%	–	79.14%
Truck 2	47.8%	–	–

Scenario 2 shows the most expensive cost per pallet. This is due to the fact that the outsourcing company defines its price based on the weight, with an additional cost per kilometer if the total weight is above 1 ton. Scenario 3 leads to a cost point per pallet between Scenario 1 and Scenario 2, although the occupancy rate of the truck is higher. As the truck is 12 years and breakdowns are more likely to occur, the Company does not have the flexibility of the second truck to overcome these constraints, having to rely on the outsourcing company for very urgent deliveries. If on the one hand there is lack of internal flexibility, on the other hand, the use of the outsourcer provides additional capacity slack. A problem that can emerge in this scenario is that the outsourcer might not have enough flexibility to respond to very short delivery times (a few hours), leading the Company to be exposed to penalties from the customers for not being able to fulfill the service level agreements. As so, a second truck in the fleet of the Company emerges as a positive solution. Additionally, this scenario shows an occupancy rate that is higher than the one from truck 1 in Scenario 1, but not much higher (under 80%), which is an unexpected result. It is possible that this result emerges from the fact that the uncertainty of demand leads to pallets that are not full pallets or truckloads that need to be sent even without full truckload for a specific client. The fluctuation of demand, regardless of the Class of the customer, also leads to days in which there are no deliveries, contributing to decrease the overall occupancy rate of the trucks. These results are interesting as most literature [1–3, 5–9] argues towards the use of outsourcing instead of own fleet as a way to reduce cost (among other advantages). For this particular case, this is not true. The fact that the Company is using trucks with 12 years, and therefore amortizations are no longer considered, substantially reduces the cost for Scenarios 1 and 3. Once the trucks have to be replaced, even if the Company buys used ones, the cost for these two scenarios (1 and 3) will increase. Nonetheless, due to the flexibility introduced by the self-owned fleet, aligned with the fact that Class A customers have a very short lead time and a very demanding service level agreement, full outsourcing (Scenario 2) would still present serious limitation.

The cost level per Scenario may also be the consequence of the very short lead times the Company has to fulfill, not allowing the outsourcing company enough time to aggregate demand and be able to reduce its price per pallet. This is under the scope of the argument of keeping internal capacity available for very critical situations and outsource for other situations, which is argued in [15].

As the Company's trucks have 12 years each, they are likely to require maintenance quite often. Although this maintenance can be performed outside the labor hours of the truck drivers, it is possible that an occasional malfunction occurs leading to immediate lack of ability to fulfill the short lead times, and to the inevitable penalties imposed by the customers. Nonetheless, if these penalties are lower than the saving exposed in Scenario 1 from the fact that the Company used its own fleet, it would still be worth maintaining the fleet with 2 trucks.

Other companies using the proposed roadmap should be careful about the amortization issue. For the specific company analysed, there were not considered as the current fleet is 12 years old. But it should be taken into consideration that the cost for Scenario 1 and Scenario 3 would increase if new(er) vehicles were included. In this case, as Scenario 1 involves 2 vehicles and Scenario 3 only one, it is possible that the cost per pallet would end up being higher for Scenario 1 than for Scenario 3. Nonetheless, the qualitative approach has to be taken into consideration: in Scenario 1 there is more flexibility and more slack in capacity for urgent and more demanding orders from the main customers than in Scenario 3. This balance between the qualitative and the quantitative approach should be considered by every company using the proposed roadmap otherwise the all approach would be not more than an optimization problem.

As a last remark regarding the use case, it is worth mentioning that the Company has a privileged location, 66 kms from the delivery points of Class A customers, which represent about 50% of its volume of sales. If the distance was longer, not only the lead time of only a few hours would not be possible to fulfill, but the empty return of the trucks could increase the price per pallet. In this case, outsourcing could emerge as a more interesting solution.

This research, although focusing on a single case, was able to propose a methodology that can be used by other companies addressing the same challenge, thus contributing to the knowledge in this area. The proposal has to be adjusted to the specific situation of each company, but the overall approach, the roadmap that is proposed considering both a quantitative and a qualitative approach, can be followed by other companies.

5 Conclusions

This research is based on a real case and aimed at analyzing a proposed roadmap for analysis of fleet solution in companies wanting not only to reduce cost but also to address service quality in their fleet decision. A specific Company is used and the current situation is compared with alternative scenarios based on cost, truck occupancy rate and ability to fulfill service level agreements.

Arguments in literature recommend outsourcing transportation as a solution for lowering costs and even achieve improved service quality as experts will be conducting the route planning and will be able to aggregate cargo and therefore increase truck occupancy rate [1–3]. Nonetheless, findings showed that for this Company keeping its own fleet (and even not reducing it) is the best solution (Scenario 1). A context of very short lead times, demand uncertainty, and high service levels encourage the Company to pursue maintaining its own fleet, which is in line with recommendations from [15] for the outsourcing decision.

As a case study, this research contributes directly to the analyzed Company. Nonetheless, it provides reflection material for other companies with similar constraints regarding lead times and service level agreements. In terms of the overall knowledge in the area, this research proposed a roadmap to address the challenge of comparing alternative transportation scenarios when both quantitative and qualitative issues need to be addressed.

This research is limited for the fact that the number of pallets per order in the case study had to be estimated. Nonetheless, the statistical analysis allowed concluding that the estimates are reliable. Additionally, the costs for the Company were based on the fact that amortization no longer exists, which reduces the costs used for the simulation. It would be interesting to assess if newer trucks and correspondent amortization were considered, the recommendation for the Company would remain the same. In fact, once the current fleet has to be replaced, and the Company faces the challenge of having to buy new trucks or outsource its total operations, the problem that was analyzed using the proposed roadmap will have to be reassessed, and the same roadmap can be followed. A second limitation of this research is that the proposed roadmap was tested using a single case. Although further testing should be developed, this roadmap was based on [4] and [16], so consistency is already imbedded in the proposal. The issue of amortization should be considered by other companies using the proposed roadmap as it might apply to their specific situation.

Acknowledgments. This work is supported by National Funding from FCT-Fundação para a Ciência e a Tecnologia, under the project UID/MAT/04561/2019.

References

1. Carvalho, J.C.: Logística e Gestão da Cadeia de Abastecimento. Edições Sílabo, Lisboa (2017)
2. Rushon, A., Croucher, P., Baker, P.: The Handbook of Logistics and Supply Chain Management: Understanding the Supply Chain, 6th edn. Kogan Page Limited, London (2017)
3. Stock, J., Lambert, D.: Strategic Logistics Management, 4th edn. McGraw-Hill, Irwin (2001)
4. Yin, R.: Case Study Research and Applications: Design and Methods, 6th edn. Sage, London (2017)
5. Mangan, J., Lalwani, C.L.: Global Logistics and Supply Chain Management, 3rd edn. Wiley, Chichester (2016)
6. Christopher, M.: Logistics & Supply Chain Management, 5th edn. Financial-Times/ Pearson, Edinburgh (2016)

7. Chopra, S.: Supply Chain Management, 7th edn. Pearson, London (2018)
8. Bowersox, D., Closs, D., Cooper, M.B., Bowersox, J.: Supply Chain Logistics Management: Strategy, Planning and Operation, 5th edn. McGraw Hill, New York (2019)
9. Ballou, R.: Business Logistics Management, 4th edn. Pearson/Prentice Hall, New Jersey (2004)
10. Dantzig, G., Ramser, J.: The truck dispatching problem. Manag. Sci. **6**, 80–91 (1959)
11. Prins, C.: Efficient heuristics for the heterogeneous fleet multitrip VRP with application to a large-scale real case. J. Math. Model. Algorithms **1**, 135–150 (2002)
12. Clarke, G., Wright, J.R.: Scheduling of vehicle routing problem from a central depot to a number of delivery points. Oper. Res. **12**, 568–581 (1964)
13. Groër, C., Golden, B., Wasil, E.: A library of local search heuristics for the vehicle routing problem. Math. Program. Comput. **2**(2), 79–101 (2010)
14. Groër, C.: The VRPH software (2010). https://sites.google.com/site/vrphlibrary/. Accessed 27 July 2019
15. Simchi-Levi, D., Kaminsky, P., Simchi-Levi, E.: Designing and Managing the Supply Chain: Concepts, Strategies, and Case Studies. McGraw-Hill (2009)
16. Voss, C., Trikriktsis, N., Frohlich, M.: Case research in operations management. Int. J. Oper. Prod. Manag. **22**(2), 195–219 (2002)

Optimize Capacity for a Uniform Waste Transportation Collection

José Tiago Silva[1], André Filipe Oliveira[1], Ana Lúcia Martins[2(✉)], and João Carlos Ferreira[1,3]

[1] Instituto Universitário de Lisboa (ISCTE-IUL), ISTAR-IUL, Lisbon, Portugal
{jtbpc, afmao, jcafa}@iscte-iul.pt
[2] Instituto Universitário de Lisboa (ISCTE-IUL),
Business Research Unit (BRU-IUL), Lisbon, Portugal
almartins@iscte-iul.pt
[3] INOV INESC Inovação—Instituto de Novas Tecnologias,
1000-029 Lisbon, Portugal

Abstract. Transportation-related costs are responsible for a large portion of the waste collection process. In the past several optimization approaches in routing having been the proposal with a diversity of algorithm. In this work we propose a novel approach where we analyze waste deposition volume and try to identify patterns for a deterministic and uniform waste collection. Instead of routing optimization we propose a capacity determination based on location, year period, special events and weather conditions. An IoT sensor transmitted volume every time the wasted door is open and provide real-time value.

Keywords: Frequency-capacity · Logistics · Transportation · Waste collection · IoT

1 Introduction

In smart cities, the use of technology is common to optimize several services provided by the city council. One of the areas where technology can be used is in waste collection. By adding sensors to containers with the ability to measure the volume of waste in it, each time the container is opened, it's possible to know, in real time, the volume of waste in every container of the city. In Portugal, this is already used in cities such as Castelo Branco, but all the data generated by the sensors are typically used for routing optimization only.

Problems like frequency-capacity optimization with a fixed frequency of waste collection or the correlation of waste data with other datasets are not typically addressed. The frequency-capacity optimization problem consists in, given a frequency of waste collection (like twice for a week), what is the best number of containers by geographic area so that there are no filled containers.

This work aims to explore the data generated by the sensors and the correlation of that data with other data sets, according with, events or atmospheric conditions. It also aims the design and implementation of an algorithm-based analysis to solve the problem of container frequency-capacity optimization by location. To do this, we

A. L. Martins et al. (Eds.): INTSYS 2019, LNICST 310, pp. 108–128, 2020.
https://doi.org/10.1007/978-3-030-38822-5_8

analyze real data on the volume of containers over time in Portuguese cities between in the years of 2017 and 2018 with 18 thousand registers.

The problem of calculating the required capacity of containers by geographic location, fixing the frequency of waste collection, has not yet been addressed in the literature, which increases the interest of the topic addressed in this article. The results obtained can be used to save resources and costs to the city councils that decide to implement the algorithms under study. The correlation between waste volume data sets can also provide interesting information about the habits of the citizens.

2 Literature Review

Most of what has been studied about the waste collection are focused on routing problems. It's possible to associate the waste collection routing problem with the generic Traveling Salesman Problem (TSP) or Vehicle Routing Problem (VRP) [1]. The TSP consists in, given a set of n cities and the distance between them, and the best path for a Salesman to visit all the cities once and only once and return to the initial city. In the VRP, instead of one salesman or vehicle, we have m vehicles to visit n cities. In waste collection optimization, the containers represent the cities and the garbage trucks represent the vehicles. To limit the waste collection schedule, it can be added time windows restrictions to this problem [2]. Despite their simple statement, both these problems are too complex to solve obtaining the optimal solution when the number of containers is large [3], so it's typical to see heuristic approaches to obtain good solutions in less time [4].

Several articles study this problem, proposing algorithms for the calculation of good routes using optimization and/or machine learning. In [5], a mathematical formulation of the problem is presented and several papers in the literature are classified by the type of algorithms proposed. In [6], a genetic algorithm is presented for the identification of optimal routes for Municipal Solid Waste collection, supported by a geographic information system. Good solutions were achieved but for a small and simplified waste collection routing problem. In [7], the proposed algorithms differ from the previous ones in the literature because they are dynamic algorithms and at the same time robust, being prepared for the recalculation of the routes in the event of any failure or of a collection truck reaching the limit of capacity.

Some papers focus on optimizing time and costs of waste collection in particular cities, like Xangai (Pudong area) [8] or Allahabad [9], proposing municipal solid waste management systems suitable for those particular places. [10] summarizes similar papers for the United Kingdom. Focused on the logistics involved in waste collection in several European cities, [11] carries out a detailed study on how to manage waste collection and what standards are imposed by the European Union. This study provides a set of current and interesting information about the problem as well as what is expected in the resolution of the problem.

More focused on cloud technologies, the article [12] presents a whole system for the collection of waste in smart cities, proposing different solutions for different stakeholders in a city. To collect data, the authors use not only the sensors but also the surveillance system of a city and it addresses several possible problems in the collection of waste in the containers. Similarly, [13] used sensors that can read, collect and transmit trash volume and used this data to calculate new routes in real time, guaranteeing that when trashcans become full, they are collected on the same day. However, by doing that, they increased the waste collection frequency too much, incrementing the daily collection cost between 13–25%.

In [14], the authors focused on forecasting quantity and variance of solid waste and its correlation with other sets of data, like residential population, consumer index and season, in Shanghai. The work [15] proposes a new architecture for the dynamic scheduling of waste collection considering the capacity of the same using sensors for their measurement. This is one of the most complete articles in the use of measurements of capacities of the containers for the calculation of the frequency of garbage collection and the calculation of routes in real time taking these data into account.

Even though there's many articles dedicated to routing optimization, it can't be found in literature a study about the frequency-capacity optimization with a fixed frequency of waste collection. This can be modelled by a generic optimization problem where we want to have the minimum number of containers needed by the geographic area that guarantees enough capacity (or maximize that capacity) with the constraints of the collection frequency. It can also be viewed as a multi-objective optimization problem where we want to minimize the total number of containers and maximize the capacity by geographic area.

3 Approach Developed

The data collected from a Lora volume sensor. Every time the door is open a volume measurement is sent to a management system. We use data from a Portuguese company Evox (www.evox.pt). The central system provides visual information about the status of every monitor waste container. Based on a pre-defined filled volume a collection route is defined, like the example provided in Fig. 1.

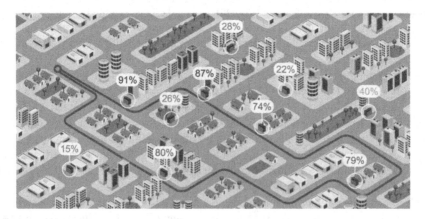

Fig. 1. Current solution of the waste management system, with route optimization based on capacity available.

Our approach is the data analysis to identify deposition patterns for years periods (e.g. summer, winter), correlate with special events and weathers conditions in order to determine what container capacity should be installed, for a uniform week garbage collection. To study this problem of capacity optimization given a fixed frequency, we start by analyzing sets of data of containers volume in time. Each container has a sensor that measures the volume of waste in it, every time the container is opened. The data from each container consists on the following elements: *container Id*, *description*, *container type*, *waste type*, *geographic localization*, *address*, *localization zone* and sets of reading *date and time* and respective *volume* filled in percentage. Table 1 shows an example of those elements, representing the core data of the container and data about the volume reading.

Table 1. Data set examples.

Field	Example
Container id	15415
Description	Container 611
Container type	Four weal with 1000 L
Waste type	Solid urban waste
Geo localization	39.826069/−7.493849
Address	R. do Arco do Bispo 21
Localization zone	Castle zone
Reading date and time	08/06/2018 12:04; 08/06/2018 17:21; …
Volume	59%; 83%; …

This data must be cleaned and organized in appropriate structures to begin their mining. To do so, we decided to work with the Python, because of its simplicity to manipulate datasets.

We added also weather information from the National Centers for Environmental Information (NCEI) using the information on temperature and rain that we divided into pre-defined classes. For events, we've created a crawler to find local news from 2017 to 2018 and identify the type of occurrence. Hence, with this new evidences, new classes have been added: *precipitation [mm]*; *air-temperature [Celsius]*; *type of day*; *events*, that we collected from local news, such concerts, parties, public holidays and others.

The dataset containing the information from all classes provides a big portion of the information we intend to use in the study of the capacity-frequency problem. However, because the volume is measured each time a container is opened, these discrete data doesn't have a fixed time period between readings. One container can be opened ten times in a day, while others might not be opened in that space day.

To deal with this, we created a function that generates another dataset in which the volume data frame is defined with a fixed time period of every x hours (8 h, 16 h, or even 1 day). Each line of the data frame has, for each container, information about the last measured volume and the mean and median measure of volume in that time period. This can also be viewed as a continuous dataset in which the volume of a container on a *datetime* is the last measure or the average volume in the time period containing that *datetime*. We expect with this dataset to easily get information about the average volume growth by container or zone and to have two different approaches in this study.

With the datasets defined, we present in the next section a detailed study of the information on those datasets and a visualization of the data.

4   Data Visualization

The main dataset is composed of almost eighteen thousand rows, and each row accords to a waste volume measure, a date and time, and an id of the corresponding container. In total, there are eighteen waste containers, identified by a unique id, his geographic coordinates, type of container and his total capacity. There are three types of containers: the standard ones, with 800 L and 1000 L capacity and the surface containers which can also store 1000 L.

4.1   Visualization by Zone

The containers are split across the district of Castelo Branco, making up about eight streets, as shown in Fig. 2, we can visualize the number of containers that are for disposal for each street, following by their id number and capacity.

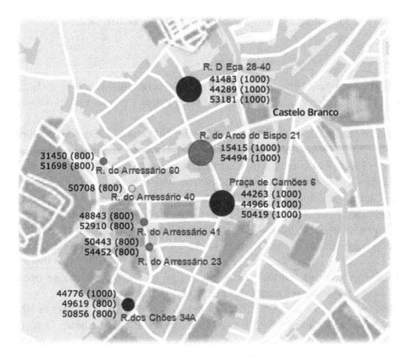

Fig. 2. Container's streets locations with a perspective view.

Here we grouped all the data by their locations mentioned before, between the dates of 08-jun-2017 to 08 jun-2018. In Fig. 3 is shown the average volume of waste inside the containers in percentage, by each street, for each month. We can see that even for an average calculation, the values seem to appear quite aleatory, however, seems to be increasing over the time. Despite the noise, we can notice that most of the volumes are between the range of 30% to 60%.

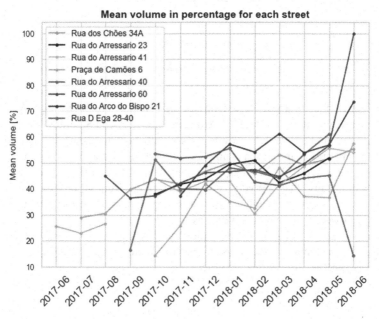

Fig. 3. Average volume of waste in the containers by street location, and their according months.

Another interesting fact is that, 90% of the times, the *volume* is below the 60%. In other words, from the full cycle of data (366 days), only in 36 days the *volume* was higher than 60% and those days mostly correspondent to the Wednesdays. This could be important later, when defining a collection day.

4.2   Deposits and Collections

With the container's locations and dates been set, the next step is to calculate the frequency of waste collection. Hence, we split the volume of waste into two types: *volume-deposits [Liters]*, which is when the volume of the containers gets filled, and *volume-collections [Liters]*, when the volume is emptied. With the class *day-of-week*, on calculated the amount of volume deposited and collected, for each day of the week. The result shown below is the average volume of liters, for every container, regardless the time of the year (Fig. 4):

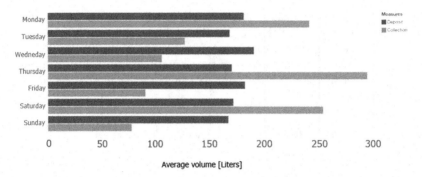

Fig. 4. Average volume of liters deposited and collected per day.

Observing at the volume collected, on can see that there are three main days of week where the waste volume is collected, at Monday, Thursday and Saturday, so the average frequency calculated is three times a week, taking into account the mean result for every container at any time of the year meaning that the frequency may vary, depending of the time of the year. We'll deduce that all the containers have the same collection day programmed, because they are very close to each other, from 40 to 80 m.

Looking at the average volume of waste deposits, we can see that there is no discrepancy between the days of week, as they vary just from 166 to 190 L, so the amount of deposits is not influenced by the day of week. However, the volume of the containers, in percentage, is always higher on Wednesdays, because is when the interval between two collections is higher.

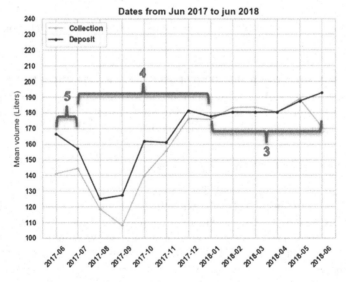

Fig. 5. Average volume of waste collection and deposit, for each month and it's waste collection frequency (Color figure online)

In Fig. 5, is registered the average volume of waste collection and deposits. By reducing the graph to the scale of one year, we can observe the volume had a higher low on august 2017, this may be due to the period correspondent to the end of seasonal time, were people come back from holydays. At that time, the deposits have been increased linearly until December 2017, and then the trend remained slightly constant from that time period (December to June). The red marked numbers shown are the occurred frequency per week, for each month. As we can notice, the frequency is dynamic, that is, it changes from month to month in order to fit the needs.

According to the frequency, observing the months from July to December 2017, the frequency was four times a week, the collections days were on Monday, Tuesday, Thursday and Saturday. From among the months between January to June 2018, the frequency has changed to a fixed amount of three (removal of Tuesday as a collection day).

4.3 Collection Analysis

Considering the amount of waste *volume* in the containers in each day and moments of waste collection, it is possible to evaluate, for each container, how well the current waste collection frequency performs. To do so, let us consider the following definitions: we consider a **needless collection** as the collection of waste in a container with less than 35% of volume waste and a **critical point** as point where the volume of a container is 100% for more than one day.

According to the collections of each container, the percentage of *needless collections* is presented in Fig. 6. On the other hand, we can see the total amount of critical points for each container in the Fig. 7.

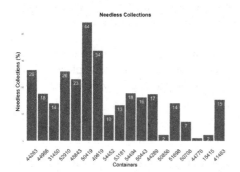

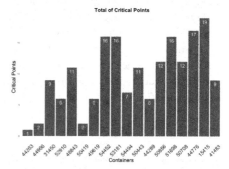

Fig. 6. Percentage of *needless collections* by container.

Fig. 7. Number of *critical points* for each container.

On a first analysis, we can assume that containers *44263*, *44966*, *50419* and *49619* should have less waste collection frequency, because they have high percentage of needless collections and low number of critical points. On the other hand, the containers *54452*, *53181*, *51698*, *44776* and *15415* should have a more frequent waste collection frequency, because of their high number of critical points. This data shows that the waste collections frequency and/or the capacity of the containers can be changed and improved for each container. Ideally, there would be no critical points or needless collections, but our focus will not be to minimize these points individually for each container but to consider all the containers grouped by their location and address the frequency-capacity problem.

4.4   Data Correlation

In this section, on will try to find patterns that may influence the amount of deposits. This case studies four scenarios, according to the class *type-of-day,* the database is divided into three types of day, the celebrative days but not holidays, the holidays and normal days and weekends. The class *season,* which represents the partition of the database into the different seasons, *precipitation [mm],* which can be rainless, rain or heavy rain and *air-temperature [Celsius],* that vary from a frosty day, cold day, warm day and hot or very hot day.

Relatively to the levels of precipitation, we can notice the average waste deposits are very close to each other, showing our lower value of 165 with heavy rain, and the higher value of 180, with a normal raining day. Concerning to the air temperature, the verified values of waste deposits differ from 149 to 180 L. The amounts are also very similar, on exception of the variable *very hot day,* which is a much lower value. This may be due to the seasonal time corresponding to the summer. Comparatively to the season, on can observe the volume of deposits in the summer is significantly lower than in the rest of the seasons, as said before, there seem to appear some sort of correlation between the variables *summer* and *very hot day* and so, the values can be interpreted as the seasonal time of the year, where a set of families go out to another cities which decreases the demographic population of Castelo Branco. According to the type of day, we can relate that, in average, the amount of waste deposits is similar between the type of days, as the values are close to each other. By having a broad view of the deposit's interactions, the results vary from 160 to 190 L.

In short, on can observe that the type of day isn't really an important class, as we can see, the volume of waste deposit doesn't seem to alter from, for example a holiday to a normal day, plus, a normal day (175,6 L) presented higher volume than in a holiday (160,6 L).

4.5   Major Findings

In this section it was shown a lot of information about the dataset and a good data visualization and analysis, which will be used as leverage information for the algorithms coming in the following sections.

Regarding the class *day-of-week* on saw that that the frequency of collection is dynamic, as it may vary according to the time of the year. Also, the days of week for collection are fixed on Monday, Thursday and Saturday. Tuesday is also added when the frequency is increased to four.

The daily average volume of the containers is mostly between 30% and 60% (330 days of 366), and those few days where the volume is higher than 60%, are correspondent to Wednesdays. As the volume of deposits are, in average, about

180 L per day and the containers have capacity between 800 to 1000 L, it is possible to decrease the frequency to three times a week and in the summer to two times a week (Fig. 8).

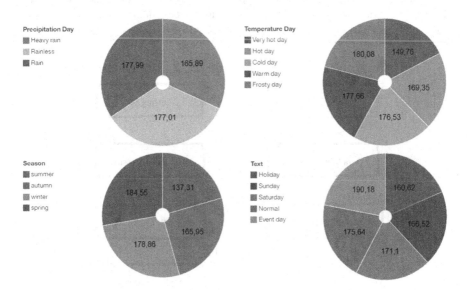

Fig. 8. Pie chart representation of the deposits by the levels of precipitation, temperature, season and type of day.

A quick analysis on the current collection shown that a large percentage of the collections are *needless collections* and some of the containers have a considerable amount of critical points, which leads to the idea that waste collection can be improved.

On data correlation, it was found that the classes *type-of-day, precipitation [mm]* and *Air-temperature [Celsius]*, haven't shown concrete results, as the variation was very low, and so, on decided to omit them, in order to delete ambiguity and posteriorly apply machine learning with the less noise as possible. Relatively to the class *season*, this indicated us that in the period accorded to summer, the volume of waste deposits decayed 175 to 130 L, which may be due to fire forests or less population density and we must take that into account.

5 Predictions

Using information such as season, events, weekday, precipitation and temperature can provide good predictions on whether a container waste must be collected or not. To do so, we used data from the main data set and several datasets with fixed time periods. In both cases we considered that a waste container must be collected if his capacity gets higher than 60%. We pretend to compare the results of the several datasets.

The classes *day-of-week, month, season*, are the main inputs and the target is *volume-filled [%]*. The inputs were used to train our machine learning model through the workflow processes illustrated in Fig. 9. Train dataset is pre-processed to align data on the same scale. Then, the processed data are fed to train the Machine Learning (ML) models where they will be hold-out and cross-validated with 80% of data. Finally, the model with chosen hyperparameters will be tested with 20% of data for testing.

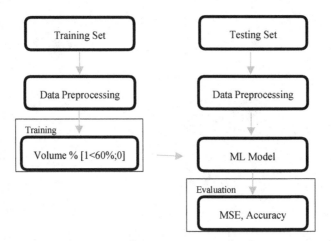

Fig. 9. Machine learning prediction process.

5.1   Data Preparation

Raw data with categorical values, such as *day-of-week, month* and *season*, are pre-processed using dummy techniques, where the number of columns is equal to the number of categories.

The target, the *volume* is what we want to predict. More specifically we want to predict if a container has to be collected. To improve the performance and match the points of interest of the article, we transferred the values, which vary from 0% to 100%, to binary data. When the volume filled is inferior to 60%, returns 1, otherwise equals to 0.

Since all the data now is composed of binary data, in exception of the class *season*, which vary from 1 to 12, we won't need to standardize nor normalize the data as all classes have the same weights.

5.2   Evaluate Algorithms

Regarding the procedures of [16], we will test the accuracy with linear and nonlinear algorithms and use 10-fold cross validation to evaluate algorithms using the **Mean Squared Error** (MSE) metric and default tuning parameters. MSE will give a gross idea of how wrong all predictions are (0 is perfect), Fig. 10.

The six algorithms selected included for the baseline of performance on this problem are:

- Linear Algorithms: Linear Regression (LR), Lasso Regression (LASSO) and Elastic Net (EN).
- Nonlinear Algorithms: Classification and Regression Trees (CART), Support Vector Regression (SVR) and k-Nearest Neighbours (KNN).

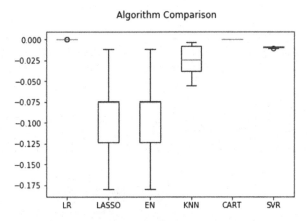

Fig. 10. Algorithm comparison (LR, LASSO, EN, KNN, CART AND SVN), using de mean square error.

On Fig. 10, represents a plot of the algorithm evaluation results and the comparison of the spread and the MSE of each model. We can see that the algorithms have a pretty good behavior, as their MSE calculated are very close to zero, in particular, LR, CART and SVR have their box and whisker plots squashed at the top of the range.

Using the metric of **accuracy** to evaluate models, which is a ratio of the number between correctly predicted and the total number of instances in percentage and using 10-fold cross-validation to estimate accuracy, we'll evaluate five different algorithms:

- Linear Algorithms: Logistic Regression (LR).
- Nonlinear algorithms: k-Nearest Neighbours (KNN), Classification and Regression Trees (CART), Gaussian Naive Bayes (NB), Support Vector Machines (SVM).

Ensuring the evaluation of each algorithm is performed using the same data splits, the results are directly comparable, in Fig. 11.

This plot shows that the accuracy of the algorithms is at least 0.92, which is a great result. This happens because of the strong correlation between the inputs and the volume data. On top of that, 90% of the time, the volume of waste is below 60%, which makes the prediction data very unbalanced and easier to predict. A study on a more balanced dataset will be made in the following subsection.

The decision tree algorithm shows, on Fig. 12 show relevant weekday on the *volume* class. In fact, the first ramification splits the dataset in Wednesday data and other weekdays data. This is consistent with the conclusions on Sect. 4, where it was shown that Wednesdays were in average the days with more waste volume.

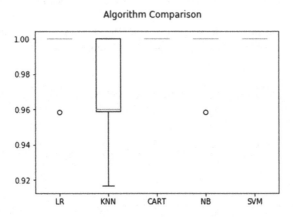

Fig. 11. Algorithm comparison (LR, KNN, CART, NB and SVN), using the accuracy score.

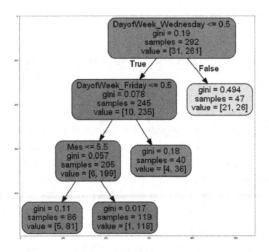

Fig. 12. Decision tree example.

5.3 Prediction with Time Periods

Considering a dataset with volume values every 8 h, for every container and using information about season, events, weekday, precipitation and temperature, we predicted if a container waste should be collected using, in this case, five algorithms: k-nearest neighbours (KNN), Latent Dirichlet Allocation (LDA), decision tree (cart) and random forest (RF). An example of the training results is presented in Fig. 13:

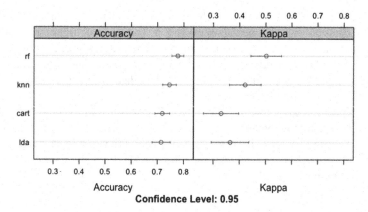

Fig. 13. Training results.

In this example, we can see that the random forest algorithms present the better results, with up to 80% of accuracy. With this, random forest was the elected algorithm for the remaining tests. Although this is not a bad accuracy result, when making predictions to compare with the validation set, the predictions accuracy doesn't go further that 75%, for most of the containers data used.

Table 2. Prediction results by time period.

Container/TP	6H	8H	12H	24H
44263	0.90	0.93	0.92	0.93
44966	0.62	0.69	0.68	0.69
31450	0.73	0.76	0.72	0.72
52910	0.76	0.79	0.73	0.76
48843	0.65	0.68	0.69	0.63
50419	0.92	0.91	0.92	0.91
49619	0.83	0.83	0.77	0.82
54452	0.58	0.58	0.57	0.61
53181	0.68	0.62	0.56	0.60
54494	0.65	0.66	0.71	0.59
50443	0.69	0.66	0.68	0.68
44289	0.64	0.69	0.71	0.73
50856	0.64	0.61	0.53	0.77
51698	0.60	0.62	0.68	0.71
50708	0.67	0.58	0.66	0.67
44776	0.58	0.67	0.63	0.75
15415	0.65	0.73	0.63	0.74
41483	0.68	0.70	0.59	0.65
Mean	0.69	0.71	0.69	0.72

All results are shown on Table 2. The mean of the accuracy obtained was around 71% for the datasets with volume values every 8 h. The same algorithm was applied for datasets with time periods of 6 h, 12 h and a day. The mean of accuracy obtained was 69% 69% and 72% respectively. We conclude with this results that classification algorithms provide better predictions using the main dataset and there is no advantage of using time periods information.

The results presented show that information like season and weekday provide good predictions on whether a container waste must be collected or not. This can be useful on creating new models of collection frequency, providing a way to study how they change as the amount of volume, not only for the dates on the datasets but also to predict how they behave in the future.

6   Capacity-Frequency Models

After the data analysis shown in section four, we concluded that the current waste collection frequency in Castelo Branco a collection between three to four times a week, most of the time on Monday, Thursday and Saturday. On the other hand, if we consider that we just need to collect a container waste if the container has more than 60% of waste volume, it was shown that more than 40% of the past collections were needless collections, meaning the collection frequency should be easily decreased.

In this section, we pretend to analyze what is the capacity needed if we reduce the waste frequency to once or twice a week and present good models to find the best day or days for waste collection. To validate these models, an analysis of the containers overload (new volumes provided by the model higher than 100%) will be made.

With the historical data from each container, it's possible to simulate what happens to the volume waste if the frequency of waste collection was fixed once a week or twice a week, for every container. For that, we fix a date (nd) and time (nt) for the new collection and, from a set with time period of one hour, we generate an entire new set of volume data, for each container. Initializing $gap = 0$, this process works like this:

1. *For every* entry of the dataset we check date (d), hour (h) and volume (v);
2. *If* $d = nd$ and $t = nt$ it's time for a new collection so we set $gap = -v$, otherwise, *if* $prev\_v - v > 10$ this was an old collection and we set $gap+ = prev\_v$, otherwise gap stays the same;
3. We set the new volume for this date and time $nv = v + gap$.

The model data is the set of the new volume generated, of each container. For a model with a collection frequency of more times a week, the algorithm has several days and hours as its input.

6.1   Collection Once a Week

Considering a period dataset with time period of 2 h and a waste collection frequency of once a week (Wednesday at 10 P.M.), Fig. 14 shows an example of the new model volume, compared to the real volume with the current collection frequency:

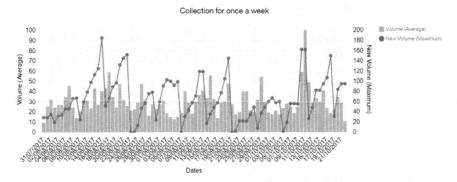

Fig. 14. First 1000 records of once week frequency for container 49619.

As we can see, a waste collection frequency of once a week is not enough for container 49619 between 06/08/2017 and 15/10/2017, with too many occurrences of waste overload.

Table 3. Once a week frequency results.

Container	Average volume	Count >100%
44263	38	46
44966	157	115
31450	108	106
52910	118	104
48843	159	124
50419	65	60
49619	80	89
54452	195	137
53181	188	139
54494	183	127
50443	152	121
44289	172	122
50856	164	153
51698	183	122
50708	140	130
44776	195	164
15415	219	109
41483	177	130
Mean	149%	117

Table 3 shows the mean of the new volume by container and the amount of waste overloads for each container. We can see by the results that a collection frequency of once a week is clearly not enough for these containers. This asks for an improvement of the container capacity or the collection frequency.

6.2   Collection Twice a Week

Considering the same container and time period, Fig. 15 shows the simulation for a twice a week frequency (Wednesday and Sunday at 10 P.M.):

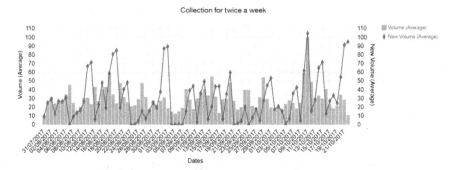

Fig. 15. First 1000 records of twice week frequency for container 49619.

We can see in this example that a waste frequency of twice a week is perfectly enough for container 49619 between 06/08/2017 and 15/10/2017, with only two occurrences of waste overload.

Table 4. Twice a week frequency results.

Container	Average volume	Count >100%
44263	19	3
44966	74	57
31450	56	59
52910	57	40
48843	77	64
50419	31	11
49619	44	34
54452	100	75
53181	90	67
54494	95	64
50443	76	55
44289	89	60
50856	81	70
51698	96	73
50708	71	49
44776	99	90
15415	117	75
41483	90	73
Mean	76%	56

Table 4 shows the mean of the new volume by container and the amount of waste overloads for each container. The results are much more reasonable, with a total average of 76% of volume.

Now, for this model we have to check the capacity by zone. The average by container or the total average do not guarantee that the current capacity is enough for this collection frequency. Grouping by streets the mean volume by month, as in Sect. 4, for these new volume sets, we have the result shown in the next figure (Fig. 16):

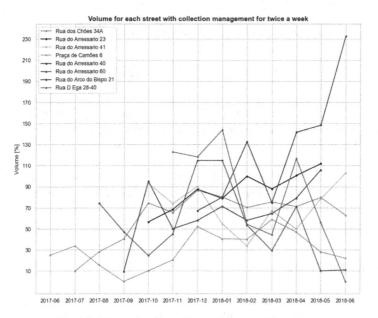

Fig. 16. Mean of volume by month grouped by streets.

This shows that the zone with more capacity problems is Rua do Arco do Bispo 34. For this zone, we have to add a container with a 1000 L capacity. For Rua D Ega and Rua do Arressário, a new container with 400 L is enough. With these improvements, we have a model with a good capacity frequency, as pretended.

6.3   Prediction on Model

To validate the new model of a collection frequency of twice a week, we applied the prediction process of Sect. 5 for each street group. The target, the *new volume* is what we want to predict, but instead of predicting if a container needs waste collection, we want to know if a container is likely to have a waste overflow. To do that, when the volume filled is inferior to 100%, returns 1, otherwise equals to 0.

The algorithm used was decision tree. The data set of the model was divided in partitions of 80% for training set and 20% for accuracy validation. The results are shown in Fig. 17.

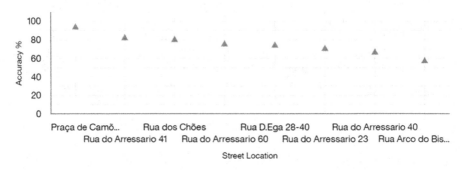

Fig. 17. Prediction model for two times a week.

The accuracy obtained are around 75% and the predictions for this model states that the with a waste collection frequency of twice a week and the capacity changes on Rua D Ega and Rua do Arressário, represent a good solution for these containers, without waste overload.

This is a major improvement on the current collection frequency that is between three to four times a week. The addition of the containers to guarantee the capacity needed have a fixed cost, while reducing the collection frequency one or two times a week represent cost reduction every week.

7 Major Findings

In this study, it was shown (from Visualization approach) that grouping the containers by streets, the monthly average volume was always between 30% to 60% and the average volume of waste deposit was never above 20% of waste a day. On the other hand, the waste collection was, in most cases, done wrong, with a high number of *needless collections* and *critical points*. It was also found that the classes *type-of-day, precipitation [mm]* and *Air-temperature [Celsius]* had a week correlation with the volume data while *day-of-week, month* and *season* had a strong correlation.

Using machine learning algorithms, we predicted if a container waste has to be collected or not with a 95% accuracy, just using information on *season, month* and *week day*. These predictions can be used to propose more complex models where the waste collection frequency varies by season.

We propose two different models of frequency-capacity. The first proposal was a waste collection frequency of once a week. For this model, we saw that almost every container had an average waste volume over 100% which shows that a frequency of once a week is not enough for this case. The second proposal was a waste collection frequency of twice a week. This model needed a capacity adjustment for the street of Rua do Arco do Bispo, by adding a container with a 1000 L capacity and For Rua D

Ega and Rua do Arressario, a new container with 400 L. With this adjustment, the containers waste doesn't overload through all year, which makes it a successful capacity-frequency model for our containers.

8 Conclusion

In this paper we addressed the waste collection process with a different approach by studying the capacity-frequency problem.

We successfully correlated waste volume data and were able to extract information, with the variable's *year*, *season* and *weekday* which allowed us to make predictions on whether a waste container needs to be collected with a precision above 90% of accuracy.

It was possible to analyze waste deposition volume and to identify patterns for a determinist and uniform waste collection. For this case, we concluded that a uniform collection of twice a week, with small improvements on containers capacity, proved to be enough for these containers, which is a major improvement to the current collection frequency of three to four times a week.

This process is easy to implement for other sets of data because the process to generate the model's new volume data is scalable, so it's easy to apply this study for other use cases. It also allows the simulation of different waste collection frequencies in multiple periods of time.

For future work, we pretend to use the season information to propose mixed different waste collection frequencies by season and to automate the calculation of the needed capacity for a given frequency.

References

1. Nuortio, T., Kytöjoki, J., Niska, H., Bräysy, O.: Improved route planning and scheduling of waste collection and transport. Expert Syst. Appl. **30**(2), 223–232 (2006)
2. Kim, B.I., Kim, S., Sahoo, S.: Waste collection vehicle routing problem with time windows. Comput. Oper. Res. **33**(12), 3624–3642 (2006)
3. Laporte, G.: The traveling salesman problem: an overview of exact and approximate algorithms. Eur. J. Oper. Res. **59**(2), 231–247 (1992)
4. Bautista, J., Fernández, E., Pereira, J.: Solving an urban waste collection problem using ants heuristics. Comput. Oper. Res. **35**(9), 3020–3033 (2008). Part Special Issue: Bio-inspired Methods in Combinatorial Optimization
5. Ghiani, G., Lagana, D., Manni, E., Musmanno, R., Vigo, D.: Operations research in solid waste management: a survey of strategic and tactical issues. Comput. Oper. Res. **44**, 22–32 (2014)
6. Karadimas, N.V., Papatzelou, K., Loumos, V.G.: Genetic algorithms for municipal solid waste collection and routing optimization. In: Boukis, C., Pnevmatikakis, A., Polymenakos, L. (eds.) AIAI 2007. ITIFIP, vol. 247, pp. 223–231. Springer, Boston, MA (2007). https://doi.org/10.1007/978-0-387-74161-1_24

7. Anagnostopoulos, T., Zaslavsky, A., Medvedev, A.: Robust waste collection exploiting cost efficiency of IoT potentiality in smart cities. In: 2015 International Conference on Recent Advances in Internet of Things (RIoT), pp. 1–6, April 2015
8. Minghua, Z., et al.: Municipal solid waste management in Pudong new area. China. Waste Manag. **29**(3), 1227–1233 (2009)
9. Sharholy, M., Ahmad, K., Vaishya, R.C., Gupta, R.D.: Municipal solid waste characteristics and management in Allahabad. India. Waste Manag. **27**(4), 490–496 (2007)
10. Burnley, S.J.: A review of municipal solid waste composition in the United Kingdom. Waste Manag. **27**(10), 1274–1285 (2007)
11. Bing, X., Bloemhof, J.M., Ramos, T.R.P., Barbosa-Povoa, A.P., Wong, C.Y., van der Vorst, J.G.A.J.: Research challenges in municipal solid waste logistics management. Waste Manag. **48**, 584–592 (2016)
12. Medvedev, A., Fedchenkov, P., Zaslavsky, A., Anagnostopoulos, T., Khoruzhnikov, S.: Waste management as an IoT-enabled service in smart cities. In: Balandin, S., Andreev, S., Koucheryavy, Y. (eds.) ruSMART 2015. LNCS, vol. 9247, pp. 104–115. Springer, Cham (2015). https://doi.org/10.1007/978-3-319-23126-6_10
13. Gutierrez, J.M., Jensen, M., Henius, M., Riaz, T.: Smart waste collection system based on location intelligence. Procedia Comput. Sci. **61**(2015), 120–127 (2015)
14. Vicentini, F., et al.: Sensorized waste collection container for content estimation and collection optimization. Waste Manag. **29**(2009), 1467–1472 (2008)
15. Anagnostopoulos, T., Zaslavsy, A., Medvedev, A., Khoruzhnicov, S.: Top k query based dynamic scheduling for IoT-enabled smart city waste collection. In: 2015 16th IEEE International Conference on Mobile Data Management, vol. 2, pp. 50–55, June 2015
16. Brownlee, J.: Machine Learning Mastery with python (2016)

Tracking and Prediction

Automatic Generation of Spider Maps for Providing Public Transports Information

Sara Santos[1]([✉]), Teresa Galvão Dias[1,2], and Thiago Sobral[1,2]

[1] Faculty of Engineering of University of Porto, Porto, Portugal
{up201402814,tgalvao,thiago.sobral}@fe.up.pt
[2] INESC TEC, Porto, Portugal

Abstract. With the continuous growth and complexity of public transport systems, it is essential that the users have access to transport maps that help them easily understand the underlying network, thus facilitating the user experience and public transports ridership. Spider Maps combine elements from geographical and schematic maps, to allow answering questions like "From where I am, where can I go?". Although these maps could be very useful for travellers, they still are mostly manually generated and not widely used. Moreover, these maps have several design constraints, which turns the automation of the generation process into a complex problem. Although optimisation techniques can be applied to support the generation process, current solutions are time expensive and require heavy computational power. This paper presents a solution to automatically generate spider maps. It proposes an algorithm that adapts current methods and generates viable spider map solutions in a short execution time. Results show successful spider maps solutions for areas in Porto city.

Keywords: Spider maps · Schematic maps · Public transports · Automation

1 Introduction

Every major city has a complex public transport system that is part of everyday mobility of millions of citizens. These systems are vital for cities mobility and ought to be encouraged as an alternative to private transport. Thus, public transport maps provide simplified representations of the public transport networks, making them easy to interpret, facilitating the user experience and public transports ridership.

These maps are often represented by schematic maps, since they fulfilled the need for better and simpler representation of complex networks [6], presenting the readers the available services and navigation possibilities. A specific type of schematic map is designated spider map, used to represent complex areas, such

© ICST Institute for Computer Sciences, Social Informatics and Telecommunications Engineering 2020
Published by Springer Nature Switzerland AG 2020. All Rights Reserved
A. L. Martins et al. (Eds.): INTSYS 2019, LNICST 310, pp. 131–149, 2020.
https://doi.org/10.1007/978-3-030-38822-5_9

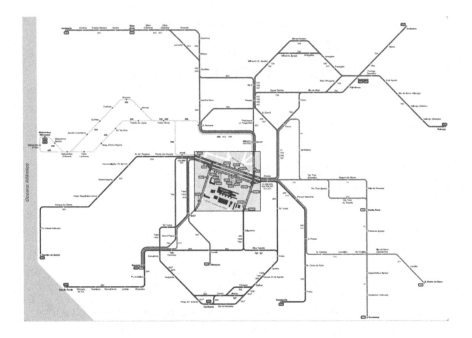

Fig. 1. São João hospital spider map [11]

as bus networks in city centres. For instance, Fig. 1 depicts a spider map created for the São João hospital area in Porto, Portugal.

Even though spider maps are a favourable representation for providing passengers public transport information, the generation process is still manual and relies on the expertise of the designer. There are several methods and techniques that can be applied to automate the spider map generation, but current solutions are complex and time expensive.

This work produces a solution able to generate a feasible spider map at run time, presenting an algorithm that modifies and adapts current techniques. The goal is to tackle the complexity of the problem and present viable solutions with short execution times and using less computational power. Thus, it aims at simplifying the traditional spider map generation process and potentially make an impact on the use of spider maps for providing public transports information.

In Sect. 2 a brief overlook of relevant state-of-the-art methods and concepts are depicted, while Sect. 3 presents the problem approach and the developed methods. The last section concludes this paper and proposes future work and improvements.

2   Maps for Providing Public Transports Information

Transportation maps support complex public transport networks providing essential information (routes, stops and points of interest) for representing the transport network [4]. An important process associated with these maps is schematisation, where certain aspects are giving emphasis and unimportant information is removed.

There are many methods for guiding this process. For instance, line generalisation methods, such as **simplification**, where some line points are removed, only maintaining those that ensure the overall line shape; **exaggeration**, that amplifies certain portions of objects; and **enhancement**, where certain features are emphasised to elevate the message [6]. Among other techniques is adapting the initial map (where points correspond to geographical locations) to a grid [5]. In this technique, line points are moved to grid intersections, while ensuring certain constraints, such as orientation and distance between points. The result is a map with a simpler overall shape, where incremental optimisation processes can be applied to improve the result.

Nonetheless, adapting maps to a grid can lead to very saturated areas, for instance, representing complex centre areas that have lines ending on city outskirts. Hence, Sarkar and Brown [10] proposed a method denominated fish-eye that applies different scales throughout the map, thus enabling magnification of crowded areas [2]. This is a *Focus+Context* technique of great value to the schematization process, since it emphasises important information, while maintaining the global context [9].

Spider maps combine elements from both geographical and schematic maps [1] and are used for represent the travel possibilities of complex public transport areas, for instance, bus networks in a city centre [7].

These maps are characterised by a central area called the hub, generally depicted by a rectangular shape which details a geographic map of the location, proving better spatial context [8]. From the hub emerges the schematic lines that represent the network routes. The location where lines emerge from the hub is not arbitrary and should considered route orientation and the stop location within the hub.

The lines in the spider map do not follow the geographic layout, since they are the result of several simplification and displacement operations, introducing the concept of *map point*. A **map point** is a relevant location in the map (e.g. stops or group of stops along the line routes), with coordinates associated to a map canvas that result from several operations during the map generation [9].

Spider maps have many elements in common with schematic maps, thus similar methods can be applied. However, they have extra constraints, e.g., determine the location where lines emerge from the hub, that makes the spider map generation process even more complex. Furthermore, overall topology should be assured, i.e., the general relations between map points should be maintained in order guarantee spatial awareness.

Spider maps' schematic lines are defined by a set of segments and map points, some of them shared by different lines. Shared segments should be drawn parallel separated by a distance greater than zero and each line has a colour associated. Moreover, angles between segments should be octilinear, i.e., should only follow horizontal, vertical or diagonal orientations (0, 45 or 90° angles) [9].

Though spider maps have a great potential for providing public transports information, there is not much information in literature about this type of maps and how to automate the generation. Most studies focus on the efforts made by Mourinho [9] in the development of techniques to automate the generation of spider maps.

In the proposed method, Mourinho [9] models the spider map as a graph with restrictions associated with points (vertexes of the graph) and lines (edges of the graph). The initial algorithm state is a map where map points and lines resemble the geographic location, then a multi-criteria algorithm is applied to determine the best location of each point, while ensuring a set of constraints and design guidelines. The solution successfully attained the proposed goals. However, this is a complex multi-criteria optimisation problem with great computational effort, since it aims at finding the best solution possible.

3 Automatic Generation of Spider Maps

3.1 Problem Definition

The spider map generation process is a complex problem, since these maps have several design constraints as depicted in Sect. 2. Additionally, the process is mostly done manually, relying on the expertise of the map maker. Even though some current solutions can automatically generate spider maps, they are complex and time expensive for producing results.

Thus, the objective of the proposed solution is to develop an algorithm capable of producing a spider map by creating, adapting and modifying techniques. The solution must take as input the spider map hub area selected by the user and generate as result a viable spider map. A result is considered viable if it satisfies the design restrictions of spider maps aforementioned in Sect. 2. The goal is to develop a prototype that integrates the developed algorithm capable of producing spider map results in short execution times, since it will affect the prototype usability.

Along with automating the spider map generation process, the prototype should also integrate interaction and visualisation techniques, taking advantage of the benefits of digital maps over the traditional form and thus potentially achieve better usability. Such techniques can be integrated before generating the map, for instance, during the hub selection process, and when visualising the map result, e.g. different levels of zoom and clickable items for additional information.

The developed prototype is focused on Porto city and all the public transport data was provided by OPT[1]. The user is presented a geographic map of Porto for choosing the hub area that will be used as input for generating the spider map.

The next section, Sect. 3.2, will describe the algorithm for generating a spider map solution, while Sect. 4 will present the prototype development. Results and evaluation of the developed solution will be analysed in Sect. 5.

---

[1] http://www.opt.pt/.

3.2   Map Generation Algorithm

Beforehand, the algorithm needs as input the coordinates of the hub, that will allow querying the server for information relating the stops inside the selected area and the routes that belong to the spider map. The server will gather and process all the information needed and return to the client the set of stops inside the hub and the lines of the map. Each line is defined by a sequence of map points.

The spider map is modelled as a graph $G(V,E)$ with vertexes V that represent the map points and edges E, the connection between two vertexes, translating the segments of routes defined by two map points. A graph representation was chosen since map points and route segments are shared between multiple lines, thus avoiding duplicated information and making it easier to ensure the relations between points.

Nonetheless, the map points returned from the server have as coordinates the latitude and longitude of the accurate geographical location. Hence, they need to be projected to the map canvas, which is defined as an SVG (Scalable Vector Graphics) using the tool *D3.js*. Thus, all the latitude and longitude coordinates are projected using the Mercator projection centred on the hub centre. The result is a map where the lines and map points are close to the geographical locations, but now map points have as coordinates x and y associated with the defined canvas.

The next step is to insert the hub and determine the location where the lines should emerge from. Therefore, the intersection points between the line segments and the hub boundaries are calculated and those will be the emerging points and all the other segments inside the hub are eliminated. The intersection represents an approximation of the orientation and path of the route, since the hub is a geographical representation of the area. The following step is to resize the hub, translating the lines to new locations considering the centre and the new hub dimensions and insert the hub image depicting the geographic location. Figure 2 exemplifies a hub in Casa da Música area in Porto, after the aforementioned operations.

Furthermore, before beginning the displacement operations to satisfy the spider map restrictions, a matrix containing the topological relations between points is built. It is important to build the matrix before the generation process starts, since at this stage all the points relate to each other close to their real geographical location. Thus, for each map point is calculated the relation to every other map point. A map point can be north or south and east or west of another point. When two points have an equal coordinate (x or y), they are called *in line* of each other.

(1) **Grid Adaptation.** The following algorithm step is to adapt the initial map to a grid, which will lead to an overall simpler shape, closer to fulfil the spider map restrictions. To build the grid, the bounds of the map are calculated, i.e., the maximum and minimum x and y coordinates are determined, that will correspond to the boundaries of the grid. Then, a grid is built with an initial cell size

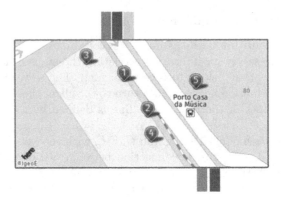

Fig. 2. Hub example of Casa da Música area

length and all the grid intersection points are calculated. The grid intersection points will be the possible displacement options.

The next step is to move each map point to a neighbour grid intersection with the best score. Thus, for each map point the nearest grid intersection points are determine and a score that translates the quality of the displacement is calculated. The score combines the distance between the map point and the grid intersection and how well the topological relations are maintained if the map point is moved to that location. Thus, for each topological relation that is violated a penalty is given. However, if a topological relation changes to *in line* a smaller penalty is attributed, e.g., if point P1 is north of P2 and, with the displacement, P1 becomes in line with P2, a smaller penalty is credited than if P1 becomes south of P2. This loosen the topological constraints and will result in more straight lines after the grid adaptation process. The map point is moved to the grid intersection with the smaller score. Figure 3 depicts the grid adaptation process, illustrating initial locations in the left image and the displacement result in the right image.

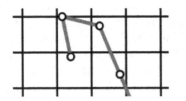 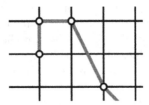

Fig. 3. Grid adaptation process

However, not all the nearest grid intersections are valid displacements. Grid intersection points that will cause hub occlusion, i.e., will intersect the hub, and that will cause line segments to overlap or pass through map points that do not belong to that segment are removed as possible displacement locations. The addition of this restriction will lead to, in some cases, map points that will not have any possible displacements. When this happens, the graph is returned to the original state, the grid cell size is decrease and the grid adaptation process is restarted. By decreasing the grid cell, the granularity is increased which leads to more displacement options. This process is repeated until all points are displaced to a grid intersection or the grid cell size reaches a defined minimum. In this last case, the grid adaptation process may not be possible, thus a map solution will not be produced.

(2) Correcting Non-octilinear Angles. After the grid adaptation, the result will be a map with simpler line shapes that respect the topology relations, however some of the angles between segments will still not be octilinear. Thus, the next step is to identify the map points where the octilinear angle restriction is not satisfied and correct them. It is important to note that the non-octilinear angles resulting from the segments emerging from the hub are not taken into consideration in this step and will be corrected using a different approach.

Afterwards, for each map point identified with an incorrect angle, the algorithm will try to identify a near grid intersection that will correct the angle. Similar to the grid adaptation process, some of nearest grid intersection points will be removed as possible displacements. Grid intersections points are considered not valid if at least on of the following situations occur: (1) the displacement will cause octilinear angles to become non-octilinear; (2) the displacement will disturb the topological relations between points (changes to in line do not count as disturbance); (3) the displacement will cause occlusions, line overlapping or segments passing through map points that do not belong to that line. Figure 4 illustrates the correction of the non-octilinear angle (depicted in the left image) by displacing a point to a new grid location (right image).

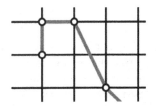 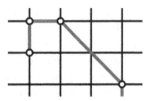

Fig. 4. Non-octilinear angle correction by displacement

However, some map points will not have any possible valid displacements that will correct the non-octilinear angles, thus making them candidates for a break point introduction. A break point will transform one segment in two new ones, which allows correcting the angles without any displacements. Moreover, a break point insertion also has restrictions, since it cannot cause occlusions and

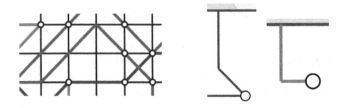

Fig. 5. Non-octilinear angle correction

line overlapping. In some cases, angles cannot be corrected with only a break point, thus two break points are introduced.

The non-octilinear angles of segments that emerge from the hub will be corrected using a different approach. If a segment that emerges from the hub has a non-octilinear angle with the next segment, a perpendicular line to the hub segment is inserted an then a break point is introduced to connect to the next map point. The break point is inserted in a grid intersection that will cause a 90° angle or, if not possible, a 45° angle. Figure 5 depicts the correction of non-octilinear angles by introducing two break points (left image) and the correction of hub related angles.

Even though the several angle correction steps aim at correcting non-octilinear angles through various approaches, in some cases it may not be possible to correct all angles, thus the generated map solution may have some errors.

(3) Draw the Spider Map. After correcting the angles, the final map point locations are determined, and the drawing process can begin. The first is to obtain and place the hub image, that is a geographical representation of the area. The image is obtained using the API Here[2] that returns an image of the geographical map giving a boundary box. Moreover, the stops are identified with markers.

Map points are drawn in the associated locations and do not need further processing. However, segments are shared between lines and need to be drawn parallel, thus making it necessary introducing an offset between shared segments.

In order to introduce an offset that will lead to parallel segments, it is necessary to calculate the slope of the line. Thus, identifying the correct orientation (vertical, horizontal or diagonal), is possible to introduce a correct offset to the x and y coordinates, just as illustrated in Fig. 6.

The final step is to draw the labels that identify the map points. Not all map points need to be labelled, only the last and the most important of each line. Nonetheless, the label's position needs to be determined. Thus, a score is calculated that translates how many occlusions will the label cause. For that, a bounding box of the label is placed at top, bottom, left and right of the corresponding map point and a penalty score is given for each line intersection. The chosen place will be the one with the smaller score.

---

[2] https://developer.here.com/.

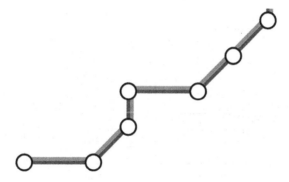

Fig. 6. Shared line segments

After this step, the generation process is finished and a valid spider map solution is presented to the user. Figure 7 depicts the algorithm generation process in a flowchart. Hence, a valid spider map solution is generated if all the aforementioned algorithm steps are successfully completed. In some cases the algorithm is not capable of producing a valid solution, for instance, if grid adaptation fails, no solution will be presented, or if not every non-octilinear angle is corrected, the spider maps will have errors.

The developed algorithm is integrated in the developed prototype depicted in Sect. 4 and results will be illustrated and evaluated in Sect. 5.

4 Prototype Development

For the purpose of testing how the developed algorithm performs in real situations, a prototype was created integrating the algorithm depicted in Sect. 3.2 and taking advantage of digital map characteristics by combining visualisation and interaction techniques.

4.1 Use Cases

The main use cases consist of selecting the desired hub area, and the generation of the corresponding spider map. Figure 8 illustrates the prototype use cases. Moreover, there is the ambition to integrate interaction and visualisation techniques to enhance the user experience.

In the first screen, a map of Porto city with interaction capabilities is presented to the user, i.e., the user can zoom and navigate through the map. Furthermore, in the top right corner, the user can access control buttons illustrated in Fig. 9 left. In this controls users can show/hide the pre-defined grid, check stops inside the grid selection and finally generate the spider map.

The pre-defined grid lays over the Porto city corresponding to the boundaries of the available data. Then, the user can select one or combine several grid cells to create a personalised hub area. Figure 9 right shows an example of grid selection,

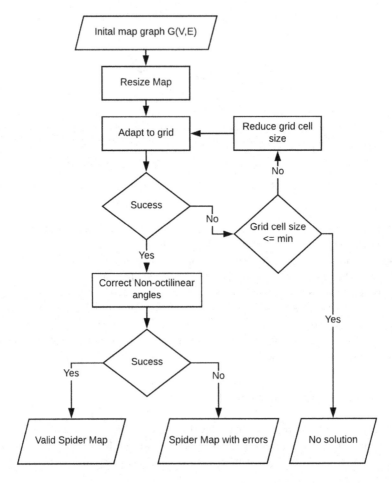

Fig. 7. Generate spider map algorithm

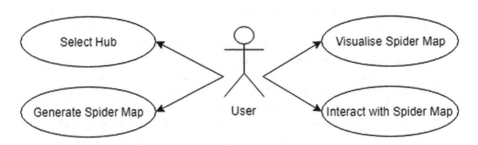

Fig. 8. Prototype use cases

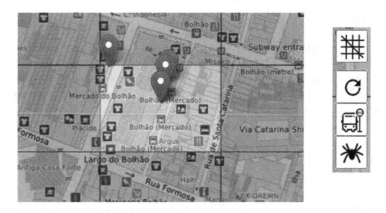

Fig. 9. Example of grid selection (left) and control buttons (right)

where selected cells are shown in orange and markers depict stops inside the hub selection.

After the user chooses the desired hub and selects *"Generate Spider Map"*, the algorithm takes the hub coordinates as input and generates a spider map result. In the next screen the user can visualise and interact with the map result. The user can navigate, zoom and click on map points to check additional information. All these interaction features were developed using *D3.js Behaviour* plugin that allow to catch and handle interaction events. Figure 10 depicts an example of a portion of a spider map result where it is possible to check the additional information box when a map point is hover or clicked on.

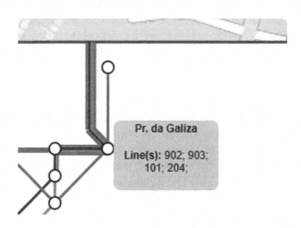

Fig. 10. Interaction with spider map: click on map points to obtain additional information

4.2 Architecture

The developed solution follows a simple two-tier architecture or client-server, illustrated in Fig. 11. This architecture style is commonly used in distributed systems to separate operations into the client and server, where the server provides services to the client [3]. Thus, the server is responsible for dealing with all the necessary data operations, while the client is responsible for the spider map generation and rendering operations.

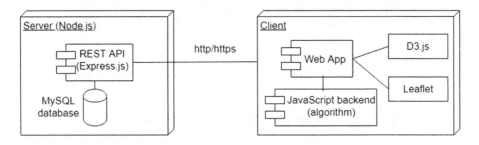

Fig. 11. Solution architecture

The server was implemented using *Node.js*[3] and *Express.js*[4] for the REST API. Moreover, the server establishes a connection with a *MySQL*[5] database that stores all the public transport data, that will be depicted in detail in the next section. Hence, the server is responsible for gathering and processing all the data needed for the spider map generation.

On the other hand, the client consists of a web application based on the two major use cases described in Sect. 4.1. For the geographic maps and hub selection *Leaftlet*[6] and *OpenStreetMap*[7] were used, while the spider map drawing and generation was developed using *D3.js*[8] and *Javascript* technologies.

4.3 Data Model

The data related to public transports of Porto was provided by OPT and stored in a MySQL database following the model depicted in Fig. 12.

Lines are made comprise of several stops that can belong to multiple lines. Moreover, routes are defined by a series of stops associated with an order and recorded in the Path table. The OPT data also identifies map points, which group several stops in a single point. Hence, when gathering the data for the

---

[3] https://nodejs.org.
[4] https://expressjs.com/.
[5] https://www.mysql.com/.
[6] https://leafletjs.com/.
[7] https://www.openstreetmap.org/.
[8] https://d3js.org/.

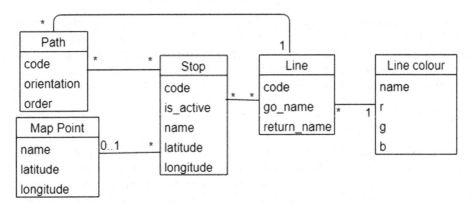

Fig. 12. Data model

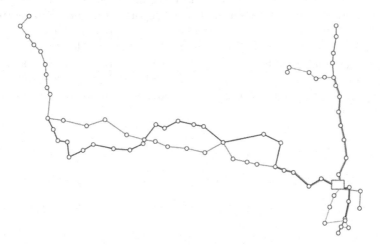

Fig. 13. Initial map state for *Praça da República* hub area

spider map generation, stops along the routes will be replaced or grouped by a map point record and those will be the considered map points during the map generation process.

Furthermore, stops and map points have associated geographical coordinates (latitude and longitude), which will represent the initial position of the points. Moreover, lines and stops also have other attributes associated, such as names and line colours.

5 Evaluation and Validation

Current solutions are complex and take very long to produce spider map results. Hence, the ambition is to tackle the complexity of the generation process of spider maps and develop a solution capable of automatically generate spider maps in real-time. Thereby, the two variables taken into consideration during the evaluation and validation are if the map is correctly generated, i.e., the spider map follows the establish design rules, and the execution time needed to produce the result. A result is considered valid if it complies with the spider map restrictions aforementioned in Sect. 2.

5.1   Tests and Results

Performed tests aim at testing if the solution is capable of generated valid spider maps at real-time using the prototype develop to select the input hub area and generate and evaluate map results. Several tests were performed by choosing different hub areas as input and evaluating the results. Even though tests were only performed for Porto's bus network, the number of possible hub inputs is very extensive. Hence, the tests focused on testing areas where the network is denser, i.e., areas served by many public transports' lines like city centres. In Porto, some of the busiest areas are *Aliados*, *Casa da Música*, *Hospital São João*, *Castelo do Queijo* and others. Tests demonstrated that the developed algorithm produces successful spider map results for the city of Porto. Figures 13 depicts the initial map state for *Praça da República* and Fig. 14 depicts the corresponding generated spider. Figure 15 also depicts a spider map result for *Aliados*, a busy centre area in Porto.

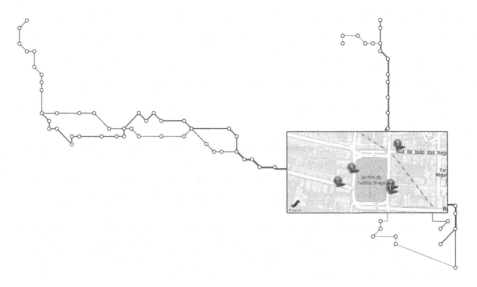

Fig. 14. Spider map result for *Praça da República* hub area

The complexity of the generation process and, subsequently, the spider map is directly related to the number of map points, i.e., the complexity increases as the number of map points also increases, since more displacement operations

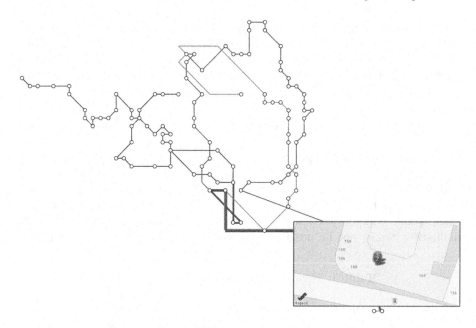

Fig. 15. Spider map result for *Aliados* hub area

and angle corrections will be needed to generate a valid map. Hence, to control the continuous increase in complexity, a limit to the number of lines in the spider map was set, as well as a limitation on the hub size. This prevents the user to select very large areas for the algorithm, preventing the exponential increase in complexity.

There is not much literature in automating the generation process of spider maps, and most of the efforts made in this area were through Mourinho's [9] work. However, in his work the goal was to find the optimal spider map solution, hence the quality was valued over fast results. Thus, the solution required great computational effort and long execution times. For instance, in tests accessing the quality versus the number of algorithm iterations, the average execution times were of 2797 s.

Even though is not possible to establish a direct comparison with the tests performed by Mourinho, it is possible to conclude that the developed solution was able to produce results faster. The developed solution produced spider maps under 500 ms for complex centre areas. Table 1 depicts tests results for valid solutions, describing the number of map points, the numbers of different lines of the map, hub area and the execution time (ET) in milliseconds. In addition, Table 2 depicts the success of test results, identifying how frequently a valid solution was obtained, the number of times where a solution was not possible and the number of incorrect solutions (i.e., spider map results that contain some non-octilinear angles).

It can be concluded that the developed algorithm successfully produces results, i.e., the solution generates valid spider map results in real time, taking significantly less time compared to state-of-the-art solutions. Thus, this work successfully tackles the complexity of the spider map generation process and contributes to the identified gap of current work.

5.2 Limitations and Future Work

The quality of the result depends on how and if all the stages of the algorithm are successful. In the grid adaptation stage, the algorithm will adapt the cell size until the initial map is successfully adjusted to the grid; however, in some cases, grid adaption may not be possible. In very dense areas, a vast number of map points compete for a grid allocation. Thus, even by increasing the grid granularity, it may not be possible to assign a grid point to every map point.

Table 1. Tests results for generated spider maps

No. map points	No. lines	Hub area	ET (ms)
153	6	Castelo do Queijo	844.29
153	6	Castelo do Queijo	710
32	1	Av. Boavista	122.21
153	6	Casa da Música	419.23
144	1	Casa da Música	298.64
10	1	Aliados	35.04
108	4	Aliados	387.71
130	4	Trindade	664.88
52	2	Boavista	215.83
88	2	Hosp. São João	272.87
106	4	Hosp. São João	432.53
102	4	Av. Boavista	5445
32	1	Av. Boavista	102.67
105	4	Praça da República	482.9
105	4	Aliados	496.27
27	1	Bolhão	95.45
39	1	Campo Lindo	177.45
66	3	Marquês	244.62
177	6	Marquês	599.46
37	6	Passeio Alegre	105.96
51	6	Foz do Douro	159.23
33	6	Ramalde	102.33
79	6	Parque Real	194.93

Table 2. Outcome of performed tests

Solution	No. of results
Valid solution found	22
No solution found	3
Solution with errors	5

Moreover, since the subsequent algorithm steps depend on the success of grid adaptation, a solution may not be found.

Nevertheless, introducing a restriction to the maximum number of lines solved contained the occurrence of this problem, and tests showed that the grid adaptation process is successfully completed even in complex areas, and with just one or two iterations. Therefore, reducing the cell size in each iteration to increase the grid granularity was proven successfully.

The next algorithm step that will influence the quality of the solution is the correction of non-octilinear angles. In the developed solution, the algorithm has several iterations that aim correcting the non-octilinear angles through several approaches. The first approach is identifying a valid grid allocation to displace the identified map points and correct the angle. Nevertheless, in some cases is not possible to find a valid displacement that corrects the angle, thus the next iterations try to correct the remaining non-octilinear angles by inserting one or two break points. The integration of different approaches to correct identified non-octilinear angles was effective in producing valid spider map results.

Notwithstanding, in some cases the algorithm may not produce a valid spider map (i.e., some angles may not be corrected) or, in the worst-case scenario, not produce a solution. Most invalid algorithm results derive from the non-octilinear angle correction, not the grid adaption as depicted in Table 2. Thus, even for invalid results, the algorithm can present a solution that may not be completely correct (some angles may not be octilinear).

Some errors are the result of incorrect map point coordinates, that lead to incorrect projections, which subsequently cause the failure of grid adaptation or angle correction.

On the other hand, circular lines are viewed as a special case, since they sometimes lead to particular results. For instance, results with circular lines often cross themselves, which may be valid according to spider map restrictions, but is not very aesthetically pleasing. Also, the rescaling the hub operation may lead to undesired distortion, that in some cases may preclude the success of the non-octilinear angle correction.

Even though some limitations were identified and the algorithm may be improved so it becomes more robust to certain cases, results have proven that the developed solution was successful and provides enhancements in the current state-of-the-art solution. The solution is able to produce viable spider map solutions at real-time and taking in consideration the hub area as user input. Furthermore, the prototype demonstrates the the successful integration of the algorithm with the advantages of digital maps by incorporating visualisation and interaction techniques.

Finally, the spider map solutions can be aesthetically improved in a post-processing stage, with more line simplifications. Nonetheless, the developed solution provides advances in the simplification of the generation process of spider maps, thus potentially making an impact on the use of spider maps in providing public transports information. Through the developed prototype, the user is able to choose a desire hub area and visualise all the travel possibilities by the generated spider map.

6   Conclusions

Spider maps are a type of transportation map that presents all the public transport possibilities available in an area. These maps are very useful for passengers, but their production is still mostly manual. Some efforts have been made to automate the generation of these maps, but state-of-the-art solutions require great computational effort and long execution times to produce results. Hence, the proposed approach aims at developing a solution capable of automatically generate spider maps, tackling the complexity gap of current solutions, and thus possibly making an impact on the use of spider maps for providing public transport information.

The state-of-the-art review identified a gap in current solutions. The generation process of spider maps could be simplified, enabling the automatic creation of map results in real-time. Furthermore, human-computer interaction techniques can be applied to spider maps to enhance the user experience while manipulating such maps.

Henceforward, this work is focused on two goals: develop an algorithm that automatically generates spider maps results in real-time and considering the hub as input; and to develop a prototype that integrates the map generation algorithm, adding interactive capabilities to map results. The algorithm adapted techniques used in schematic maps generation, such as adapting a map to a pre-defined grid, and developed new processes that apply several operations to produce a spider map compliant to all the design restrictions. The prototype used the $D3.js$[9] tool to assist the visualisation and interaction with the map. $D3.js$ is a powerful open-source tool that provides several data manipulation operations and integrated interaction events, ideal for the prototype goals.

Throughout the validation and evaluation process, the objective was to test if the solution could produce valid spider map solutions at real-time, reducing the execution time needed to produce map results. The prototype and tests focused on Porto bus network.

Performed tests showed that the solution is successful and can produce map results in shorter execution times than state-of-the art solutions. Furthermore, the prototype developed validated that the algorithm can be successful integrated in a web application that provides an interface for passengers to interact and customise the map generation.

---

[9]   https://d3js.org/.

Future work may improve the map aesthetics in a post-processing phase by applying more simplification to the spider map schematic lines, which will increase the quality of the solution, and other algorithm improvements so it becomes more robust to complex network data. Notwithstanding, the developed solution contributed to the identified gap in state-of-the-art solution, producing spider map solutions at real-time and considering user input.

Acknowledgements. This work is financed by the ERDF - European Regional Development Fund through the Operational Programme for Competitiveness and Internationalisation - COMPETE 2020 Programme and by National Funds through the Portuguese funding agency, FCT-Fundação para a Ciência e a Tecnologia within project PTDC/ECI-TRA/32053/2017 and POCI-01-0145-FEDER-032053.
Furthermore, special gratitude to OPT (http://www.opt.pt/) for supporting this project by providing all the data related to Porto's bus network, thus making it possible to evaluate the solution with real data.

References

1. Avelar, S., Hurni, L.: On the design of schematic transport maps. Int. J. Geogr. Inf. Geovis. **41**(3), 217–228 (2006). https://doi.org/10.3138/A477-3202-7876-N514
2. Baudisch, P., Good, N., Stewart, P.: Focus plus context screens - combining display technology with visualization techniques. In: Proceedings of the International Symposium on User Interface Software and Technology, UIST 2001, pp. 31–40 (2001). https://doi.org/10.1145/502348.502354
3. IBM: The Client/Server model (2019)
4. International Cartographic Association: History of ICA (2019). https://icaci.org/research-agenda/history/
5. Klippel, A., Kulik, L.: Using grids in maps. Theory and application of diagrams. In: Proceedings of First International Conference, Diagram 2000, Edinburgh, Scotland, UK, 1–3 September 2000, pp. 486–489 (2000)
6. Klippel, A., Richter, K.F., Barkowsky, T., Freksa, C.: The cognitive reality of schematic maps. In: Meng, L., Reichenbacher, T., Zipf, A. (eds.) Map-based Mobile Services: Theories, Methods and Implementations, pp. 55–71. Springer, Heidelberg (2005). https://doi.org/10.1007/3-540-26982-7_5
7. Maciel, F., Dias, T.G.: Challenging user interaction in public transportation spider maps: a cobweb solution for the city of Porto. In: Proceedings of IEEE Conference on Intelligent Transportation Systems, ITSC, pp. 181–188 (2016). https://doi.org/10.1109/ITSC.2016.7795551
8. Maciel, F.M.A.: Interactive spider maps for public transportation. Ph.D. thesis, Faculty of Engineering of University of Porto (2012)
9. Mourinho, J.: Automated generation of context-aware schematic maps: design, modeling and interaction. Ph.D. thesis, Faculty of Engineering of University of Porto (2015). https://hdl.handle.net/10216/79324
10. Sarkar, M., Brown, M.H.: Graphical Fisheye views of graphs. In: Proceedings of the SIGCHI Conference on Human Factors in Computing Systems, pp. 83–91 (1992). https://doi.org/10.1145/142750.142763
11. Sociedade de Transportes Colectivos do Porto: São João hospital spider map (2019). https://www.stcp.pt/fotos/spider_map

Public Transportation Prediction
with Convolutional Neural Networks

Dancho Panovski$^{(\boxtimes)}$ and Titus Zaharia

IP Paris, Télécom SudParis, ARTEMIS Department,
UMR CNRS 5157 SAMOVAR, Évry, France
{dancho.panovski,titus.zaharia}@telecom-sudparis.eu

Abstract. Good, efficient and reliable public transportation systems are of crucial importance for all major cities today. In this paper, we propose a concrete solution to a particular problem: improve the prediction of the bus arrival time at each bus stop station on a given itinerary, by taking to account global and local traffic contexts. The main principle consists of modeling the traffic data as an image structure, adapted for applying CNN deep neural networks. The results obtained shows that the proposed approach outperforms traditional machine learning techniques, such as OLS (Ordinary Least Squares) or SVR (Support Vector Regression) with different kernels (RBF or Polynomial), with more than 18% better accuracy prediction, while being computationally faster.

Keywords: Machine learning · Deep learning · Convolutional neural networks · Public transportation · Traffic prediction · Traffic simulation

1 Introduction

In all urban areas around the world, mobility is of the most crucial importance, and the question that needs to be solved is the following: how to minimize the time spent in transport going from one point of the city to another?

In addition, let us underline that vehicular transports in the urban areas performed by individuals or public transportation vehicles contributed heavily on the carbon footprint, called greenhouse gas. The data [1] obtained from the French government in 2015 gives an extensive overview of the key numbers about production of the greenhouse gas. Transport, in general, is responsible for 27% of the production of greenhouse gas. Transport operated by road represents 94,8% of these emissions. The logical solution to this problem is to decrease the number of vehicles used for private transportation, by proposing more reliable public transportation systems. The question of reliability is here highly important since the user acceptancy strongly depends on. Within this framework, disposing of efficient traffic prediction tools, dedicated to public transportation, is a challenging issue, for both users (which want to be informed precisely and in real-time) and transport operators (which want to optimize their transport networks/itineraries).

© ICST Institute for Computer Sciences, Social Informatics and Telecommunications Engineering 2020
Published by Springer Nature Switzerland AG 2020. All Rights Reserved
A. L. Martins et al. (Eds.): INTSYS 2019, LNICST 310, pp. 150–161, 2020.
https://doi.org/10.1007/978-3-030-38822-5_10

2 Related Work

In this paper, we specifically tackle the issue of bus arrival time prediction in urban areas. The main objective is to minimize the predicted time error of bus arrival at each bus stop while taking to account global and local traffic data at the itinerary of the bus.

In order to obtain this particular data type, we decided to simulate the scenario with the help of a traffic simulation software. Traffic simulation can be defined as the mathematical model of transportation systems, implemented through the application of dedicated algorithms [2]. Two main branches exist for traffic simulation software, including macroscopic [3] and microscopic [4] approaches. Each traffic simulation has its own pros and cons. In our work, a microscopic traffic simulator has been adopted, since it can provide a highly detailed picture (with velocity, location, time, speed...) of each individual entity in the system. More precisely, among the various well-established simulation frameworks [5–7] available, the SUMO [8] traffic simulator has been retained. SUMO (*Simulation of Urban MObility*) [8] is an open-source, microscopic, multimodal traffic simulator that can simulate various scenarios with different type of traffic data and it is supported by a large developer community.

Different algorithms, techniques, and applications have been introduced in the last years in order to address the issue of traffic prediction [9–12]. A conventional commercial application like Google Maps [13] and Citymapper [14] have been widely adopted by the general population. Among other applications, let us mention Transilien [15] for Paris and MVV [16] for Munich. Traditional techniques include time-series analyses [17], ARIMA models [18] with its variations [19] and Kalman Filter [20]. They have been successfully implemented and still intensively exploited today. However, in recent years, with the rapid growth of computational powers, notably GPUs, such approaches have been surpassed in many applications by machine learning techniques [21] and more specifically by deep learning approaches [22]. Different neural networks have also been introduced for solving similar issues, including LSTMs (Long Short Term Memory) [23, 24], CNNs (Convolutional Neural Networks) [25, 26] and GNNs (Graph Neural Networks) [27, 28].

Our main contribution is twofold and concerns the development of the data model involved as well as the prediction approach exploiting the dedicated data model. Thus, the vehicular traffic data is in our case modeled and represented as an image. This makes it possible to exploit an original, dedicated convolutional neural network (CNN) that yields the predicted arrival times of the bus as a regressor.

The rest of the paper is organized as follows, Sect. 3 describes the simulation scenario and the data model. In Sect. 4, the proposed CNN method is described in details. Experimental results are presented and discussed in Sect. 5. Finally, Sect. 6, concludes the paper and opens some perspectives of future work.

3   Simulation Scenario and Data Model

3.1   Simulation of a Real-Live Scenario

Obtaining data that contains information about vehicles, public transportation, pedestrians…. is not obvious and easy to acquire, for various reasons, including economic barriers and regulation issues. In our work, we have considered instead synthetic data, that we have created with the help of the SUMO (*Simulation of Urban MObility*) [8] open platform.

The simulation scenario under consideration concerns two real bus lines, that are fully operational in the city of Nantes, France. They are illustrated in Fig. 1. The decision of choosing these lines is based on the geographical location of the bus itineraries, which globally cover the same geographical region. This makes it possible to include two different bus lines in a single simulation scenario. The bus data, including itineraries, location and names of the bus stops have been recovered from TAN (*Transport de l'Agglomeration Nantaise*) [29] and Nantesmetropole [30] – open data repository, while the map was loaded from OSM (*Open Street Map*) [31].

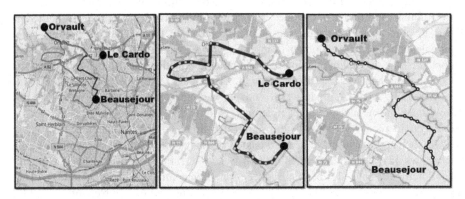

Fig. 1. A geographical area in city of Nantes, with Bus line 89 (middle) – 36 bus stops and 13,4 km, bus line 79 (right) – 25 bus stops and 9,64 km

The simulation scenario has been developed and executed by the SUMO traffic simulator with the following tools and parameters:

- The 2D map of the considered region of the city of Nantes has been converted and imported from OSM.
- The bus itineraries and the bus stop have been manually added to the simulation.
- The total number of simulations performed is 12000.
- The total number of vehicles inserted into the system varies between [8000, 25000].
- Each vehicle itinerary is calculated using the shortest path algorithm of Dijkstra [32], presented with Origin/Destination matrix.
- The total number of pedestrians was set for all simulations to 3600. Let us note that it is important to use pedestrians in the simulation due to the impact of pedestrian

traffic lights. This makes it possible to increase the degree of realism of the entire simulation.

- The simulation time was set to 19000 s, which ensures that all the vehicles will get in and out of the system, as presented in Fig. 2(A).
- The bus time spends at each bus stop was fixed to 20 s.

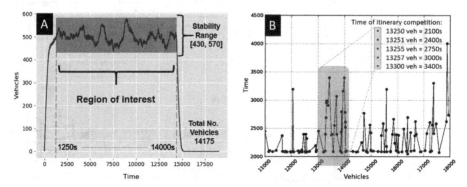

Fig. 2. A – region of interest and stability range; B - time needed to compute the whole itinerary

Each consecutive simulation differs from the previous one by the number of vehicles inserted within the system. This may be questionable because of the small number of vehicles inserted into the system between two consecutive simulations. However, huge disparities from one simulation to another can appear, even though the number of vehicles is increased by small units. This phenomenon is illustrated in Fig. 2 (B), which show the time of completion of the bus itinerary with respect to the total number of vehicles that are inserted in the system. This can be explained as a result of the random distribution of the initial vehicle starting point to the systems, and also by the fact that for each vehicle the shortest route algorithm is calculated, taking to account the global situation.

In the same time, the results in Fig. 2(B) demonstrate that attempting to make a global prediction of the time of completion of an itinerary is impossible.

3.2 Data Model

Our initial goal is to take into account the traffic situation around the bus itinerary. Each simulation is used to create a specific traffic density map that later on can be transformed into one channel (grayscale) image as presented in Fig. 3.

In order to represent traffic as a grayscale image, first, we need to compute and create a so-called TDM (*Traffic Density Matrix*). This matrix represents the traffic situation at each measurement station. Measurement stations are points in space that detects and counts how many vehicles pass in a given period of time. In real-life scenarios, such information can be acquired with the help of loop detectors. In our work, for the convenience of the simulation, each bus stop location has been considered as a measurement station. In this particular scenario, the detection radius around the

considered measurement station was set to 100 m. This representation can be interpreted as a traffic density matrix evolving over time, which is traversed by the considered buses. The last step is to normalize the values of the traffic density matrix by the
maximum value of 255 as one channel (grayscale) image.

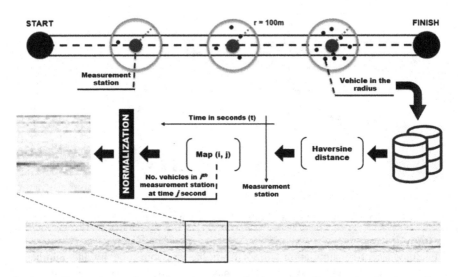

Fig. 3. Traffic density matrix, computation, normalization and traffic data visualized as an image

For each bus generated at each simulation, we create in this way a local density map
simulation matrix, denoted by D, of size (Mstations x T), where Mstations is the
number of measurement stations and T is the number of time instances measured. In
order to simplify and speed up the process, we have evenly sampled the simulation
interval with a step of 10 s. This helps reduce the amount of data and consequently the
related storage/computational requirements.

The simulation yields the following two outputs, controlled by a global parameter
which is the total number of vehicles injected within the system:

- A vector $a = (a_1, a_2, a_{Nstops})$ of size N_{stops}, storing the bus arrival times in all the
  stations of the itinerary
- The density matrix D, of size $(M_{staions} \times T)$
- $M_{stations}$ is (25, 36) for bus 79 and 89 respectively
- T - the time is 4000 s, but since is measured every 10 s, $T = 400$
- The final image was developed by the grayscale (min/max) normalization
  procedure:

$$I = 255 \frac{X - \min(X)}{\max(X) - \min(X)} \tag{1}$$

- *X:* the value of the original image
- *I:* the output - grayscale value of the image after the normalization procedure.

The objective is then to predict the arrival vector *a*, given as an input the image *I*. In order to solve such a problem, we have adopted a CNN architecture, described in the following section.

4 Proposed CNN Architecture

The (Convolutional Neural Network) CNN architecture proposed is illustrated in Fig. 4.

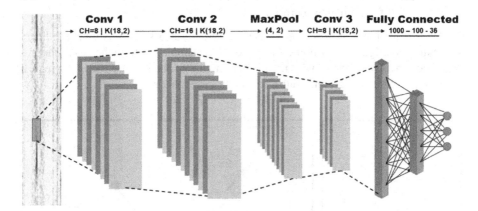

Fig. 4. A proposed convolutional neural network with 3 convolutional layers, one max-pooling and 3 fully connected layers, ReLU as an activation function

It includes the following elements:

- 3 convolutional layers with kernel size (18, 2) and channels (8, 16, 8) respectively,
- 1 max-pooling layer of size (4, 2),
- 3 fully connected layers with size (1000, 100, 36).

The specific kernel size was chosen because of the particular elongated shape of the image data considered (*cf.* Section 3.2). The size and structure of the fully connected layer depend heavily on the vector that is received after the convolutions and down-sizing step. Padding was chosen as 0, so it was not used in this scenario because the traffic information at the beginning and the end of the image is not relevant for the prediction process. The SGD (*Stochastic Gradient Descent*) algorithm (with learning rate of 0.001) has been considered for the learning stage.

For implementation purposes, we have considered the PyTorch [33] deep neural network framework for the CNNs.

5 Experimental Results

For comparison purposes, we have considered several machine learning techniques: Linear Regression (OLS) [34], Support Vector Regression (SVR) [35] (with different kernels). We have retained the Scikit-learn [36] machine learning toolbox with their respective implementations. All the data has been structured in .csv format and compressed with the MsgPack [37] library. The next step is to split the data randomly into three different sub-set and performing 10-fold cross-validation. The training/test split was performed as follows:

- Total number of simulations 12000
- Training dataset - 80% (9600)
- Test dataset – 20%, (2400), from which: 10% (240) were used for validation, and 90% (2160) for evaluation purposes

Our first approach is based on Linear Regression also known as OLS (Ordinary Least Squares). Figure 5 illustrates a snapshot of the simulation from the bus during the scheduled itinerary, together with the prediction curves obtained by the linear regression model (versus the ground truth), for booth buses 79 and 89.

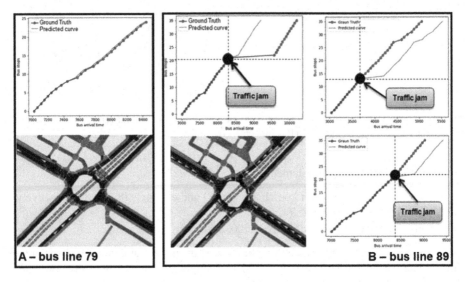

Fig. 5. Prediction results and snapshot from the simulation software. A - bus line 79, the traffic situation is normal and fluid. B - bus line 89 on the right with a traffic jam.

The corresponding MAE (Mean Absolute Error) scores are summarized in Table 1.

Table 1. Prediction results for bus 79 and 89 both directions

	79 Beau > Ovra	79 Ovra > Beau	89 Beau > Le Cr	89 Le Cr > Beau
MAE	4.96	3.18	134.18	133.2

MAE = Mean Absolute Error (s), Beau = Beausejour, Ovra = Ovrault, Le Cr = Le Cardo

For bus line 79, the results are highly accurate, with an MAE inferior to 5 s. In this case, we can observe that the traffic is mostly fluid and the OLS model is perfectly adapted for prediction purposes. However, the prediction results degrade significantly in the case of bus line 89. We can observe from Fig. 5(B), that some localized singularities events (traffic jams) occur in some places and introduce a certain non-linearity. As a consequence, the MAE value increases up to 134,18 s.

In order to investigate this behavior, we have considered a second approach, based on SVR (kernel = 'Poly' and 'RBF'). The polynomial kernel is of second degree known as Quadratic kernel, and the RBF (Radial Basis Function) kernel with gamma = 1/n_features and C = 1.0. The obtained prediction curves are presented in Fig. 6.

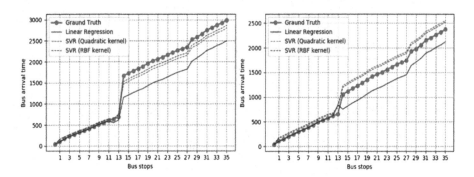

Fig. 6. Support vector regression ('Poly' and 'Rbf') vs linear regression

We can observe that the SVR method with both kernels significantly outperforms the Linear Regression model. These results are also confirmed by the global MAE values and computational time reported in Table 2. We can observe that the CNN training process is faster than the other two methods.

Table 2. Prediction error and computational time for bus 89 direction Beausejour > Le Cardo

	OLS	SVR (rbf)	SVR (poly)	CNN
MAE	134.18	71.23	72.06	59.38
cTime	818	12063	11727	768

MAE = Mean Absolute Error (s), cTIME = Computational Time in (s), OLS = Ordinary Least Squares, Poly = Polynomial, Rbf = Radial Basis Function

The results obtained confirm our original intuition: more complex, non-linear machine learning techniques are required, in order to be able to obtain more accurate predictions while taking to account this localized, non-linear phenomena. Let us now investigated if the proposed CNN can further confirm this intuition.

Figure 7 presents the prediction curves between the different machine learning techniques considered.

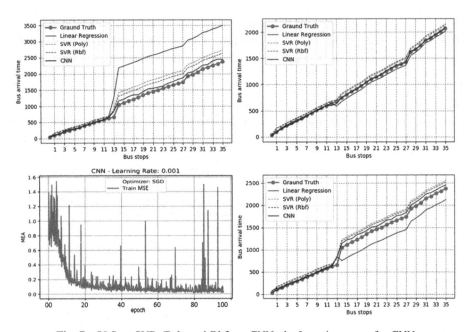

Fig. 7. OLS vs SVR (Poly and Rbf) vs CNN, the Learning curve for CNN

The proposed CNN method outperforms the two previously considered techniques, with overall gains accuracy (Table 2) of 18,5% with respect to SVR and 77,7% better over OLS. The learning curve evolution of the CNN training model (for 105 epochs) is also illustrated here.

In Fig. 8, the histogram and cumulative histogram plots are presented.

From the plot (left) we can observe that 50% of the simulations have an MAE lower than 34 s (which corresponds to the median of the MAE). Moreover, in 80% of cases the MAE is inferior to 86 s.

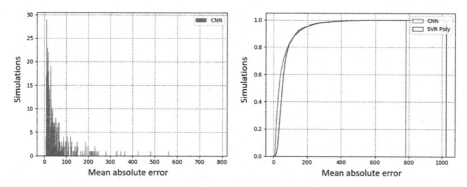

Fig. 8. CNN histograms (left), CNN and SVR Poly cumulative histogram (right)

6 Conclusion and Perspectives

In this paper, we have proposed a new approach for the prediction of bus arrival times in the various bus stops over their itinerary.

We have shown that modeling the traffic data as a 2D image can offer multiple benefits for structuring the information in a meaningful and exploitable manner.

A dedicated CNN network architecture has been proposed, which makes it possible to predict the bus arrival time while taking into account the current traffic situation. The experimental results obtained showed that the proposed CNN outperforms the traditional prediction techniques based on linear regression or SVR approaches, in both prediction accuracy and computational complexity.

Our perspectives of future work concern the consideration of different neural network-based approaches able to deal with the temporal nature of the data, such RNN (Recurrent Neural Networks) and LSTM (Long Short Time Memory).

Acknowledgment. Part of this work has been carried out within the framework of the French FUI project ETS (*Electronic Ticketing System*), supported by the Conseil Départemantal de l'Essonne and the Systematic Paris Region competitivity cluster.

References

1. SOeS: Mars 2015 Chiffres clés du transport
2. Azlan, N.N.N., Rohani, M.M.: Overview of application of traffic simulation model. In: MATEC Web Conference, vol. 150, p. 03006 (2018). https://doi.org/10.1051/matecconf/201815003006
3. Geroliminis, N., Daganzo, C.F.: Macroscopic modeling of traffic in cities (2007)
4. Toledo, T., Koutsopoulos, H., Ben-Akiva, M., Jha, M.: Microscopic traffic simulation: models and application. In: Simulation Approaches in Transportation Analysis, pp. 99–130. Springer, New York. https://doi.org/10.1007/0-387-24109-4_4
5. Balmer, M., Rieser, M.: MATSim-T: architecture and simulation times. In: Multi-Agent Systems for Traffic and Transportation Engineering (2009). https://doi.org/10.1140/epjb/e2008-00153-6

6. Fellendorf, M., Vortisch, P.: Microscopic traffic flow simulator VISSIM. In: Fundamentals of Traffic Simulation (2010). https://doi.org/10.1007/978-1-4419-6142-6_2

7. Rickert, M., Nagel, K.: Dynamic traffic assignment on parallel computers in TRANSIMS. Future Gener. Comput. Syst. **17**, 637–648 (2001). https://doi.org/10.1016/S0167-739X(00)00032-7

8. Krajzewicz, D., Erdmann, J., Behrisch, M., Bieker, L.: Recent development and applications of SUMO - Simulation of Urban MObility. Int. J. Adv. Syst. Meas. **5**, 128–138 (2012)

9. Panovski, D., Zaharia, T.: Simulation-based vehicular traffic lights optimization. In: 2016 12th International Conference on Signal-Image Technology & Internet-Based Systems (SITIS), pp. 258–265. IEEE (2016). https://doi.org/10.1109/SITIS.2016.49

10. Lin, Y., Yang, X., Zou, N., Jia, L.: Real-time bus arrival time prediction: case study for Jinan, China. J. Transp. Eng. **139**, 1133–1140 (2013). https://doi.org/10.1061/(ASCE)TE.1943-5436.0000589

11. As, M., Mine, T.: Dynamic bus travel time prediction using an ANN-based model. In: Proceedings of the 12th International Conference on Ubiquitous Information Management and Communication - IMCOM 2018, pp. 1–8. ACM Press, New York (2018). https://doi.org/10.1145/3164541.3164630

12. Petersen, N.C., Rodrigues, F., Pereira, F.C.: Multi-output bus travel time prediction with convolutional LSTM neural network. Expert Syst. Appl. **120**, 426–435 (2019). https://doi.org/10.1016/j.eswa.2018.11.028

13. Google Maps. https://www.google.com/maps

14. Citymapper - The Ultimate Transport App. https://citymapper.com/paris

15. Schanzenbacher, F., Chevrier, R., Farhi, N.: Fluidification du traffic Transilien : approach prédictive et optimisation quadratique, 2p (2016)

16. Munich Transport and Tariff Association | MVV. https://www.mvv-muenchen.de/

17. Karimpour, M., Karimpour, A., Kompany, K., Karimpour, A.: Online traffic prediction using time series: a case study. In: Constanda, C., Dalla Riva, M., Lamberti, P.D., Musolino, P. (eds.) Integral Methods in Science and Engineering, Volume 2, pp. 147–156. Springer, Cham (2017). https://doi.org/10.1007/978-3-319-59387-6_15

18. Kumar, S.V., Vanajakshi, L.: Short-term traffic flow prediction using seasonal ARIMA model with limited input data. Eur. Transp. Res. Rev. **7**, 21 (2015). https://doi.org/10.1007/s12544-015-0170-8

19. Zhang, N., Zhang, Y., Lu, H.: Seasonal autoregressive integrated moving average and support vector machine models. Transp. Res. Rec. J. Transp. Res. Board. **2215**, 85–92 (2011). https://doi.org/10.3141/2215-09

20. Mir, Z.H., Filali, F.: An adaptive Kalman filter based traffic prediction algorithm for urban road network. In: 2016 12th International Conference on Innovations in Information Technology (IIT), pp. 1–6. IEEE (2016). https://doi.org/10.1109/INNOVATIONS.2016.7880022

21. Panovski, D., Scurtu, V., Zaharia, T.: Simulation and prediction of public transportation with maps of local density blobs. In: 2019 IEEE International Conference on Consumer Electronics (ICCE), pp. 1–4. IEEE (2019). https://doi.org/10.1109/ICCE.2019.8661921

22. Panovski, D., Scurtu, V., Zaharia, T.: A neural network-based approach for public transportation prediction with traffic density matrix. In: 2018 7th European Workshop on Visual Information Processing (EUVIP), pp. 1–6. IEEE (2018). https://doi.org/10.1109/EUVIP.2018.8611683

23. Ke, J., Zheng, H., Yang, H., Chen, X.M.: Short-term forecasting of passenger demand under on-demand ride services: a spatio-temporal deep learning approach. Transp. Res. Part C Emerg. Technol. **85**, 591–608 (2017). https://doi.org/10.1016/J.TRC.2017.10.016

24. Yu, R., Li, Y., Shahabi, C., Demiryurek, U., Liu, Y.: Deep learning: A generic approach for extreme condition traffic forecasting. In: Proceedings of the 2017 SIAM International Conference on Data Mining, pp. 777–785. Society for Industrial and Applied Mathematics (2017)
25. Ma, X., Dai, Z., He, Z., Na, J., Wang, Y., Wang, Y.: Learning traffic as images: a deep convolutional neural network for large-scale transportation network speed prediction. Sensors **17**(4), 818 (2017)
26. Fouladgar, M., Parchami, M., Elmasri, R., Ghaderi, A.: Scalable deep traffic flow neural networks for urban traffic congestion prediction. In: 2017 International Joint Conference on Neural Networks (IJCNN), pp. 2251–2258. IEEE (2017). https://doi.org/10.1109/IJCNN.2017.7966128
27. Wu, Z., Pan, S., Chen, F., Long, G., Zhang, C., Yu, P.S.: A comprehensive survey on graph neural networks (2019)
28. Li, Y., Yu, R., Shahabi, C., Liu, Y.: Diffusion convolutional recurrent neural network: data-driven traffic forecasting (2017)
29. Webmaster: Tan - Ma vie sans arrêt - tan.fr
30. Accueil—Open Data Nantes Métropole. https://data.nantesmetropole.fr/pages/home/
31. Jokar Arsanjani, J., Zipf, A., Mooney, P., Helbich, M.: An introduction to OpenStreetMap in geographic information science: experiences, research, and applications. In: Jokar Arsanjani, J., Zipf, A., Mooney, P., Helbich, M. (eds.) OpenStreetMap in GIScience. LNGC, pp. 1–15. Springer, Cham (2015). https://doi.org/10.1007/978-3-319-14280-7_1
32. Dijkstra, E.W.: A note on two problems in connexion with graphs. Numer. Math. **1**(1), 269–271 (1959)
33. Paszke, A., et al.: Automatic differentiation in PyTorch (2017). https://openreview.net/forum?id=BJJsrmfCZ
34. Seber, G.A.F., Lee, A.J.: Linear Regression Analysis. Wiley, Hoboken (2003)
35. Undefined: support vector regression (2004). cmlab.csie.ntu.edu.tw. Science, M.W.-D. of C., of, U
36. Pedregosa, F., et al.: Scikit-learn: machine learning in Python. J. Mach. Learn. Res. **12**, 2825–2830 (2011)
37. Ching, T., Eddelbuettel, D.: RcppMsgPack: messagepack headers and interface functions for R (2018)

Tourism Guidance Tracking and Safety Platform

Frederica Gonçalves[1,6(✉)], Ana Lúcia Martins[2,3],
João Carlos Ferreira[2,4,5], Eduardo Marques[6], Magno Andrade[6],
and Luís Mota[6]

[1] ITI/LARSyS - Universidade da Madeira, Funchal, Portugal
`frederica.goncalves@staff.uma.pt`
[2] Instituto Universitário de Lisboa (ISCTE-IUL), Lisbon, Portugal
[3] Business Research Centre (BRU-IUL), Lisbon, Portugal
[4] Information Sciences, Technologies and Architecture Research Center
(ISTAR-IUL), Lisbon, Portugal
[5] Inov Inesc Inovação – Instituto de Novas Tecnologias, Lisbon, Portugal
[6] Universidade da Madeira, Funchal, Portugal

Abstract. We propose a platform for tourism Guidance Tracking and Safety (GTS) based on beacons Bluetooth Low Energy (BLE), mobile device App and a central cloud server. Context information is provided to improve tourism transportation options taking into account local offer and a collaborative gamified approach is applied to share trips and advice natural trails walk. Guidance, safety is provided in remote natural walks and a case application in Madeira, island Levadas, natural trails. This work is the results of a submitted project between ICSTE-IUL and Madeira University used to create a tool to get tourism data, advice and orient tourism for ecological trails.

Keywords: Beacons · App · Mobile device · Orientation

1 Introduction

Every tourism activity has specific geography and temporal sequence, and contemporary tourism geography is a growing field of study. Considering this reality, we propose the creation of a shared platform to collect tourist data in a non-intrusive way that provides context personalized and safety information based on the new approach of beacons interaction with mobile devices. The management of the collected data supports better policy taken decision as well as touristic operators' new offers to best meet tourist needs. Improving touristic experiences was in the scope of Human-Computer Interactions researchers in the past [1]. Poon [2] refers in his study the importance of technology as a strategic tool to tourism. Research on information technology and tourism has reflected the general understanding of how technology changes our society and economy [3]. There are now possibilities to access a variety of data, in massive quantities, in different formats and potentially real-time [3]. Fuchs et al. [4], presents a knowledge infrastructure which has recently been implemented as

A. L. Martins et al. (Eds.): INTSYS 2019, LNICST 310, pp. 162–171, 2020.
https://doi.org/10.1007/978-3-030-38822-5_11

a genuine novelty at the leading Swedish mountain tourism destination by applying a business intelligence.

The main goal is the acquisition of quality data to create new and improve tourist product offers while also supporting informed policy decisions and prepare better transportation offers. Smart destinations enable a city to achieve a unique selling proposition and to make the overall experience of tourists visiting the destination more fun-filled and convenient [5]. Some authors stated [6], that the evolution and convergence of several technologies, such as wireless communications, machine learning, real-time computer decision–making, sensors, cameras, and embedded computing are promoting the fast growth of the Internet of Things (IoT). Most of the IoT sensors are expected to operate using a battery for months or years without resorting to external power sources. To satisfy this expectation, suitable wireless sensor network technologies are required [7] including low power WPAN (Wireless Personal Area Network) standards such as Bluetooth Low Energy (BLE) [8]. Schöning et al. [9] evaluated how information generated on-the-fly about a point of interest (POI) can be presented interactively using an augmented reality approach. In another way, Marshall et al. [10] analyses how tangible multi-touch surfaces could be adapted to multi-user interactions between users in a touristic centre in the planning phase of a trip. More recent Zhang et al. [11] investigate how generating touristic trips differs when performed by a group of people, including inter-group communication, labour & information search division, and cultural difference between the tourists.

Based on IoT technologies, information on how tourists move can be acquired and complemented by other tourists' related data (e.g., range age, gender, country, visiting days, visited places and impressions) collected from social networks for additional information about their impressions about a place. Data is then processed to extract knowledge for Tourists Offices and local Operators.

A Mobile App shall be developed for tourism usage, giving integrated context information about the local region to help tourists decide/choose Point of Interests to visit and to know the best way to get there, and to receive safety advises and related recommendations.

2 Context

2.1 Madeira Tourism

Tourism potential on Madeira Island lays on natural resources available for the activity, in the exceptional laurel forest UNESCO World Heritage site [12]. A special interest on this ecological unit enforced building the highland waterway levadas. The circa 1400 km of manmade-infrastructures are constantly channelling water from the Northern part of the island, where is more humid because of the higher amount of precipitation, to the southern part of the island where the climate is drier in comparison. They supply water for agriculture and plantations of sugarcane and at later stage to vineyards to produce Madeira wine [13]. They play a very important role supplying water to the hydroelectric plants installed on the island. The levadas offer the possibility to walk through the laurel forest, a unique sightseeing in the world; they still an alternative way on land connecting villages and urban structures, often used for tourism activity. During the period between October and April is when most of the cruise ships disembark on Madeira, being a great contribution to tourist arrivals, but due to the reduced time on land, just few levadas are visited. Tourists booking a longer stay on Madeira Island and traveling by plane are the ones visiting more often the trails. Regardless of the importance of levadas sustaining local economy, there are few studies centred on their tourism potential. Authors like, Almeida, et al. [14] are studying their use for tourism and their contribution to the variety of offers. For three months, 150 tourists interested on walking routes registered their opinion on a tailor-made survey provided on the most visited trails on Madeira Island. Tourists gave value to this experience as an opportunity to have direct contact with nature, but not necessary engaging on physical activities. The region offers excellent natural resources for tourism activity, cultural assets and ages-old architecture; however, motivation to visit the Destination lays on enhancing their well-being through the unique island landscape, trekking on levadas and the climate. Although, there is a lack of studies centred on tourism on the levadas.

2.2   Tourism Carrying Capacity of Natural Tourist Attractions

Tourist managers concerned with possible impacts from visitors' flow, use operational data for planning and managing of the attractions [15]. In Spain, García and Ventura [16] studied tourism and the public use of natural protected areas with the intention to assess impacts of visitors by using carrying capacity. In Mexico, some authors [17] used this methodology to determine tourism capacity on the mass tourism destination of Cozumel. They adjusted the methodology by creating local indicators for sustainability based on independent variables thought more feasible to quantify. In Portugal, [18] assessed tourist capacity to provide thresholds for beach management. Queiroz et al. [19] determined the tourism carrying capacity in the Azorean Islands using Cifuentes's correction factors for social, precipitation, light and accessibility, highlighting the social factor affecting greatly his calculation by considering groups of 15 people and a minimum group distance of 250 m. Moreover, tourism capacity shall be taken as a borderline relating actions to minimizing impacts from tourist activity.

Despite of the methodology being commonly accepted, several concerns point out the subjectivity by using variables requesting permanent revision. Tourism capacity can be the visitors' perception linking rhetorical thresholds. As human values influence the calculation of such limit, it is very difficult to find the real threshold for visitation [20]. For example, local people being more familiar with a tourist attraction, register different satisfaction levels related to sense of crowding. Patterns for local and foreign visitors' variate greatly as behavioural attitude differs also [18].

However, the assessment of tourism carrying capacity provides a start point for managing tourism; it carries the ability to understand boundaries for visitation related to sustainability. The process itself is not extremely technical, which reduces the need for specialised people and costly equipment.

2.3 Beacons

A Beacon is a small Bluetooth Radio Transmitter that repeatedly broadcasts synchronous Bluetooth Low Energy (BLE) [21] signal in a restrict region/area. Each signal contains configurable data that can be received by a smart device. A beacon example can be observed in Fig. 1.

Fig. 1. Estimote Proximity Beacon (left) and BlueCats AA Beacon (BC-313) (right).

Estimote Beacon. It was implemented by Estimote, Inc - a company founded in 2012 by Jakub Krych and Łukasz Kostka, graduates from Jagiellonian University and AGH University of Science respectively. Nowadays, Estimote sells five types of products [22]: Location UWB Beacon, Location Beacon, Proximity Beacon, Sticker Beacon, and Video Beacon. The most appropriated Estimote product to use in an Indoor Location concept is the Proximity Beacon. This device holds an average of 2–3 years of battery life and a configurable range of maximum 70 m in open field.

BlueCats Beacon. In 2011, BlueCats was founded by Cody Singleton, Kurt Nehrenz and Nathan Dunn in USA and Australia. Indoor location devices are the core of this company. There are 3 types of beacons available on the marked: AA Beacon(BC-313) [23], Coin Beacon [24] and USB Beacon [25]. The most designated BlueCats product for complement this project is the AA Beacon (BC-313). This indoor location device holds waterproof and a battery life of maximum 5 years depending on the device performance.

Beacons are the most recent indoor location technology, it is easy to configure and to maintain. It has its own API for the developers that want to implement an ILS. The security and Privacy of the users are safe, and the cost of each equipment is not expensive. Both beacon types, Estimote and BlueCats, have very similar characteristics so we are sure that both would fulfill all the requirements of this project. Since the price and the characteristics of both beacons are similar, we chose the Estimote beacon because the design of the product holds a better look. Figures 2 and 3 shows the design of both products, Estimote Proximity Beacon and BlueCats AA Beacon (BC-313).

3 Architecture of GTS

Taking into account our research goals our platform are based on: GPS tracking in a mobile App, an App that performs user interaction, Central cloud server to store data and perform data analytics with a dashboard, beacon configurator.

GPS Tracking – module to track tourists in cities so that patterns of movement can be recognized and preferred routes identified. This process runs in the APP, and it will record the location of the tourists periodically by GPS and store the information which can be synchronised when tourists reach a Wi-Fi point. A gamification approach could be added to increase tourist's attachment to their apps.

Beacon locater and context information - Using new technology based on Bluetooth Low Energy the beacons can be configured and implemented near each PoI (Point of Interest). Given the hyper-local and contextual capabilities of beacons, they are of immense value to both travellers as well as players in the tourism industry. The beacon signal will the captured by mobile device App, and context information can be sent to the mobile APP, and we take mobile device Bluetooth address and date/time (way of checking the tourists present in a specific place). We aim at implementing a new approach to context information used in the commercial area applied to the tourism business. For example, tourists can be alerted about useful information when they are close to a PoI, transportation schedules, weather updates and public services in multiple languages, and at relevant times during the day.

Cloud Server and dashboard - A cloud platform will store data and run all developed process for data analyses. All developed will be available and since it is a cloud environment can be shared. During the project, we will discuss with each Tourism Office existing local server and how local information can be stored.

We incorporate the most advanced techniques of data visualization, especially for what concerns the ease of discrimination of the target of interest vs the rest of the picture. To achieve this, a Dashboard will be developed. Dashboards present potentially disparate and complex pieces of information in a unified presentation view and are becoming common place.

4 Context Information and Beacons

These BLE devices are responsible for sending data that is going to be after received by the End User smartphone (as a BLE signals receptor) that is going to be after converted as user current location by the app. To validate the source of each BLE signal, each beacon needs to be configured and placed separately by System and Database Administrators in order to distinguish each beacon separately. As long as the End User smartphone receives a different BLE signal when walking through, the user current location is updated.

Beacon Physical Placement
The role of this process is to get the number of beacons needed, the position where each one is going to be placed in each building and the broadcasting power in order to get a good performance of the ILS, avoiding BLE signals overlap. If there is BLE signals

overlap the correct user location can't be assured. An external mobile App was developed to test the beacons, named Nearest Beacons App. The first step is the Beacon Manager. This entity is responsible, as the name says, to manage the beacons that the smartphone can intersects while the user is walking. Estimote provides an SDK that offers an API to handle the BLE connection, so there's no need to monetize and process all the packets that are nearby the smartphone because this API fulfils the requirements of what is needed in this entity. To import this SDK, we need to add it as a dependency of the Android Studio project. In Gradle Scripts, into the build. Gradle, we just need to add the dependency. Until now, version 1.4.0 is the most viable to use, so that is the one that we choose to work. The second step is the BLE signal parametrization.

Broadcasting Power and Range

Broadcasting Power is the power with which beacon broadcasts its signal. The range is described as the area where the BLE signal can be intersected/received by other smart devices. Broadcasting Power directly impacts the signal range. High power values mean that the range is going to be bigger/longer. The Broadcasting Power can be set from −40 dBm (minimum) to +4 dBm (maximum) – corresponding to a minimum range of 2 m and maximum range is 70 m, without obstacles between the Beacon and the receiver.

Advertising Interval

The beacon's transmission packets can be configured in a restrict interval, this interval is the time when the beacon is "sleeping", which means how long the beacon will be freeze until sending another Ibeacon packet. For example, if the interval configured is 100 ms, it means that the beacon will broadcast its signal once every 100 ms (or 10 times per second). It can be set from 100 ms to 2000 ms. Choosing the interval can affect the battery life of the equipment: when the interval is low, more packets are sent, which means that the battery life will be shorter.

Beacon Identification Parametrization (Using the IBeacon Protocol)

The IBeacon protocol [26] was developed by Apple in 2014. This protocol enables the configure which data, and its format that is going to be sent in BLE signals of the beacon.

In each IBeacon packet there are the following features:

- UUID: 16 bytes, usually represented as a string, e.g., "B9407F30-F5F8-466E-AFF9-25556B57FE6D";
- Major number: 2 bytes, or an "unsigned short", i.e., a number from 1 to 65,535;
- Minor number: 2 bytes, same as Major.

This data format offers the user/developer the ability to create a hierarchy of beacons and lets the app get the information it is inside or outside the Beacon Region. This protocol is suitable for this project because in each BLE packet three fields are sent so it is possible to have more combinations and be more specific when identifying the beacons signal origin.

BLE Signal Characteristics

The Received Signal Strength Indicator (RSSI), is the strength of beacon's signal as received on the smart device. This is related to distance and Broadcast Power, i.e., the strength depends on distance and broadcasting power values. Considering the maximum Broadcasting Power, +4 dBm, the Received Signal Strength Indicator range from approximately −26 (close distance, few meters) to −100 (40–50 m). The RSSI can be used to estimate the distance between the device and the beacon.

NearestBeacons App

A mobile app called NearestBeacons was developed by the author based on the Estimote API [27]. This auxiliary application has the objective of evaluating the BLE signal, depending on the position of the user, as a monitor of BLE signals intersected. This app, when scanning and detecting one or more BLE signals, print the following fields of each signal order by signal strength (RSSI) on the smartphone screen:

- Major and Minor: to identify which beacon we are evaluating;
- Measured Power: "indicates what's the expected RSSI at a distance of 1 m to the beacon". [28].
- RSSI: Signal strength value that depends on distance and broadcasting power [29].

The string format that is printed on the screen, for each intersected BLE signal, follows the next nomenclature: [incremental intersected BLE signal counter value] + "– Major:" + [Major value] + "|Minor:" + [Minor value] + "|Measured Power:" + [Measured Power value] + "dbm" + "|Rssi:" + [RSSI value] + "**". Figure 2 shows an example of NearestBeacons app showing two intersected beacons ordered by RSSI value, with the corresponding fields referred above.

Fig. 2. NearestBeacons scan values example

5 Levadas App

Trail map and all related information are loaded in our App storage. GPS gives position and related information is represented based on users position. If GPS is not available beacon can generated alerts information. For example dangerous zones, guidance when alternative paths were available. This still a conceptual work that we intend to implement under TABS project (Interreg Atlantic submitted project). Previous load information in the app can give details about the places. Major output is the alerts in dangers places, where we allocate beacons. When mobile device is in the range (we configure 70 m), the mobile app is awaked by beacon signal and information is displayed about the problem. We validate the concept at our university in an indoor guidance system [30]. Tested in a population of the system around 100 walks were measured an evaluated system location and information. Indoor location with BIM information gives a good location.

Testing @Iscte Campus - Due to delays on project we prove concept at our university campus and wait for this installation. We use a set of 26 Estimote beacons. Test Cases to perform these tests, we needed to choose where would be the current position/location of the user in Edificio 1 and also pick the final destination. But before that, we decided to split these tests into two approaches: the current location floor is the same of the destination and the other one, the current location floor is different from the destination floor. Also, in the end we tested the situation of running the mobile App in a position that is not covered by a beacon region.

The current location floor is the same as the destination. In this test, the current location floor is the same as the destination floor so there is no need to use stairs or elevator, so we expected that the App only renders one map floor. The user is going to choose the room 1E02 as a destination, and his current location is going to be on the west side of the floor on the left bottom. Each location can be confirmed in Fig. 3 (left), the current location in yellow and destination in red color. Having this current location and destination on the same floor, the Find Me! App can calculate two possible paths to reach the destination. One is through the south corridor and the other through the east corridor. Figure 3 (right) represents the two expected possible path.

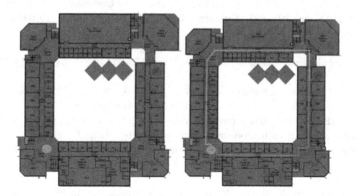

Fig. 3. Floor 1 map with current (yellow) and destination (red) locations marked (left) and - Floor 1 with paths possible options marked (right) (Color figure online)

6 Conclusions

This beacon solution with pre-loaded information can play an important role in natural trails where there is no cellular network, giving guidance and safety alarms. The app can track also tourists to better understand their behaviour. In spite off not being installed in a natural trail, the solution has more than one-year working experience in indoor guidance environment and also for emergency evacuations. With a very easy installation process, the current solution is limited by beacon battery duration each is also related to beacon range, but at local university tests, we are running the same beacon for more than two years. This solution can be applied also in a point of interesting to track tourists and give them useful information about the place.

Acknowledgements. The authors would like to thank "Tourism Project: Characterization, Impact and Sustainability of Madeira Tourism", co-financed by the Operational Program of the Autonomous Region of Madeira 2014-2020 (Portaria No. 92/2015), M14-20-01-0145- FEDER-000007, and SMARTDEST, MAC/1.1b/133, of the University of Madeira.

References

1. Samsonov, P., Heller, F., Schöning, J.: Autobus: selection of passenger seats based on viewing experience for touristic tours. In: em MUM, Stuttgart, Germany (2017)
2. Poon, A.: Tourism, Technology and Competitive Strategies. CAB, Wallingford (1993)
3. Xiang, Z.: From digitization to the age of acceleration: on information technology and tourism. Tour. Manag. Perspect. **25**, 147–150 (2018)
4. Fuchs, M., Höpken, W., Lexhagen, M.: Big data analytics for knowledge generation in tourism destinations – a case from Sweden. J. Destination Mark. Manag. 3(4), 198–209 (2014)
5. Boes, K., Buhalis, D., Inversini, A.: Conceptualising smart tourism destination dimensions. In: Tussyadiah, I., Inversini, A. (eds.) Information and Communication Technologies in Tourism 2015, pp. 391–403. Springer, Cham (2015). https://doi.org/10.1007/978-3-319-14343-9_29
6. Gubbi, J., Buyya, R., Marusic, S., Palaniswami, M.: Internet of Things (IoT): a vision, architectural elements, and future directions. Future Gener. Comput. Syst. **29**(7), 1645–1660 (2013)
7. Gruman, G.: Beacons are harder to deploy than you think. http://www.infoworld.com/article/2983166/bluetooth/beacons-are-harder-to-deploy-than-you-think.html
8. Nield, D.: IBeacon technology powers a new smart public transport project in Bucharest. http://www.gizmag.com/ibeacon-smart-public-transport-bucharest/37901/
9. Schöning, J., Hecht, B., Starosielski, N.: Evaluating automatically generated location-based stories for tourists. In: CHI 2008 Extended Abstracts on Human Factors in Computing Systems (2008)
10. Marshall, P., Morris, R., Rogers, Y., Kreitmayer, S.: Rethinking 'multi-user': an in-the-wild study of how groups approach a walk-up-and-use tabletop interface. In: CHI 2011 Proceedings of the 29th Annual ACM Conference on Human Factors in Computing Systems (2011)
11. Zhang, L., Sun, X.: Designing a trip planner application for groups: exploring group tourists? Trip planning requirements. In: CHI 2016 Extended Abstracts on Human Factors in Computing Systems (2016)
12. UNESCO: UNESCO, 1999. https://whc.unesco.org/en/list/934
13. Quintal, R.: Levadas and Footpaths of Madeira 4ª Edição. Francisco Ribeiro, Funchal (2010)
14. Almeida, A., Soares, J., Alves, A.: As levadas da Madeira no contexto da afirmação e da confluência do turismo de natureza com o turismo ativo. Rev. Port. Estudos Regionais 27–42 (2013)
15. González-Guerrero, G., Olivares Robles, A.K., Valdez Pérez, M.E., Morales Ibarra, R., Castañeda Martínez, T.: The application of the tourist carrying capacity technique and its critical analysis for tourism planning. Tour. Plann. Dev. **13**(1), 72–87 (2016)

16. García, J.G.-L., Ventura, D.G.: Capacidad de acogida de uso público en los espacios naturales protegids. In: em Cuadernos de la Red de Parques Nacionales, vol. 3. La Trébere, Madrid (2014)
17. Segrado, R., Muñoz, A.P., Arroyo, L.: Medición de la capacidad de carga turística de Cozumel. El Periplo Sustentable (13), 33–61 (2008)
18. Zacarias, D.A., Williams, A.T., Newton, A.: Recreation carrying capacity estimations to support beach management at Praia de Faro. Portugal. Appl. Geogr. **31**(3), 1075–1081 (2011)
19. Queiroz, R.E., Ventura, M.A., Guerreiro, J.A., da Cunha, R.T.: Carrying capacity of hiking trails in Natura 2000 sites: a case study from North Atlantic Islands (Azores, Portugal). Rev. Gestão Costeira Integrada-J. Integr. Coast. Zone Manag. **14**(2), 233–242 (2014)
20. Saarinen, J.: Traditions of sustainability in tourism studies. Ann. Tour. Res. **33**(4), 1121–1140 (2006)
21. Developers, A.: Bluetooth low energy. https://developer.android.com/guide/topics/connectivity/bluetooth-le.html. Accessed 08 Jan 2018
22. Inc., E.: Estimote products specification. https://estimote.com/products/?gclid=Cj0KCQiAyszSBRDJARIsAHAqQ4om91_Co4TM8pBLM44BeJlQAkwcc4JNeazH2sXqhaENhVX0f2HOOcaAh51EALw_wcB. Accessed 08 Jan 2018
23. BlueCats: BlueCats AA Beacon. https://www.bluecats.com/aa-bluetooth-beacon/. Accessed 08 Aug 2018
24. BlueCats: BlueCats Coin Beacon. https://www.bluecats.com/coin-mobile-beacon/. Accessed 08 Aug 2018
25. BlueCats: Blue Cats USB Beacon. https://www.bluecats.com/usb-beacon/. Accessed 08 Aug 2018
26. Belwariar, R.: A* Algorithm. https://www.geeksforgeeks.org/a-search-algorithm/. Accessed 08 Dec 2017
27. Inc., E.: Estimote Cloud Settings Values. https://cloud.estimote.com/#/beacons/b238d205630607db4bb08ed5703fb201/settings. Accessed 14 Sep 2018
28. Inc., E.: Estimote Monitoring API. https://developer.estimote.com/android/tutorial/part-2-background-monitoring/. Accessed 08 Aug 2018
29. Inc., E.: Beacon Signal Characteristics. https://community.estimote.com/hc/en-us/articles/201636913-What-areBroadcasting-Power-RSSI-and-other-characteristics-of-a-beacon-s-signal. Accessed 08 Aug 2018
30. Ferreira, J., Resende, R., Martinho, S.: Beacons and BIM models for in-door guidance and location. Sensors **18**(12), 4374 (2018)

App Guidance for Parking Occupation Prediction

Gonçalo Alface[1] , Joao C. Ferreira[1,2(✉)] , and Ruben Pereira[1]

[1] Instituto Universitário de Lisboa (ISCTE-IUL), ISTAR-IUL,
1649-026 Lisbon, Portugal
{gpaea,jcafa,rfspa}@iscte.pt
[2] INOV INESC Inovação - Instituto de Novas Tecnologias,
1000-029 Lisbon, Portugal

Abstract. This research work presents a prototype model, focused on an android application, to handle the problem of finding an available parking space during driving process for all type of road vehicles in a city using historical data and prediction methods, where there is not any type of real-time system to provide information about the current state of the parking lot. Different source data integration were performed to improve the process of prediction, namely events in the surrounding areas, traffic information on the vicinity of the park and weather conditions on the city of the parking lot. This type of system aims to help users on a daily basis to find an available parking space, such as recommending the best parking lot taking into account some heuristics used by the decision algorithm, and creating a route to it, this way removing some anxiety felt by drivers looking for available spaces.

Keywords: Parking occupancy · Prediction · Mobile App

1 Introduction

Wanting to leave home and knowing that the parking lot will have an empty space for your car when you reach it, is an increasingly necessity in the lives of people. We all have been in the situation of trying to locate a free parking place to park the car, and after minutes and minutes of looking, we start to get frustrate and our stress levels increases, making us angrier and therefore increasing the probability of making an error, possibly causing an accident [6]. The strategy used from most of the drivers looking for a free parking space is called "Blind Search" [14] and is used by the drivers when there is no information given regarding the current status of the parking lot. This strategy is based on the driver going around the park looking for an empty parking space until they find a free parking space.

Every day, vehicles in search of free parking spaces negatively impact traffic conditions and the environment, making people lose a lot of time looking for a free parking space. This impact on traffic conditions goes up to 30% [1] and

A. L. Martins et al. (Eds.): INTSYS 2019, LNICST 310, pp. 172–191, 2020.
https://doi.org/10.1007/978-3-030-38822-5_12

pollution in cities for up to 40% [10], as drivers looking for a parking space often slow down or even double-park their cars, which blocks other cars, causing the traffic behind them to slow down too. Another problem lifted with the search for a free parking space, when there is no information, is that drivers often are distracted, putting cyclists and pedestrians in danger [6]. Another emerging problem in the transportation systems in cities is the management of the spatial resource since it is limited, as well as the parking cost being to expensive [14]. This limited resource contributes to cars spending to much time looking for parking places and consume to much gas/energy during the search for an available parking space.

Cars where initially invented to increase convenience and comfort in everyday life of people, however car congestion in a city causes unpleasant problems such as environment issues, energy consumption, parking space shortage, traffic jams, noise, air pollution, and even minor psychological damage to some people [14]. From all of those, we can check that the parking space shortage is regarded as one of the major issues in city transportation management since spatial resource of a city is limited and the construction of new parking spaces is expensive, and as a result, cars will need more time and have a larger energy consumption while looking for a parking space. A study on the parking situation in Schwabing (Germany) was done and it concluded that the annual total economy damage due to traffic caused by the search of an empty parking space had been estimated as much as 20 million euros [2].

If the city has means to inform the drivers in advance about the availability of parking spaces at and around their intended destination, the traffic congestion can be efficiently controlled [18]. On average it takes 12 min to a driver to find a free parking place [10] and a nation-wide survey done in Netherlands says that if employer-provided and residential parking are excluded, a total of 30% of car trips end with the search for a free parking space [1]. In the United States of America, a car looking for a free parking space in Los Angeles needs to go around a block at least two and half times to find a clear space to park, adding a total of around 1,500,000 excess kilometers traveled, resulting on almost a total of 178,000 L of gas wasted and a total of 730 tons of carbon dioxide produced in one year [7].

Is important to define parking availability to be the remaining parking spaces in a parking lot, and as of what was said earlier, parking availability is among the most important factors affecting car-based trip decisions and traffic conditions in urban areas. Drivers decisions are influenced by past experience, as well as real-time (on road) perceptions [16], meaning that parking is such a case where prior knowledge on possible prevailing conditions (e.g. difficulty in finding a parking space, parking costs, and so on) affects drivers parking decisions, just like the knowledge of current conditions (e.g. day of the week, if it is raining and how much, temperature, events around the parking spaces, and more) affects parking availability [13]. Predictive parking information reveals to be a very useful information for all drivers, as users will make informed choices, improving and optimizing parking searching in a way that people could start to plan their route depending on the availability of parking spaces at the destination.

Taking all this into consideration, in this paper we propose a system that offers the user the shortest path to the most optimal parking lot considering various conditions, namely the distance from the parking lot to the destination the user wants to get to, the duration of the trip, the occupancy of the parking lot at the time of arrival and the price per hour of parking the vehicle in the park. Information about the parking availability on the parking lot at a respective time must be predicted by taking into consideration historical data from the parking data occupancy, as well as other external factors, like weather, events and traffic and characteristics of the parking lot, like the price per hour and the total number of parking spaces.

This paper will be organized as follows. The following section will be about previous research works for parking lot availability prediction. In Sect. 3 the conceptual model of the proposed system is explained. For Sect. 4 the predictive model is developed and feature selection is made. Next, in Sect. 5 validation for the proposed system is made. Finally, we conclude our paper and suggest future work in Sect. 6.

2   Literature Review

In this section we will focus which features show to be more important and have a bigger impact on the prediction of the park availability, as well as the type of models created to deal with this type of problem.

2.1   Feature Selection for Parking Prediction

Systems based on historical available data are cost-effective and, if it has enough data, can cover cyclical variations over a year (e.g. seasons of the year, holidays period, and so on) which may prove to be important [15]. In [16] six months of historical data was used, and in [10] only two months, revealing to be a short time to cover all possible outcomes and not showing the full impact of cyclic features like seasons of the year.

Having access to historical data is really important when dealing with this type of problems, being easier to monitor and retrieve data from closed parking lots than on-street parking. Monitoring each single parking space could reveal expensive, so monitoring the flow of entering and leaving the parking lot [7] it is easier and this way the monitor park will always have the exact number of cars in the parking lot at a reasonable cost. However, this type of monitoring will not be able to give the exact position of a free parking space and can only be implemented on closed parking lots.

There are some factors that can influence the search for a free parking space. Weather information is one of the features that reveals to be important when evaluating the parking occupancy, like rain intensity, temperature and wind strength [8]. Bad weather conditions could lead to lower traffic flow than expected, but parking occupancy would just be affected in shopping malls, iconic locations, and other, not on parks close to apartments and offices [13]. The period of the day and time of year are also important [18], as holidays, week-days and hour of the day could have direct impact on park occupancy. Holiday features reveal to be really important, as parking availability is really different between a normal day and an holiday, showing bigger parking occupancy in park close to apartments and shopping malls, and quiet less in office parks [13]. The time of the day can generate more information like, the day, the month and the hours of the day, affecting, once again, the traffic and park occupancy [10]. The location of the parking lot is also an important factor [10], since if the parking lot is in the proximity of some type of shopping mall or close to an important public highway, or even if events happen regularly around the parking lot, like football games and concerts, those can cause a significant increase in the amount of traffic, consequently increasing the demand for free parking spaces [6]. In [13] each parking lot is categorize into seven categories of the parking lot, being those, apartment, office, mall, food, hospital, park and entertainment. If the parking lot is close to shopping centers or supper markets, it categorized as a mall parking lot, and so on. The idea is that shopping malls will have a different availability from 8 AM to 5 PM, than a park from an office building, and models created for a type of category can be replicated to other parking lots inside the same category.

As we can see throughout all features we can conclude that traffic information is one of the most important factors when predicting the availability of a parking space, as it directly influence the parking occupancy [16].

For [14] the parking cost and estimated queuing time outside the parking lot are important factors to be taken into consideration, which can be used to evaluate the effectiveness of parking guidance.

When predicting parking availability, factors like spatial and temporal have varying importance [13], so first there must be a evaluation on which features should really be used, since data like traffic and events are harder to get and the effort to integrate that information is increasingly higher [10].

2.2 Modelling for Parking Occupancy Prediction

In [16] data obtained wirelessly from a IoT sensor network available in the "smart" city of Santader, Spain, giving the current status of the parking space (free/occupied). The model was developed using a methodology of two modules, the first using Neural Network (NN) for the prediction of the time series of park-ing occupancy in different regions of an urban network, and the second module using some factors (e.g. weekday, weekend, time period, morning evening) with survival analysis for estimating the probability of finding a free parking space in the following time interval, resulting on visual representations, to help the user decide. A naïve prediction is used as baseline, proving that the model gen-erated as better accuracy values than the baseline when the predictive horizon gets larger, revealing a robustness of the NN model in dealing with problems of ranging levels of complexity up to half an hour prediction ahead.

For the development of the application Du-Parking, Recurring Neural Network (RNN) with the incorporation of Long Short-Term Memory (LSTM) were used [13]. RNN have been successfully applied to sequence learning tasks, and with help of LSTM, RNN will be able to continue to learn long-term temporal dependency. For performance analysis, the model built was compared with other two methods, namely Linear Interpolation being a distance-weighted interpolation algorithm with the idea that as the distance between parking lots, its parking availability is similar. The other method used was Gradient Boosting Decision Tree GBDT, and the reason to choose this algorithm goes from its effectiveness on training and on classification. The results of this experiment show that GBDT outperforms Linear Interpolation, and in the case of the Du-Parking model it gives a bigger improvement over the baseline algorithms implemented.

The idea behind [6] study is creating a demand profile, reflecting the parking occupancy in a determined time and area, with the idea to apply this profile to other areas with similar conditions. This solution reveals to be a good option to reduce the implementation costs of this type of model in other areas of the city, since the sensors installation and maintenance has a very high cost. A step to take into account when implementing a system like this in a new area, is that the data needs to be coherent with the new location. Aggregated features like date and time, traffic value, temperature, precipitation, payment type and payed amount, under a location unit id, are used to train the model and the target variable is the occupancy rate. With the use of similar functions like cosine similarity and earth mover's distance, the authors were able to compare different locations between booth projects, establishing which models best adapt to the areas of each other. Algorithms used on model training using SFpark data, applying algorithms like Decision Trees, Support Vector Machine (SVM), Multilayer Perceptrons and Gradient Boosted Trees. Extreme Gradient Boosting was had the best accuracy result of all of them.

For [18] the modelling of the occupancy rate is done after applying different features with the help of methods like Regression Trees, SVR and NN. Predictions are made for periods of 15 min ahead and all three algorithms were used, but for predictions higher than 15 min, SVR was not, due to the long computation time needed. The first feature set has the input of time and day of the week and the second feature set has the input previous observations of the occupancy rate on a certain time and the number of steps ahead to be predicted (each step represents 15 min). After applying all algorithms results show that Regression Trees, the least computationally intensive algorithm from all three, is better when comparing with the NN and SVR, for all feature sets. The feature set that reveals better results is the feature set that includes the history of the occupancy rates along the time of the day and the day of the week.

As a way to deal with the parking problem and to cope with the limitations from Parking Guidance and Information System, the study in [14] focus on creating a concept of smart parking guidance system, as well as a parking guidance algorithm to assign the driver to the most appropriate parking facility considering various factors, like parking cost, traffic congestion, distance to parking facility and walking distance to the destination. This system will monitor the parking lot status in real-time with the help of sensors. This information is then evaluated by the parking guidance algorithm in the central server, suggesting the most appropriate parking facility based on the current status of parking lots and the information inputted by the driver. The user then has the opportunity to reserve the specific parking lot until he/she arrives, and subsequently parking costs occurs from this point on, or just drives to the suggested option without a reservation.

3   Conceptual Model

In this section we show the conceptual model of the system being developed. As we can see in Fig. 1, the central part of this system is the android application where the user can interact with the system. This application integrates all services present in the study, having access to the predictive model being developed, which are exploited in Sect. 4, with the help of the complete dataset, that combines weather, traffic, events and parking occupancy data, being described in this section. Other services are necessary for the development and proper functioning of the application, namely some Google API Services, like Directions API, Maps API and Firebase. In the following sections we explain the components of the proposed solution being created.

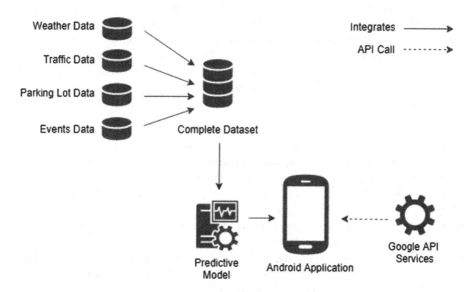

Fig. 1. Conceptual model diagram for the proposed system.

3.1 Android Application

The android application, as have been said, integrates all of the previous services taking into account the predictive model responsible to predict the available parking places in a respective parking lot. The main idea of the application is to contain information about various parking lots so that each one has associated a predictive model that provides the occupancy rate of the parking lot at a given time. By having several parking lots added, this allows a better management of the occupation of these parks, not allowing one park to have high occupancy and the others to be empty, but rather indicating better parking options to the user taking into account a decision algorithm that takes weight dimensions such as, distance from the parking lot to the final destination, duration of the trip to the park, the hourly price of the park, the distance the user is willingly to walk, and more importantly, the occupancy rate on arrival to the parking lot considering the current position of the user. With those heuristics in mind, the decision algorithm provides the most optimal parking lot for the driver. In this case, we focused on a single park, but the robustness of the model allows it to be implemented in more than one nearby parking lot.

The application firstly shows some options that the user needs to fill, namely the destination and how many meters it would like to walk from the parking lot to the final destination. With the all options filled up, the application creates the most optimal route between the start location and the closest parking lot to the end location, by running the decision algorithm, as well as taking into account the range off how many meters the user would like to walk from the parking lot. In [11], if no park is in the surroundings of the end location inside the range defined by the user, the system gives information to the user about which parking lot in the surroundings of the destination has the most probability of having a free parking space, as we have done, while also providing information about the distance from the final destination.

3.2 Complete Dataset

The complete dataset is used to create the predictive model. This dataset is composed by four datasets combined during the period from 1 of October of 2018 to 31 of January of 2019, making it a total 4 months of data. The data was gathered every hour making a total of 4 months of data, resulting on a 2952 row dataset. The first dataset being used is the parking occupancy data from a parking lot in Lisbon situated around the Marquês de Pombal area, plus weather data of Lisbon, events on the surroundings of the parking lot and the traffic data surrounding the parking lot. This data is then merged by the date and time each measurement was made for each dataset. In the following sections we explore each dataset and its composition.

3.3 Parking Lot Dataset

At first we have the parking lot dataset being used in this study, this parking lot has a total of 336 parking spaces and is open 24 h a day from Monday to Sunday.

Even though the dataset as not an extensive size to see the annual pattern of the parking lot, this intercepts a key moment for park affluence, namely during the Christmas period. This period allow us to analyze and perceive how the parking occupancy changes during festive periods, as holidays can have an huge impact on the parking lots [3]. Analysing this dataset we were able to conclude that the months of October, November and January show very similar patterns of occupancy over time, yet the month of December shows a very high variety, much because it is a festive month and because it contains several holidays. Another important factor is that this parking lot is located on a area which is surrounded by office buildings, so we categorize this parking lot as an office parking lot which may prove important in terms of their affluence and time periods [13]. A decisive characteristic for the parking lot occupancy is that it has an associated cost per hour [14] that will be further explain. The following information represents the composition of each row of the dataset:

- Hour - representing the time the measurement was made;
- Date - representing the date the measurement was made;
- Rotation - number of rotation cars inside the parking lot;
- Covenants - number of covenants cars inside the parking lot.

The measurements of Rotation and Covenants gives us the total of cars inside the parking lot from each type of client, and by adding the two we can have the complete parking occupancy in the parking lot for the determined date and hour.

The parking lot has two types of clients, the ones from rotation and from covenants. The rotation vehicles are the ones that enter and leave the parking lot without any kind of commitment, besides having to pay the ticket for the total number of hours spent in the car park. Users of type rotation need to pay a fee per hour, more specifically 2.15€. In the case of the covenants, where a use has unlimited entry and exit from the park during the time period in which he made the advance payment, the cost must be negotiated depending on external factors.

It is important to note that the parking lot to be studied is an underground park with a total of 336 parking spaces and is equipped with extra services like CCTV, so the security is higher, WC for the drivers and passengers, parking places for people with reduced mobility and car wash, and can therefore be differentiating factors at the time the users decide which parking lot they should park the car. The location of the parking lots also turns out to be quite important at the moment of decision by the users [4], since a good location can define the use of a park.

3.4   Weather Dataset

The weather dataset was obtained from the OpenWeatherMap using the API service History Bulk [9] from 1 of October of 2012 to 14 of March of 2019. This dataset comes with 50947 rows, representing a total of almost 6 and a half years of weather data from Lisbon, where each row of the dataset represents a measurement done for a respective date and time. The weather dataset was collected in intervals of 1 h, as the weather conditions typically do not change much during short time horizons [3]. From this dataset we used the following columns:

- dt_iso - date and time in UTC format;
- temp - current temperature in Kelvin;
- temp_min - minimum temperature at the moment in kelvin;
- temp_max - maximum temperature at the moment in kelvin;
- pressure - atmospheric pressure (on the sea level) in hPa;
- humidity - humidity in %;
- wind_speed - wind speed measured in meter per second;
- clouds_all - cloudiness in %;
- weather_main - group of weather parameters (Rain, Snow, Extreme etc.);
- weather_description - weather condition within the group.

Weather_main represent the weather condition within the following categorizations: clear, clouds, drizzle, fog, haze, mist, rain, smoke, snow and thunderstorm. The weather_description gives some more information within the weather_main condition, like if it raining heavily.

It is important to know that temp_min and temp_max are deviations from the current temperature that is possible to happen in large cities and megalopolises geographically expanded.

We transformed some columns to a unit that is clearer and simpler to analyze, such as passing the columns temp, temp_max and temp_min from the Kelvin unit to Celsius. In the case of wind_speed, we decided to convert it from meters per second to kilometers per hour.

3.5 Traffic Dataset

Other type of data used for enrichment of the analysis were the traffic data. As it has been concluded in the literature review, traffic information is one of the most important factors when predicting the availability of a parking space, as it directly influence the parking occupancy [16]. This data gives us information about the traffic state on certain roads and it was obtained the same period as the parking lot data. The data was gathered for the surroundings of the parking lot since those areas in Lisbon are heavily influenced by traffic, and came in the format of a JavaScript Object Notation (JSON), with various interesting components like the average speed, average travel time and speed limit on certain roads, but in our case we opted to use the sample size values that gives us the total number of vehicles that passed through the segment of the road in the respective date and time.

3.6 Events Dataset

One important factor that may over-saturate the parking lot are the events on the surroundings of the location of the park [17]. If rich historical can be implemented and information regarding the events is known in advance, the prediction can better adjust itself to take into account those special occasions. For the events dataset case, we collect all major events that occur within the surroundings of the parking lots for the same data period. Having said that, 13 events were referenced due to their large size and proximity to the parking lot under study, namely the following ones: SIL - Salão Imobiliário de Portugal (03/10/2018–07/10/2018), Web Summit (05/10/2018–08/10/2018), Lisbon Fashion Week (11/10/2018–14/10/2018), Greenfest (11/10/2018–14/10/2018), Lisbon Marathon'18 (14/10/2018), Lisboa Games Week (15/10/2018–18/10/2018), Doclisboa (18/10/2018–28/10/2018), Concert: Kodaline (24/10/2018), Super Bock em Stock Festival'18 (23/11/2018–24/11/2018), Feira Outlet (07/12/2018–09/12/2018), São Silvestre de Lisboa Race'18 (29/12/2018), Wonderland Lisboa (01/12/2018–01/01/2019) and Beethoven's Violin Concert (18/01/2019–19/01/2019).

We did the same to define the holidays, resulting on total of 10 holidays with different importance, meaning that for the same time span of the parking lot data not all of the holidays have the same importance. We decided to give the holidays an importance between the range 0 to 2, where 0 is a normal day, as those do not represent any type of public holiday, value 1 represents a festive day, but it's not officially a holiday, and 2 a very important one. For example, Christmas Day has a bigger impact then the Kings' Day, as we can see in Table 1.

Table 1. Public holidays importance inside the period being analyzed.

Date	Public holiday	Importance
05/10/2018	Implementation of the Republic	2
01/11/2018	All Saints Day/Bread Day by God	2
01/12/2018	Restoration of Independence	2
08/12/2018	Immaculate Conception Day	2
25/12/2018	Christmas Day	2
26/12/2018	Boxing Day	1
31/12/2018	Réveillon	1
01/01/2019	New Year's Day	2
06/01/2019	Kings Day	1

We also defined a school vacation period between 14 December 2018 to 31 January 2019 and a work vacation period between 22 December 2018 to 1 January 2019.

3.7 Google Services

The Google API services are of great importance in this application, as the entire application works around the maps service provided by Google. The Maps API allows the presence of a map based on Google Maps data, that the user can explore by the route to the parking lot. Another service used in the application is the Directions API, that allows the application to obtain direction information and draw a route between two points, taking into consideration traffic stats. This service provides us with information for different transport modes, waypoints and travel times, as well as one or more travelling routes to the destination while checking the distance and time it takes from one point to another. In this application, the only considered transport mode is a car, since all of the studies focus on the parking lot state. Other Google service used is Firebase that supplies the means to build an authentication system for the login and register option, as well as the database to keep information about the users and the parking lots.

4   Development of the Predictive Model

In this section we be developed the predictive model while taking into consideration the different features previously referenced, as a way to understand which features best help the prediction problem reach better accuracy values.

4.1   Data Analysis and Processing

In this step we initially started by combining all the previously referenced datasets by the *datetime* column all of them have and processing and combining some data so it would be easier to analyze it and help take conclusions.

We then did a quick analysis of the data and we came across two incorrect parking occupation measurement, where the total number of cars was greater than the maximum capacity of the car park, which is 336. Having said that, we removed the measurement with values greater than this capacity.

With the help of the *datetime* column, 4 new columns were created, namely year, month, day and hour, representing the hour and the measurement was made, respectively, and after that we dropped the *datetime* column.

To verify which features suits best to predict the total occupation in the parking lot, we firstly created the column *total* that is calculated by joining the rotation values with the covenants values to gives us the total number of vehicles in the car park. We then used the Pearson's Correlation Coefficients, as this method give us a way to establish the relationship between two values, by indicating that if one variable changes in value the other variable tends to change its value too, in a specific direction. The Pearson's Correlation uses two metrics to evaluate the relationship between two variables, namely the strength and the direction. The strength metric makes it possible to understand the absolute correlation between two variables, so the stronger is the relationship, the higher is the number in absolutely from a range between -1 and 1. A relationship of 0 means that there is no type of relationship between two variables is meaningful, and in contrast, if the coefficient is 1 that reveals a really big correlation. The other metric used is the direction of the correlation, namely the sign of the value, where negative values means that, when one variable increases the other

Table 2. Correlation of weather features with the target total.

Feature	Correlation coefficient
road_tunel_marques	0.57
road_mouzinho	0.74
road_duque	0.39
road_castilho	0.63
road_braamcamp	0.55
road_herculano	0.54
road_praca_marques	0.63
hour	0.28
day	0.01
month	0.004
year	0.0075
humidity	−0.24
wind_speed	−0.17
clouds_all	0.11
pressure	0.04
temp_max	0.36
temp_min	0.29
temp	0.32

decreases, and when the value is positive, as one variable increases the other increases as well.

We then applied the Pearson's Correlation to the continuous variables, as this method evaluates the linear relationship between two continuous variables, obtaining the results shown in Table 2.

As we can see from the results shown in the Table 2, the most meaningful features are the traffic data, reaching values of 0.74 and not lower than 0.39. In terms of weather data, we can conclude that only the temperature features show a high correlation values which may be due to the fact that the car park is categorize as an office park [13]. The resulting column features resulting from the *datetime* feature, namely the year, month, day and hour, only the hour feature revealed a bigger correlation value with a total of 0.28, the other features reveal real poor correlation values, no greater than 0.004 in the case of month feature.

Having said, from the features evaluated by the Pearson's Correlation we selected the following columns for the rest of the work: *road_tunel_marques, road_mouzinho, road_duque, road_castilho, road_braamcamp, road_herculano, road_praca_marques, year, month, day, hour, temp_max, temp_min* and *temp_min*. Even though the *year, month* and *day* features had low values of correlation, this values may be needed to retrain the model with data from other months and years, just like in [10].

Next, as a way to have better predictive results we created a column named *occupation_tax* that divides the total column by the total park capacity. This method results in better predictions and a more intuitive result to show to the user, meaning that for the case of a total of 280 cars in the parking lot, it represents a 83% occupation that we always round up to multiples of 10, resulting on a total of occupation of 90%, as the system to be developed needs to generate precise parking availability values, because if the system returns more free parking spaces than there really are, it would forward a user to a parking lot with no free parking spaces, revealing a problem for the user and smear the confidence on the system [12] so we always round up to prevent those types of problems. We then removed the covenants, rotation and total columns, as those columns are highly dependent and highly correlated with the *occupation_tax* target.

Various flag columns were added, the first one was *flag_weekend* that identifies if the current day of the measurement is on a weekend, having value true if so, and false if it is a workday. The *flag_holiday* has also been added, providing information on whether the current date represents a holiday or not. The value of the *flag_holiday* feature, for a respective measurement, is given depending on the importance of the holiday, as we can see previously presented in Table 1. Also, a *flag_event* was included, having value 1 when the day of the measurement corresponds to one of the date intervals previously mentioned in Sect. 3.5.

Two columns identifying vacation periods were also added, the first being *flag_vacationperiod* representing the festive period when several people take their holidays. This flag as value 1 for every measurement made between 22 December 2018 to 1 January 2019 and 0 for every other case. The second *flag_vacationschool* represents the vacation period from school, that lasts approximately between 14 December 2018 to 31 January 2019, where once again, all measurements made inside this time period have value 1, and the rest has a value of 0.

The latest flags added represented the current weather condition based in the *weather_main* column. The first one was the *flag_fog*, identifying measurements where the atmosphere had any type of fog, this column would have value 1 if the *weather_main* column had one of the following results: fog, mist, haze or smoke. The *flag_rain* was also added giving information if during the measurement it was raining having value 1, and 0 if not. The same happens with the *flag_storm* representing whether a thunderstorm was occurring during the measurement.

To conclude, we have total of 2950 rows for the complete dataset, composed by 23 columns, more specifically the following ones: *temp, temp_min. temp_max, flag_rain, flag_fog, flag_storm, year, month, day, hour, flag_weekend, flag_event, flag_holiday, flag_vacationperiod, flag_vacationschool, road_tunel_marques, road_mouzinho, road_duque, road_castilho, road_braamcamp, road_herculano, road_praca_marques, tax_occupation.*

4.2   Algorithm Testing

In this section we started to perform algorithms tests to predict the total occupation of the parking lot. The algorithms chosen to test this were Neural Networks

(NN) like in [16], has it is a good solution for a time series prediction like our problem of parking occupancy. Distributed Random Forest (DRF) were also used, as those are a forest of classification or regression trees, rather than a single classification or regression tree, as in [18], where Regression Trees had better results and less computationally needs comparing to SVR and NN. At last, Gradient Boosting Machine (GBM), that corresponds to a sequentially regression trees on all the features of the dataset in a fully distributed way, being a good option as those gave the best results in [6]. Those algorithms were applied to the complete dataset, where the datasets where divided in 70% to train and 30% to test and to validate the results obtained we used a 5-fold cross validation, has it helps to prevent the over-fitting [18]. To test the impact of each feature type, we decided to test each of these feature in the complete dataset (Events, Traffic and Weather) with the park occupancy data, as well as the park occupancy data alone. All these algorithms were implemented with the help of the python library H2O [5]. We then tested the algorithms with the complete dataset, resulting in the accuracy metric and the execution time metric values shown in Table 3.

Table 3. Accuracy and mean execution time results.

Dataset	GBM	Execution time	DRF	Execution time	NN	Execution time
Completed Dataset	72%	10 s	71%	13 s	67%	25 s
Park + Events Dataset	76%	5 s	76%	9 s	60%	23 s
Park + Weather Dataset	74%	5 s	73%	10 s	61%	21 s
Park + Traffic Dataset	73%	6 s	70%	9 s	65%	24 s
Park Dataset	69%	3 s	71%	8 s	53%	24 s

The results obtained in Table 3, show that overall the GBM model had the best results in terms of accuracy, with a maximum 76% accuracy result with the park plus events dataset, where the RDF model showed an equal value of 76% and the NN model 60%, respectively. We were also able to verify that for all the other datasets, we obtained very uniform results, where GBM reached values no lower than 69% and with a maximum of 76%. For the DRF model we obtained values as low as 70% when using the park plus weather dataset and as high as 76% using the park plus the events dataset. In the case of the NN model the complete dataset have shown the best result with a total of 67% accuracy and, for the case of the lowest accuracy, the park dataset showed again the worst accuracy results, with only 53%. One of the possible reasons for the accuracy values of the NN being so low when comparing to the rest of the methods used, may be because of the small size of the dataset to be used, with only 2950 rows.

Some reasons for the results obtained and the features not giving much more information in terms of predicting the park occupancy, could be due to three reasons. The first being the parking lot categorised as an office category park, where people will have to move to their work and park the vehicle there often regardless of the weather, traffic and events. The second reason may be because the park is underground, which can cause the weather condition not to be so critical to the affluence of the park. In contrast, data from events in the vicinity of the park show to be quite useful when forecasting the occupation of the park, this is due to the fact that the occupation, mainly of the total number of rotation vehicles, changes considerably at the times when an event occurs in the vicinity. And the last is that the user with a covenants will park there regardless of the weather, traffic and events on the surroundings, since they have already paid a sum to secure a place in that park.

Being this a solution to be implemented in the application the execution time is important for the application efficiency and speed. When analyzing this metric, we see that GBM overall reveals the lowest executions times with a maximum of 10 s to run while using the complete dataset, being this the largest dataset. In comparison, with the complete dataset the RDF needs 13 s and the NN needs 25 s. The GBM model also had the lowest execution time with only 3 s needed and an average of 6 s for all of the cases. Like the GBM model, the DRF model also show low mean execution times with an average of 10 s and for the case of the NN model we see the biggest execution times with an average execution time for all datasets of 22 s.

Taking those conclusions into consideration, we choose the GBM model with the complete dataset as the model to be exported and used in the android application to provide the parking occupancy levels for a certain time interval. Although this is not the model with the best values of accuracy and execution time, it does not depend on one type of data, meaning that if a problem occurs with one of the sources of data the efficiency of the model is not fully

Table 4. Confusion matrix for the GBM model built with the complete dataset.

0	10	20	30	40	50	60	70	80	90	100	Error	Rate
85	51	0	1	0	0	0	0	0	0	0	0.3795	52/137
9	1497	13	1	0	0	1	0	0	0	0	0.0158	24/1521
0	55	200	6	2	2	1	0	0	0	0	0.2481	66/266
0	15	12	111	10	2	0	0	0	0	0	0.2600	39/150
0	5	6	13	77	3	2	1	0	0	0	0.2804	30/107
0	2	2	0	3	45	1	1	2	2	0	0.2241	13/58
0	5	3	0	0	4	118	1	2	2	0	0.1259	17/135
0	2	0	0	0	1	6	55	8	3	1	0.2763	21/76
0	0	0	0	0	0	4	3	132	18	1	0.1646	26/158
0	0	0	0	0	0	1	2	18	263	3	0.0836	24/287
0	0	0	0	0	0	0	0	1	16	38	0.3091	17/55
94	1632	236	132	92	57	134	63	163	304	43	0.1115	329/2950

compromised and the difference between the best accuracy and the accuracy of the complete dataset is only 4%.

After that we decided to analyze the confusion matrix of the GBM Model built with the complete dataset, as the results can be see in Table 4.

By analyzing Table 4, we can see that the dataset is unbalanced because it has almost half of the records at the expected value of 10%. To try and avoid this problem of unbalanced, we aggregated certain values with fewer counted records to try to balance the categories with more data. In this case, we then divided the occupation of the park into categories of 0–10%, 20–30%, 40%–50%, 60%–70% and 80%–90% and 100%, thus balancing the number of each category and, in turn, making it easier to predict new values within those categories. w in our case we implemented the above categories. After this treatment, we obtained an increase on accuracy levels to a total of 79%, an increase of 7%, and an execution time of 6 s, having an increase in performance of 4 s. The new results for the confusion matrix can be seen in Table 5.

Table 5. Confusion matrix for the GBM model built with occupancy categorization.

0%–10%	20%–30%	40%–50%	60%–70%	80%–90%	100%	Error	Rate
1212	51	1	1	0	0	0.0419	53/1265
84	615	15	1	0	0	0.1400	100/715
1	32	187	6	1	0	0.1762	40/227
3	12	5	169	12	5	0.1996	37/206
0	1	0	8	299	29	0.1101	37/336
0	0	0	0	28	173	0.1393	28/201
1300	711	208	184	340	207	0,1	295/2950

As we can see by evaluating the results in Table 5, we have a better distribution of the results than in Table 4, so thus increasing the rate of correct forecasts. To conclude the model being used in the rest of study it is built using the GBM model with the help of the complete dataset, to predict one of previously presented six categories. These models are built using historical information with an interval of one hour from the parking lot occupancy, weather data, traffic data and events data.

5   Results Evaluation

In this section we focused on the consolidation of the proposed system and test its efficiency and functionality. For this assessment we considered the example where a user is trying to find an available place at a peak hour in Lisbon.

For this example, the user started at ISCTE (Instituto Superior de Ciências do Trabalho e da Empresa) in Lisbon, looking for a place to leave the car in the area of Marquês de Pombal with a radius of 500 m of search between the destination and a parking lot, where all the parks outside of this range will be discarded. If there is not a single option inside the range defined by the user, the application will suggest the closest parking lot and a pop up will appear asking the user if the application should show the route to that park. This search will be performed at the 9:00 am to simulate the peak hour on the area of Marquês de Pombal.

Fig. 2. Navigate option with Marquês de Pombal as the destination.

As we can see in the Fig. 2, the user inserted Marquês de Pombal on the first input box and 500 m on the second input box. After this, the user clicked on navigate and the decision algorithm would run to calculate the weight of each option. This algorithm takes into consideration four heuristics to find the best suitable parking lot. First it takes into account the occupancy of the parking lot at the time of arrival, secondly the duration it takes from the current location of the user to the park, next the distance from the parking lot to the destination provided by the user, in this case Marquês de Pombal and lastly, the price per hour for having the vehicle parked in the parking lot. By taking this information the algorithm was executed and provided the result of each option, while also giving the value for the weight feature. The option with the biggest value on the weight feature will be chosen and the route to that parking lot will be created.

After executing the navigate option, the decision algorithm will run and decide which of the parking lots is the best option, in this case we only have

Table 6. Decision algorithm heuristics and weight outcome.

Parking lot	Route duration (s)	Distance to the parking lot (m)	Distance from Destination to parking lot (m)	Parking lot occupancy (Percentage)	Price per hour (€)	Weight
Park 1	939	3029	348	40%–50%	2.15	184.85

one parking lot added, so the output of the decision algorithm can be seen in Table 6.

By analyzing Table 4, we can see that the occupancy at the time of arrival is between 40%–50%, being this the most important heuristic to take into consideration by the decision algorithm. The duration from the current location to the destination is also an important heuristic to take into consideration and in this case the user was at 939 s away (15 min and 39 s). For the third heuristic to take into consideration we have the distance from the destination and the parking lot chosen, in this case the parking lot is at 348 m away from the destination provided by the user. At last, the algorithm takes into consideration the price per hour it costs the user to have their vehicle in the parking lot and for the parking lot in consideration it is 2.15€. By providing all these features to the decision algorithm it will produce an output (weight), which will be used for the decision of the best parking lot, as the best option will have the highest weight value, and the route to that vehicle park will be created, as we can see in Fig. 3.

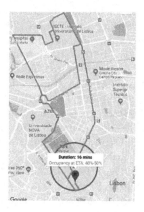

Fig. 3. The route to the Park 1 chosen from the decision algorithm.

6   Conclusions

This work provides a solution to real-time guidance to parking places in a general solution to the problem that is increasingly real in large cities which is to find a free place to park the vehicle. A solution like the one shown has the potential to reduce traffic within cities and in turn allow users to better manage their time and route. In this study we consider three types of data to help predict the occupation of a park categorized as an office park, namely events, traffic and weather in the vicinity of the park, concluding that the data types with the greatest impact are the events, mainly in the rotation type users. We were also able to conclude that the traffic data show a high correlation with the occupation situation of the park. This park contains the option of covenants, which does not suffer much disturbance, since the user has already paid a fee to be able to guarantee the car inside the park over a given period, forcing the user in a certain way to leave the car in the same parking lot. Good accuracy values were obtained, however, the fact that the data are short and that the month of December has patterns of parking not very common, due to the fact that it is a festive month and with many holidays, can condition the forecast values. As a future work it would be interesting to add more car parks to understand how the decision algorithm behaves in several cases and to understand the impact of the same types of data on those same car parks.

References

1. Bock, F., Sester, M.: Improving parking availability maps using information from nearby roads. Transp. Res. Procedia **19**(June), 207–214 (2016). https://doi.org/10.1016/j.trpro.2016.12.081
2. Caliskan, M., Barthels, A., Scheuermann, B., Mauve, M.: Predicting parking lot occupancy in vehicular ad hoc networks. In: 2007 IEEE 65th Vehicular Technology Conference - VTC 2007-Spring, pp. 277–281 (2007). https://doi.org/10.1109/VETECS.2007.69. http://ieeexplore.ieee.org/document/4212497/
3. Chen, B., Pinelli, F., Sinn, M., Botea, A., Calabrese, F.: Uncertainty in urban mobility: predicting waiting times for shared bicycles and parking lots. In: IEEE Conference on Intelligent Transportation Systems, Proceedings, ITSC (ITSC), pp. 53–58 (2013). https://doi.org/10.1109/ITSC.2013.6728210
4. Giuffrè, T., Siniscalchi, S.M., Tesoriere, G.: A novel architecture of parking management for smart cities. Procedia - Soc. Behav. Sci. **53**, 16–28 (2012). https://doi.org/10.1016/j.sbspro.2012.09.856. https://linkinghub.elsevier.com/retrieve/pii/S187704 2812043182
5. H2O: H2o documentation (2019). http://docs.h2o.ai/h2o/latest-stable/h2o-docs/index.html. Accessed 8 Apr 2019
6. Ionita, A., Pomp, A., Cochez, M., Meisen, T., Decker, S.: Where to park?: predicting free parking spots in unmonitored city areas. In: Proceedings of the 8th International Conference on Web Intelligence, Mining and Semantics, pp. 22:1–22:12 (2018). https://doi.org/10.1145/3227609.3227648
7. Klappenecker, A., Lee, H., Welch, J.L.: Finding available parking spaces made easy. Ad Hoc Netw. **12**(1), 243–249 (2014). https://doi.org/10.1016/j.adhoc.2012.03.002
8. Lijbers, J.: Predicting parking lot occupancy using prediction instrument development for complex domains (2016)
9. OpenWeatherData: Openweatherdata history bulk (2019). https://openweathermap.org/history-bulk. Accessed 23 Apr 2019
10. Pflügler, C., Köhn, T., Schreieck, M., Wiesche, M., Krcmar, H.: Predicting the availability of parking spaces with publicly available data. Lecture Notes in Informatics (LNI), Gesellschaft für Informatik, Bonn, pp. 361–374 (2016). http://cs.emis.de/LNI/Proceedings/Proceedings259/361.pdf
11. Pullola, S., Atrey, P.K., Saddik, A.E.: Towards an intelligent GPS-based vehicle navigation system for finding street parking lots. In: ICSPC 2007 Proceedings - 2007 IEEE International Conference on Signal Processing and Communications (November), pp. 1251–1254 (2007). https://doi.org/10.1109/ICSPC.2007.4728553

12. Richter, F., Martino, S.D., Mattfeld, D.C.: Temporal and spatial clustering for a parking prediction service. In: Proceedings - International Conference on Tools with Artificial Intelligence, ICTAI 2014-December, pp. 278–282 (2014). https://doi.org/10.1109/ICTAI.2014.49

13. Rong, Y., Xu, Z., Yan, R., Ma, X.: Du-parking: spatio-temporal big data tells you realtime parking availability. In: Proceedings of the ACM SIGKDD International Conference on Knowledge Discovery and Data Mining, pp. 646–654 (2018). https://doi.org/10.1145/3219819.3219876

14. Shin, J.H., Jun, H.B.: A study on smart parking guidance algorithm. Transp. Res. Part C: Emerg. Technol. **44**, 299–317 (2014). https://doi.org/10.1016/j.trc.2014.04.010

15. Tilahun, S.L., Di Marzo Serugendo, G.: Cooperative multiagent system for parking availability prediction based on time varying dynamic Markov chains. J. Adv. Transp. **2017** (2017). https://doi.org/10.1155/2017/1760842

16. Vlahogianni, E.I., Kepaptsoglou, K., Tsetsos, V., Karlaftis, M.G.: A real-time parking prediction system for smart cities. J. Intell. Transp. Syst.: Technol. Plan. Oper. **20**(2), 192–204 (2016). https://doi.org/10.1080/15472450.2015.1037955

17. Xiao, J., Lou, Y., Frisby, J.: How likely am I to find parking? - a practical model-based framework for predicting parking availability. Transp. Res. Part B: Methodol. **112**, 19–39 (2018). https://doi.org/10.1016/j.trb.2018.04.001

18. Zheng, Y., Rajasegarar, S., Leckie, C.: Parking availability prediction for sensor-enabled car parks in smart cities. In: 2015 IEEE Tenth International Conference on Intelligent Sensors, Sensor Networks and Information Processing (ISSNIP), 7–9 April (2015)

Visualization

Evaluation of SIMMARC: An Audiovisual System for the Detection of Near-Miss Accidents

Florian Krebs[1(✉)], Georg Thallinger[1], Helmut Neuschmied[1],
Franz Graf[1], Georg Huber[2], Kurt Fallast[2], Peter Vertal[3],
and Eduard Kolla[3]

[1] Joanneum Research, Graz, Austria
`florian.krebs@joanneum.at`
[2] Planum, Graz, Austria
[3] University of Žilina, Žilina, Slovakia

Abstract. In this paper, we present and evaluate a system that automatically identifies hazardous traffic situations using visual and acoustic sensors. The system has been installed at three locations in Austria and several months of audio and video data have been analyzed. We evaluate the accuracy of the employed data analysis algorithms as well as the usefulness of the detected events for the overall task of assessing the risk potential of a road intersection. Our results show that the long-term analysis made possible by the proposed system leads to a better understanding of the risk potential of traffic areas, and can finally serve as a basis for defining and prioritizing improvements.

Keywords: Near-miss accidents · Accident detection · Automatic event detection

1 Introduction

Nearly 1.35 million people die in road accidents each year, according to the annual report of the World Health Organization [1]. The reduction of fatalities is therefore one of the most important aims of humanity which drives the development of safer vehicles and road infrastructure.

Authorities in many countries have a predefined procedure for assessing and optimizing the safety of their road infrastructure. For example, the Austrian research association for roads, railways and transport (FSV[1]), defines a crossing or street section as *accident black spot*, if either at least three similar accidents with bodily injury have occurred within three years, or at least five accidents with bodily or material damage have occurred within one year[2]. Once such an accident black spot is identified, the FSV suggests carrying out a safety inspection of the involved road section to investigate the underlying causes of the accidents.

---

[1] http://www.fsv.at/.

[2] RVS 02.02.21.

© ICST Institute for Computer Sciences, Social Informatics and Telecommunications Engineering 2020
Published by Springer Nature Switzerland AG 2020. All Rights Reserved
A. L. Martins et al. (Eds.): INTSYS 2019, LNICST 310, pp. 195–202, 2020.
https://doi.org/10.1007/978-3-030-38822-5_13

As this is a purely reactive approach, where accidents must occur before a black spot is identified, methods were proposed to identify dangerous traffic spots based on near-miss scenarios [2, 3, 8]. These systems are able to detect near-miss scenarios semi-automatically by analyzing data gathered at a traffic area. Suspicious events are identified automatically and then presented to a human expert to decide whether the detected events are relevant and which actions to take.

In this paper, we present an evaluation of the audiovisual analysis system proposed in [2], after analyzing three traffic spots in Austria over a period of several months. Once the methodology has been reviewed, we outline the strengths and limitations of the system and present ideas for future improvements.

2   System Overview

In this section, we shortly describe SIMMARC [2], a system for the audiovisual detection of dangerous scenes. The system gathers audio and video traffic data from sensors that are installed on poles at the traffic area (see Fig. 1).

Fig. 1. Camera and microphone installation at Wickenburggasse (left) and Dietrichsteinplatz (right) in Graz, Austria.

The sensor data is then used to detect the following events in real-time:

- Emergency braking actions (video)
- Car horns (audio)
- Tire squealing (audio)
- Tram bells (audio)

Once an event is detected, the corresponding audiovisual footage (including 30 s before and after the event) is captured to an incident store. This incident store is periodically analyzed by a traffic expert.

In the following, we describe the methodology to extract the events mentioned above.

2.1   Detection of Audio Events

For the detection of acoustic events we have selected a recurrent neural network due to its computational efficiency. To extract the three acoustic events (car horn, tire squealing, tram bell) from the raw audio signal, the signal is segmented into overlapping time frames (length 46 ms) to obtain a frame rate of 50 fps. From each time frame, we compute the logarithm of the mel-filtered magnitude spectrogram. We chose a filter bank with 120 mel frequency bands between 200 and 16000 Hz, in order to capture all important harmonics of the target sounds. These features are fed into a recurrent neural network, which consists of two Gated Recurrent Unit [9] layers with 30 hidden units each and a final classification layer which outputs a scalar that indicates the presence of the corresponding audio event. We apply exponential smoothing to the activation function with a time constant of 0.24 s. Once the smoothed activation function exceeds a certain threshold, an event is considered to be present.

2.2   Detection of Video Events

The aim of the visual analysis is to detect the position, type (car, bus, pedestrian, etc.), speed and acceleration resp. deceleration of various road users. We divide this task into two steps: First, we recognize the rough vehicle position (bounding box) and the type of road user with the Yolo v3 neural network [7]. Then, we determine speed, acceleration and a refined position (the used traffic area) with the feature-based point tracking method proposed in [5]. Distinguishable points in the image are tracked and an algorithm similar to [6] is used to cluster the resulting trajectories and assign them to individual objects. The outcome of the whole process is illustrated in Fig. 2 and the process is described in the following.

To determine the object velocity, the first step is to calculate the velocity of the object points with the assumption that they are all at ground level. In reality, however, points have different heights which yields different velocities for the same object. These speed differences are used to calculate the actual height of the points and thus correct their velocities. With plausibility checks (e.g. the height of the object must be above the road level) and by rejecting outlier points, the point velocities are refined and merged into an object velocity. As an additional result we get a 3D point cloud of each object, from which the used traffic area (the projection of the vehicle onto the ground plane) can be calculated. In order to ignore shadows, points near the ground plane are discarded (see Fig. 2).

The speed of an object is then used to calculate the acceleration of a traffic user. If the braking acceleration falls below -4 m/s^2, the corresponding time is reported as emergency braking.

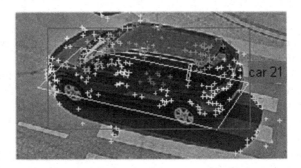

Fig. 2. In video images, objects are detected by the Yolo v3 detector (red rectangle with the object label). From the tracked feature points the speed, acceleration, and the used traffic area (green rectangle) are calculated. (Color figure online)

3 Evaluation

3.1 Data

In order to evaluate the system, data was recorded at three locations in Austria (see Fig. 3):

Graz, Dietrichsteinplatz. The Dietrichsteinplatz node (Fig. 3 left) is a heavily frequented, unregulated intersection, with peak loads of 1,000 vehicles/h at the evening on working days. The diversity of traffic participants (tram, regional bus, taxi, car, truck, bicycle, foot), the cramped space conditions and the short distance to a neighboring light signal-controlled intersection have repeatedly led to structural and traffic-related adaptations in recent decades. In total, we recorded 5 days in June 2017.

Graz, Wickenburggasse/Körösistraße. The highly frequented, signal controlled junction (Fig. 3 center) features an intersection of two main cycle routes. The sum of the access loads in the morning peak on working days is around 1,800 vehicles/h and around 900 cyclists/h. In total we recorded 52 days between April and July 2018.

Velden, Kärntner Straße. This location (Fig. 3 right) is a shared space. A large number of pedestrians use this area, especially during the summer months. We recorded 15 days in August 2018.

Fig. 3. Camera view of the recording locations (from left to right: Dietrichsteinplatz, Wickenburggasse, Kärntner Straße).

At each location, one microphone and one camera were installed on a pole at approximately 6 m and 10 m height respectively. In total, we recorded 72 days of video and audio footage.

3.2   Detection of Audio Events

In the following the audio detection algorithms are evaluated.

Datasets. We randomly sampled 32 h of the recorded data for training, 8 h for validating, and 34 h for testing the algorithms and annotated the occurrence of the three target audio events (horn, tire squealing, and tram bell). We made sure that there is no overlap between the three sets.

Evaluation Metrics. In contrast to other sound event detection evaluations we are not interested in the exact start and stop time of an event. For our application it suffices to know whether an event has occurred within a certain temporal window. Therefore, we use the following approach: An event is counted as true positive if there is at least one frame overlap between a detected and an annotated event. If a detection occurs outside of an annotated event, it is counted as false positive. An event is counted as false negative, if all detections of the corresponding event are below the threshold. Then, we compute three metrics: F-measure, Precision, and Recall [10]. The threshold was determined by maximizing the F-measure on the validation set.

Table 1. Audio event classification results on the 34 h test set.

Event	F-measure	Precision	Recall
Horn	0.76	0.89	0.66
Tire squealing	0.51	0.47	0.56
Tram bell	0.81	0.85	0.83

Results. The results on the test set are shown in Table 1. In total, there were 61 horn events, 21 tire squealing events, and 17 tram bell events in the 34 h test set. As can be seen, the tram bell detector was found to perform best, probably because the tram bell sound does not vary much and the sound stands out from the remaining sounds. The most common (false positive) errors of the detectors are:

Horn detector: Ambulance siren, shouting children, brake squealing, tram bell
Tire squealing: Car brake squealing, children squealing
Tram bell: Children squealing

3.3   Detection of Braking Actions

Groundtruth. In order to assess the accuracy of the visual speed and acceleration measurements, we selected 11 scenes which cover a variety of dangerous situations. A 3D model of the scenes including the vehicles was constructed by mapping simulated vehicles onto the video recordings using the software PC-Crash[3]. Once a 3D model of a scene was constructed, the speed and acceleration trajectories of all traffic participants was obtained and compared to the output of the video analysis system. Measuring location and speed trajectories by 3D reconstruction is commonly used for accident reconstruction [4].

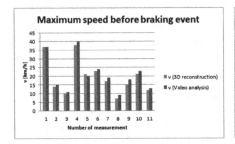 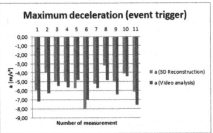

Fig. 4. Comparison of speed and deceleration values from the video analysis system and the 3D model reconstruction.

Results. Figure 4 shows the maximum speed and deceleration values before a braking event of the video analysis system and the 3D reconstructions. As can be seen, the speed measurements closely match the 3D reconstructions (mean error 1.45 km/h). However, the measurement of the deceleration is less precise (mean error 1.07 m/s^2). Since the deceleration is calculated from successive velocity values, changes in velocity measurement errors have a large influence on the error of the deceleration values. Results could probably be improved by averaging the deceleration over a longer period of time, with the disadvantage that shorter braking maneuvers would not be recognized.

3.4   Detection of Relevant Situations

In this section we evaluate the relevance of the detected scenes for improving the safety of a road section. To that means, we performed two experiments:

Experiment 1. In the first experiment, we addressed the question *"What percentage of the detected scenes is actually relevant for traffic experts?"*. In this regard, the scenes detected at Dietrichsteinplatz were presented to a traffic expert, who classified them as relevant or not.

Results. In the 78 h of recording at Graz, Dietrichsteinplatz, the system detected 505 events. Of these 505 events, 430 events were detected correctly, and 39 events were identified as relevant by the traffic expert. The relevant scenes contained various disregards of traffic regulations (from drivers, pedestrians, cyclists and motorists) like ignoring the right of way or road markings, and frequent strong decelerations at parts of

---

[3] http://www.dsd.at.

the junction. The traffic experts concluded that the traffic participants often are not aware of the priority situation at the crossing, which could be improved by further road markings or traffic signs.

If the manual inspection of one recorded scene is assumed to take 10 s, it takes roughly 1.4 h to watch the 505 detected scenes for the observation time period of 78 h. This means a reduction to 1.8% of the original material. These numbers are expected to vary from location to location according to different traffic volumes and intersection layouts.

Experiment 2. This experiment addressed the question *"Are the detected scenes representative of the actual traffic situation?"*. Therefore, a manual observation at the location Wickenburggasse/Körösistraße was carried out at the same time the automatic system was present. A representative period on a working day from 07:00 to 10:00 o'clock was selected and both video and audio was recorded. Then we compared the detections of (i) an expert on site, (ii) another expert watching the footage in the office, and (iii) the automatic detection system.

Results. The evaluation showed that the expert on site recorded 55 noteworthy incidents within 3 h, while the expert in the office identified 98 incidents. Among these, 31 incidents were detected of both experts. As the expert in the office had a restricted field of view, it can be assumed that the real agreement is higher. During the same reference period, the automatic system detected 19 incidents, 16 that were also identified by the experts, and three additional ones. Obviously, the current automatic system cannot detect incidents that do not coincide with braking or acoustic cues (e.g. bikes crossing the street at red traffic light). Therefore, we plan to extend the set of detected events in future work. Nevertheless, the automatic system outperforms the human eye in detecting rapid decelerations, as these happen at very short time scales.

4   Conclusions and Future Work

In this paper, we evaluated various aspects of an automatic system that detects potentially dangerous events on three road intersections in Austria. We showed that the detection of four event types (car horn, tire squealing, tram bell, and emergency braking) already yields scenes that are relevant for traffic planners to assess the risk potential of an intersection. Using a semi-automatic system, the time needed to inspect a location can be drastically reduced (in the described case to 1.8% of the original time period) and therefore enables long-term analyses. Future work will be extending the set of reported events by exploiting the position and distances between traffic participants and to automatically derive an assessment of the severity of a detected traffic event.

Acknowledgements. This research was partially funded by the Austrian Research Promotion Agency (FFG) within the program "Mobilität der Zukunft".

References

1. Global status report on road safety 2018. World Health Organization (2018)
2. Thallinger, G., et al.: Near-Miss Accidents – Classification and Automatic Detection. In: Kováčiková, T., Buzna, Ľ., Pourhashem, G., Lugano, G., Cornet, Y., Lugano, N. (eds.) INTSYS 2017. LNICST, vol. 222, pp. 144–152. Springer, Cham (2018). https://doi.org/10.1007/978-3-319-93710-6_16
3. Foggia, P., Petkov, N., Saggese, A., Strisciuglio, N., Vento, M.: Audio surveillance of roads: a system for detecting anomalous sounds. IEEE Trans. Intell. Transp. Syst. 17(1), 279–288 (2016)
4. Edelman, G., Bijhold, J.: Tracking people and cars using 3D modeling and CCTV. Forensic Sci. Int. 202, 26–35 (2010)
5. Lucas, B., Kanade, T.: An iterative image registration technique with an application to stereo vision. In: Proceedings DARPA Image Understanding Workshop, pp. 121–130 (1981)
6. Saunier, N., Sayed, T.: A feature-based tracking algorithm for vehicles in intersections. In: Proceedings of the 3rd Canadian Conference on Computer and Robot Vision, pp. 59–59. IEEE (2006)
7. Redmon, J., Farhadi, A.: Yolov3: an incremental improvement. arXiv preprint arXiv:1804.02767 (2018)
8. Green, E.R., Agent, K.R., Pigman, J.G.: Evaluation of auto incident recording system (AIRS) (2005)
9. Cho, K., van Merrienboer, B., Bahdanau, D., Bengio, Y.: On the properties of neural machine translation: encoder-decoder approaches. arXiv preprint arXiv:1409.1259 (2014)
10. van Rijsbergen, C.J.: Information Retrieval, 2nd edn. Butterworth, London (1979)

Assessing the YOLO Series Through Empirical Analysis on the KITTI Dataset for Autonomous Driving

Filipa Ramos[1]([✉]) [iD], Alexandre Correia[1] [iD], and Rosaldo J. F. Rossetti[2] [iD]

[1] Bosch Car Multimedia S.A., 4705-820 Braga, Portugal
{Filipa.Ramos, Alexandre.Correia}@pt.bosch.com
[2] Artificial Intelligence and Computer Science Lab,
Department of Informatics Engineering, Faculty of Engineering,
University of Porto, 4200-465 Porto, Portugal
rossetti@fe.up.pt

Abstract. Computer vision and deep learning have been widely popularised on the turn of the 21st century. On the centre of its applications we find autonomous driving. As this challenge becomes a racing platform for all companies, both directly and indirectly involved with transportation systems, it is only pertinent to evaluate exactly how some generic, state-of-the-art models can perform on datasets specifically built for autonomous driving research. With this purpose, this article aims at directly studying the evolution of the YOLO (You Only Look Once) model since its first implementation until the most recent version 3. Experiences carried out on the respected and acknowledged driving dataset and benchmark known as KITTI Vision Benchmark enable direct comparison between the newest updated version and its predecessor. Results show how the two versions of the model have a performance gap whilst being tested on the same dataset and using a similar configuration setup. YOLO version 3 shows its renewed boost in accuracy whilst dropping minimally on detection speed. Some conclusions on the applicability of models such as this to a real-world scenario are drawn so as to predict the direction of research in the area of autonomous driving.

Keywords: YOLO · Deep learning · Autonomous driving · KITTI Vision Benchmark

1 Introduction

Autonomous driving has established itself as the topic of the future. Most international news outlets are filled with information on research and tests being carried out on such vehicles operating in innumerable urban environments. These scenarios have already stirred much confusion and created barriers for further research. Indeed, failures of such systems are identified in tragic ways that are

© ICST Institute for Computer Sciences, Social Informatics and Telecommunications Engineering 2020
Published by Springer Nature Switzerland AG 2020. All Rights Reserved
A. L. Martins et al. (Eds.): INTSYS 2019, LNICST 310, pp. 203–218, 2020.
https://doi.org/10.1007/978-3-030-38822-5_14

counterproductive towards the full implementation of autonomous vehicles on real-life roads, while ensuring safety and public acceptance.

The idea of autonomous vehicles entails many complex requirements that need to be fulfilled. It certainly starts with the vehicle's perception of the surrounding environment. If the transportation system does not have a good grasp of its outside system, there is no possibility of ensuring safety. On this topic, many non-trivial tasks unfold such as object detection and tracking, traffic signs interpretation, lane detection and many more. All of these are tasks that are not fully computationally solved as of today. As such, autonomous driving imposes invaluable research opportunities and challenges for the technological world.

Specifically on RGB camera detection, there is also the impingement of hardware limitations. As a camera captures almost the same information a human eye would, it also suffers in worse scenarios such as darkness, storms, rain showers and many others in which even the human eye has difficulties detecting objects. These are frontiers hard to overcome and with still much exploration to be made as reporeted in previous studies [14, 15].

Furthermore, if computational models are to be applied to these vehicles in real time, real-world ensembles, the speed of inference and reaction of the independent intelligence centre of the system is paramount. Accidents on the roads happen in a fraction of second and are many times triggered by the delay between the tasks of object detection and classification, risk assessment and corresponding body movement performed by humans when they drive any vehicle.

Broadly on the topic of computer vision and two dimensional object detection, one model that has been keeping up with the state of the art over its improvements and evolution is the YOLO model. Standing for You Only Look Once, this neural network is able to detect and classify objects on camera images. When it launched, the model devised by Redmon et al. [17] showed that real-time, unified object detection and classification was possible. YOLO was one of the first detectors that only ran through the image once, detecting and classifying all objects within this single step. This enabled the model to outperform every other alternatives in the indispensable metric of detection speed. Supporting this, its accuracy was approximately parallel to that of much slower running models.

The research for object detection has gone through an exponential growth in which many models surfaced namely the Faster R-CNN [21] and others in the search for a valid solution. In order to keep up with the evolution in the field, the YOLO version 2 [18] was born, presenting many elements of significant improvement. With these upgrades, YOLO once more proved to be an already mature, strong detector and classifier even if it still had more room for improvement. However, as it becomes more and more of a huge public topic of research, new models keep rising almost every day and most recently, Facebook AI Research (FAIR) launched its Retinanet [11], based on the use of focal loss in order to diminish more effectively the effects of class imbalance. In the current research scenario, this model is considered one of the leading references in both accuracy and speed. Even more fresh, the newest update for YOLO has launched, namely version 3 [20]. The paper describing YOLO version 3 reports an accuracy parallel to that of the commonly found best detectors on the .50 IoU mAP metric (even Retinanet). Unfortunately and opposed to this improvement, the model has become more heavy and slower at performing detection.

On an ensemble system that draws information over a panoply of sensors, this model can certainly be a good candidate for real-world autonomous driving applications. In order to dwell in more depth how this new model can really achieve such impressive results, this article reflects on the distance spanning YOLO version 2 and the newest updated version 3, all the same applying it to a prestigious urban driving dataset in several configurations in order to ascertain how the improvements have reflected on its application.

On the topic of the dataset, the KITTI Vision Benchmark Suite [5] aims at connecting research with the real-world application which makes it ideal in order to predict more informed data on how researched models will perform outside of the laboratory. Sporting scenarios from highways to urban and rural areas of Karlsruhe, frames can contain up to 15 cars and 30 pedestrians either truncated, occluded or fully visible which makes it a dataset with abundance of easy, medium and hard cases. Many respected models with good results on other benchmarks have been found to have a poor performance on this benchmark comparatively. This paper also intends to demonstrate how YOLO – which has been evaluated on general object detection datasets like PASCAL VOC [2] and COCO [12] – can cope with the complex and challenging autonomous driving scenario.

2 State of the Art

Ever since deep learning established itself as the path to follow for object detection, the evolution on the field of generally referred to as two dimensional object detection has been characterised by two main different approaches. These methodologies seem to divide themselves in two stage detectors, which seem to prime in accuracy and the one stage detectors which are usually the fastest.

The concept of two stage detectors really kicked off with the surface of the R-CNN [7] (Regions with CNN features) model. What this model had in accuracy, it did not have in detection speed which invalidated it for such scenarios as autonomous transportation systems. In fact, the original system took over 40 seconds to perform detection on a single image. Over the years, many updates were proposed namely the R-CNN minus r [9], Fast R-CNN [6], the Faster R-CNN [21] and most currently the Mask R-CNN [8] specialised in object instance segmentation. Lenc et al. even proposed R-CNN minus r [9] which used static bounding box proposals instead of the selective search [24]. Furthermore, through further improvements made on R-CNN, specifically from Faster R-CNN [21], the selective search [24] ended up being substituted for a fully qualified region proposal neural network. Selective search proposals were estimated to take around 2 s per image which invalidates its application on a real-time scenario. Incrementally, the updates that the model suffered unified the network, reducing the strenuous process of having to train or tune independently the feature extraction convolutional neural network, the box scoring SVM, the bounding box adjustment linear model and the non-max suppression step. Unifying this pipeline meant the network became much faster, however, its speed is still incomparable to that of the current YOLO model.

On the topic of one stage detection, the field was dominated by such models as SSD [13] and YOLO [20] for quite some time. The SSD, Single Shot MultiBox Detector, relied on loosing the feature re-sampling step and the evaluation of default boxes for feature maps of different sizes. This model surpassed, at the time, its competitor YOLO version 1. Following SSD, Fu et al proposed DSSD [4] which introduced feed forward modules with deconvolutional layers which improved accuracy over the original model. However, the contribution did not seem to be significant in terms of detection speed, having approximately equal and at some resolutions even worse detection times than its predecessor.

Recently as well, Facebook's FAIR proposed a novel network, the Retinanet which has been performing outstandingly well in both accuracy and speed. This network is inserted in that of 1 stage detectors, however, it uses a new balanced focal loss which reduces the impact of imbalance between foreground and background classes on the data. The Retinanet detector's backbone is based on the feature pyramid network [10] which has established itself as a strong architecture choice on the field of deep learning for object detection and convolutional related tasks. This network uses an hierarchy of pyramidal features each merged and combined following a top-down order. The existence of both lateral and top down connections in between feature maps enables the network to be more accurate and fast at the same time.

On the other hand, YOLO has been one of the longest standing one stage detectors. The fact that YOLO's premise focus so specifically in detection speed makes it ideal to use in autonomous driving systems. Moreover, with the evolution of the network, the trade off between its performance in terms of results and detection time is even smaller. Hence the importance of studying its behaviour in urban scenarios specially to ascertain if and how the newest version outperforms its predecessor as advertised.

3   KITTI Dataset for Object Detection

The KITTI dataset used for training and testing the models scoped by this paper is described in a work by Geiger et al. [5] in more detail. This section sums up on some general information that may be relevant for the experiences presented below.

The KITTI dataset was collected using a test vehicle equipped with a panoply of cameras (both RGB and grayscale), a laserscanner, one inertial navigation system and varifocal lenses. The raw dataset contains all the information mustered through the movement inside urban areas. 3D tracklets are provided for all labelled classes. The labelled classes that can be found in this dataset are explained below.

Car	Any standard vehicle.
Van	All kinds of vehicles that present an intermediate size and shape in between that of a Car and a Truck.
Truck	The largest kind of moving vehicles.
Pedestrian	People in movement or in position of initiating movement.
Person (sitting)	People that do not seem to be in movement on the scenario. For example, people on a park bench.
Cyclist	Any moving person on a bicycle.
Tram	A standard, urban tram.
Misc	Other kinds of objects attached to vehicles such as trailers or segway.

The raw dataset provided by KITTI explores a variety of urban scenarios. Some statistics on the tracklets can be found in Fig. 1. As we can denote on the left graph, the most frequent label is Car, followed by Van. Classes such as Truck, Pedestrian, Cyclist and Misc have approximated frequency of labels. The rare classes are Tram and Person (sitting) with special emphasis on the last as it is particular hard to find examples of this behaviour on the dataset. The graph on the right explores the frequency of tracklets per frame. From what can be seen, the largest percentage of frames seem to have around 2 and 6 tracklets.

In order to evaluate identification on the KITTI Vision Benchmark Suite, the objects are separated according to their difficulty of identification. Levels of difficulty are extracted according to the occlusion and truncation of the object to be found on the tracklet. The three levels span from **Easy** and **Moderate** to **Hard**.

The 2D labelled dataset available in KITTI's 2D object detection benchmark page contains labels for all these classes. Benchmark evaluation is done over three levels of difficulty for classes *Car* which requires an overlap of 70% with the ground truth, *Cyclist* and *Pedestrian* which require an overlap of 50%.

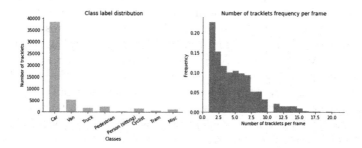

Fig. 1. Statistics on the KITTI raw data.

4 "You Only Look Once"

The You Only Look Once model looks at the full image once. This was the original premise and with this, YOLO was able to efficiently extract context from

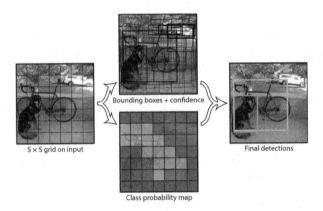

Fig. 2. From the You Only Look Once: Unified, Real-Time Object Detection [17] paper, YOLO detection pipeline.

the whole consumed image, joining both the global features and each object's specific characteristics. Taken from its original paper [17], image 2 shows the pipeline proposed initially for object detection.

As one can denote in Fig. 2, the pipeline starts from the division of the image into an $S \times S$ grid. Each cell will then predict B bounding boxes along with a confidence score for each of them. A box confidence is evaluated over the multiple classes conditional probabilities and the overall intersection over union of the predicted box with the ground truth one. All classes are predicted at the same time for the whole image and that is the premise that makes the model as fast as it has always been. The resulting tensor encodes both the number of grids, the number of classes to classify and the number of bounding boxes that each cell predicts.

A cell on the grid is responsible for a detection and classification if the object's centre is found within it. A bounding box is then represented by 5 different variables: (x, y) is the tuple that represents the centre coordinates of the box, the (w, h) contain the width and height of the box according to the image proportion and a confidence value that the box contains the object. As such, the loss function is modelled over these 5 parameters, being a combination of the sum of squared errors with some characteristics added in order to balance errors in large or small boxes and distinguish between classification and localisation mistakes.

The whole YOLO model is implemented using the Darknet framework [19] and its classifier was previously trained on Imagenet [23]. The architecture is quite simple, being a standard convolutional network with 24 layers followed by 2 fully connected layers. Non maximum suppression is also used in order to eliminate duplicated boxes.

Just like any other model, YOLO has its strengths and weaknesses. The incremental work done with the updates was in the sense of reducing the handicaps and augment even more the existent strengths. The most flagrant obstacle to tackle is the reduction of the sources of error from wrong localisation. In a comparison in between Fast R-CNN and YOLO, Redmon et al. reported that whilst their network makes much less false positive classifications coming from background image areas, it looses most of its mAP on localisation errors. Moreover, detection of small objects specially grouped together has been a great challenge to overcome.

4.1   Version 2

The 2016 paper [18] introduced the second incremental version of the model alongside a joint training algorithm that enables training on both detection and classification data namely YOLO9000.

On the newest architecture, some changes were made which focused directly on the region proposal setup, diminishing the number of location errors and the low recall achieved by its predecessor. All the while, the objective was to always maintain the classifier's accuracy. One direct point of approach was the difficulty that the original YOLO model had with small objects.

The incremental approaches taken are described below.

Batch Normalisation. Its application on all convolutional layers improved mAP and stabilised the model. It also eliminated the need for dropout.

Higher Resolution. The classifier is tuned for 448×448 input resolution on ImageNet which helps adjust the filters for higher resolutions on the detection step. Opposed to the initial model which trained the classifier at a 224×224 resolution and used 448×448 for detection.

Anchors. Inspired by Faster R-CNN's offset prediction, anchor boxes are used. Network resolution is reduced to 416×416 in order to have only one cell at the centre of the image. Higher resolution output after the removal of one pooling layer.

Clustering. Anchor priors are chosen through $k-$means clustering. With a $k = 5$, anchors are defined using a distance metric that involves the intersection of union between the box and its centroid.

Location Predictions. Bounding boxes are predicted according to the responsible cell. Sigmoid activation is used in order to constraint the ground truth to a range between 0 and 1. Parameters t_x, t_y, t_w, t_h, t_o are used to calculate the boxes centre/dimensions alongside with the top left corner offset coordinates (c_x, c_y) and the prior width and height p_w, p_h.

Fine-Grained Features. Additional feature map of larger resolution (26×26) stacked with the 13×13 feature map through a pass-through layer.

Multi-Scale Training. Training done with random net resolutions switched at each 10 batches.

Darknet-19. Classifier network changes to Darknet-19, a more mature and evolved model with 19 convolutional layers and 5 max pooling layers. Data augmentation, hue, saturation, crops, rotations and exposure shifts used in order to introduce variety in the data.

4.2   Version 3

Most recently, the YOLO project web page[1] has launched a newer update – version 3. On a preprint arXiv archive the changes are described and the newer results are advertised as still being much faster than any model and on par with accuracy on the AP .50 metric. However, on the newer .95 metric, the model can not keep up with Retinanet in terms of accuracy, having around 7% less mAP. This fact immediately leads us to the conclusion that this model seems to be great at localising and classifying objects but not great at giving an exact, almost perfect bounding box that contains the object.

Objectness. Objectness score was introduced in version 2. However, on the newest update, this score is calculated using logistic regression which represents the ratio of overlapping in between the ground truth object and the bounding boxes prior.

Classification. Softmax is removed and independent logistic classifiers are added instead. Predictions are then obtained using binary cross-entropy.

Pyramid Extraction. Much like feature pyramid networks [11], YOLOv3 extracts features at several scales and concatenates the upsampled feature maps with ones obtained on earlier stages.

Anchors. Box priors are still extracted through $k-$means clustering, only now with 9 clusters and 3 arbitrary scales.

Darknet-53. The classifying network evolves towards 53 layers and adds short-cut connections in order to process the connected feature maps with more fine grained information. This network is also trained on ImageNet [23] and achieves top classification on par with ResNet-152 but much faster.

With these newer updates, the model moves towards more accuracy. Even whilst loosing some speed, it is still a very powerful and fast network. It is reported that small objects are not such a challenge for the model anymore however, it seems that more difficulties arise on the larger and medium objects.

5   Experiments

In order to ascertain how the model would perform on the KITTI dataset, several experiments were conducted. The bulk of experiences were carried out using the raw dataset available at KITTI's website[2] since the objective of this work was not to benchmark the YOLO series but rather to observe its performance under different conditions and versions. The dataset used contains around 12932 different images. Since this collection encompasses all frames taken during the trips made with the test vehicle, several consecutive images are very similar with small changes. A validation dataset was drawn from 355 frames. The validation

---

[1] Found at https://pjreddie.com/darknet/yolo/.
[2] Download at http://www.cvlibs.net/datasets/kitti/raw_data.php.

set always contains frames from different drives since inside the same drive the variation of data is very small. Even though the validation set is small compared to the number of existent frames, the data extracted is very significant since it eliminates any kind of repetition and similarity in between most of the frames from training.

All experiments described below were run on a single NVIDIA Geforce GTX 1080 Ti with 11GB of dedicated memory. Libraries CUDA and CudNN are used on version 9.0 and 7.0 respectively. Also, all models were trained until they stabilised and reached a convergence stage. The weights chosen for each result comparison are those at the best early stopping point in order to avoid overfitting. Loss values displayed are taken from an average around the early stopping point. Val time corresponds to the time that takes to validate performance on the whole testing dataset (which means detection time for 355 images). The threshold used for mAP calculations is 0.25. Training thresh equals 0.6.

Experiments follow an incremental evolution pattern. In fact, if a parameter is found to be better than the others in a given experiment, in following experiences these best performing configurations are kept, varying only the tweaks in study.

5.1   RGB

All training was carried out using the colour left images of the dataset from all available drives and frames with tracklet information.

Network Resolution. A study that was found to be interesting was the variation of the network resolution. Since the input images have a rectangular resolution (width larger than height by approximately 3.6 times), when training was deployed on squared resolutions, the end results seemed to be much lower. For a squared resolution test, the 416×416 size was chosen. Since resolutions over 832 are not advisable, the testing rectangular resolution 256×832 was used. This is approximately a factor of 1.5 (closer resolution multiple of 32 as expected by the model) times smaller than the original dataset image size.

Anchors. YOLO comes with default anchors. However, for each dataset, using the specified $k-$means approach for each version, it is possible to generate new anchors that are supposedly more appropriate for the training in question. Training was carried out for both versions with the default priors and with calculated ones. The results can be observed in Table 2.

Random. One of the new introductions made by the YOLOv2 paper [18] was the enabling of the model to switch its own resolution at random in order to enable the model to generalise better for other input dimensions. Tests with this configuration were also carried out. The comparison is made between random training runs, starting either with a squared or a rectangular resolution for both models.

Table 1. Results obtained for the variation of the network resolution. The evaluation metrics are mAP, which stands for mean average precision, and IOU, which represents the intersection of union.

Network	Resolution	Loss	mAP	IOU	Val time
YOLOv2	416 × 416	0.30	56.06	55.05%	4 s
YOLOv3	416 × 416	0.9	72.58	65.72%	8 s
YOLOv2	256 × 832	0.28	69.91	59.27%	4 s
YOLOv3	256 × 832	0.43	**75.51**	**73.12%**	9 s

Table 2. Results obtained for the variation of the anchors.

Network	Anchors	Loss	mAP	IOU	Val time
YOLOv2	standard	0.28	69.91	59.27%	4 s
YOLOv3	standard	0.43	**75.51**	**73.12%**	9 s
YOLOv2	generated	0.3	68.59	59.71%	4 s
YOLOv3	generated	0.56	73.48	69.56%	9 s

5.2   Grayscale

Having trained the model on RGB images and using the exact same validation set, however this time with grayscale left pictures, the model was validated. YOLO uses saturation, hue changes and other techniques referred on previous sections for data augmentation. This experiment shows how this technique can help the model generalise better to other environments. The results were quite positive and are described in Table 4. Figure 3 shows a detection with the model on a painting, as an example for other kinds of generalisation.

5.3   Version 2 vs Version 3

Wrapping up all the experiences previously exposed, the best configurations from each version are chosen in order to directly compare how both models wage on the dataset. On this dataset, the best configuration found for both models does not use random training but a rectangular resolution and the standard anchors. Table 5 shows a strong improvement on mean average precision of around 5 points and an increase for intersection of union of over 13% which are incredibly substantial results for YOLO version 3 over its predecessor.

From the bundle of experiments carried out, it is possible to conclude that, overall, the YOLO model has improved considerably. Even so, there is still a visible trade-off in the newest update such as the loss of detection speed in detriment of accuracy, which is obvious in all previous experiments. In most cases, it has approximately doubled the detection time for 355 images, properly observable in Table 5 through the column *Val time*. There certainly is a trade-off between accuracy and speed which may influence the applications of this model

Table 3. Results obtained for the variation of the random resolution switch.

Network	Random	Resolution	mAP	IOU	Val time
YOLOv2	0	256 × 832	69.91	59.27%	4 s
YOLOv2	1	416 × 416	61.05	55.59%	4 s
YOLOv2	1	256 × 832	22.21	54.27%	4 s
YOLOv3	0	256 × 832	**75.51**	**73.12%**	9 s
YOLOv3	1	416 × 416	72.58	65.72%	8 s
YOLOv3	1	256 × 832	11.42	50.13%	9 s

Table 4. Results obtained for the tests on grayscale data.

Network	mAP	IOU	Val time
YOLOv2	63.79	57.59%	**5 s**
YOLOv3	**71.45**	**70.27%**	8 s

in certain real-world situations. However, it is still the fastest model known publicly, producing detection in around 25 ms per image on the newest update at a large resolution (of 832 in one parameter). This behaviour was more than expected as the number of layers was more than doubled from Darknet-19 to Darknet-53.

As for resolution, the YOLO model shows different behaviours in version 2 and in the newest update. It seems reasonable to conclude that keeping the aspect ratio of the original training images is the best approach regardless of the model being used. However, it is also obvious to conclude that YOLO version 2 was much more sensible to the object's original ratio. This is proved by the astounding improvement in mAP of 13.85 points gained by using a rectangular

Fig. 3. Output of YOLO version 3 on a painting that did not have a coincident resolution with the network's training resolution. Painting by Tom Brown [1], 2015.

Table 5. Compilation of the best results obtained for each version of the YOLO system.

Network	Loss	mAP	IOU	Val time
YOLOv2	0.28	69.91	59.27%	4 s
YOLOv3	0.43	**75.51**	**73.12%**	9 s

resolution as seen in Table 1. Meanwhile, the improvement in version 3 is only of around 3 points. This may be due to the use of connection of the different scales and feature maps that make it more invariable to natural scales on the newest update. The lack of sensibility in between resolutions is certainly a good aspect as it may increase the capacity of the model to generalise better in new conditions.

When it comes to the prior generation, the results seem a bit puzzling. Even if the standard anchors have been properly tuned on larger datasets such as COCO [12] and PASCAL VOC [2] with a large abundance of classes and cases, it is still surprising to find that the standard anchors produce slightly better end results for both models. Nevertheless, this is good news as it means that YOLO can be adapted to new datasets with minimal pre-processing overhead. Table 2 shows small differences between using standard and generated anchors, having only an increase around 1–2 points on mean average precision. Even though slightly, the use of generated anchors over the standard ones for version 3 seems to produce worse results compared to the behaviour of version 2.

The possibility to variate resolution during training was also tested and yielding interesting results. The use of random for training with a starting squared resolution gives good results even though the testing images are rectangular in both version 2 and 3. Even so, training for a rectangular resolution specifically proves to the best approach, assumption proved by the results showcased in Table 3.

Moreover, the use of random training from a starting rectangular resolution produces rather poor results on both metrics even if more heavily on average precision. This seems to be a limitation in the classifier. Both versions of the model have the same kind of behaviour towards this parameter. From Table 3 one can denote that having a direct rectangular resolution produces superior outcomes compared to having a randomly sized training process which consumes more gpu resources and takes around twice the time to train. When the ratio of the images is known beforehand, it is preferable to keep the network's resolution parallel to that of the original aspect whilst still keeping it under 832 for width or height since larger resolutions have a directly proportional decrease in detection speed that would nullify the objective of trading off speed over accuracy. This was also tested in extra experiments.

YOLO is able to generalise to different resolutions, environments, lightning conditions and even paintings. On the grayscale experience, with results showcased in Table 4, it is only noticeable a little drop in mean average precision compared to the colour validation set. This is an invaluable quality for an

Fig. 4. Output of YOLO version 3 on the KITTI dataset for lane detection [3].

autonomous driving situation. On the road, many unplanned, new scenarios arise and the model needs to be elastic enough to respond to all of them with the degree of safety and confidence as the cases it was trained for. On this aspect, YOLO maintains and in some aspects even increments on its generalisation value. Table 4 depicts less loss in average precision in the newest version than in its predecessor whilst comparing these with the best obtained on the RGB set.

6   Conclusions

It was intuitively expected that the additional layers would decrease the speed of the network whilst boosting its performance. However, there are more tweaks on the newest version that prove that the YOLO series has even more room to grow and expand itself into a possible alternative to meet the demanding requirements of the autonomous driving scenario. However, its behaviour with the prior generation must be more deepened in order to ascertain its true advantages to the model. Using random resolution training is an expensive alternative that must only be applied to certain use cases.

Overall, YOLO version 3 is a much superior object detection model over version 2. The model has reached new heights in accuracy in all configurations, keeping a standard mean average precision around 70% which was rare and quite hard to obtain by using version 2 on this dataset. The improvements are expressed as well on the placement of more correct bounding boxes, supported by the increasing intersection of union.

Moreover, the fact that the YOLO series is able to generalise so well to grayscale images is a step forward towards solving the problem of object identification in such complex environments as night time, rain conditions, storms and such. If the model were to show such results on applications of thermal images, it could be a reliable solution for the more demanding conditions to be faced on the road. Furthermore, if YOLO could perform detections on these types of cameras whilst only having been trained on RGB images, the gathering of such powerful, mixed information would be a gigantic step for autonomous driving as it would allow having less sensors on the vehicles and less training processes in order to make them operational. Very much similarly to YOLO9000 [18] that generalised to 9000 classes, future work on the direction of enabling YOLO to perform just as accurately on several types of cameras could be an interesting step moving forward. Another study of great interest would be the thorough analysis of the relationship between the number of layers in the classifier network and its impact on speed degradation, so as to identify the optimal point for the reasonable trade-off between accuracy and speed.

Finally, this study contributes with a thorough analysis of YOLO version 2 and version 3, emphasising on the improvements of the latter version towards supporting the autonomous driving scenarios. Currently YOLO is underlying the development of an Artificial Transportation Systems platform, coined MAS-Ter Lab [22], endowing such an environment with computer-vision-as-a-service functionality. Both traffic and transport control and management, as well as the simulation of autonomous vehicles in urban settings [16] are under development within the MAS-Ter Lab platform using the YOLO model.

Aknowledgements. This work is supported by: European Structural and Investment Funds in the FEDER component, through the Operational Competitiveness and Internationalization Programme (COMPETE 2020) [Project n° 037902; Funding Reference: POCI-01-0247-FEDER-037902].

References

1. Brown, T.: Plein Air Oil Painting (2015). http://tombrownfineart.blogspot.com/2015/06/25-cars-8x10-plein-air-oil-painting-by.html
2. Everingham, M., Eslami, S.M.A., Van Gool, L., Williams, C.K.I., Winn, J., Zisserman, A.: The PASCAL visual object classes challenge: a retrospective. Int. J. Comput. Vis. (2014). https://doi.org/10.1007/s11263-014-0733-5
3. Fritsch, J., Kuehnl, T., Geiger, A.: A new performance measure and evaluation benchmark for road detection algorithms. In: International Conference on Intelligent Transportation Systems (ITSC) (2013)
4. Fu, C.Y., Liu, W., Ranga, A., Tyagi, A., Berg, A.C.: DSSD: deconvolutional single shot detector. CoRR abs/1701.06659 (2017)

5. Geiger, A., Lenz, P., Stiller, C., Urtasun, R.: Vision meets robotics: the KITTI dataset. Int. J. Robot. Res. **32**(11), 1231–1237 (2013). https://doi.org/10.1177/0278364913491297

6. Girshick, R.: Fast R-CNN. In: Proceedings of the IEEE International Conference on Computer Vision 2015 Inter, pp. 1440–1448 (2015). https://doi.org/10.1109/ICCV.2015.169

7. Girshick, R., Donahue, J., Darrell, T., Malik, J.: Rich feature hierarchies for accurate object detection and semantic segmentation. In: Proceedings of the IEEE Computer Society Conference on Computer Vision and Pattern Recognition, pp. 580–587 (2014). https://doi.org/10.1109/CVPR.2014.81

8. He, K., Gkioxari, G., Dollar, P., Girshick, R.: Mask R-CNN. In: Proceedings of the IEEE International Conference on Computer Vision 2017, pp. 2980–2988, October 2017. https://doi.org/10.1109/ICCV.2017.322

9. Lenc, K., Vedaldi, A.: R-CNN minus R. In: British Machine Vision Conference (2015)

10. Lin, T.Y., Dollár, P., Girshick, R., He, K., Hariharan, B., Belongie, S.: Feature pyramid networks for object detection. In: 2017 IEEE Conference on Computer Vision and Pattern Recognition (CVPR), pp. 936–944, July 2017. https://doi.org/10.1109/CVPR.2017.106

11. Lin, T.Y., Goyal, P., Girshick, R., He, K., Dollar, P.: Focal loss for dense object detection. In: Proceedings of the IEEE International Conference on Computer Vision 2017, pp. 2999–3007, October 2017. https://doi.org/10.1109/ICCV.2017.324

12. Lin, T.-Y., et al.: Microsoft COCO: common objects in context. In: Fleet, D., Pajdla, T., Schiele, B., Tuytelaars, T. (eds.) ECCV 2014. LNCS, vol. 8693, pp. 740–755. Springer, Cham (2014). https://doi.org/10.1007/978-3-319-10602-1_48

13. Liu, W., et al.: SSD: single shot multibox detector. In: Leibe, B., Matas, J., Sebe, N., Welling, M. (eds.) ECCV 2016. LNCS, vol. 9905, pp. 21–37. Springer, Cham (2016). https://doi.org/10.1007/978-3-319-46448-0_2

14. Loureiro, P.F.Q., Rossetti, R.J.F., Braga, R.A.M.: Video processing techniques for traffic information acquisition using uncontrolled video streams. In: 2009 12th International IEEE Conference on Intelligent Transportation Systems, pp. 1–7, October 2009

15. Neto, J., Santos, D., Rossetti, R.J.F.: Computer-vision-based surveillance of intelligent transportation systems. In: 2018 13th Iberian Conference on Information Systems and Technologies (CISTI), pp. 1–5, June 2018. https://doi.org/10.23919/CISTI.2018.8399240

16. Pereira, J.L.F., Rossetti, R.J.F.: An integrated architecture for autonomous vehicles simulation. In: Proceedings of the 27th Annual ACM Symposium on Applied Computing, SAC 2012, pp. 286–292. ACM, New York (2012)

17. Redmon, J., Divvala, S., Girshick, R., Farhadi, A.: You only look once: unified, real-time object detection. In: 2016 IEEE Conference on Computer Vision and Pattern Recognition (CVPR), pp. 779–788, June 2016. https://doi.org/10.1109/CVPR.2016.91

18. Redmon, J., Farhadi, A.: Yolo9000: better, faster, stronger. In: 2017 IEEE Conference on Computer Vision and Pattern Recognition (CVPR), pp. 6517–6525, July 2017. https://doi.org/10.1109/CVPR.2017.690

19. Redmon, J.: Darknet: Open source neural networks in C (2013–2016). https://pjreddie.com/darknet/

20. Redmon, J., Farhadi, A., Ap, C.: YOLOv3 : an incremental improvement. Technical report (2018). https://doi.org/10.1109/CVPR.2017.690

21. Ren, S., He, K., Girshick, R., Sun, J.: Faster R-CNN: towards real-time object detection with region proposal networks. IEEE Trans. Pattern Anal. Mach. Intell. **39**(6), 1137–1149 (2017). https://doi.org/10.1109/TPAMI.2016.2577031
22. Rossetti, R.J.F., Oliveira, E.C., Bazzan, A.L.C.: Towards a specification of a framework for sustainable transportation analysis. In: 13th Portuguese Conference on Artificial Intelligence, EPIA, Guimarães, Portugal, pp. 179–190. APPIA (2007)
23. Russakovsky, O., et al.: ImageNet large scale visual recognition challenge. Int. J. Comput. Vis. **115**(3), 211–252 (2015). https://doi.org/10.1007/s11263-015-0816-y
24. Uijlings, J.R., Sande, K.E., Gevers, T., Smeulders, A.W.: Selective search for object recognition. Int. J. Comput. Vis. **104**(2), 154–171 (2013). https://doi.org/10.1007/s11263-013-0620-5

Evaluation of Broadcast Storm Mitigation Techniques on Vehicular Networks Enabled by WAVE or NDN

Oscar Gama[⊠], Alexandre Santos, Antonio Costa, Bruno Dias,
Joaquim Macedo, Maria Joao Nicolau, Bruno Ribeiro,
and Fabio Goncalves

Algoritmi Center, University of Minho, Braga, Portugal
{b2583,b7214,b7207}@algoritmi.uminho.pt, {alex,costa,
bruno.dias,macedo}@di.uminho.pt, joao@dsi.uminho.pt

Abstract. A vehicle in a vehicular ad-hoc network (VANET) can perform wireless broadcasting by flooding to find a route to a node or to send an emergency warning, for example. However, this is usually a very demanding operation because it may originate broadcast storms, with high impact on redundancy and collision of packets, as well as channel bandwidth waste. Diverse strategies have been proposed by the research community to mitigate the broadcast storm problems. To contribute to this important topic, this work evaluates on a simulation scenario the network performance of a VANET in terms of content delivery time, signal-to-interference-plus-noise ratio (SNIR) packet loss and duplicate packets, considering the use of broadcasting by flooding on two prominent network paradigms: wireless access in vehicular environment (WAVE) and named data networking (NDN). Afterwards, these network technologies are used to study two distinct strategies to mitigate the flooding problems. One strategy uses a counter-based scheme and the other a geographic location scheme. Simulation results show that both strategies are effective in mitigating the broadcast storm problems in terms of the considered metrics.

Keywords: Vehicular ad-hoc network (VANET) · Broadcast storm · Named data networking (NDN) · Wireless access in vehicular environment (WAVE)

1 Introduction

A vehicular ad-hoc network (VANET) is formed by vehicles equipped with one or more wireless communication devices, named on-board units (OBU). Vehicles can communicate one another without any infrastructure support, or with the infrastructure through a fixed road side unit (RSU), or with electronic devices able to connect to a VANET, such as smart-phones carried by pedestrians. Therefore, VANETs include vehicle-to-everything (V2X) communications, which is a collective name for vehicle-to-vehicle (V2V), vehicle-to-infrastructure (V2I), and vehicle-to-pedestrian (V2P) communications. Vehicles can communicate directly if they are within signal range, or using multi-hop routes computed in a cooperative way through specific routing protocols. Since vehicles may move at high speeds along restricted and predictable road paths, VANETs

© ICST Institute for Computer Sciences, Social Informatics and Telecommunications Engineering 2020
Published by Springer Nature Switzerland AG 2020. All Rights Reserved
A. L. Martins et al. (Eds.): INTSYS 2019, LNICST 310, pp. 219–236, 2020.
https://doi.org/10.1007/978-3-030-38822-5_15

have distinctive characteristics and communication requirements, such as, short contact time, connectivity disruption, and dynamic topology. Another characteristic of VANETs is the communication heterogeneity, as vehicles may have multiple interfaces with distinct wireless communication technologies, as discussed next.

Ideally, a vehicle should be able to choose the best technology or use multiple technologies in parallel to communicate with other nodes. The most prominent communication technologies for VANETs are currently the long term evolution - vehicle (LTE-V) [1], dedicated short-range communications (DSRC) [2], and intelligent transport systems - 5 GHz band (ITS-G5) [3]. LTE-V is a modified version of LTE [4] to provide the high speed, and low latency communications required by VANETs [5]. DSRC is a set of standards to allow short-to-medium range wireless communications with high data transmission in V2X environments. It is based on IEEE 802.11p and the IEEE 1609 family of standards, which constitute the key parts of the wireless access in vehicular environment (WAVE) protocol stack [6]. ITS-G5 is a V2X European wireless short-to-medium range communication technology for fast transmission of small size messages using the IEEE 802.11p. All those characteristics make VANETs a very challenging communication environment. Furthermore, named data networking (NDN) [7] is a recent communication architecture focused on content delivery by naming, which has been proposed as an alternative to the end-to-end connection paradigm of TCP/IP. Due to the viability of NDN becoming the future network paradigm, diverse works have been published on the use of NDN in VANETs environments [8].

Besides the communication technology to be used, the broadcast nature of the wireless communications should be also considered in order to optimize the communication performance in VANETs. A simple solution for wireless communication in VANETs is broadcasting by flooding. However, broadcasting has inherent drawbacks, namely unreliability due to its unacknowledged mode, increment of potential collisions in the wireless channel, packet redundancy, and channel bandwidth waste. Therefore, new strategies and/or mechanisms are required to control collisions and packet redundancy.

In light of such considerations, the goal of the present paper is the following. Firstly, a traffic scenario, based on a use-case, is deployed in a VANET simulator and then the network performance is evaluated in terms of content delivery time, signal-to-interference-plus-noise ratio (SNIR) lost packets, and duplicate packets, considering the use of broadcast by flooding in two distinct network paradigms: NDN, and DSRC/WAVE (hereafter named WAVE, for simplicity's sake). Afterwards, the VANET performance is evaluated for both NDN and WAVE using two distinct mitigation techniques against broadcast storm. One strategy uses a counter-based scheme and the other a geographic location scheme, as discussed later.

The rest of this paper is structured as follows: Sect. 2 presents an overview of the WAVE communication technology, NDN architecture, NDN in VANETs, as well as the relevant aspects regarding broadcast storm mitigation techniques, and the related work. Section 3 presents the two strategies evaluated in this paper to mitigate broadcast storm problems in VANETs; Sect. 4 introduces the connected ambulance use-case, and its implementation in the VANET simulator. Section 5 shows the results obtained in the simulated VANET scenario; Sect. 6 analyses these results; and, finally, Sect. 7 presents the conclusions and the future work.

2 Background and Related Work

The WAVE and NDN technologies are discussed generically next, as well as NDN enabled VANETs. A brief overview of the relevant aspects regarding broadcast storm mitigation techniques is also presented.

2.1 Communication Architecture for VANETs

The WAVE standard was designed to support public safety operations in V2X communication environments. It was developed to meet the short latency requirement for road safety messaging and control. The allocated spectrum is structured in 10 MHz wide channels, with one control channel (CCH) and multiple service channels (SCHs). The CCH is dedicated for safety communication with low latency and for initialization of regular communications. The SCHs are used for safety and non-safety exchange of data. The physical and medium access control (MAC) layers are defined by the IEEE 802.11p standard [6]. At scenarios with high densities of vehicles, the wireless channels can become very congested, which leads to a high probability of packet collisions. To prevent this phenomena, IEEE 802.11p uses the carrier sense multiple access/collision avoidance (CSMA/CA), combined with a random back-off procedure, to reduce packages collisions and to ensure latency and accuracy requirements of vehicle safety applications. Over the IEEE 802.11p plays the IEEE 1609.4 standard, which enables multi-channel operations without requiring knowledge of the physical layer parameters. Then comes the IEEE 1609.3 standard, which defines the network and transport layer services, including addressing and routing. It also defines the WAVE Short Messages Protocol (WSMP) to support secure data exchange without using IP addresses. WSMP supports high priority and time sensitive communications. IEEE 1609.3 specifies a maximum WSMP message size of 1400 bytes.

2.2 Named Data Networking Architecture

The communications in NDN involve the exchange of interest packets and data packets between consumers and producers. Basically, a consumer sends an interest packet to the network asking for a content and a data packet carrying the requested content is replied by a provider. No IP addresses are carried by these packets. Both the requested data and the replied data are identified by hierarchical names. The data packet contains the name, the content, and a signature. An interest packet is uniquely identified by the combination of name and nonce. The nonce is a random number used to detect looping interests. Data and interest packets are forwarded by the routers based only on the names. NDN also provides data muling, which allows a moving node to be a physical carrier of data packets. These nodes are called packet mules.

Three major data structures are present in the NDN routers: content store (CS), pending interest table (PIT), and forwarding information base (FIB). The CS is a temporary cache of data packets received by the router, and it is used to satisfy future interests. The PIT stores the names of all interest packets received by the router that were not still satisfied and the respective incoming interfaces (face, in NDN terminology). The PIT table is used to register the return path for possible data packets in response to the interests forwarded upstream. The data mules cache all data packets heard over a broadcast channel, even if there is no matching pending interest in the PIT. The interest lifetime field in the interest packet defines for how long the interest packet is hold in the PIT. The FIB stores information related with routing, namely the outgoing faces to forward the interests that match the longest name prefix. A name prefix in the FIB can have multiple output faces.

When a NDN router receives an interest packet, it checks firstly the CS in order to find the requested content. If this is cached in the CS, the router returns a data packet through the interface that received the interest. Else, the router checks the PIT for a matching record of the interest name. If the record exists in the PIT, it adds the incoming face of the interest to the record, and discards the packet. In the absence of a matching entry, a new record is created in the PIT, and then the FIB is checked to find out where the interest should be forwarded to. If no face is found in the FIB, then the interest is dropped and a negative acknowledgement (NACK) of the interest is sent to the downstream node. When a router receives interests for the same name from multiple downstream nodes, it forwards only the first interest upstream towards the data producer. When a data packet arrives to an NDN router, this finds the matching PIT entry and forwards the data to all downstream interfaces listed in that PIT entry. It then removes that PIT entry, and caches the data in the CS to satisfy future interests.

There are several cache placement strategies proposed in literature [9]. Leave copy everywhere (LCE) is the default cache placement policy used in the NDN architecture, whereby a data packet will be cached in all active routers between the producer and consumer, without any selection criterion. However, this simple scheme may produce significant cache redundancy. Moreover, due to the limitation of cache size, caches need a replacement policy, such as first-in-first-out (FIFO), least recently used (LRU), least frequently used (LFU), most frequently used (MFU), and most recently used (MRU). The replacement policies more used in NDN are LRU and LFU.

2.3 Named Data Networking in VANETs

Vehicular networking is a domain where the NDN architecture may offer diverse advantages over the TCP/IP architecture, such as reduced delay, robustness to disruptions, increased content availability, and content decoupling from producers. Although NDN can improve the connectivity, there are still a number of challenges to solve due to the variable network densities, network partitions (caused by vehicles being unable to send/forward packets to other subsequent vehicles), message redundancy, broadcast storms, security and privacy. As a car in vehicular NDN can play the role of producer, consumer, forwarder and data mule, the high mobility of the receiver and/or producer must be also considered carefully in the deployment of NDN over VANETs. It is claimed in [10] that, in the NDN-enabled VANETs, the packets are usually flooded, because there is no role for the FIB in these environments. As the cache size of vehicles is very large, the placement strategy usually adopted in VANETs is the LCE.

According to [11], modifications to the regular NDN operations are necessary for VANET environments. Instead of only accepting data with matching entries in PIT, a vehicle should cache all received data, in order to facilitate rapid data dissemination in highly dynamic environments. Vehicles should also serve as data mules in order to carry a copy of the content to other areas. Moreover, since it is very difficult to run a routing protocol to build and maintain the FIBs in a VANET, due to the high dynamics of connectivity among vehicles, other means to forward interest packets should be developed.

A few works have studied the performance of NDN over VANETs, such as [11, 12]. Although these works experimentally demonstrated the effectiveness of VANET via NDN with infrastructure support, no performance comparative study was conducted with host-centric networks. In [13], a comparison study for two connected vehicle systems powered by NDN and IP solutions, respectively, was conducted for image dissemination. The simulation results showed that the NDN may be effectively a promising alternative to the conventional IP networking.

2.4 Broadcast Storm Mitigation Techniques

In a traffic scenario with high density of vehicles, the wireless channel can become very congested, which leads to high probability of packet collisions and broadcast storms. Hence, strategies to mitigate these problems are required. As discussed in [14], there are a few schemes proposed to alleviate the broadcast storm problem, namely the (*i*) probabilistic, (*ii*) counter-based, and (*iii*) distance-based schemes. Basically, these schemes try to inhibit some hosts from rebroadcasting in order to reduce the redundancy and collision of packets.

The simplest way to reduce the number of rebroadcasts is to use probabilistic rebroadcasting. According to this method, after receiving a message, a host will rebroadcast it with a defined probability. The distance-based scheme measures the relative distance between hosts to decide whether a packet should be rebroadcast or not. It is based on the fact that when the distance between two cars is very small, there is little additional coverage provided by the rebroadcasting of one of those cars.

Another way is to use a counter-based scheme, as described in [14]. A defer time is calculated before each packet transmission, and if the same packet is overheard during the defer time a certain number of times, the transmission is canceled.

Other mechanisms have been proposed to decide which nodes should forward the packets in order to alleviate the broadcast storm problem. For instance, candidate forwarders could be the vehicles that have maximum connectivity time and good link quality with the consumer [15], or only the vehicles in the path towards the data producer, as discovered during a preliminary flooding stage [12]. A scheme based on hop counts to control the packet flooding/broadcast storms is proposed in [16]. As discussed in the next section, a broadcasting mechanism based on geographical location (geolocation) of the vehicles is also considered in this paper to reduce the broadcast storm problems.

A nonce is a random number that can be used just once in the network. Nonces may be used, for example, in cryptography and networking. Nonces are used in NDN to discard duplicate packets received over different paths [7]. As the nonce allows a packet being retransmitted by the intermediate nodes only once at most, then nonces may be used to reduce the number of (re)broadcast packets too.

The geolocation and the counter-based schemes will be evaluated in this work, as well as the effect in the network performance of the use of nonces.

3 Evaluated Strategies to Mitigate Broadcast Storms in VANETs

This work evaluates two strategies to mitigate the broadcast storm problems in VANETs enabled by WAVE and NDN: (*i*) the counter-based strategy; and (*ii*) the geolocation strategy. The effect in the network performance of the use these strategies with nonces is also evaluated.

The counter-based strategy was implemented following the algorithm proposed in [14]. Basically, as a host may hear multiple times the same message from other hosts before starting to transmit its message, a counter keeps track of the number of times the broadcast message is received during a certain time interval. If this counter reaches a predefined value, then the rebroadcasting is canceled.

The geolocation strategy is a broadcasting solution based on geographical location. According to this strategy, the producer and the consumer communicate each other using preferably the vehicles circulating on a set of roads connecting the producer and the consumer. In case of communication failure after a number of trials using the geolocation transmission mode, the packet is rebroadcast by flooding. The set of roads is chosen through an algorithm that takes into consideration, for example, the minimum distance between the producer and the consumer and/or the density of vehicles in the roads. By receiving an interest packet containing the GPS location of the consumer, the producer is able to define a list of contiguous roads and send this list in the data packet. In the same way, by receiving a data packet containing the GPS location of the producer, the consumer is able to define such list and send it in the interest packet. When the forwarder nodes receive a data/interest packet, only those located in the roads defined in the list are allowed to rebroadcast it. Otherwise, the forwarder node discards the received packet.

4 Connected Ambulance Use-Case

In order to evaluate the efficiency of the counter-based and geolocation strategies against broadcast storm, a use-case inspired on a connected ambulance care assistant was considered for this work, as described next.

During the trip of an ambulance transporting a patient to the hospital, the electronic equipment of the paramedics in the ambulance send patient's data, such as video images of patient's injuries and data of vital signs, to the health specialists in the hospital, allowing them to know more exactly the clinical health state of the patient carried in the ambulance. In this way, the first aids can be properly carried out in the ambulance, and when this vehicle arrives to the hospital everything is ready to receive the patient. The data is sent to the hospital through a wireless communication infrastructure. A similar use-case is considered in the SliceNet Project [17].

The consumer (receiver) of the content (hospital) is static and the producer (ambulance) is dynamic. Since NDN communications are driven by the consumers, in the NDN scenario the producer only sends a data packet after receiving the respective interest from the consumer. In the WAVE scenario, the ambulance only sends the data packet of sequence number n after receiving the ACK of the packet $n - 1$ from the hospital.

This work considers the transmission from the ambulance to the hospital of a certain number packets, each one containing a set of physiological signals of the patient, such as the electrocardiography (ECG), arterial pressure, oximetry, respiration rate, heart rate, and body temperature.

4.1   Use-Case Simulation

In order to evaluate the performance of the geolocation and counter-based strategies, it was considered a VANET with an ambulance able to provide the service described above. This scenario was implemented in a simulator. The simulation setup and the simulation test conditions are presented next.

Simulator. It was used the simulator Veins-4.7.1. This is a vehicular network simulation framework that couples the mobility simulator SUMO [18] with a wireless network simulator built on the discrete event simulator OMNeT++. Veins has a manager module to synchronize the mobility of the vehicles between the wireless network simulator and SUMO. Veins implements fully detailed models of IEEE 802.11p and IEEE 1609.4 DSRC/WAVE network layers, including multi-channel operation.

The simulator was programmed so that cars take diverse actions to help decrease the ambulance trip delay, as described next. The use-case was implemented over this functionality. During the trip, the OBU of the ambulance broadcasts periodically emergency warning messages using the WAVE short message protocol (WSMP) [19] over IEEE 802.11p. In each warning message is sent the current road and next $n - 1$ roads of the ambulance. For example, if the number of roads is equal to two, then the current road and the next road of the ambulance are sent in the message. Basically, when a car receives an emergency warning message from a nearby ambulance, it checks if the car is moving in the same direction of the ambulance. If this is true, and if the car is moving ahead the ambulance, then the car checks if the ambulance is not overtaking. If true and if the current road of the car is included in the set of ambulance next n roads, then the car tries to change lane to pull to the road side. If this is done with success, then the car stops until being passed by the ambulance. If the car and the ambulance are moving in crossing or opposite directions, then if the next junction is the same for the car and the ambulance, and if the car is near this junction, then the car stops at the end of the road to let the ambulance pass. The cars moving in the opposite direction of the ambulance also stop at the road end to make easier the flow of the cars moving ahead the ambulance. This helps to reduce the traffic volume ahead the ambulance. When the ambulance is overtaking, the cars rolling in the opposite road also tries to change lane and stop, in order to leave the road free to the ambulance.

If the RSU of a traffic light receives the emergency warning message from an ambulance, the traffic light switches as soon as possible to green in the direction of the emergency vehicle and to red to block the vehicles in the crossing directions. The signal keeps green while the ambulance does not pass through the traffic light. Once crossed by the ambulance, the traffic light runs the regular sequence loop of color light signals.

Road Grid. The simulation was carried on a road grid with seven horizontal roads and seven vertical roads, as shown in Fig. 1a. The length of each road is 200 m. To simulate the pull of the car to the side of the road in order to give way to the ambulance, the roads of the grid have two lanes, as shown in Fig. 1b. Although a map with two lanes in every road is not very representative of a city, where often only one lane exists, it should be noted that all cars in the simulation roll mostly on the internal lanes, and the external lanes are only used by cars to help free the internal lanes to the approaching ambulance. An ambulance never uses the external lanes. So, the external lanes are used to simulate the real situation of cars pulling to the side of the road to let the ambulance pass.

Routes. Along the simulation time, the ambulance follows a predefined closed pattern, covering most of the grid edges. After running a sinuous trajectory through 56 edges, which corresponds to a distance of 11.11 km, the ambulance reaches the start position, thus completing one cycle. Then, it starts another cycle, repeating again the same closed pattern route. This scheme continues until the simulation time is over. The routes of the cars were generated with the SUMO traffic generator (randomTrips.py). A route with a new traffic profile is generated every time a simulation is run.

Number of Vehicles. Simulations were run for 200, 400, 600, and 800 vehicles in the road grid. The ambulance started rolling and transmitting messages only when the stipulated number of vehicles was present in the road grid.

NDN. The essential aspects of the NDN architecture were implemented at Veins. The CS can store 1000 data packets, and the PIT 1000 interest packets. For simplicity's sake, LCE and FIFO were the strategies used for the cache placement and the cache replacement, respectively. As OBUs have only one face to receive and transmit packets, the FIB role was not considered in this work, just as in [11, 12, 20]. The mule strategy was also not implemented.

Communications. All vehicles had an OBU with IEEE 802.11p. The transmission power was 20 mW, which corresponds to a signal range of 530 m. The total length of the MAC frames containing the warning messages was 166 bytes. The service channel was not used, the simple path loss propagation model was used, and no buildings were considered in the simulation scenario. As Veins does not simulate acoustic signals, these were simulated using wireless communication messages. The cars able to "listen" the siren are those that receive such messages directly from the ambulance. It should be noted that the siren messages are always transmitted via WSMP, even when NDN is used in the VANET to access the producer's content.

Traffic Lights. Simulations were carried out with three traffic lights. One traffic light was placed exactly at the central junction of the grid and the other two at the junctions indicated in Fig. 1a. The traffic lights switch between red and green every 50 s. For simplicity, the yellow light was not used. The ambulance crosses twice each junction with traffic lights during a complete route cycle (Fig. 1b).

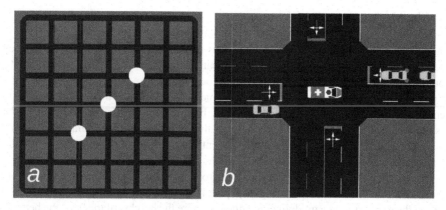

Fig. 1. (*a*) Road grid of size 7 × 7, with white dots marking the location of the traffic lights. (*b*) Ambulance crossing a junction with traffic lights. Note the two lanes per edge. (Color figure online)

Parameters. The values of the parameters used in the simulations are shown in Table 1. The simulation finishes when the consumer receives the full content from the producer. It is required 1000 packets to transmit the full content. Each packet carries an application payload of 100 bytes. This size is enough to contain a sample set of physiological signals of the patient, because the arterial pressure, oximetry, respiration rate, heart rate, and temperature are quantified by decimal values.

Table 1. Parameterization used in the simulated scenario.

Parameter	Value	Parameter	Value
road grid size	7 x 7	communication protocol	IEEE 802.11p
number of traffic lights	3	service channel (SCH)	unused
road length	200 m	MAC frame size	166 bytes
number of hundreds of vehicles	2, 4, 6, 8	application payload size	100 bytes
minimum car trip distance	2000 m	transmission data rate	18 Mbps
vehicle velocity	10 m/s	transmission power	20 mW
vehicle acceleration	3 m/s²	time-to-live (TTL)	31
vehicle deceleration	10 m/s²	data payload size	100 bytes
lane stay time	6 s	full content size	1000 packets
emergency warning period	0,2 s	CS size	1000 data packets
max. time for car to change lane	20 s	PIT size	1000 interests
time for car to send change lane mesgs.	3 s	PIT entry lifetime	1 s
change lane warning mesg. period	1 s	packet retransmission period	0,1 s
traffic light changing period	50 s	cache placement	LCE
number of ambulance roads (*n*)	2	cache replacement	FIFO

5 Simulation Results

The wireless communication performance was evaluated on the simulated emergency scenario considering the use of V2X communications in WAVE and NDN environments, combined with the use of the counter-based or geolocation strategies, as well as the nonces. The use of nonces means that every time the consumer or the producer needs to send a packet, a number is generated randomly by that node and sent in the packet. The results obtained for the content delivery time, the SNIR lost packets, and the duplicate packets are presented next. The results represent the average values of multiple simulations, each one with a different traffic profile. All results are relative to the content consumer (hospital). The number of cars in the road grid is constant along the simulation. The results were obtained considering respectively the presence of 200, 400, 600, and 800 cars on the road grid. As a guideline rule, the lower are the heights of the bars, the better is the communications performance of the VANET in terms of the considered metrics.

The bar graphics of Figs. 2, 3, 4, 5 and 6 show the results obtained for the proposed use-case, using both WAVE and NDN technologies. In all graphics, the x-axis contains the number of cars, and the y-axis the percentage values of the considered performance metrics. The meaning of the three bars obtained for each specific number of cars in the road grid is presented next.

The blue bar (at left) shows the content delivery time, which is the time required to receive the full content from the producer. It is expressed in a percentage relatively to a reference time, which is equal to the maximum content delivery time found in all simulations. Considering all 292 simulations carried out in this work (see Table 2), the maximum content delivery was equal to 1434,0 s, which occurred for a test in NDN with 600 cars, using the counter-based strategy with nonces. For example, if the blue bar indicates 40%, it means that the average content delivery time for this particular case was 1434,0 × 0,40 = 573,6 s. So, the content delivery time is calculated by:

$$content\ delivery\ time = delivTime/refTime * 100\%$$ (1)

where *delivTime* was the time required to deliver the full content from the producer to the consumer, and *refTime* is the reference time (1434,0 s).

The red bar (at middle) shows the average SNIR lost packets at the producer (*P*) and the consumer (*C*). This parameter reflects the number of collisions on the OBUs of both nodes, and may be used as an indirect indication of the bandwidth occupancy of the wireless channel, in that the higher is its value, the more occupied is the wireless channel used by both OBUs. The SNIR lost packets (%) is calculated by:

$$SNIR\ lost\ packets(\%) = (SNIRlostPkts(P) + SNIRlostPkts(C))/2$$ (2)

where SNIRlostPkts(X) means "SNIR lost packets at X", with X = {P, C} (P is the producer, C is the consumer), and is calculated by this expression:

$$SNIRlostPkts(X) = SNIRlostPkts(X)/(SNIRlostPkts(X) + recvdPkts(X)) * 100\%$$ (3)

where recvdPkts(X) means "received packets by X", with X = {P, C}.

The orange bar (at right) shows the duplicate packets sent in average by the producer (data packets) and the consumer (ACK packets). Note that the value shown in the graph must be multiplied by four to get the real value of duplicate packets. The duplicate packets (%) is calculated by the expression:

$$duplicate\,packets(\%) = (duplPkts(P) + duplPkts(C))/2 \qquad (4)$$

where $duplPkts(X)$ means "duplicate packets sent by X", with X = {P, C}, and is calculated by this expression:

$$duplPkts(X) = (nrSentPkts(X) - nrUniquePkts(X))/nrUniquePkts(X) * 100 \qquad (5)$$

where nrSentPkts(X) is the number of packets sent by X and nrUniquePkts(X) is the number of unique packets sent by X, with X = {P, C}. The number of unique packets is equal to the number of packets used to transmit the full data content, which is equal to 1000 packets.

The meaning of the legends in the bar graphics is the following:

(i)   *flood* means that all packets were sent in broadcast by flooding. This is obviously the transmission mode more susceptible to originate broadcast storms in the VANET.

(ii) *geoX* means that the flooding mode is used after X trials in geolocation mode without successful delivery of the packet to the destination node. This is valid to all packet types, i.e. interest, data, and acknowledgement packets. So, if $X > 1$, the first packet is sent in geolocation mode, as well as the eventual next $X - 1$ retransmissions of this packet, and the eventual retransmission number X is done in flooding mode. The eventual retransmission number $X + 1$ is done again in geolocation mode, restarting in this way the retransmission mode cycle. For example, *geo10* means one transmission in geolocation mode followed by nine eventual retransmissions in geolocation mode too, and then one eventual retransmission in flooding mode. Afterwards, the cycle restarts again.

(iii) *cntX* means that the counter-based strategy is used with a counter threshold equal to X for all types of messages (*i.e.*, data and interest packets in NDN, WSM and ACK packets in WAVE).

(iv) *non* means that a nonce is attributed to each packet sent by the producer or the consumer, so that a packet is retransmitted by the intermediate nodes only once at most. So, each packet has a sequence number and a nonce. If the consumer or the producer retransmits a packet, this packet is sent again with the same sequence number of its last transmission, and a new nonce.

Table 2 shows the number of simulations run, with distinct traffic profiles, for each type of transmission strategy with a specific number of cars. For example, fifteen simulations were run using geo10 with nonces (geo10 non) on a scenario with two hundred cars. A few simulations were run just a little number of times, or not run at all, because they require a very long time to finish. For example, a conventional laptop requires more than one month to run in WAVE the flooding strategy with 600 cars. In this very specific case, the results were linearly extrapolated from those obtained with the flooding strategy in WAVE using 200 and 400 cars.

Figures 2, 3, 4, 5 and 6 show the bar graphics of the average values obtained for the three evaluated metrics, which are discussed in the next section.

Table 2. Number of simulations run in WAVE and NDN for each transmission mode with a specific number of cars.

	WAVE				NDN			
	200	400	600	800 cars	200	400	600	800 cars
flood	1	1	0	0	1	1	1	0
flood non	3	0	0	0	1	0	0	0
cnt1	16	13	16	10	17	10	10	5
cnt1 non	11	4	2	3	10	4	2	1
geo10	14	10	5	4	14	10	10	12
geo10 non	15	10	10	4	10	10	9	2

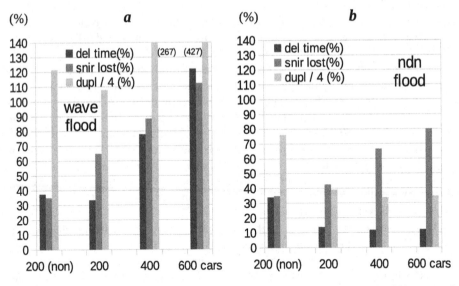

Fig. 2. Results for flooding in WAVE (*a*) and NDN (*b*), with nonces (non) for 200 cars, and without nonces for 200, 400 cars, and 600 cars. The results for WAVE with 600 cars were extrapolated. For WAVE with 400 and 600 cars, the *dupl/4* bar gets 267% and 427%, respectively. (Color figure online)

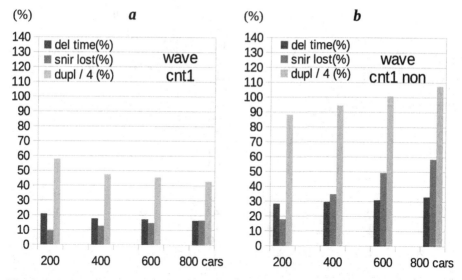

Fig. 3. Results for counter-based strategy in WAVE, with counter threshold equal to one (cnt1), without nonces (*a*), and with nonces (non) (*b*). (Color figure online)

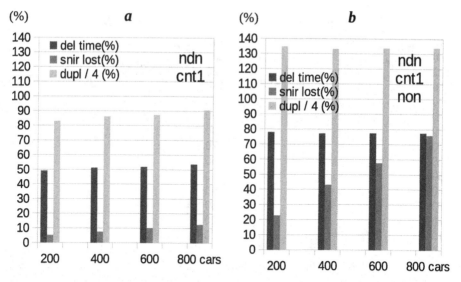

Fig. 4. Results for counter-based strategy in NDN, with counter threshold equal to one (cnt1), without nonces (*a*), and with nonces (non) (*b*). (Color figure online)

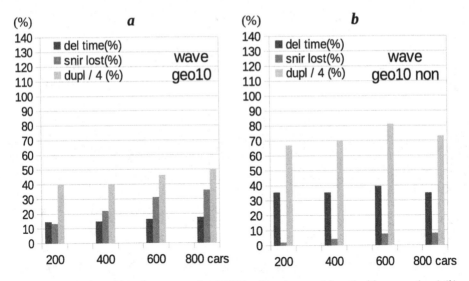

Fig. 5. Results for geolocation strategy in WAVE, without nonce (*a*), and with nonces (non) (*b*). Flooding is used after ten trials in geolocation mode without successful delivery of the packet to the destination node (geo10). (Color figure online)

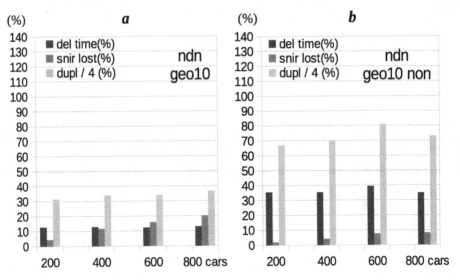

Fig. 6. Results for geolocation strategy in NDN, without nonces (*a*), and with nonces (non) (*b*). Flooding is used after ten trials in geolocation mode without successful delivery of the packet to the destination node (geo10). (Color figure online)

6 Analysis of the Results

The results obtained in the simulated VANET scenario for NDN and WAVE are discussed next. It is analyzed firstly the NDN results, and then the WAVE results.

When flooding is used in NDN without nonces (Fig. 2b), it is noted that the network performance, regarding the three considered metrics, was clearly better than that obtained with WAVE (Fig. 2a). This is justified by the operation of PIT in NDN. Indeed, all interest packets already registered in the PIT are discarded, because a similar interest packet has already been sent to the network. So, the number of broadcasts in the VANET becomes lower. Moreover, Fig. 2b (and Fig. 2a) shows that, when 200 cars are rolling in the road grid, the use of nonces in NDN (and WAVE) does not help to decrease neither the content delivery time nor the duplicate packets, comparatively to the situation where the nonces were not used. When nonces are not used, Fig. 2b shows that the SNIR lost packets increases considerably with the number of cars, which does not occur for the content delivery time and the duplicate packets. When compared with the flooding results, Fig. 6a shows that the use of geolocation strategy reduces considerably the SNIR lost packets, although the content delivery time and the duplicate packets do not change so considerably. Figure 4a shows that the use of the counter-based strategy in NDN presents a considerably higher content delivery time and duplicate packets when compared with the use of flooding and geolocation transmission schemes, but the SNIR lost packets is smaller than that obtained with these two schemes. Comparing Fig. 4a with Fig. 4b, it is noted that the use of nonces in the counter-based strategy increases clearly the SNIR lost packets, the content delivery time, and the duplicate packets. However, the use of nonces in the geolocation strategy (Fig. 6b) helps to decrease the SNIR lost packets, but increases considerably the content delivery time and the duplicate packets too, when compared with the geolocation strategy without nonces (Fig. 6a). So, the best global performance in NDN was obtained with the use of the geolocation strategy without nonces.

Let us analyze now the results obtained with WAVE. When flooding is used in WAVE without nonces (Fig. 2a), the content delivery time, the SNIR lost packets and the duplicate packets increase considerably with the number of cars. When the geolocation scheme is used without nonces, Figs. 5a and 6a shows that the most significant difference between WAVE and NDN is the SNIR lost packets, which is almost the double in WAVE than in NDN. The duplicate packets are also higher in WAVE than in NDN. In WAVE, the use of nonces in the geolocation scheme (Fig. 5b) helps to decrease the SNIR lost packets, but increases the content delivery time and increments considerably the duplicate packets, when compared with the geolocation without nonces (Fig. 5a). In WAVE, the use of the counter-based strategy revealed lower SNIR lost packets than the geolocation strategy. However, the counter-based and the geolocation strategies present similar performances in terms of content delivery time, specially when there are at least four hundred cars in the road grid. Once again, Figs. 5a and b show that the use of nonces on the geolocation scheme helps to decrease the SNIR lost packets, but increases the content delivery time and the duplicate packets, comparatively to the geolocation without nonces. Figure 3b shows that the use of nonces on the counter-based strategy deteriorated the performance of all parameters when compared with Fig. 3a, where nonces are not used. In WAVE, without nonces, the difference observed in the network performance between the counter-based and geolocation strategies is not so notorious as that observed in NDN. However, one may say that the best global performance in WAVE was obtained with the counter-based strategy without nonces, since it presents a significant smaller SNIR lost packets than the geolocation strategy. This is particularly true when there are at least four hundred cars rolling in the road grid.

Tables 3 and 4 summarize the analysis of the results for each broadcast strategy in the form of replies to the following questions. Table 3 answers to the question: "Using the considered transmission strategy, had NDN better performance than the WAVE in terms of content delivery time, SNIR lost packets, and duplicate packets?" Table 4 answers to the question: "For the WAVE/NDN technology, had the transmission strategy B globally better performance than the transmission strategy C in terms of the considered three metrics?" The meaning of the replies is the following: Y means "yes"; YY means "yes, considerably better"; N means "no"; NN means "no, considerably worst"; and $\approx$ means "almost equal", where "considerably" means a difference, in module, above twenty percentage points (pp). Table 4 is composed of two subtables: table A for WAVE, and table B for NDN. For example, table A indicates that, in WAVE, the geolocation strategy (geo10) performed worst (N) than the counter-based strategy (cnt1). Yet, table B indicates that, in NDN, geo10 performed considerably better (YY) than cnt1. Table 4 does not consider "flooding with nonces", because the results available for this case are limited to 200 cars in the road grid.

In summary, the best global performance was obtained in NDN with the geolocation strategy, {NDN geo10} (Fig. 6a), and in WAVE with counter-based strategy, {WAVE cnt1} (Fig. 3a), both without nonces. Comparing Fig. 3a with Fig. 6a, it is noted that the content delivery time was always lower in {NDN geo10}, with differences to {WAVE cnt1} between 3,5 pp and 8,1 pp. The duplicate packets was also always lower in {NDN geo10}, with differences to {WAVE cnt1} between 6,2 pp and 26,5 pp. The SNIR lost packets was lower in {NDN geo10} for 200 and 400 cars, but higher than {WAVE cnt1} for 600 and 800 cars, with differences, in module, below 5,1 pp. So, globally, the NDN with the geolocation strategy performed moderately better than the WAVE with counter-based strategy, in terms of the considered metrics.

Table 3. Summary of the results in the form of replies to the formulated question (Y = yes; YY = "yes, considerably better"; N = no; NN = "no, considerably worst"; $\approx$ = almost equal).

Had NDN better performance than WAVE ?			
transmission strategy	content delivery time	SNIR lost packets	duplicate packets
flooding	YY	Y	YY
counter	NN	Y	NN
counter with nonce	NN	N	NN
geolocation	Y	Y	Y
geolocation with nonce	N	Y	$\approx$

Table 4. Summary of the results for WAVE (table A) and NDN (table B) in the form of replies to the formulated question (Y = yes; YY = "yes, considerably better"; N = no; NN = "no, considerably worst").

Had the transmission scheme at the column better performance than the scheme at the row ?										
WAVE						**NDN**				
table A	cnt1	cnt1 non	geo10	geo10 non		cnt1	cnt1 non	geo10	geo10 non	table B
flood	NN	NN	NN	NN		Y	Y	NN	Y	**flood**
cnt1	*	YY	Y	Y		*	YY	NN	N	**cnt1**
cnt1 non	NN	*	NN	N		NN	*	NN	NN	**cnt1 non**
geo10	N	YY	*	Y		YY	YY	*	YY	**geo10**

7 Conclusions and Future Work

In this paper, an evaluation study was conducted for two mitigation strategies against broadcast storm problems on a VANET enabled with NDN and WAVE technologies. For this goal, a connected ambulance care assistant was implemented on a vehicular simulated scenario. The results show that the best global performance in NDN was obtained with the use of the geolocation strategy without nonces. In WAVE the best global performance was obtained with the counter-based strategy without nonces, although the difference to the geolocation strategy is more contained than that observed in NDN. Globally, the geolocation strategy in NDN performed moderately better than the counter-based strategy in WAVE, regarding the considered three metrics.

The use of nonces in the geolocation and counter-based schemes tends to increase the content delivery time and the duplicate packets, and so they do not help to improve the global network performance. Comparatively to the broadcast by flooding, the results show that, in WAVE, the geolocation and counter-based strategies are effective in mitigating the broadcast storm problems in terms of the considered metrics. In NDN, the geolocation strategy is able to improve the network performance by reducing significantly the SNIR lost packets obtained with flooding.

This study was conducted for a specific use-case. The efficiency of the geolocation and counter-based strategies should be tested with other use-cases, including scenarios with a fraction of cars equipped with V2X communications, and different road configurations. The effect of the buildings along the roads on the radio signals should be also considered. Other strategies based, for example, on probabilities and distances should be evaluated too, as well as the use of different strategies operating together in a VANET scenario. These issues should be tackled in future work.

Acknowledgement. This work has been supported by national funds through FCT – Fundação para a Ciência e Tecnologia within the Project Scope: UID/CEC/00319/2019 and by the European Structural and Investment Funds in the FEDER component, through the Operational Competitiveness and Internationalization Programme (COMPETE 2020) [Project n° 039334; Funding Reference: POCI-01-0247-FEDER-039334].

References

1. Araniti, G., Campolo, C., Condoluci, M., Iera, A., Molinaro, A.: LTE for vehicular networking: a survey. IEEE Commun. Mag. **51**(5), 148–157 (2013)
2. Kenney J.: Dedicated short range communications (DSRC) standards in the United States. In: Proceedings of the IEEE, pp. 1162–1182 (2011)
3. ETSI Intelligent Transport Systems (ITS): European profile standard for the physical and medium access control layer of intelligent transport systems operating in the 5 GHz frequency band. ETSI Draft - ES 202 663 v1.1.0. European Telecommunication Standards Institute, Sophia Antipolis, France (2009)
4. Sesia, S., Toufik, I., Baker, M.: LTE: The UMTS Long Term Evolution. Wiley, Hoboken (2009)
5. Chen, S., et al.: Vehicle-to-everything (V2X) services supported by LTE-based systems and 5G. IEEE Commun. Stand. Mag. **1**(2), 70–76 (2017)
6. Weigle, M.: Standards: WAVE/DSRC/802.11p. Vehicular Networks CS, vol. 795, p. 895 (2008)
7. Zhang, L., et al.: Named data networking. ACM SIGCOMM Comput. Commun. Rev. (CCR) **44**, 66–73 (2014)
8. Liu, X., Li, Z., Yang, P., Dong, Y.: Information-centric mobile ad hoc networks and content routing: a survey. Ad Hoc Netw. **58**, 255–268 (2017)
9. Zhang, G., Li, Y., Lin, T.: Caching in information centric networking: a survey. Comput. Netw. **37**(16), 3128–3141 (2013)
10. Deng, G., Xie, X., Shi, L., Li, R.: Hybrid information forwarding in VANETs through named data networking. In: Proceedings of the 26th IEEE International Symposium on PIMRC, pp. 1940–1944 (2015)
11. Grassi, G., Pesavento, D., Pau, G., Vuyyuru, R., Wakikawa, R., Zhang, L.: VANET via named data networking. In: IEEE INFOCOM 2014 Workshops, pp. 410–415, April 2014
12. Amadeo, M., Campolo, C., Molinaro, A.: Enhancing content-centric networking for vehicular environments. Comput. Netw. **57**(16), 3222–3234 (2013)
13. Xu, X., Jiang, T., Pu, L., Qiu, T., Hu, Y.: A comparison study of connected vehicle systems between named data networking and IP. J. Internet Technol. **16**(2), 343–350 (2015)
14. Ni, S., Tseng, Y., Chen, Y., Sheu, J.: The broadcast storm problem in a mobile ad hoc network. Wirel. Netw. **8**(2/3), 153–167 (2002)
15. Ahmed, S.H., Bouk, S.H., Yaqub, M.A., Kim, D., Song, H.: DIFS: distributed interest forwarder selection in vehicular named data networks. IEEE Trans. Intell. Transp. Syst. **19**(9), 1–5 (2018)
16. Ahmed, S.H., Bouk, S.H., Yaqub, M.A., Kim, D., Song, H., Lloret, J.: CODIE: controlled data and interest evaluation in vehicular named data networks. IEEE Trans. Veh. Technol. **65**(6), 3954–3963 (2016)
17. SliceNet Project. https://slicenet.eu/5g-ehealth-smart-connected-ambulance-use-case. Accessed 15 June 2019
18. Krajzewicz, D., Erdmann, J., Behrisch, M., Bieker, L.: Recent development and applications of SUMO-simulation of urban mobility. Int. J. Adv. Syst. Meas. **5**(3–4), 128–138 (2012)
19. 1609.3-2010 - IEEE Standard for Wireless Access in Vehicular Environments (WAVE) - Networking Services, pp. 1–144 (2010)
20. Duarte, J.M., Braun, T., Villas, L.A.: Receiver mobility in vehicular named data networking. In: Proceedings of the Workshop on Mobility in the Evolving Internet Architecture (MobiArch 2017), pp. 43–48. ACM, New York (2017)

Non-destructive Diagnostic Methods for Smart Road Infrastructure Evaluation

Lenka Mičechová[1(✉)], Anna Krišková[1], Jozef Jandačka[2],
Ján Mikolaj[3], and Michal Veselovský[1]

[1] Research Centre, University of Žilina,
Univerzitná 8215/1, 010 26 Žilina, Slovakia
{lenka.micechova, anna.kriskova,
michal.veselovsky}@rc.uniza.sk
[2] Faculty of Mechanical Engineering, University of Žilina,
Univerzitná 8215/1, 010 26 Žilina, Slovakia
jozef.jandacka@uniza.sk
[3] Faculty of Civil Engineering, University of Žilina,
Univerzitná 8215/1, 010 26 Žilina, Slovakia
jan.mikolaj@fstav.uniza.sk

Abstract. Nowadays, high emphasis is placed on the efficient use of resources for optimum management of transport infrastructure. The use of non-destructive diagnostics is the main application for visualization and support of intelligent infrastructure models. Moreover, such models also have enormous potential to support the "smart city" concept. Disaster management, 3D cadaster, energy assessment, pavement performance, pollution monitoring and visibility analysis could benefit from regular pavement diagnostic and its surroundings. To demonstrate this potential, the authors present examples of non-destructive diagnostics on the roads in the Žilina region. As a result, the importance of using non-destructive diagnostics is highlighted, because of the potential for saving money and streamlining planning for smart city needs.

Keywords: Non-destructive diagnostic · Pavement performance · Smart City · Intelligent road infrastructure · ITS

1 Introduction

Intelligent transport processes cannot be carried out on the demanded level without being able to rely on a synergistic transport infrastructure. This means that we need to focus not only on innovation in transport technology, transport and logistics processes, but also on changing user behaviour, innovative planning and building processes. Current trends in the area of transport infrastructure for smart cities projects include e.g. development and implementation of technologies enabling the collection of selected technical, material, environmental and physical data on its current state. These are followed by technical and software solutions designed to determine the infrastructure's predictive status in order to optimize the management of traffic processes by the operator. Selected examples include solutions that work together to manage winter

A. L. Martins et al. (Eds.): INTSYS 2019, LNICST 310, pp. 237–246, 2020.
https://doi.org/10.1007/978-3-030-38822-5_16

maintenance by monitoring the road temperature profile [1], the degradation status of asphalt pavement layers [2, 15] or innovations to improve the communication structure between smart application sensors [3] as well as tunnel safety enhancement features [4, 17] or overall optimization of transport processes in terms of economic context [16]. From the perspective of improving the quality of transport infrastructure elements, the trend is focused on activating the philosophy of the circular economy as a complement to the complex philosophy of Smart Cities. This is accompanied not only by the need to reuse the demolition and construction waste, but also by focusing on building parts with a longer lifespan. Emphasis is also placed on improving the quality of monitoring itself. Interesting solutions in this area include innovations in bridge object diagnostics procedures through mathematical modal analysis procedures [5], following the possibility of performing it in full operation. A concrete example of new bridge infrastructure solutions can also be found in [6] where preconditions for efficient functioning of precast concrete frames are presented.

2   Application of Approach of Non-destructive Diagnostics to Sustainable Pavement Management

The key resources for implementing the Smart City strategy are information and intelligent processing systems designed to ensure a stable link between individuals and knowledge. Smart urban construction can be supported by the benefits of new technologies that enable a stable interconnection in urban planning. One of the most reliable methods for collecting selected technical and physical road parameters is the use of non-destructive deformation diagnostics. Non-destructive diagnosis has two main advantages over destructive tests. First, destructive testing interferes with the underlying pavement or requires removal of materials, which are tested under laboratory conditions. However, in the case used to innovative technology to collect data it is indeed in-situ testing without undesirable damage to the road cover or possible modification. Another big advantage is fast road testing, in most cases without traffic restrictions or without traffic limitation and one ride can get large amounts of data to test the roadway from multiple perspectives at once [8] (Table 1).

Non-destructive diagnosis data combined with survey data, such as traffic flow composition or traffic intensity, are used to select the best alternative to maintenance and road renewal, which is a very important aspect on the way of sustainable transport and its benefits philosophy Smart City.

2.1   Data Collection with Lynx SG1

The Mobile Mapping System (MMS) enables contactless determination of spatial coordinates of points via sensors and associated evaluation software that are part of the vehicle. The mobile laser scanner is able to collect a huge number of points (point cloud) with minimal separation in a very short time. For field data collection, a mobile mapping device combines multiple technologies at the same time (LiDAR, Global Navigation Satellite System, Inertial Measurement Units and Distance Measurement Unit) [7, 11] (Fig. 1).

Table 1. Diagnostic device - Research Centre of University of Žilina

---

ROAD SCANNER_georadar:

Is a diagnostic facility for collecting data on road and bridge faults by a non-destructive method using ground penetrating radar (GPR) technology.

DYNAMIC ROAD SCANNER (in developing):

The instrument for measuring the transverse and longitudinal unevenness.

3D scanner LYNX SG1:

The Mobile Mapping System (MMS) allows contactless determination of spatial coordinates through sensors and the corresponding evaluation software that are part of the Lynx SG1.

Deflectometer FWD KUAB :

Impact Load Test - The goal is to simulate a truck crossing in the measured point. The resulting value is referred to as deflection.

Fig. 1. Point cloud from experimental measurement of highway tunnel - Považský Chlmec 27. September 2017

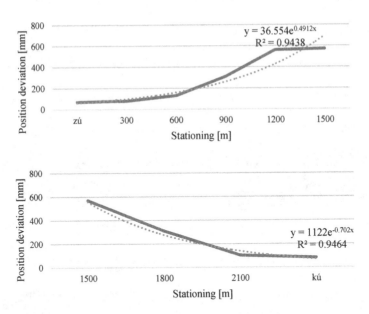

Fig. 2. Exponential accuracy of measurement at the reach of the GNNS signal – highway tunnel - Považský Chlmec 27. September 2017

Fig. 3. Example of 3D visualization with 3D Lynx SG1, which creates space for potential Smart City applications.

Terrasolid's Terrascan program has been used for *.las cloud point processing as an extension for MicroStation V8i. In order to obtain the clearest possible rendering, the first step is to classify the points, which consists of separating the individual objects (e.g. paths, sidewalks, lawns) and then removing unnecessary objects (e.g. cars, faulty objects). Points can be filtered by colour, reflected signal strength, altitude, and other criteria, and linked to groups with common attributes. Good point cloud classification is the basis for further analysis and work. After the drawing is created, the output can be exported to various standard CAD formats dgn, dwg, shp [9] (Fig. 2).

In this case, all data including vectorization is processed in the ETRS89 coordinate system. Finally, a.dgn drawing is created, which is transformed into the SJTSK system (Unified Trigonometric Network System) using a transformation service. This transformation allows the measured data to be located in the territory of the Slovak Republic and subsequently it is possible to work with such data also in the area of the real estate cadastre for support more sophistic urban planning [9] (Fig. 3).

Fig. 4. Location of mapped setting into cadastral map SR for support more sophistic urban planning.

2.2 Data Collection with Dynamic Road Scanner

Mobile high-capacity contactless measuring device for road surface profiles with the precision needed to determine the IRI index (Fig. 4).

Fig. 5. Results of Dynamic Road Scanner measurements of Bus stop Hurbanova and Mostná in Žilina 17.10.2017 and standardized measurements according to STN EN 13036-7.

The device is able to measure road profiles while driving and is able to filter out the measuring beam oscillation based on gyroscopes and accelerometers. The data processing software provides both the raw height data of the measured profile x, y (*.txt) as well as the determination of IRI values based on the determined algorithm (Fig. 5).

2.3   Data Collection with Georadar

The principle of the georadar method consists of the repeated transmission of radio frequency electromagnetic pulse through transmitting antenna into the examined environment. In locations where the electromagnetic pulse change occurs, the reflection that receives the antenna takes place. It, therefore, shows different types of layers, material continuity disorders. The laser scan method is based on the laser beam time transmitted from the scanner to the measured surface and back from which the distance is calculated. Using a laser beam can be determined, for example, depth of the ruts [10].

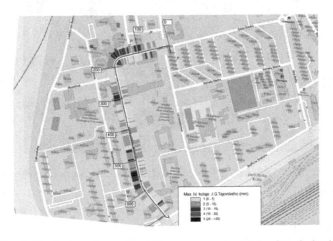

Fig. 6. Evaluation of experimental measurement - depth of track depth.

In the Fig. 6, the authors present the results of experimental measurements that determine the depth of rutted tracks. Results from experimental measurements form the basis for assessing roadworthiness to optimize traffic infrastructure management.

2.4   Data Collection with FWD KUAB

Diagnostic devices - deflectometers work on the principle of in-situ impact loading test. The impact load test is one of the dynamic impulse methods, the aim of the method is to simulate the truck's passage at the measured point. When tested, a roadblock is applied to the road that is damped by a rubber pad and the change in impact load and deformation at the point and outside of the vertical direction, known as deflection [12].

The paper presents the results of the authors from the diagnostics of the newly built transport infrastructure, but also from the analysis of the long-term monitored sections in the Žilina region - road section Poluvsie - Porúbka Road 1/64, where the technical parameters were analysed and evaluated diagnostics (Fig. 7).

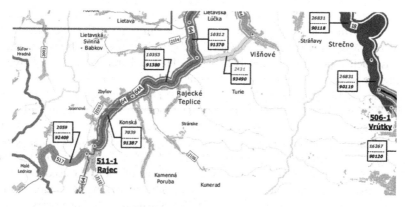

Fig. 7. Road section 91380 - Polúvsie – Porúbka 1/64

The assessment based on the equivalent resilient modulus is based on the greatest (maximum) time deflection amplitude on the road surface in the centre of the y_0 loading plate. The equivalent resilient modulus E_{ekv} is calculated from the general relationship [14]:

$$E_{ekv} = 2.\left(1 - \mu^2\right).\frac{\alpha.\sigma}{y_{0(50,T20)}} \quad (1)$$

Eekv   Equivalent resilient modulus [MPa]
$Y_{0(50,\ T\ 20)}$ deflection in the centre of the load plate calculated at 50 kN comparative force and 20 °C comparative temperature [m]
α loading plate radius [m]
σ contact load stress [MPa]
μ Poisson's number

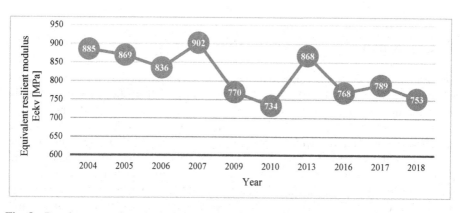

Fig. 8. Development of equivalent resilient modulus - Long term monitored road section Poluvsie – Porúbka - Diagnostics with Deflectometer FWD KUAB

By evaluating and thoroughly analysing the given parameters, we obtain detailed information on the status of the transport infrastructure as part of the Smart Cities philosophy, for the need of urban engineers and planners to benefit from such created models as much as possible, especially with regard to rapid urbanization, which requires obtaining the most accurate information about the environment in the most effective time so that it can be reached soon with the lowest possible financial costs [13].

It is clear from the evaluation of the equivalent modulus of elasticity that all grading stages (5) are located on the entire monitored road section Poluvsie - Porúbka, with the highest percentage of grades 1–3 (excellent, very good, good), namely the 1st grading grade 31.37%, 2nd classification 27.45% and 3rd classification level again 31.37% of which we can conclude that based on the assessment of the road according to the equivalent resilient modulus in good to excellent. Graphically, the evaluation is shown in Fig. 9 is the percentage of all 5 grades. The remaining grading grades have the following percentages: 4. grading grade 3.92% (sufficient) and 5. grading grade 5.88% (insufficient). Figure 8 shows the development of the equivalent modulus of elasticity from 2004 to 2018.

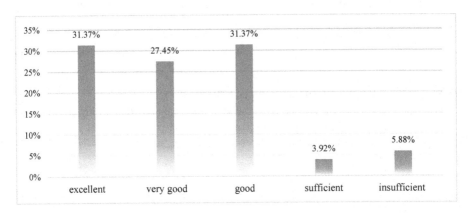

Fig. 9. Percentage of classification grades by module E_{ekv}

3   Conclusion

The technologies for non-destructive diagnostic and technologies for capturing and processing 3D geodata are rapidly advancing. As a result of these developments in geodata acquisition technology, the availability of 3D geodata is steadily increasing.

The current use of diagnostic of pavement and its ambient is mainly used to the visualization of damage, which leaves many other potential applications for the approach to the smart city. This is a chance for change, since urban managers and planners have benefited tremendously from road infrastructure models. This is especially true in light of the rapid urbanization worldwide, which requires continuous monitoring of energy consumption, noise pollution and many other 'smart city' applications. This paper presents the results of several experimental measurements, which are the basis for optimal management of roads and present sustainable approach for intelligent urban construction for smart mobility.

The development of transport means and their characteristics requires a corresponding adjustment of the technical parameters of the transport infrastructure and its gradual modernization. This problem must also be resolved due to the increasing transport performance and the number of means of transport on the roads. The current state of the infrastructure is not able to provide sufficient traffic stream throughput. Additional infrastructure expansion is not possible especially in urbanized areas and the construction of new infrastructure is very demanding. The solution is to use non-destructive diagnostics to quickly determine and predict roadway development almost without any traffic restrictions - without limiting the transport infrastructure logistics processes. The basic goal is to reduce the financial costs involved and to determine the optimal time for repair, maintenance or reconstruction while maintaining the longest possible road life. The cost of repairing roads by using non-destructive diagnostics can be effectively reduced and added value to urban modelling with 3D mobile mapping tools. By optimizing the cost of repair, road maintenance contributes to reducing user costs, improving service delivery and reducing pollution. Last but not least, the aim is to increase road traffic safety, increase the efficiency of transport, expressed by saving time for transport, as well as increasing the quality of the environment and improving the productivity of the company's commercial activity.

Acknowledgment. "This work was supported under the project of Operational Programme Research and Innovation: Progressive systems and technologies for industry and infrastructure., No. ITMS2014+: 313011T415. The project is co-funding by European Regional Development Fund".

References

1. Dudak, J., Gaspar, G., Sedivy, S., Pepucha, L., Florkova, Z. : Road structural elements temperature trends diagnostics using sensory system of own design. In: Building up Efficient and Sustainable Transport Infrastructure 2017, BESTInfra 2017; Prague; Czech Republic; 21 September 2017 through 22 September 2017; IOP Conference Series: Materials Science and Engineering, vol. 236, no. 1. Institute of Physics Publishing, 15 September 2017. ISSN: 17578981

2. Šrámek, J.: Stiffness and fatigue of asphalt mixtures for pavement construction. Slovak J. Civil Eng. J. Slovak Univ. Technol. **26**(2), 24–29 (2018). ISSN 1210-3896

3. Dudak, J., Gaspar, G., Sedivy, S., Fabo, P., Pepucha, L., Tanuska, P.: Serial communication protocol with enhanced properties-securing communication layer for smart sensors applications. IEEE Sensors J. **19**(1), 378–390 (2019). Article number 8486988, ISSN: 1530437X, Publisher: Institute of Electrical and Electronics Engineers Inc.

4. Rázga, M., Jančaříková, E., Danišovič, P.: Research of selected factors of safety in road tunnels for practice. In: Advances and Trends Engineering Sciences and Technologies II, Conference ESaT 2016, pp. 829–834. CRC Press/Balkema, Taylor and Francis Group (2017). ISBN 978-1-138-03224-8, eBook ISBN 978-1-315-39382-7

5. Kortis, J., Daniel, L., Farbak, M., Maliar, L., Skarupa, M.: Operational modal analysis of the cable-stayed footbridge. Civil Environ. Eng. **13**(2), 92–98 (2017)

6. Bujňák, J., Farbák, M.: Tests of short headed bars with anchor reinforcement used in beam-To-column joints. ACI Struct. J. **115**(1), 203–210 (2018). **ISSN:** 08893241, Publisher: American Concrete Institute, Publisher: DE GRUYTER OPEN LTD, BOGUMILA ZUGA 32A ST, 01-811 WARSAW, POLAND, ISSN: 1336-5835

7. Tao, C.V., Li, J.: Advances in Mobile Mapping Technology. International Society for Photogrammetry and Remote Sensing Book Series, vol. 4. Taylor & Francis Group, London (2007). ISBN 0-415-42723-1

8. Shahin, M.Y.: Pavement Management for Airports, Roads, and Parking Lots (2005). ISBN-10: 0-387-23464-0, ISBN-13: 978-0387-23464-9

9. Duris, L., Florkova, Z., Veselovsky, M.: System 3D mobilneho mapovania a jeho vyuzitie v cestnom inzinierstve. In: Silniční obzor [print] = Road Review : mesicnik pro otazky vystavby a udrzby silnic, dalnic, mistnich komunikacii... ISSN 0322-7154. - Roc. 79,c. 1 (2018), s. 16-20 [print]

10. Al-Qadi, I.L., Lahouar, S.: Measuring layer thicknesses with GPR - theory to practice. In: 2003 10th International Conference on Structural Faults and Repairs, vol. 19, no. 10, pp. 763–772 (2003). ISSN: 0950-0618

11. Wan, R., Huang, Y.C., Xie, R.C., Ma, P.: Combined lane mapping using a mobile mapping system. Remote Sens. **11**(3), 305 (2019)

12. Wen, H.F., Tharaniyil, M.P., Ramme, B., Krebs, S.: Field performance evaluation of class C fly ash in full-depth reclamation - case history study. Transp. Res. Rec. **1869**(1), 41–46 (2004). ISBN: 0-309-09463-1

13. Ng, K., Hellrung, D., Ksaibati, K., Wulff, S.S.: Systematic back-calculation protocol and prediction of resilient modulus for MEPDG. Int. J. Pavement Eng. **19**(1), 62–74 (2018). ISSN: 1029-8436, eISSN: 1477-268X

14. Kováč, M., Remišová, E., Čelko, J., Decký, M., Ďurčanská, D.: Diagnostika parametrov prevádzkovej spôsobilosti vozoviek. Žilinská univerzita v Žiline, EDIS – vydavateľstvo Žilinskej univerzity (2012). ISBN 978-80-554-0568-1, 265 s., prvé vydanie

15. Florkova, Z., Sedivy, S., Pepucha, L.: Analysis of results of the aggregate microtexture evaluation by volumetric characteristics. In: RSP 2017 - XXVI R-S-P Seminar 2017 Theoretical Foundation of Civil Engineering, MATEC Web of Conferences, vol. 117 (2017). ISSN: 2261-236X

16. Remek, L., Danisovic, P., Pepucha, L., Sedivy, S.: Novel cost-benefit analysis method performed in highway development and management software for economic impact evaluation of a motorway noise barrier. In: 16th International Multidisciplinary Scientific Geoconference (SGEM 2016), Ecology, Economics, Education and Legislation Conference Proceedings, SGEM 2016, Albena, Bulgaria, vol. III (2016). ISBN: 978-619-7105-67-4

17. Danisovic, P., Razga, M., Sedivy, S.: Road tunnel operation and simulation. In: XXIV R-S-P Seminar, Theoretical Foundation of Civil Engineering (24RSP) (TFOCE 2015), Procedia Engineering, 24th Russian-Polish-Slovak Seminar on Theoretical Foundation of Civil Engineering, Samara, RUSSIA (2015). ISSN: 1877-7058

Sensing

Towards Dynamic Monocular Visual Odometry Based on an Event Camera and IMU Sensor

Sherif A.S. Mohamed[1(✉)], Mohammad-Hashem Haghbayan[1],
Mohammed Rabah[3], Jukka Heikkonen[1], Hannu Tenhunen[1,2], and Juha Plosila[1]

[1] University of Turku (UTU), 20500 Turku, Finland
samoha@utu.fi
[2] Royal Institute of Technology (KTH), 11419 Stockholm, Sweden
[3] Kunsan National University (KNU), Gunsan 54150, South Korea

Abstract. Visual odometry (VO) and visual simultaneous localization and mapping (V-SLAM) have gained a lot of attention in the field of autonomous robots due to the high amount of information per unit cost vision sensors can provide. One main problem in VO techniques is the high amount of data that a pixelated image has, affecting negatively the overall performance of such techniques. An event-based camera, as an alternative to a normal frame-based camera, is a prominent candidate to solve this problem by considering only pixel changes in consecutive events that can be observed with high time resolution. However, processing the event data that is captured by event-based cameras requires specific algorithms to extract and track features applicable for odometry. We propose a novel approach to process the data of an event-based camera and use it for odometry. It is a hybrid method that combines the abilities of event-based and frame-based cameras to reach a near-optimal solution for VO. Our approach can be split into two main contributions that are (1) using information theory and non-euclidean geometry to estimate the number of events that should be processed for efficient odometry and (2) using a normal pixelated frame to determine the location of features in an event-based camera. The obtained experimental results show that our proposed technique can significantly increase performance while keeping the accuracy of pose estimation in an acceptable range.

Keywords: Event-based camera · Monocular · Visual-odometry · IMU

1 Introduction

Visual odometry (VO) is one of the most popular topics in machine vision (MV) that is used in broad types of applications, such as autonomous navigation, object avoidance, and 3D scene reconstruction. VO estimates the position and orientation of a moving platform by analyzing the variations induced by the

© ICST Institute for Computer Sciences, Social Informatics and Telecommunications Engineering 2020
Published by Springer Nature Switzerland AG 2020. All Rights Reserved
A. L. Martins et al. (Eds.): INTSYS 2019, LNICST 310, pp. 249–263, 2020.
https://doi.org/10.1007/978-3-030-38822-5_17

motion of the camera on a sequence of consecutive images, i.e., *ego-motion esti-mation*. *Frame-based cameras* are widely used in conventional VO approaches, because they can provide high-resolution images with low cost and have a similar output to human vision. In VO techniques based on frame-based camera, the location of the camera is reconstructed by computing the optical flow (OF) from key information extracted from two consecutive *frames*. The key information in a frame, e.g., corners, is extracted using a *frame feature detector*, such as *Moravec* [1] or *Harris* [2], and the reconstructed scene can be refined using bundle adjustment [3] or another offline optimization method. Even though there has been significant advancement in the field of odomery based on frame-based cameras, there still exist practical problems in using such cameras in odometry, for example high latency of image delivery, motion blur phenomenon, and low dynamic range, which negatively affect the efficiency of the odometry algorithm w.r.t. the accuracy of the result and performance.

Another type of camera that can be used for odometry is the *event-based camera* [4]. Opposite to frame-based cameras that acquire the intensity of all pixels simultaneously and generate frames at fixed rates, event-based cameras use biologically inspired vision sensors to output pixel-level temporal intensity changes, i.e., *events*. This feature of event-based cameras makes them very appealing and efficient for odometry. An event is triggered whenever the brightness of a pixel changes. In such a case, the location of an event in a pixelated image (u,v), polarity of the brightness change (1 or 0), and time-stamp, are passed as a single event to the camera output. Therefore, such cameras produce a stream of events that has no redundant data and can thereby reduce the latency (response time) down to 10 µs. Moreover, the power consumption of odometry can be significantly reduced, even by the factor of 50, which is an important aspect especially for resource limited devices.

The benefits event-based cameras provide make them attractive for odometry in navigation and tracking on high speed agile robotic platforms that operate under challenging lighting conditions. However, processing data of event-based cameras for odometry is not straightforward, since the output of these cameras is fundamentally different from that of frame-based cameras. For example, unlike in frame-based cameras, features cannot be extracted easily in event-based cameras, making odometry difficult in practice. Moreover, reconstruction of a frame based on data captured by an event-based camera is problematic. The main question here is that how many events should be considered together to form an instantaneous frame? There are recent studies that aim at solving these problems by defining the new features of event-based cameras and by determining the number of events per frame in a given time interval [5]. However, such techniques are efficient only in special situations, e.g., when the number of events is not changing for different scenes, and, therefore, they do not offer general solutions. The main drawback of such techniques is that their efficiency, in terms of performance and accuracy, is dependent on the velocity of the camera and the number of events in a scene. In dynamic situations, where the scene and velocity of the camera change drastically, i.e., the number of events in a frame changes rapidly in time, processing the events for accurate and fast (real-time) odometry poses still a big challenge.

In this paper, we propose a hybrid technique for odometry based on data captured by both frame-based and event-based cameras, combining the ability of frame-based cameras to detect and track features and the low latency and high dynamic range of event-based cameras to achieve fast and accurate odometry. To do this, our proposed techniques can be divided into two main novel methods that are: (1) defining dynamically the number of events for a frame to reach a minimized amount of data processing for a scene while keeping the accuracy of pose estimation, and (2) using a frame-based camera as a reference guide for an event-based camera to recognize and track features in an event-based camera output. To determine the number of events to construct a frame in run-time, we define two factors that together affect the number of events in an instantaneous scene: (1) *entropy* of the scene that is the entropy of a pixelated image [6], i.e., the amount of *information* the image can convey from an event-based camera, and (2) velocity of the camera that determines how fast the environment changes and is one of the main factors in ego-motion. In this definition, we assume all the objects in a scene are stationary and only the camera is moving. To estimate the velocity of the scene, we use IMU data that can report the acceleration of motion in run time. To extract features from the output of an event-based camera, we use a common method, FAST [7], to first extract features from a frame-based image and then use this information to initiate tracking of those features in the event-based camera output. After this, the detected features on the event-based camera are tracked. Periodically, features from the frame-based camera are used to correct the error of feature tracking in the event-based camera.

We organize the remaining part of this paper as follows. In Sect. 2, we demonstrate motivation to show the existing problem in odometry based on event-based camera and review the related work in visual odometry for both traditional and event cameras. In Sect. 3, we illustrate the overall system workflow, which consists of three steps: event frame generator, feature tracking, and visual odometry. In Sect. 4, we present the experimental results. Finally, in Sect. 5, we draw the conclusions.

2   Motivation and Related Work

In standard frame-based cameras, e.g., those cameras with global-shutter or rolling-shutter sensors, images are generated at a fixed rate by obtaining the intensity of pixels in the whole image simultaneously. To estimate the pose based on these cameras, two main problems might occur. The first problem is the amount of redundant repetitive data that the next frame might contain in the case where the scene does not change much, i.e., the information in the image is low or the movement of the camera is slow. Such amount of redundant data takes unnecessary transfer and process cost and does not add any new information w.r.t. the previously captured data. The second problem, from the other side, is the amount of information that might be missed between two frames, i.e., *blind time*, when the change in the scene is too fast due to rapid movement of the camera and high amount of information in the scene between two frames. To solve this problem, one solution is to dynamically change the frame rate of the camera based on the speed and entropy of the captured image[1]. However, this solution does not solve the problem of redundant repetitive data between two frames, and also there is a strict limitation to change the frame rates of those cameras.

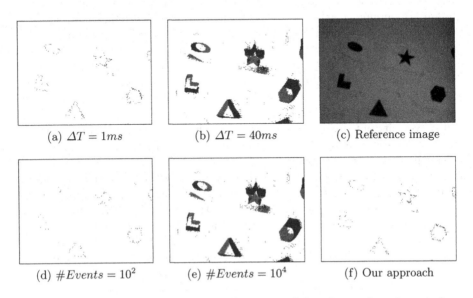

(a) $\Delta T = 1ms$ (b) $\Delta T = 40ms$ (c) Reference image

(d) #$Events = 10^2$ (e) #$Events = 10^4$ (f) Our approach

Fig. 1. The effect of applying different techniques to define the number of events for a frame on the resolution of the output image while rapid movement

Event-based cameras solve this problem by transmitting a stream of asynchronous events that happen in the pixels of an image. Therefore, instead of reporting the scene at each time interval, like in the case of frame-based cameras, only the events are reported, and the new scene can be updated based on the events and the current history of the scene. If the change in the scene is slow, then the number of generated events is small, and the information can be processed fast. Since the accepted interval between two events is small, in the range of microseconds, such cameras can transfer the information at a very high resolution in the cases where the change in the scene is very fast, making this approach well-suited for cases where fast actions are needed due rapid changes in the scene.

As mentioned in the introduction part, even though an event-based camera provides rich and small data that is suitable to be transferred and computed

---

[1] This technique is widely used in cinema to show the importance or inferiority of a scene by applying slow-motion, fast motion, and time-elapsed photography.

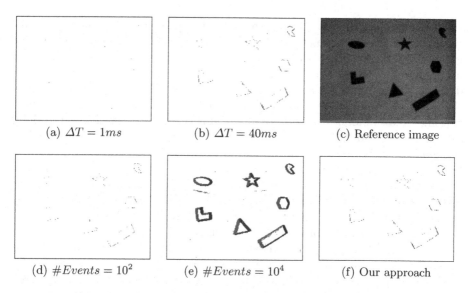

(a) $\Delta T = 1ms$ (b) $\Delta T = 40ms$ (c) Reference image

(d) $\#Events = 10^2$ (e) $\#Events = 10^4$ (f) Our approach

Fig. 2. The effect of applying different techniques to define the number of events for a frame on the resolution of the output image while slow movement

fast and accurately, the captured data requires specific processing to be used for odometry. To process a scene that is constructed from event-based camera data, a frame of such a scene should be first constructed based on the captured events. The first issue that makes such processing challenging is the number of events that can be considered to make a frame. Indeed, since an event-based camera only reports a stream of events, determining the suitable amount of events to make a frame becomes an important problem. In [8], the authors propose a fixed time interval, i.e., ΔT, and the events accumulated during this interval are considered a frame. In [5], the author proposes a fixed number of events, i.e., $\#Events$, to form a frame. Using a fixed ΔT or $\#Events$ causes a problem corresponding to a fixed frame rate in frame-based cameras, i.e., inflexibility in dynamic situations

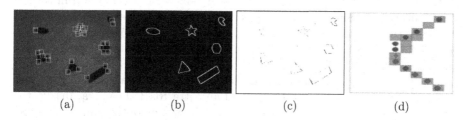

(a)   (b)   (c)   (d)

Fig. 3. Feature detection and matching. (a) Frame with detected corners and patches (green boxes). (b) edge map using Canny detector. (c) accumulated events in ΔT time. (d) (zoom for a patch) point sets used for feature matching: edges (in gray) and events in (red and blue). (Color figure online)

where the number of events for different frames varies significantly. Inspired by this observation, we propose a technique to dynamically calculate the number of events based on the velocity of the camera and entropy of the capture pixelated image of the scene. Figures 1 and 2 show the reconstructed frames based on two different values for ΔT and $\#Events$ and in two different situations wherein the velocity of the camera is high (a high amount of information per unit time) and low (a low amount of information per unit time), respectively. At the right side of Figs. 1 and 2, the result of our proposed dynamic frame construction technique is shown to demonstrate how dynamicity in detecting $\#Events$ can help to reconstruct the frame in these two different environmental conditions. As can be seen in these two figures, while using a large ΔT and $\#Events$, the constructed frame is blurry and non-informative when the velocity of the camera is slow. In contrary, small ΔT and $\#Events$ result in a weakly depicted frame for rapid motion and is not suitable for odometry.

After frame construction, the next step is to utilize the reconstructed frame for odometry. As indicated above, the event-based approach requires a specific technique to process the frame, differing from traditional odometry that is based on frame-based cameras. Generally, the traditional odometry techniques can be divided into two main strategies that are (1) *feature-based*, also know as *indirect*, and (2) *direct* methods. In a feature-based method, instead of processing all the pixels in an image, some selected interest points, i.e., features, are processed. Feature-based techniques can be further categorized into two main branches that are *sparse* and *dense* methods. The sparse feature-based method is the most widely used algorithm to estimate the 6-Dof pose from a set of features that are extracted from an image. The optimization process is performed by minimizing the estimated geometric error without any notion of neighborhood [9, 10]. Dense approaches [11] use the geometric error estimation and geometric prior, i.e., smoothness of the flow field, together for odometry. Direct approaches analyze the intensity of pixels in the image to recover the pose of the camera [12–14]. Sparse direct methods, such as SVO [15] and DSO [16], use only selected pixels in an image, which reduces the computational cost drastically. However, direct methods do not cope very well with large frame-to-frame motions, because they obtain the pose by minimizing the photometric error.

Recently, odometry based on event-based cameras has been used in several SLAM algorithms. Since an event-based camera generates asynchronous events, obtaining the ego-motion, i.e., the 6-DoF motion, is a challenging problem. In [17], the authors propose an algorithm to estimate the rotational ego-motion and reconstruct intensity images based on captured events. In [18], a 2D SLAM system is presented to estimate the planar motion based on captured events. This is extended for 3D in [19] with the help of an extra RGB-D camera. In [20], the authors propose an approach to estimate the 3D rotation of the camera based on a particle filtering framework. In [21], the authors propose a VO system which first extracts features from intensity images and then tracks those features in events produced by an event-based camera. In [22], the authors present a system to estimate the motion and depth of a 3D scene, by reconstructing the image intensity based on captured events. Most of the mentioned techniques are computationally intensive due to high amount of processing needed to understand the events and process the additional data, especially in the cases where an extra frame-based camera is used.

3   System Architecture of the Proposed Framework

The overall system architecture of the proposed hybrid algorithm is shown in Fig. 4. The system consists of two main novel parts as explained earlier: (1) dynamic frame generation based on captured events and (2) feature extraction and tracking. For the rest of the algorithm we use conventional methods of 3D mapping component and pose optimization.

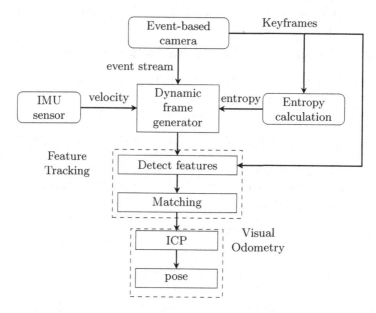

Fig. 4. A overall system architecture of the proposed framework for visual odometry

3.1   Dynamic Event-Based Frame Generation

As mentioned in the previous sections, generating a suitable frame highly depends on richness of information captured by a scene. To estimate this richness, we propose two metrics that are the velocity of the camera and the entropy of the pixelated image of the scene. Entropy or average information in a pixelated image is a common metric used in different vision applications, e.g., automatic image focusing, and can be determined approximately from the histogram of the image, where the histogram shows the different grayscale probabilities in the image. For example, in automatic image focusing, the state of a camera's focus can be determined by image entropy, i.e., whenever the focus state varies, so does its entropy [23]. Even though image entropy provides richness of a scene, in a moving object, the scene changes over time based on the velocity of the camera in ego-motion. Therefore, velocity is needed as additional information to model the change of entropy over time. This combination results in a suitable metric to estimate how many events are needed to construct a frame. To properly determine such a metric, the relationship of velocity and entropy on the number of events has to be discussed. To find such a relationship, we first show the relationship between the camera velocity and the number of events.

Definition 1: Let V and W be two vector spaces based on the same field F. linear map is a function $f : V \to W$ if for any two vectors u and v in V and any scalar $c \in F$ the following two conditions are always satisfied: $f(u + v) = f(u) + f(v)$ and $f(cu) = cf(u)$. The former condition is called additivity and the latter is called the operation of the scalar multiplication.

Based on this definition we can formulate the following lemma:

Lemma 1: In a pinhole camera with a projection matrix, the velocity of the 2D pixels associated to a constant object in 3D environment is the result of *linear map* of the camera velocity.

Proof: In a pin hole camera, a 3D point in the *world metric coordinate system* $X = [X, Y, Z, 1]^T$ can be mapped onto a 2D point in the *image pixel coordinate system* $x = [u, v, 1]^T$ by knowing the mathematical model of the camera, i.e., the intrinsic and extrinsic parameters of the camera[2]. If it is assumed that the origin of the world coordinates and camera projection are the same, and the Z axis of the camera, i.e., the principal axis, and the world coordinate lie on each other, then the point x is calculated as follows:

$$\begin{bmatrix} x_p \\ y_p \\ 1 \end{bmatrix} = \frac{1}{Z} \begin{bmatrix} f_u & \alpha_u & u_0 & 0 \\ 0 & f_v & v_0 & 0 \\ 0 & 0 & 1 & 0 \end{bmatrix} \begin{bmatrix} X \\ Y \\ Z \\ 1 \end{bmatrix} \tag{1}$$

where f_u and f_v are the focal length in the dimension of pixels, and u_0 and v_0 are the principle point. The parameter α is determined when the pixels are rectangular and is called the *skew factor* [24]. According to the formula of velocity, which is $v = dx/dt$, where x is the pose and t is the time, we get:

$$v_p = d \begin{bmatrix} x_p \\ y_p \\ 1 \end{bmatrix} / dt = \frac{1}{Z} \begin{bmatrix} f_u & \alpha_u & u_0 & 0 \\ 0 & f_v & v_0 & 0 \\ 0 & 0 & 1 & 0 \end{bmatrix} d \begin{bmatrix} X \\ Y \\ Z \\ 1 \end{bmatrix} / dt \tag{2}$$

---

[2] The points are represented by homogeneous vectors in projective geometry.

The above equation shows that the velocity of pixels in an image is a linear map of the velocity of the camera.

In an event-based camera, any variation in the pixels of an image causes an event. Such variation is caused by movement of pixels. Based on this and Lemma 1, it can be concluded that the number of events in an even-based camera has a relationship with the linear map of the velocity of the camera and can be modeled by the transformation matrix of the camera. In other words, to use the velocity as a parameter in the model, we need to consider the velocities of all the linear-mapped pixels. Based on this, we propose our metric value for the velocity, to be considered to determine the number of events in a frame, as follows:

$$\iint_{(x_p, y_p)} d \begin{bmatrix} x_p \\ y_p \\ 1 \end{bmatrix} / dt \, dx_p \, dy_p \tag{3}$$

which shows the average summation of all the velocities of the pixels in x and y directions.

Even though the number of events generated by an event-based camera has an relationship with the velocity of the camera, the velocity alone cannot provide us with a good metric to estimate a suitable number of the events in a frame. To understand this fact, let us imagine that the camera is moving very fast but in an empty area with a totally black scene. In such a case, regardless of the velocity of the camera, no data will be generated as an event. Based on this simple example, it can be concluded that another factor should be included in the estimation of the number of events in a frame. This factor highly depends on the amount of contrast a scene provides. Such contrast is directly connected to the amount of information a scene contains. The entropy $H(x)$ of a pixelated frame gives us a metric to measure the amount of information and is calculated as follows:

$$H(x) = -\sum_{i=1}^{n} p_i \log_2 p_i \tag{4}$$

where p denotes the occurrence probability of a given intensity and n is the number of pixels in the image.

Figure 5 shows the linear relationship between the number of high intensity pixels in a totally black image and entropy. As can be seen, by increasing the amount of contrast in an image, the entropy linearly increases. Our final metric to determine the number of events in a frame, is the product of the entropy and the result of Eq. 3, providing us a suitable method to estimate the number of events in a scene. It should be mentioned that usually event-based cameras provide also the pixelated normal image that can be used to calculate the entropy. Another important fact is that, calculating the entropy is not necessarily needed to generate each frame, and entropy estimation can be done in a longer epoch than frame reconstruction. As mentioned earlier, in this estimation, we assume

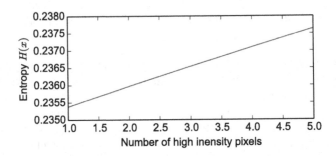

Fig. 5. Relationship between entropy and pixel intensity

for simplicity that all the objects in a scene are stationary and only the camera is moving.

In our proposed techniques in Fig. 4, we use an IMU sensor to estimate the velocity of the camera. IMUs typically consist of an accelerometer and gyroscope unit to obtain linear and angular acceleration at a high data rate, up to 5kHz. Three-axis accelerometer gets merged with the three-axis gyroscope to measure the sensor's angular rate and linear acceleration. In order to acquire the velocity of an object, the current orientation of the IMU is calculated by integrating the gyroscope output. Next, the obtained orientation of the IMU is used to construct a rotation matrix that will transform the accelerometer readings from the IMU "body frame" of reference to the "world frame" of reference. Finally, by integrating the transformed accelerometer output, the current speed of the IMU in the world frame is obtained. After determining the velocity of the camera, this velocity, accompanied by the camera parameters needed for estimating the velocity of pixels in different parts of the image, and the estimation of the image's entropy, are passed to the frame generation module to create a frame based on the estimated number of events.

3.2 Feature Extraction and Tracking

After reconstructing the frame based on the determined number of events, feature extraction and tracking for the captured events is performed. It should be noted that most event-based cameras provide also normal frames that can be used whenever needed. In our proposed algorithm, which is based on the DAVIS [25] event-based camera, we use features extracted from the normal frame-based output of the camera to initiate tracking in event-based frames. To detect features, we use FAST [7] due to its low computational cost and high performance as is shown in Fig. 3. We also use the Canny detector [26] to detect edges as other key features inside patches. To reduce the computational complexity of feature detection in normal frame-based images, the initialization process is performed infrequently (with a long interval), to correct potential errors that might happen in the feature tracking process on event-based frames.

We use Iterative Closest Point (ICP) algorithm [27] to minimize the distance between the edges and events as follow:

$$T_{k,k-1} = \arg \min_{T_{k,k-1}} \sum_{i=1}^{N} \frac{1}{2} \left\| e_i R + t - f_i \right\|^2 \tag{5}$$

where the set of edge features and events in patches are denoted by f_i and e_i, respectively. The Euclidean transformation $T_{k,k-1}$ is obtained which minimizes the distance between the edges points and event points in each detected corner. The operation of this algorithm consists of three main stages: (1) finding point correspondences according to the minimum Euclidean distance, (2) estimating the transformation matrix, and (3) applying the same process on the edge features. The algorithm converges when the error difference between two consecutive iterations is below a given threshold.

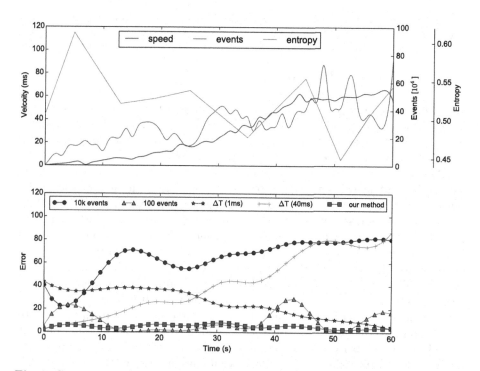

Fig. 6. Comparison of error for several odometry techniques based on an event-based camera. The instantaneous value of the number of detected events for the camera, entropy of the pixelated image of the scene, and velocity of the camera are also shown, used for analyzing the behavior of each technique w.r.t. the change in the environment setup

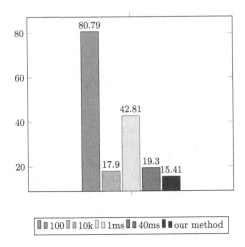

Fig. 7. The measured response time for different odometry techniques based on event-driven camera

4   Experimental Results

We evaluate the proposed event-based VO by running the algorithm considering several situations of the camera movement in normal, rapid, and slow motion. For this, we use the Event-Camera Dataset [28] which contains IMU measurements at 1kHz and many sequences captured with a DAVIS-240C camera. Kalman filtering (KF) is used to merge both accelerometer and gyroscope of noisy IMU data to obtain smooth and rather precise estimation of the acceleration. The camera can capture events and intensity images at the resolution of 240×180. In a normal motion scenario, the DAVIS camera generates up to 10^5 events per second. On the other hand, in rapid camera movements, it can generate up to 1.5 million events per second. The proposed algorithm is tested on a Jetson TX2 board with a quad-core ARM Cortex-A57 CPU @ 2GHz clock frequency.

Figure 6 shows a comparison of the obtained accuracy for different odometry techniques based on the event-based camera, including our method. The velocity of the camera, entropy, and the number of generated events are shown as separate synced graphs to demonstrate how the behavior of the camera and environment can affect the number of generated events and accuracy. In Fig. 7, the response times of the considered event-based VO techniques are depicted.

As can be seen, our proposed method outperforms the other techniques by obtaining the best accuracy, i.e., the smallest error, and the shortest response time. The technique with a large ΔT time to accumulate the events to be processed in a frame loses accuracy whenever the speed of the camera increases. On the other hand, the technique with a small ΔT provides better results when the speed of the camera is high, but for the low camera speeds the error is quite high. A similar analysis can be applied to the techniques that are based on the number of events. In these cases, since the number of events is strongly affected by the amount of information coming from the environment, together with the velocity of the camera, the effect of entropy can be clearly seen in the accuracy of the algorithms. The accuracy of the method with the fixed number of 10k events is not good, while for the technique with 100 events the accuracy is acceptable most of the time, decreasing only when entropy increases. Our proposed algorithm keeps the accuracy constantly high, because it is aware of the velocity of the camera and entropy of the environment simultaneously.

The other aspect to be discussed is the response time of the algorithm. As can be observed, the response times are quite high for the techniques with a small ΔT or $\#Events$. On the other hand, the techniques with a large ΔT or $\#Events$ can provide small response times, because their iterative processes take place in longer intervals, sacrificing the accuracy of the methods. The proposed technique, in turn, can keep the execution time at a reasonable level, making it suitable for different applications in which odometry is needed to be performed in real time.

5 Conclusion

In this paper, a hybrid technique was proposed to enable efficient odometry based on data captured by event-based cameras. The main contribution of the approach is its ability to flexibly change the number of events that are processed as a frame. To do this, we employed concepts of 3D projection and information theory to define a metric to dynamically determine the number of events that are considered for each frame. We used normal pixelated image data to extract the features in events and track those features in event-based frames. Experimental results show that the proposed hybrid method outperforms the traditional approaches that are based on considering either a fixed number of events per frame or a fixed time interval to accumulate the events. Our algorithm can operate efficiently and accurately in different environmental conditions and camera velocities.

References

1. Morevec, H.P.: Towards automatic visual obstacle avoidance. In: Proceedings of the 5th International Joint Conference on Artificial Intelligence, ser. IJCAI 1977, vol. 2, pp. 584–584 (1977)
2. Harris, C.G., Pike, J.M.: 3d positional integration from image sequences. In: Proceedings of Alvey Vision Conference, Cambridge, England (1987)
3. Triggs, B., McLauchlan, P.F., Hartley, R.I., Fitzgibbon, A.W.: Bundle adjustment - a modern synthesis. In: Proceedings of the International Workshop on Vision Algorithms: Theory and Practice, ser. ICCV 1999, pp. 298–372 (2000)
4. Lichtsteiner, P., Posch, C., Delbruck, T.: A 128×128 120 db 15μs latency asynchronous temporal contrast vision sensor. IEEE J. Solid-State Circ. **43**(2), 566–576 (2008)
5. Rebecq, H., Horstschaefer, T., Gallego, G., Scaramuzza, D.: EVO: a geometric approach to event-based 6-dof parallel tracking and mapping in real time. IEEE Robot. Autom. Lett. **2**(2), 593–600 (2017)

6. Shannon, C.E.: A mathematical theory of communication. Bell Syst. Tech. J. **27**(3), 379–423 (1948)

7. Rosten, E., Drummond, T.: Machine learning for high-speed corner detection. In: Leonardis, A., Bischof, H., Pinz, A. (eds.) ECCV 2006. LNCS, vol. 3951, pp. 430–443. Springer, Heidelberg (2006). https://doi.org/10.1007/11744023_34

8. Alzugaray, I., Chli, M.: Asynchronous corner detection and tracking for event cameras in real time. IEEE Robot. Autom. Lett. **3**(4), 3177–3184 (2018)

9. Mur-Artal, R., Montiel, J.M.M., Tardós, J.D.: ORB-SLAM: a versatile and accurate monocular SLAM system. CoRR (2015)

10. Klein, G., Murray, D.: Parallel tracking and mapping on a camera phone. In: Proceedings of Eigth IEEE and ACM International Symposium on Mixed and Augmented Reality (ISMAR 2009), Orlando, October 2009

11. Ranftl, R., Vineet, V., Chen, Q., Koltun, V.: Dense monocular depth estimation in complex dynamic scenes. In: 2016 IEEE Conference on Computer Vision and Pattern Recognition (CVPR), pp. 4058–4066, June 2016

12. Newcombe, R.A., Lovegrove, S.J., Davison, A.J.: Dtam: dense tracking and mapping in real-time. In: 2011 International Conference on Computer Vision, pp. 2320–2327, November 2011

13. Pizzoli, M., Forster, C., Scaramuzza, D.: REMODE: probabilistic, monocular dense reconstruction in real time. In: 2014 IEEE International Conference on Robotics and Automation, ICRA 2014, Hong Kong, China, 31 May - 7 June 2014, pp. 2609–2616 (2014)

14. Engel, J., Sturm, J., Cremers, D.: Semi-dense visual odometry for a monocular camera. In: 2013 IEEE International Conference on Computer Vision, pp. 1449–1456, December 2013

15. Forster, C., Pizzoli, M., Scaramuzza, D.: SVO: fast semi-direct monocular visual odometry. In: Proceedings - IEEE International Conference on Robotics and Automation, pp. 15–22 (2014)

16. Engel, J., Koltun, V., Cremers, D.: Direct sparse odometry. IEEE Trans. Pattern Anal. Mach. Intell. **40**(3), 611–625 (2018)

17. Cook, M., Gugelmann, L., Jug, F., Krautz, C., Steger, A.: Interacting maps for fast visual interpretation. In: The 2011 International Joint Conference on Neural Networks, pp. 770–776, July 2011

18. Weikersdorfer, D., Hoffmann, R., Conradt, J.: Simultaneous localization and mapping for event-based vision systems. In: Chen, M., Leibe, B., Neumann, B. (eds.) ICVS 2013. LNCS, vol. 7963, pp. 133–142. Springer, Heidelberg (2013). https://doi.org/10.1007/978-3-642-39402-7_14

19. Weikersdorfer, D., Adrian, D.B., Cremers, D., Conradt, J.: Event-based 3d SLAM with a depth-augmented dynamic vision sensor. In: 2014 IEEE International Conference on Robotics and Automation, ICRA 2014, Hong Kong, China, 31 May - 7 June 2014, pp. 359–364 (2014)

20. Kim, H., Handa, A., Benosman, R., Ieng, S.-H., Davison, A.: Simultaneous mosaicing and tracking with an event camera. In: Proceedings of the British Machine Vision Conference. BMVA Press (2014)

21. Kueng, B., Mueggler, E., Gallego, G., Scaramuzza, D.: Low-latency visual odometry using event-based feature tracks. In: 2016 IEEE/RSJ International Conference on Intelligent Robots and Systems, IROS 2016, Daejeon, South Korea, 9–14 October 2016, pp. 16–23 (2016)

22. Kim, H., Leutenegger, S., Davison, A.J.: Real-time 3d reconstruction and 6-dof tracking with an event camera. In: Computer Vision - ECCV 2016 - 14th European Conference, Proceedings, Part VI, Amsterdam, The Netherlands, 11–14 October 2016, pp. 349–364 (2016)

23. Thum, C.: Measurement of the entropy of an image with application to image focusing. Opt. Acta: Int. J. Opt. **31**(2), 203–211 (1984)

24. Grinberg, M.: Feature-based probabilistic data association for video-based multi-object tracking," Ph.D. dissertation, Karlsruhe Institute of Technology, Germany (2018)

25. Brandli, C., Berner, R., Yang, M., Liu, S., Delbruck, T.: A 240×180 130 db $3\mu s$ latency global shutter spatiotemporal vision sensor. IEEE J. Solid-State Circ. **49**(10), 2333–2341 (2014)

26. Canny, J.: A computational approach to edge detection. IEEE Trans. Pattern Anal. Mach. Intell. **PAMI–8**(6), 679–698 (1986)

27. Besl, P.J., McKay, N.D.: A method for registration of 3-d shapes. IEEE Trans. Pattern Anal. Mach. Intell. **14**(2), 239–256 (1992)

28. Mueggler, E., Rebecq, H., Gallego, G., Delbrück, T., Scaramuzza, D.: The event-camera dataset and simulator: Event-based data for pose estimation, visual odometry, and SLAM. Int. J. Robotics Res. **36**(2), 142–149 (2017)

Tracking and Classification of Aerial Objects

Marcia Baptista$^{(\boxtimes)}$, Luis Fernandes, and Paulo Chaves

INOV Inesc Inovacao, Lisbon, Portugal
{marcia.baptista,luis.fernandes,paulo.chaves}@inov.pt

Abstract. Unauthorized drone flying can prompt disruptions in critical facilities such as airports or railways. To prevent these situations, we propose a surveillance system that can sense malicious and/or illicit aerial targets. The idea is to track moving aerial objects using a static camera and when a tracked object is considered suspicious, the camera zooms in to take a snapshot of the target. This snapshot is then classified as an aircraft, drone, bird or cloud. In this work, we propose the classical technique of two-frame background subtraction to detect moving objects. We use the discrete Kalman filter to predict the location of each object and the Jonker-Volgenant algorithm to match objects between consecutive image frames. A deep residual network, trained with transfer learning, is used for image classification. The residual net ResNet-50 developed for the ILSVRC competition was retrained for this purpose. The performance of the system was evaluated with positive results in real-world conditions. The system was able to track multiple aerial objects with acceptable accuracy and the classification system also exhibited high performance.

Keywords: Object tracking · Deep learning · Residual networks

1 Introduction

Unmanned aerial vehicles (UAVs) come with numerous advantages. However, along with the positive aspects, drones present some undesirable characteristics, such as the possibility of a sudden crash, cyber attacks, and privacy issues, which could prevent the technology from developing at a faster pace in the short/mid-term. A major issue here is the safety of critical infrastructures such as airports, railways, and other transportation networks. As a response to the unauthorized and/or malicious use of drones, work has been done with the aim of protecting sensitive areas from the presence of drones [1]. One such technique consists in tracking drones within a given perimeter using a video surveillance system. Video surveillance systems work by generating alerts to the facility whenever the trajectory of a drone or other aerial object is considered suspicious. Companies such as the Nippon Electric Company [2] are already investing in the development of these systems. In this work, we propose to advance the state of the art in the field by evaluating, in real-world challenging conditions, a combination of automated vision algorithms and deep learning technologies that help detect the presence of intruding targets in prohibited airspace.

Our work is within the scope of the Advanced Low Flying Aircraft Detection and Tracking (ALFA) project, sponsored by Horizon2020, which builds on results from a

© ICST Institute for Computer Sciences, Social Informatics and Telecommunications Engineering 2020
Published by Springer Nature Switzerland AG 2020. All Rights Reserved
A. L. Martins et al. (Eds.): INTSYS 2019, LNICST 310, pp. 264–276, 2020.
https://doi.org/10.1007/978-3-030-38822-5_18

number of European Union (EU) sub-projects. The main goal of the project is the development of a system for real-time tracking, and classification of suspicious air targets. We are currently developing two modules in parallel: the tracking module and the classification module. The first module is responsible for object tracking. It collects images from the vision system and processes them using classical vision algorithms. The second module is responsible for object classification. Given a zoomed-in picture of an aerial target, it classifies the image as an aircraft, drone, bird or cloud. A deep learning pipeline is used for this purpose. The overall idea is that the tracking module should generate at each moment a list of items that are hypotheses for the presence of suspicious aerial objects. Hypotheses should be proven or disproven using the classification module. This should be done by zooming on the target, taking a snapshot and sending the image to the deep learning solution.

The remaining of this paper is organized as follows. Section 2 reviews related work. Section 3 introduces methods. Section 4 describes the datasets and experimental settings and Sect. 5 presents and discusses the results. Section 6 concludes the paper.

2 Related Work

2.1 Object Tracking

Typically, an object tracker consists of two steps (1) recognizing objects from the background, and (2) following the trajectory of the detected objects [3]. The first step is usually accomplished with motion tracking methods. In the second step, the objects detected are linked into trajectories (or tracks). When an object is detected in the current frame, the model tries to associate the observed item with an existing trajectory. This task of associating objects with trajectories is typically cast as an optimization problem. Classical deterministic approaches to this problem include dynamic programming, bipartite graph matching, min-cost max-flow network flow and conditional random fields [3]. A popular method here is the Hungarian method [4], which is able to solve the bipartite graph matching assignment problem in polynomial time, with complexity $O(n^3)$ where n is the number of trajectories. Despite its popularity, it has been shown that the Jonker–Volgenant solver [5] can obtain similar results to the Hungarian method in less time, considering both average and maximum time [6, 7]. The solver is reported to be ten times faster than a similar coding of the Hungarian code [8]. Probabilistic methods such as Kalman filter [9] and Particle filter [10] can also be utilized in tracking. Here, the state of each object is represented as a distribution with uncertainty. It is also common to find works such as [11, 12], that combine the Hungarian algorithm with Kalman filter in order to obtain a more robust tracking framework.

2.2 Object Classification

Recently, there has been an increased interest in the classification of aerial targets using deep convolutional neural networks (CNNs). Some studies have used standard CNNs to address this problem [13–15]. The advantage of these networks, compared to other more complex CNNs, is the optimized use of computational resources. In Aker et al. [14], a CNN was shown to distinguish between drones and birds with precision and recall values above 90%. Unlu et al. [13] reached detection percentages of 93.7% and 64.6%, for birds and drones respectively, with a CNN. The project SafeShore [16] proposed a "drone-vs-bird detection challenge" where the goal was to detect drones in a video where birds could also be present. The winner of the competition, Schumann et al. [15], reported 99.2%, 99.1% and 98.9% correct identification percentages for UAV, birds, and clutter (background) using a CNN.

Other works have applied more advanced CNNs [17, 18, 19]. Advanced CNNs have typically the disadvantage of being harder to tune and require more training data. To accelerate the training and improve performance, some works [17] use pre-trained models and transfer learning to build the image classification models. In Saqib et al. [17], birds and drones were classified using ZFNet, VGG16, and VGG_M_1024 (all with Faster-RCNN). Transfer learning was used to help the system converge faster and to deal with the sparse dataset used. The authors reported the best mean absolute precision (mAP) of 0.66 with VGG16. The work in Liu et al. [18] used YOLOv2 to distinguish between airplanes, helicopters, and drones with classification accuracies of 96.03%, 90.47%, and 52.13%. The authors did not report using transfer learning but mentioned the use of a comprehensive dataset of about 30,000 images. The work of Park et al. [19] compared six convolutional models in their ability to distinguish between 11 drone models, namely YOLOv2, SSD with MobileNet, SSD with Inception V2, R-FCN with Resnet 101, Faster-RCNN with Resnet 101, and Faster-RCNN with Inception Resnet. The authors reported an F-measure of 74.3% for the best model (Faster-RCNN with Inception Resnet). The authors did not mention the use of transfer learning but refer a dataset of 9,525 labeled drone images.

Despite the positive results, the previous works are, however, not totally adequate for airport or railway surveillance, as none of them is all-encompassing of the classes of birds, drones, aircraft, and clouds. Perhaps the most suitable work would be that of Schumann et al. [15], which distinguished between drones, birds, and clutter. However, Schumann et al. did not train the classifier to distinguish drones from aircraft as we do. Nevertheless, and especially in airport surveillance, it can be important to differentiate between small aircraft and drones as countermeasures can be quite different. In addition, the convolutional neural network used is standard and less advanced than our proposal. In addition, the authors report on a large dataset, with 3386 drones, 3500 bird, and 3500 background images, but only 10% of these data were used as the test set.

2.3   Contributions

In our previous work [20], in the same line of research, we used a tracker based on the Hungarian algorithm. In this work, we instead use the faster method of Jonker–Volgenant. Previously, the residual network ResNet-50 was trained and tested using images from the Internet. In this work, the network is the same but we train/evaluate it with photos acquired in real-world conditions.

3   Solution

This section describes how the overall problem of tracking and classifying aerial objects from a video stream was addressed. The proposed architecture is represented in Fig. 1. As shown, the solution consists in using classical computer vision for object tracking and deep learning for object classification. The idea is that when the tracking detects a suspicious aerial object a snapshot is taken by the camera and a deep convolutional model performs object classification using the zoomed-in image. The following sections describe the tracking and classification modules in more detail.

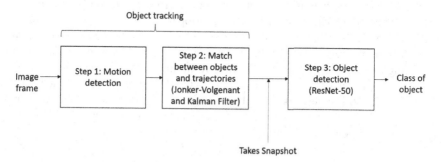

Fig. 1. The architecture proposed for tracking and classification of air targets.

3.1   Object Tracking

This section describes the methods used for locating and tracking one or more aerial objects in an input video. As shown in Fig. 1, the system receives at each moment a video frame and attempts to find relevant object observations (or detections). This is done by using a frame-difference motion detector that performs binary thresholding using a minimum and maximum threshold values (Thesh$_{Min}$ and Thresh$_{Max}$) [21]. The items detected are then dilated in order to optimize the probability of detecting well-defined targets. The dilating operation expands the found shapes, making them bigger according to a kernel (set to a 3x3 matrix) and a number of iterations (D$_I$). The outcome of this stage is a set of detections.

A multi-object tracking method based on the Jonker–Volgenant algorithm and Kalman filter is used to generate a set of reliable trajectories (or tracks) using previous information and detections in the current frame. The Kalman filter is used to help establish the tracking model, using the existing object information to predict future locations. At each moment, the filter estimates the object position and performs parameter correction. The Jonker–Volgenant algorithm is based on defining a cost matrix between tracks and detections and solving the nodes correspondence through a linear assignment method. The core of the Jonker–Volgenant algorithm is the shortest augmenting path traversal, as in the Hungarian solver, but it uses heuristics to reduce the execution time. The goal of the solver is to associate tracks with detections and also to start and remove tracks. A track is removed after a number of continuous frames are skipped (F_R) and an association is valid only if the Euclidean distance between the track and the observation is less than a certain threshold (D_V).

3.2 Object Classification

This section describes the methods used for classifying an aerial object after it is considered suspicious by the system. The deep learning model used here is a residual network. This is a state-of-the-art kind of convolutional neural network (CNN) that has achieved high classification performance on several datasets, such as ImageNet. The residual connections of residual networks make it possible to train deeper networks while reducing the probability of having overfitting problems. In addition, since these networks work by stacking modules of the same topology there is a reduced number of hyper-parameters. This simplicity also reduces the risk of overfitting. Transfer learning is used to train the residual network. Transfer learning has the advantage of reducing the training time of the neural network while resulting in a lower generalization error.

The residual network ResNet-50 was the network chosen to be retrained for our dataset. ResNet-50 is a network trained on a large set of images with 1000 categories. This training allows the network to detect generic features from images. Our re-training consisted of doing only small/simple weight adjustments in order to create the network for the intended classification. Prior to the re-training, it was necessary to remove the top layer of the ResNet-50, that considered the output of 1000 classes, and add a new layer with four outputs, one for each of the considered classes: aircraft, drone, bird, and clouds. The aircraft class contained both airplane and helicopter as well as military and civilian airplanes. The drone class included quadcopters, hexacopters, and octocopters. The output of the network was an array of classification probabilities.

4 Methodology

In this section, we present the methods and materials used to perform the evaluation of the system. We evaluate the system at two different stages: at the first stage we evaluate the tracking system and at the second stage we evaluate the deep learning pipeline for classification. This evaluation is done independently. In the following text, we describe the datasets used, the configuration of the tracking and deep learning solutions as well as the evaluation methods.

4.1 Datasets

From 24th to 28th of June 2019 a field experiment of the ALFA project took place in Cacela Velha, Portugal. The dates of the experiment were selected to guarantee good weather conditions. While different aerial targets were flying overhead (helicopter, light airplane, and drones), an off-the-shelf camera followed and recorded the moving objects. Some of these videos were collected and used in this study. Overall, they form dataset DS-1 and are further described in Table 1. In the scope of this paper, the goal of dataset DS-1 was to be used to evaluate the tracking capabilities of the system.

To evaluate the classification system we had three datasets: DS-2, DS-3, and DS-4. A total of 7763 images was collected from the Internet in order to be used to train the ResNet-50. This dataset, DS-2, consisted of images of aircraft, drones, birds, and clouds, where 2452, 2491, 2545 and 2758 were the number of images for each class, respectively. Some image examples are shown in Fig. 2. The aircraft class contained helicopters as well as military and civilian airplanes. The drones class included quadcopters, hexacopters, and octocopters. The images were cropped with the aim of having flying objects or birds against the sky. The images were resized to the proper input dimensions of the used neural networks. The number of images was augmented several times by generating new images from the original ones, which was done applying rotation, shift, shear, zoom, and flip.

Table 1. Description of videos in dataset DS-1 (videos to evaluate tracking).

Video	Description	Frames	Frames with target(s)
1	Video of a light airplane (Cessna 172)	4187	3069 (73.30%)
2	Video of a helicopter (Eurocopter AS355F1)	3225	3045 (94.42%)
3	Video of a quadcopter	5630	5530 (98.22%)

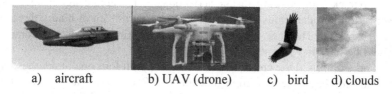

a)   aircraft   b) UAV (drone)   c)   bird   d) clouds

Fig. 2. Examples of images collected from the internet (DS-2) to train the classification system.

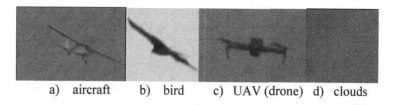

a)   aircraft   b)   bird   c) UAV (drone) d)   clouds

Fig. 3. Examples of images from dataset DS-4 used to evaluate the classification system

The images collected from the Internet had high quality (see Fig. 2). However, our previous tests indicated that zoomed-in images of aerial objects from the field do not have this same quality (please compare the images in Fig. 2 with Fig. 3). Accordingly, and in order to to make our ResNet-50 more capable of handling images collected from the field, a new dataset, DS-3, also based on the same set of internet images, was created. Here, besides rotation, shear, zoom, and flipping, the object shift was increased, the colors were randomly changed and Gaussian blur was added.

We did several field experiments to collect zoomed-in pictures of aerial objects. The purpose here was to test ResNet-50 in real-world conditions. The experiments took place in several different places of Portugal (Leiria, Nazaré) and Holland (Monster). This dataset, DS-4, was composed of 582 aircraft, 39 birds, 128 clouds and 1091 drone images. To obtain the testing images, the camera zoomed in on different objects and took a snapshot for posterior processing. The small number of bird images was increased by using 876 images from a work [22] where images were gathered in a wind farm and had relatively low quality due to capturing distant birds. Only images of birds with more than 40x40 pixels were used. This resulted in a total of 915 images with birds. Some examples of images from this dataset are shown in Fig. 3.

4.2   Configuration

The object tracking system was configured for each video in the dataset. Generally, in the implementation of the Kalman filter, we have set the process noise (Q) high (set to 10), compared to the measurement noise (R) which was set to 0.001. This allowed us to adapt more effectively to the sudden changes in the speed of the aerial objects. We also had to set the maximum Euclidean distance traveled ($D_V = 75, 200$ and 300) to a large value because the objects sometimes moved fast and traveled great distances from one frame to the other. By setting the number of dilating iterations (D_I) to 15, 30, and 40 we were able to track both close and distant aerial objects. To capture significative changes but disregard minor alterations we set the parameter $Thresh_{MIN}$ of binary thresholding to 30. The parameter $Thresh_{MAX}$ was set to 255. The maximum number of frames that a track could be idle (F_S) was set to 20 frames.

Our work comprised the creation of a ResNet-50 with four output neurons, one for each considered class. The activation function was Rectified linear unit (ReLU). The ResNet-50 had an input convolutional layer and max pooling, followed by 48 residual modules. In the end, there was a fully connected network. ResNet was trained with transfer learning. The software was implemented in KERAS (https://keras.io/) to run in graphical processing units (GPU). The training algorithm used was Stochastic gradient descent (SGD), the training error was measured by Categorical cross-entropy.

4.3   Evaluation Method

To perform an evaluation of the tracking system, we developed an automatic tool to help annotate video. All videos in dataset DS-1 were annotated with this tool by manually placing bounding boxes around aerial objects and interpolating their trajectories between keyframes. All objects were annotated, except in case of total occlusion. Each object of interest entering the scene got a unique ID, i.e. if a target left the screen to reappear later again, a new identifier would be assigned. Please note that bounding boxes were fairly aligned but not always perfectly aligned due to incorrect interpolation or mistakes made by the annotator.

To evaluate the tracking system we used the metrics referred in [23]. We chose this work because the authors define tracking performance in terms of tracks. The basis of the evaluation is the Intersection over Union (IoU) metric:

$$IoU_k = \frac{Area_{overlap}}{Area_{Union}} \tag{1}$$

Intersection over Union (IoU) for a given object in frame k is a ratio where the numerator is the area of overlap between the predicted bounding box and the ground-truth bounding box and the denominator is the area of union. We define the following binary variable based on a threshold Th_{IoU} which in our examples is set to 20%, as in [23]:

$$O_k = \begin{cases} 1, & IoU_k \geq Th_{IoU} \\ 0, & cc \end{cases} \tag{2}$$

The concept of IoU allows classifying tracks as true positive (TP), false positive (FP) or false negative (FN). Concretely, a ground truth track GT with N number of frames has been correctly detected if there exists at least one track T where:

$$\frac{\sum_{k=1}^{N} IoU_k(GT,T)O_k(GT,T)}{N} \geq Th_{spatial} \tag{3}$$

$$\frac{\sum_{k=1}^{N} O_k(GT,T)}{N} \geq Th_{temporal} \tag{4}$$

The previous conditions mean that coverage (in number of frames) should be larger than a predefined overlap threshold which we set to 15% ($Th_{temporal}$), as in [23]. We also impose that the system track has sufficient spatial overlap ($Th_{spatial}$) with the ground truth track, that is set to 20%, as in [23]. A ground truth track is considered to have not been detected correctly whenever conditions (3) or (4) do not hold for all system tracks. We also measure the number of ground truth track fragmentations (TF) as the number of system tracks that fulfill conditions (3) and (4) for a given ground truth track. For each of these system tracks, we calculate closeness of track (CT) for a given track and a ground truth track GT as the ratio of the sum of IoU over the number of frames where there is a temporal overlap. In a similar way, we compute the track matching error (TME) as the average distance error between a system track and a ground truth track GT. Distance is measured as the Euclidean distance between the centroids of the two tracks. Finally, we use the metric of track completeness (TC) and average track completeness as the:

$$TC = \frac{\sum_{k=1}^{N} O_k(GT,T)}{N} \tag{5}$$

$$TCM = \frac{\sum_{GT=1}^{N_{GT}} \max(TC(GT,T))}{N_{GT}} \tag{6}$$

In order to evaluate the classification capabilities of ResNet-50, three datasets were used for training (DS-2 and DS-3) and three datasets (DS-2, DS-3, and DS-4) were used for testing. Concretely, the dataset DS-2 was split into three sets for training, validation, and testing. The training set was used to adjust the network weights, while the validation set was used to select the best hyperparameters. The network performance was evaluated on the testing set in order to serve as a baseline. The split used for each class was 1000 images for training, 500 for validation and the remaining for the testing which resulted in a total of 4000, 2000 and 4246 images for training, validation, and testing, respectively. A similar procedure was used for dataset DS-3. Even though the testing sets of DS-2 and DS-3 were used for evaluating the models created, we also run tests using the data of DS-4, which consists of 582, 915, 128, and 1091 images of aircraft, birds, clouds, and drones, respectively. Here, we were interested in investigating how the models worked under real-world conditions.

To evaluate the ResNet-50 models we use the metric of recall, i.e. the number of items correctly identified as positive out of the total actual positives for a given class—TP/(TP+FN). We also compute the metric of precision, i.e. the number of items correctly identified as positive out of all instances where the algorithm declared the class—TP/(TP+FP). We analyze recall/precision for each class of interest. The macro-average F-Score is considered, i.e. the harmonic mean of the average recall and average precision.

5   Results

This section presents the results of evaluating the tracking system and evaluating the system classification methods. The goal here was to show that we can attain reasonable performance in a real-world scenario.

Table 2. Evaluation results for DS-1.

Video	Video 1	Video 2	Video 3
Correctly detected tracks (TP) (%)	83.33%	83.33%	100%
Incorrectly detected tracks (FN) (%)	16.67%	16.67%	0%
Average track fragmentations (TF)	1.17 ± 0.4	1.20 ± 0.4	1
Average of track closeness (CT) (%)	54.02 ± 18.8	54.03 ± 20.2	59.82 ± 16.1
Average track matching error (TME)	6.66 ± 3.7	18.44 ± 14.3	27.70 ± 9.6
Average track completeness (TC) (%)	66.63 ± 19.3	61.44 ± 30.0	55.23 ± 27.8

5.1   Tracking

We investigated the performance of the tracking system in each of the three videos of dataset DS-1. As shown in Table 2, the percentage of correctly detected tracks was consistently high. Almost all tracks were covered both spatially and temporally. In regards to tracking completeness, our results were also positive, showing that the ground truth tracks had considerable temporal overlap with their longest corresponding system tracks. Concretely, ground truth tracks were able to be covered by their longest system tracks by a considerable percentage – up to 55%. In regards to tracking closeness, the results were positive.

The track closeness was high, above 54%, meaning that the spatial coverage was on average reasonably good. It would be difficult to reach larger values in this respect. This can be explained by the fact that the bounding boxes annotated are usually larger than the bounding boxes detected, which results in low Intersection over Union (IoU) values. Moreover, the results in terms of track closeness suggest that detection by frame subtraction is a method not always robust to slow object movements or very rapid object movements. In the case of slow movement, only a small part of the object may be detected. In the case of rapid movement, the object detected may encompass the location of the object in the previous frame and in the current frame. More sophisticated object detection techniques could be used to improve the metrics of track closeness.

The metric of track matching error showed that the predicted trajectories and the real trajectories were consistently close. Please consider that the average Euclidean distances correspond to images with 1280×720 pixels. Accordingly, the TMEs obtained are considerably low, a promising result.

5.2   Classification

The results of evaluating the classification system are presented in Table 3. We were first interested in investigating the performance of the ResNet-50 trained with the original images from the Internet (dataset DS-2). When testing this ResNet-50 using the dataset of the images that the authors collected from the field (dataset DS-4), the F-1 score decreased significantly, from 98.7% to 73.5% compared to the same ResNet-50 tested on the DS-2 testing set. This was due to a decrease in both precision and recall. Concretely, the drone class decreased from a recall of 98.7%, with internet obtained images, down to 70.0%, with images from the field. The performance reduction was even more significative for the aircraft class, from 98.1% down to 45.5%. The bird class had the lowest F1-score of all the classes due to its very low precision (38.0%). This overall performance decrease was probably due to the lower quality of the images in the new test set (from dataset DS-4), namely the sky color not being from a vibrant blue and due to some blur that originated less defined shapes.

Table 3. Recall (R) (%), Precision (P) (%) and F-1 Score for different ResNet-50.

Net	Input Size	Data		Classes								F-1 Score
		Train Dataset	Testing Dataset	Aircraft		Birds		Clouds		Drones		
				R	P	R	P	R	P	R	P	
1	101×101	DS-2	DS-2	98.1	97.4	98.6	98.8	100	100	98.2	98.7	98.7
2	71×71	DS-3	DS-3	94.9	95.6	96.7	99.0	99.7	100	97.8	94.3	97.2
3	101×101	DS-2	DS-4	45.5	70.9	95.7	71.0	100	38.0	70.0	99.0	73.5
4	71×71	DS-3	DS-4	83.0	84.4	88.3	97.3	100	97.0	99.5	91.8	92.7

In order to try to make the ResNet-50 more capable of handling lower quality images, a new training set (from dataset DS-3), which consisted of internet images that were subject to blur, color change and object shift in addition to the operations of rotation, shear, zoom, and flipping, was used to make a new model. This new ResNet-50, had a high F1-score when tested on the same dataset. The F-1 score of 97.2% is comparable to the score of 98.8% obtained by the ResNet-50 trained and tested with only high-quality images from the internet (dataset DS-2). The small difference that we found is probably a consequence of the more demanding training set and also of decreasing the image sizes from 101×101 pixels to 71×71 pixels in order to limit the amount of memory necessary to create and use the datasets.

When the new ResNet-50, trained with data from dataset DS-3, was applied to the test set of images collected from the field, dataset DS-4, the F1-Score increased to 92.7%. This result suggests that this model is suitable to be used in real-world conditions. The model's recall of 83% for aircraft and 99.5% for drones is a significant improvement with respect to the previous figures of 45.5% and 70.0%, indicating that, as expected, training with different colors and blur brings robustness to classification.

6   Conclusions

The widespread use of amateur drones and other aircraft poses various safety, security and privacy threats. To address these challenges, drone surveillance is an important but not totally explored topic. In this paper, we were interested in evaluating in real-world conditions a tracking and classification system that targets drones, birds and other aircraft. This kind of methods can be integrated into surveillance systems used in airports or can be used to secure other intelligent transportation systems, such as railways or the metro network.

This paper comes from a line of work [20] in which we used a tracker based on the Hungarian algorithm and trained/evaluated a ResNet-50 for classification with images from the Internet. In this work, we use the Jonker–Volgenant for tracking and train the same network with photos acquired in real-world conditions. Our results are positive showing that we can attain reasonable performance in tracking and classifying multiple aerial targets.

As future work, we intend to improve the detection methods of close objects as we found out that by using movement subtraction to detect aerial objects we were not always able to fully detect the true boundaries of the object in the frame. Rapid and slow movements made the detection bounding box encompass both the previous and the next location of the object in the frame.

Acknowledgment. The "ALFA - Advanced Low Flying Aircrafts Detection and Tracking" project has received funding from the European Union's Horizon 2020 research and innovation programme under grant agreement No 700002.

References

1. Altawy, R., Youssef, A.M.: Security, privacy, and safety aspects of civilian drones: a survey. ACM Trans. Cyber-Phys. Syst. 1(2), 1–25 (2016)

2. "NEC's surveillance system will detect, track drones," PCWorld, 08-Oct-2015. https://www. pcworld.com/article/2990525/necs-surveillance-system-will-detect-track-drones.html. Accessed 03 Aug 2019

3. Luo, W., et al.: Multiple Object Tracking: A Literature Review, ArXiv14097618 Cs, Sep. 2014

4. Kuhn, H.W.: The Hungarian method for the assignment problem. Nav. Res. Logist. Q. **2**(1–2), 83–97 (1955)

5. Jonker, R., Volgenant, A.: A shortest augmenting path algorithm for dense and sparse linear assignment problems. Computing **38**(4), 325–340 (1987)

6. Serratosa, F.: Speeding up fast bipartite graph matching through a new cost matrix. Int. J. Pattern Recogn. Artif. Intell. **29**(02), 1550010 (2015)

7. Levedahl, M.: Performance comparison of 2D assignment algorithms for assigning truth objects to measured tracks. In: Signal and Data Processing of Small Targets 2000, vol. 4048, pp. 380–389 (2000)

8. Cao, Y.: LAPJV—Jonker-Volgenant algorithm for linear assignment problem, v3. 0. Mathworks File Exch. vol. 26836 (2013). http://www.mathworks.com/matlabcentral/fileexchange

9. Reid, D.: An algorithm for tracking multiple targets. IEEE Trans. Autom. Control **24**(6), 843–854 (1979)

10. Khan, Z., Balch, T., Dellaert, F.: An MCMC-based particle filter for tracking multiple interacting targets. In: Pajdla, T., Matas, J. (eds.) ECCV 2004. LNCS, vol. 3024, pp. 279–290. Springer, Heidelberg (2004). https://doi.org/10.1007/978-3-540-24673-2_23

11. Luetteke, F., Zhang, X., Franke, J.: Implementation of the Hungarian Method for object tracking on a camera monitored transportation system. In: ROBOTIK 2012, 7th German Conference on Robotics, pp. 1–6 (2012)

12. Sahbani, B., Adiprawita, W.: Kalman filter and iterative-Hungarian algorithm implementation for low complexity point tracking as part of fast multiple object tracking system. In: 2016 6th International Conference on System Engineering and Technology (ICSET), pp. 109–115 (2016)

13. Unlu, E., Zenou, E., Riviere, N.: Using shape descriptors for UAV detection. Electron. Imaging. **2018**(9), 128-1–128-5 (2018)

14. Aker, C., Kalkan, S.: Using Deep Networks for Drone Detection, *ArXiv170605726 Cs*, Jun. 2017

15. Schumann, A., Sommer, L., Klatte, J., Schuchert, T., Beyerer, J.: Deep cross-domain flying object classification for robust UAV detection. In: 2017 14th IEEE International Conference on Advanced Video and Signal Based Surveillance (AVSS), Lecce, Italy, pp. 1–6 (2017)

16. Coluccia, A. et al.: Drone-vs-bird detection challenge at IEEE AVSS2017. In: 2017 14th IEEE International Conference on Advanced Video and Signal Based Surveillance (AVSS), Lecce, Italy, pp. 1–6 (2017)

17. Saqib, M., Daud Khan, S., Sharma, N., Blumenstein, M.: A study on detecting drones using deep convolutional neural networks. In: 2017 14th IEEE International Conference on Advanced Video and Signal Based Surveillance (AVSS), Lecce, Italy, pp. 1–5 (2017)

18. Liu, H., Qu, F., Liu, Y., Zhao, W., Chen, Y.: A drone detection with aircraft classification based on a camera array. In: IOP Conference Series: Materials Science and Engineering, vol. 322, p. 052005, March 2018

19. Park, J., Kim, D.H., Shin, Y.S., Lee, S.: A comparison of convolutional object detectors for real-time drone tracking using a PTZ camera. In: presented at the 2017 17th International Conference on Control, Automation and Systems (ICCAS), pp. 696–699 (2017)

20. Fernandes, A., Baptista, M., Fernandes, L., Chaves, P.: Drone, aircraft and bird identification in video images using object tracking and residual neural networks. In: presented at the Electronics, Computers and Artificial Intelligence (ECAI), Pitesti, Romania (2019)
21. Singla, N.: Motion detection based on frame difference method. Int. J. Inf. Comput. Technol. 4(15), 1559–1565 (2014)
22. Image Dataset for Bird Detection. http://bird.nae-lab.org/dataset/. Accessed 04 Aug 2019
23. Yin, F., Makris, D., Velastin, S.A.: Performance evaluation of object tracking algorithms. In: presented at the IEEE International Workshop on Performance Evaluation of Tracking and Surveillance, Rio De Janeiro, Brazil, p. 25 (2007)

LiDAR SLAM Positioning Quality Evaluation in Urban Road Traffic

Franz Andert[✉] and Henning Mosebach

German Aerospace Center (DLR), Institute of Transportation Systems,
Berlin, Germany
franz.andert@dlr.de
https://www.dlr.de/ts

Abstract. This paper addresses the positioning quality of Simultaneous Localization And Mapping (SLAM) based on Light Detection and Ranging (LiDAR) sensors within urban road traffic. Based on the assumption of functional capability of existing SLAM implementations, the paper evaluates specific details of urban car drives that arise when SLAM is to be used for automatic car control. In the presented case, LiDAR-based positioning is done with the Google Cartographer software which generates real-time updates that are compared to GNSS reference. The evaluation is done by using own Light Detection And Ranging (LiDAR) sensor recordings from urban driving. Next to the overall GNSS-free path estimation, the paper zooms into some typical situations (e.g. waiting at busy intersection, driving curves) where SLAM might be inaccurate.

Keywords: GPS-free navigation · SLAM · LiDAR data processing

1 Introduction

Reliable positioning and navigation is essential for all kinds of automated vehicles. In outdoor applications, global navigation satellite systems (GNSS) are ubiquitous, however, positioning is subject to systematic errors of several meters, temporal loss due to signal interruption, reflections, or multi-path, and intentional disturbance. Low integrity is highly probable in the proximity of obstacles, e.g. when driving in urban areas. Despite the fact that there are high-quality GNSS receivers with included integrity monitoring [16], satellite-based or ground-based augmentation, multi-GNSS as combining GPS, Galileo, Glonass etc. [14], multi-antenna devices, and of course coupled navigation with inertial sensors [9], signal reception quality is still crucial. With regard to positioning performance requirements [6], automatic driving in urban canyons, car parks, or within dense traffic flow is a challenge with high demand on additional navigation technologies.

Parts of this work have been supported by the German Federal Ministry of Transport and Digital Infrastructure (BMVI) within the project *Cooperative Mobility in the Digital Test Area Düsseldorf* (KoMo:D), Grant Agreement No. 16AVF1006H.

A. L. Martins et al. (Eds.): INTSYS 2019, LNICST 310, pp. 277–291, 2020.
https://doi.org/10.1007/978-3-030-38822-5_19

Next to GNSS/INS, wheel odometry, visual lane detection, position matching to known maps, or adaptive cruise control based on distance sensing are common technologies used for automatic driving [2] and state-of-the-art for driving assistance functions [5]. However, not all cases are covered in terms of safety and reliability, preventing navigation being certified for highly automated or driverless use.

Another navigation approach is based on the idea of self-location relative to the environment using exteroceptive sensors as cameras or distance sensors and by re-finding previously measured features. In contrast to the above-mentioned techniques, arbitrary environment features can be used, i.e. there is no special need to rely on road markers, signs, or communication infrastructure. Being generally based on remote sensing ideas, the use for navigation arose in robotics. This class of technology comprises visual odometry, simultaneous localization and mapping (SLAM), or optical-aided navigation, depending on the used algorithm and special application. One advantage is that neither a-priori knowledge about the environment nor satellite positioning are required, however it can be combined to that. Typical applications are focused on mapping/exploration or on positioning/navigation; and they are various: from indoor-capable vehicle or robot navigation [18], augmented reality [12], micro air vehicles [8], and last but not least automatic car driving [13]. As a background technology, SLAM can be considered as state-of-the-art including its known shortcomings (especially position error accumulation and dependency on remarkable stationary objects), however reliable use to control a car in dynamic traffic has to be proven.

2   Towards SLAM Navigation in Urban Traffic

From its origins in robotics [3], SLAM found its way into automatic driving research as one of the navigation technologies to complement GNSS. A recent survey can be found in [1]. Together with research results, gigabytes of (raw) data are nowadays publicly available, and they are widely used for further algorithm development, optimization, and benchmarking. Next to a variety of camera data listed e.g. in [17], the popular KITTI dataset [7] as well as the Udacity dataset [4] provide LiDAR data which can be used to test the presented type of SLAM. While standard benchmarks are highly effective for evaluation of perception algorithms, they typically do not allow evaluation of closed-loop systems. Therefore, it was chosen to generate own data in this paper. In contrast to the majority of other papers in this field, no new algorithm (or an optimization of an existing one) will be presented, and the paper is not aimed at the reduction of the total position error e.g. at the end of the test drive. Instead, typical problems that arise within the drive are picked and discussed with an eye on the use for vehicle control. The evaluation data comes from urban driving tests with four LiDARs on a car (Fig. 1) driven through city traffic.

Fig. 1. Testing vehicle: Volkswagen e-Golf operated by DLR.

3   Experimental Setup

3.1   Vehicle and Sensors

Testing vehicle is an electric powered Volkswagen Golf operated by DLR's Institute of Transportation Systems. As other vehicles from the institute's fleet [11], it includes some modifications for experimental and user-defined vehicle automation and control. The modular and exchangeable equipment comprises multiple environment sensors (LiDAR, cameras, RADAR) GPS/INS with RTK capability, on-board computers for data logging, real-time data processing and vehicle control as well as various communication interfaces (WiFi, cellular, ITS-G5). Details of the sensor processing hardware are listed in Table 1.

Table 1. Details of the sensor data processing computer.

Type	Vecow ECX-1200 embedded PC
CPU	Intel Core i7-8700T, 2.4 GHz
GPU	NVidia GTX 1050 Ti, 4 GB RAM
RAM	8 GB, DDR4-2133
Hard drive	512 GB, SSD
Interfaces	6x GigE LAN, 4x RS-232/422/485, GPIO, etc.
Operating system	Ubuntu 16.04 LTS, ROS kinetic

The current testbed design considers integration into future off-the-shelf vehicles such that e.g. roof sensor racks are not used. Relevant sensors are four LiDAR sensors (see Table 2), mounted as shown in Fig. 2 so that almost a full 360° horizontal field of view is achieved. Multi-sensor integration includes extrinsic calibration and time synchronization so that data is aligned.

Table 2. LiDAR sensor specification.

Type	ibeo LUX 4L
Field of view	$110° \times 3.2°$, 4 horizontal scan lines
Range	>50 m
Range accuracy	0.1 m (range independent)
Frame rate	25 Hz

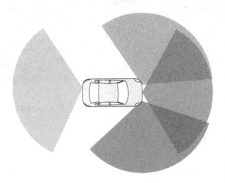

Fig. 2. LiDAR sensor setup: three at front, one at back.

As ground truth reference for SLAM evaluation, satellite navigation data is recorded together with LiDAR data during the driving tests. The device used is a NovAtel SPAN solution with RTK capability and included GPS/INS navigation filter which returns 100 Hz pose updates.

3.2 Sensor Data Processing

The major processes run within the Robot Operating System [15] including sensor drivers and data logging. As one of the components, SLAM is performed by Google Cartographer software [10]. This application can combine multiple laser range finders and is capable of generating map and pose updates in real-time. In this context, pose output (position x, y and heading ψ) is of main interest for the navigation purpose discussed in this paper. The general processing architecture is shown in Fig. 3.

The LiDAR driver returns sensor raw data which consists of a point cloud for every sensor, and multiple LiDAR point clouds are merged to scan frames for every time step. They can be optionally aligned by use of inertial data. Local matching performs registration between the scan frames and data fusion into a map, i.e. an occupancy grid. As the SLAM software is capable of matching local sub-maps into larger maps which are globally consistent (i.e. loop closure), it can optionally create globally consistent trajectory output at cost of trajectory smoothness. This is naturally only possible when previously mapped areas are entered again.

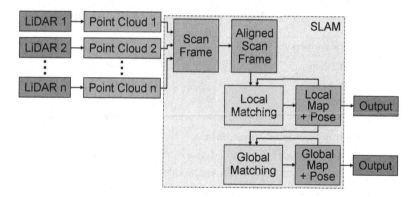

Fig. 3. Simplified SLAM architecture.

3.3 Testing Methodology

To evaluate different SLAM settings with comparable input, SLAM is executed in post-processing using sensor raw data recorded during test drives. Both data recording and SLAM are processed on on-board hardware (Table 1) and with real-time data playback so that the test comes close to live execution with regard to frame rates, timing issues, and possible frame drops. Some SLAM parameters are tuned to achieve good results, however the parameter choice is tested on different input sequences to be generally usable for the presented vehicle setup. The major parameters with non-default values are listed in Table 3.

The setup uses Cartographer's 2D map and trajectory builder with only LiDAR point cloud inputs, and without inertial or odometry data such that raw SLAM behavior will be evaluated. In the beginning, the map is empty, meaning unknown occupancy. The vehicle pose is initialized with $(x, y, \psi) = (0, 0, 0)$. At this point, true heading is close to but not exactly north. The map is empty, meaning unknown occupancy. For ground truth comparison, GPS/INS poses are transformed into the local coordinate system.

4 Driving Test

Data recording is performed during a 10-minute drive in the city center of Düsseldorf, Germany. The ride goes over two laps around a rectangular city block with close start and ending points. Figure 4 shows the mapping progress as a part of SLAM to re-calculate the vehicle's trajectory. The pictures show snapshots at different points of the drive, visualizing how the map is filled with obstacle boundaries (black) and free space (white) from the LiDAR point clouds.

5 Data Evaluation

With the used onboard computer, processing of 25 Hz LiDAR data is completely real-time capable. At default grid map resolution of 25 cm, typical delays of

Table 3. Trajectory builder parameters within Cartographer.

Software version	Release 1.0.0
min_range	1.0 m
max_range	40 m
min_z	−1.0 m
max_z	5.0 m
num_accumulated_range_data	4
ceres_scan_matcher.occupied_space_weight	2.0
ceres_scan_matcher.translation_weight	10.0
ceres_scan_matcher.rotation_weight	15.0
motion_filter.max_distance_meters	1.0 m
motion_filter.max_angle_radians	0.2 deg
submaps.resolution	0.25 m
range_data_inserter.hit_probability	0.58
range_data_inserter.miss_probability	0.48

about 5–10 ms (except jitter outliers) between LiDAR input and pose output are observed, which may allow even higher frame rates. Hence, there is much reserve for the use of higher grid resolution (see Sect. 5.3), more environment sensing, or filtering methods, e.g. integration of inertial and wheel sensors. In the next subsections, pose estimation results based on the driving test are presented.

5.1   Whole Trajectory

Figure 5 shows a top view of the SLAM-based position estimation. The used metric coordinates are related to UTM grid coordinates and thus slightly rotated to the illustration in Fig. 4. Together with Fig. 6 providing position and heading estimation over time, the plots show the two laps around the city block, one calculated with enabled SLAM loop closure, and one calculated without. Error accumulates as expected when using SLAM without any GNSS or external map hints. It can be seen that loop closure has no effect until the end of the first full circle, which is also expectable since no previously mapped areas are present until then. At the end of the sequence, SLAM accumulates a position error of about 4 m with loop closure, and 14 m without. With a total path length of about 1300 m, this equals ≈1% error compared to the distance driven. The plots do also show the typical problems of GNSS in the proximity of obstacles. There are immediate jumps of up to 3 m, which is obviously not the true driving trajectory.

5.2   Selected Data Snapshots

Now, specific driving situations are of interest. Beginning with the sequence start, and thus, the sometimes critical SLAM initialization phase, Fig. 7 compares easting of GPS and SLAM over time. At this point, no special problems are detected, i.e. error accumulation is present but as expected, and no time delays can be observed.

Next point of interest is the standing car after driving some meters. Figures 8 and 9 show easting and heading where the values should be truly constant (vibrations are supposedly very low because of electrical engine). Here, some differences are visible: The GPS/INS easting coordinate (and also northing not shown) is affected by GPS-typical jumps and secondly updates, being even less stationary than the SLAM coordinate which is only noisy. The visible 5 cm variation is about 1/5 of the grid resolution of 25 cm. In contrast to that, GPS/INS heading tends to be very stable, while SLAM is downgraded by a 0.5° noise.

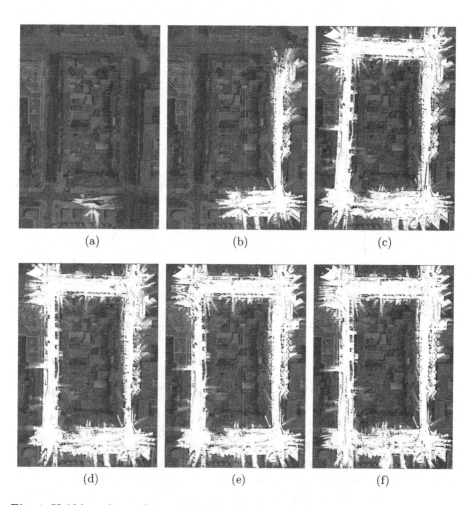

(a)   (b)   (c)

(d)   (e)   (f)

Fig. 4. SLAM results on drive within Düsseldorf city. Occupancy map, vehicle position (+), LiDAR scans (colors as in Fig. 2): (a) starting position, (b) second corner, (c) before and (d) after first loop closure, (e) re-finding corner example, (f) end of drive. Background image: GeoBasis-DE/BKG (2009), Google.

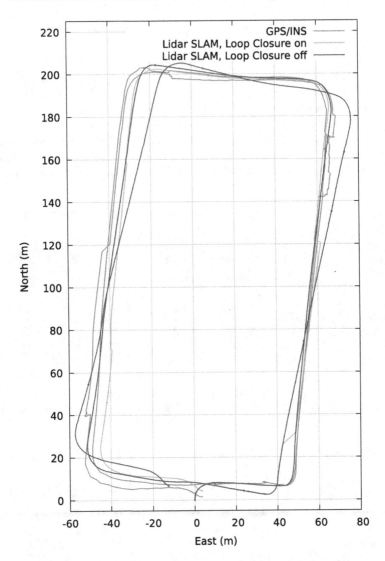

Fig. 5. Trajectories, local xy-view, Düsseldorf dataset.

Zooming out (Fig. 10) shows a wider view of this driving phase where the car waits at an intersection. Although several moving cars are in the sensors' field of view, being mapped and replaced by free space again, suitable positioning is achieved. The GPS position jump at 112 s might be the larger issue here.

At a later turn, the car does not have to stop at the intersection. As visible in Figs. 11 and 12, the curvature is reconstructed within SLAM, however there are already some absolute errors accumulated.

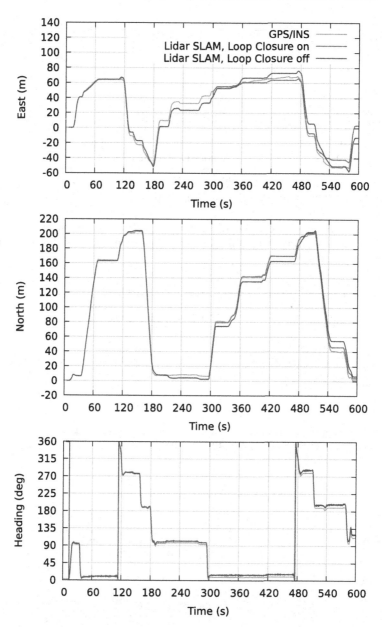

Fig. 6. Time plots, Düsseldorf dataset.

Finally, this evaluation takes a closer look at two specific points. The first is the point of first global correction (loop closure) at around 301 s from the beginning. Figure 13 shows exemplary the easting coordinate correction towards GPS/INS ground truth. Northing and heading are corrected in a similar way. A

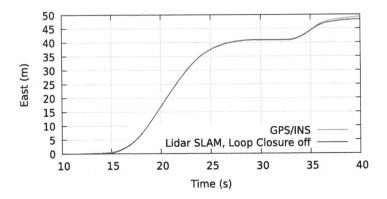

Fig. 7. Start of drive, east coordinate. (Before loop closure takes effect, SLAM with loop closure *on* is equivalent to SLAM with loop closure *off*, thus this graph is not shown in the particular figures.)

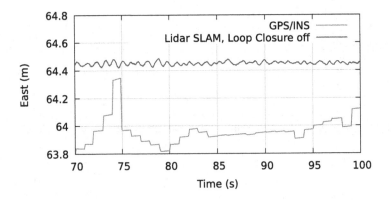

Fig. 8. Standstill, east coordinate.

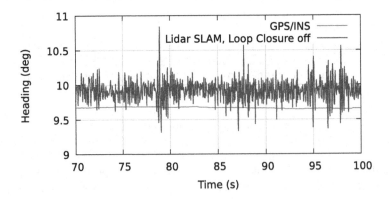

Fig. 9. Standstill, heading coordinate.

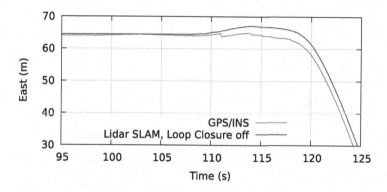

Fig. 10. Intersection waiting and curve, east coordinate.

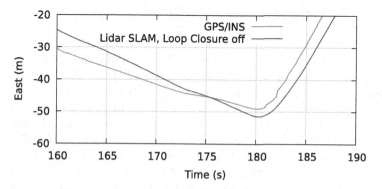

Fig. 11. Driving curve, east coordinate.

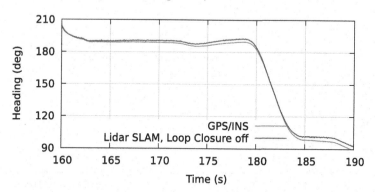

Fig. 12. Driving curve, heading coordinate.

jump of around 10 m is however critical when being used for control algorithms. Since the second lap begins now with driving within an already mapped area, later global corrections apply, too. Since they do not mark a loop closure in such a manner, the consequent position jumps are much smaller.

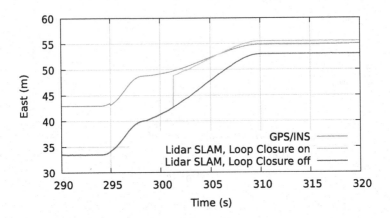

Fig. 13. Loop closure point, east coordinate.

The last close view is again more in the beginning of the data sequence where the car is standing while waiting at an intersection. The point of interest is timing at a very detailed zoom shown in Fig. 14. Ground truth data is available as specified: at 100 Hz without remarkable jitter. If the computer is fast enough, this specific SLAM implementation provides updates as fast as possible (which are also up to 100 Hz here). To provide meaningful information, only SLAM-based positions with new LiDAR data included are plotted. The 25 Hz updates are then visible in the plot, however some jitter is shown. Altogether, this seems to be very good and suitable for control inputs when the raw local SLAM output without loop closure is used.

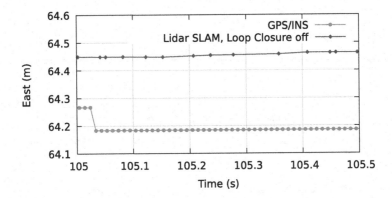

Fig. 14. Single data frames, east coordinate.

5.3   Different SLAM Settings

As listed in Table 3, all the above calculations are based on a grid resolution of 25 cm. This is one major parameter to increase or decrease depending on the available computation power. To test the effects, SLAM was run again with grid resolutions of 10 cm and 50 cm. The main result is generally comparable mapping and localization, as expected with increased or decreased accuracy. Processing time correlates quadratic with grid resolution (i.e. linear with number of grid cells). With the used hardware, real-time processing and loop closure are achieved in all cases. Major difference seems to be local positioning uncertainty, visible as noise at standstill. The plots in Figs. 15 and 16 extend the previous plots (Figs. 8/9). They show an effect on translational and rotational noise with somehow linear correlation to grid resolution. Further, total position and heading error accumulation is also lower at higher grid resolutions.

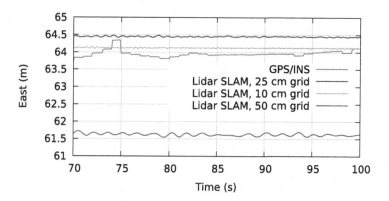

Fig. 15. Standstill, east coordinate. Extension of Fig. 8 with different grid resolutions.

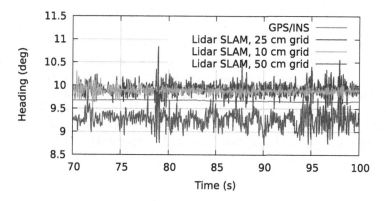

Fig. 16. Standstill, heading coordinate. Extension of Fig. 9 with different grid resolutions.

5.4 Other Datasets

To prove reproducibility, a different dataset is evaluated. Figure 17 shows the SLAM trajectory estimation result from a ride with the same car and sensor configuration around the Automotive Campus in Helmond, Netherlands. Parameters are equal as above, with a grid resolution of 25 cm.

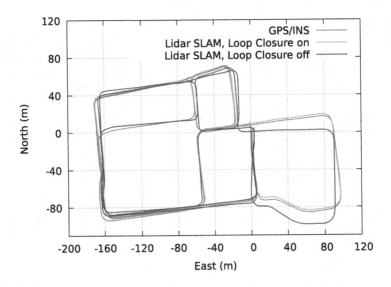

Fig. 17. Trajectories, local xy-view, Helmond dataset.

6 Conclusion and Future Work

In situations where satellite positioning and also techniques as lane detection and map matching are subject to fail, SLAM can be a reasonable complement towards safe vehicle navigation. This paper has a special focus on noise to and robustness in urban car driving, and it can be shown that up-to-date SLAM software is capable of finding its way in dynamic road traffic situations. Future work will investigate situations where SLAM is subject to fail without any optimizations or intelligent switching between different techniques. For example, stationary objects that start to move (e.g. congestion) might disturb the map and thus localization if their amount is too high. Other work will focus on specific applications, e.g. automated valet parking at very close distances when there is no need to open doors anymore.

References

1. Bresson, G., Alyased, Z., Yu, L., Glaser, S.: Simultaneous localization and mapping: a survey of current trends in autonomous driving. IEEE Trans. Intell. Veh. **2**(3), 194–220 (2017)

2. Urmson, C., et al.: Autonomous driving in urban environments: boss and the urban challenge. J. Field Robot. **25**(8), 425–466 (2008)
3. Durrant-Whyte, H., Bailey, T.: Simultaneous localization and mapping: part I. IEEE Robot. Autom. Mag. **2**(13), 99–110 (2006)
4. Gonzalez, E., Higgins, M., Cameron, O., et al.: The udacity open source self-driving car project (2016). https://github.com/udacity/self-driving-car
5. European global navigation satellite systems agency: report on road user needs and requirements - outcome of the European GNSS' user consultation platform. Tech. rep. GSA-MKD-RD-UREQ-233537 (2018)
6. European telecommunications standards institute: satellite earth stations and systems (SES); GNSS based location systems; part 3: performance requirements. Tech. rep. ETSI TS 103 246-3 (V1.1.1) (2015)
7. Geiger, A., Lenz, P., Stiller, C., Urtasun, R.: Vision meets robotics: the KITTI dataset. Int. J. Robot. Res. (IJRR) **32**(11), 1231–1237 (2013). http://www.cvlibs.net/datasets/kitti
8. Hening, S., Ippolito, C., Krishnakumar, K., Stepanyan, V., Teodorescu, M.: 3D LiDAR SLAM integration with GPS/INS for UAVs in urban GPS-degraded environments. In: AIAA SciTech Forum (2007)
9. Henkel, P., Sperl, A.: Precise RTK positioning with GPS/INS tight coupling and multipath estimation. In: International Technical Meeting of the Institute of Navigation, pp. 1015–1023 (2016)
10. Hess, W., Kohler, D., Rapp, H., Andor, D.: Real-time loop closure in 2D LiDAR SLAM. In: IEEE International Conference on Robotics and Automation, pp. 1271–1278 (2016). https://github.com/googlecartographer
11. Kaschwich, C., Wölfel, L.: Experimental vehicles FASCar-II and FASCar-E. J. Large-Scale Res. Facil. **3**, 111 (2017)
12. Klein, G., Murray, D.: Parallel tracking and mapping for small AR workspaces. In: International Symposium on Mixed and Augmented Reality (2007)
13. Levinson, J., Thrun, S.: Robust vehicle localization in urban environments using probabilistic maps. In: IEEE International Conference on Robotics and Automation, pp. 4372–4378 (2010)
14. Li, X., Zhang, X., Ren, X., Fritsche, M., Wickert, J., Schuh, H.: Precise positioning with current multi-constellation global navigation satellite systems: GPS, GLONASS, Galileo and BeiDou. Sci. Rep. **5**, 8328 (2015)
15. Quigley, M., et al.: ROS: an open-source robot operating system. In: ICRA Workshop on Open Source Software (2009). www.ros.org
16. Wang, J., Ober, P.B.: On the availability of fault detection and exclusion in GNSS receiver autonomous integrity monitoring. J. Navig. **62**, 251–261 (2009)
17. Yin, H., Berger, C.: When to use what data set for your self-driving car algorithm: an overview of publicly available driving datasets. In: IEEE International Conference on Intelligent Transportation Systems (2017)
18. Zhang, J., Singh, S.: LOAM: lidar odometry and mapping in real-time. In: Robotics: Science and Systems Conference (2014)

DORA: An Experimental Platform for Smart Cities

Vivek Prakash Nigam[1(✉)], Antero Kutvonen[1], Benjamin Molina[2],
Patricia Bellver Muñoz[3], and Jan-Niklas Willing[4]

[1] Lappenranta University of Technology,
Skinnarilankatu 34, 53850 Lappeenranta, Finland
vivek.nigam@lut.fi
[2] Universitat Politecnica de Valencia,
Camino de Vera, s/n, 46022 Valencia, Spain
[3] ETRA Investigacion y Desarrollo SA,
Tres Forques 147, 46014 Valencia, Spain
[4] VMZ Berlin Betreibergesellschaft mbH,
Ullsteinstraße 114, 12109 Berlin, Germany

Abstract (LUT). DORA (Door-to-Door Information for Airports and Airlines) is a mobility platform that aims to seamlessly integrate the real-time multimodal information flows for air mobility from airports, airlines, and regional transport. The main goal is to optimise the total travel time of air-passengers encompassing navigation from the point of origin to the departure airport, navigation within airports and finally navigation to the final destination. DORA offers a unified solution by assimilating scheduled and real-time services of all flights, terminal events (departure gates, luggage-belt, security gate), and regional transport modes. The mobility platform uses the assimilated information to assist in a door-to-door journey planning, to book or purchase tickets for regional transport of cities, and to monitor the trip in real-time. This paper presents the DORA platform and modules that enabling the concept of smart city.

Keywords: Experimental platform · Air passengers · Airports · Airlines · Public transport · Multimodal transport · Indoor navigation · Trip monitoring

1 Introduction

Since the early 90s, the concept of smart cities has been considered as the future of urban development [1]. A smart city is modelled from different perspectives and often debated for a widely accepted definition. The most eminent and frequently deliberated features are networked infrastructure, business driven development, social inclusiveness and a focus on the natural environment [2]. Urban mobility is connected to all four of these features and is gaining attention from industry, policymakers and scholars. Therefore, the technological mobility solutions with profitable potential are justifiable [3]. With economic and technological developments, air mobility has expanded and reached considerable population in developed countries. The European air mobility plays an essential role in linking people, exchanges for business, leisure and culture

© ICST Institute for Computer Sciences, Social Informatics and Telecommunications Engineering 2020
Published by Springer Nature Switzerland AG 2020. All Rights Reserved
A. L. Martins et al. (Eds.): INTSYS 2019, LNICST 310, pp. 292–302, 2020.
https://doi.org/10.1007/978-3-030-38822-5_20

within Europe and worldwide. The EU has 918 million air passengers in 2015, a growth of 4.7% from 2014 [4]. Air travellers spend considerable time in gathering information from assorted sources such as transport options and schedules between city and airport, airport navigation maps, and ticketing to commence the journey. The solution to minimize the efforts and time of air travellers is investigated through the DORA project and presented in this research paper.

The project aims to develop a seamless multimodal mobility information system that helps in optimising the total travel time of air passengers starting from point of origin to departure airport and from arrival airport to the final journey's endpoint. It includes not only the outdoor part of the trip but also the indoor part in airports. To reduce the total travel time of an average European traveller, DORA innately combines information on flights, all available modes of cities' transport and provides optimized routing and navigation to and inside airports directly to passengers' handheld devices. Moreover, the DORA platform has capabilities to integrate real time information from airports (flight information: departure and arrival times, gate information; security check queues, etc.) and ground transport system (incidents and delays on route, rerouting) to ensure timely arrival of air passengers on departure gates. To support the objectives of time optimisation within airports, the DORA platform provides technologies and services to ascertain waiting times at security check queues and estimate indoor location for use in indoor navigation (Fig. 1).

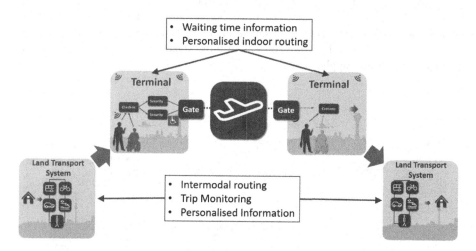

Fig. 1. DORA functionality schematic

The DORA system is under implementation between the respective airports of Berlin (TXL, SXF) and Palma de Mallorca (PMI) and real tests are envisioned to start in September 2017. The DORA platform architecture has been developed using widely adopted information technology standards to promote future expansion or third party integrations through open Application Programming Interfaces (APIs).

2 DORA Platform

The DORA platform is the central system layer integrating the different mobility data and services in order to provide those to the DORA end-user applications. With its open platform approach DORA is easily transferable to other cities and airports, and supports a straightforward integration of all transport modes and local urban mobility services such as public transport, car- and bike-sharing, taxis, charging infrastructure, ticketing, car rentals or parking facilities over the open DORA interface. The open platform is non-discriminatory as well as provider-independent and can due to its transparent and multimodal approach be harmonized with the transport strategies of cities.

All local urban mobility information and services in the both project test sites Berlin and Palma de Mallorca have been integrated and bundled in the DORA city nodes, which provide the landside mobility information for the overall door-to-door system. In this process, the transferability of the data integration approach has been successfully demonstrated in both test sites. To make all mobility information and routing services consistently available for the DORA door-to-door trip planning system, a DORA API has been specified which allows accessing all services and data sources in a common format. All cities can join and benefit from the DORA community by providing local mobility information in the defined API format.

Based on this API a DORA marketplace has been set up which will enable third parties (e.g. public transport authorities, travel portals, airports, airlines, etc.) to use the entire DORA system or single components of it for their own mobility information strategies. The DORA architecture consists of three layers: local city nodes, a service platform and end-user applications.

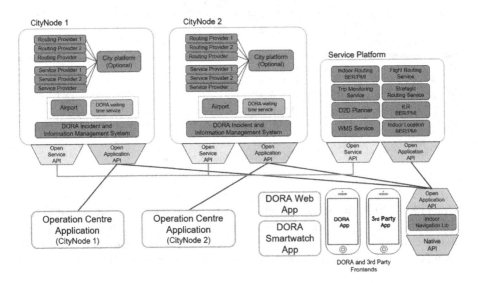

Fig. 2. DORA system architecture

The DORA service platform contains all central, not test site specific DORA services, that contribute to the route calculation, information and monitoring. Unlike the City Nodes, the DORA service platform can be located in a cloud environment since it is independent from local infrastructure and hardware. Figure 2 shows the City Nodes, the service platform as well as the end-user applications, and how they are interrelated. The service platform is connected to the City Nodes via the DORA Open Service API. Through this interface, the central platform services receive the local data and services required for the door-to-door route calculation and information from the City Nodes. The indoor router and the landside router, for instance, receive the required waiting time detection data and the local mobility information respectively via the Open Service API.

Different applications will be connected to the system. These include a Web-GUI, mobile applications as well as an Operation Centre Application. All applications, both internal and third party applications, communicate with the service platform and the City Nodes over the Open Application API. This interface is especially designed to meet the requirements that applications have regarding communication processes. Over this API to the DORA service platform the applications request and receive the central door-to-door information provided by the Door-to-Door Journey Planner. From the City Nodes the applications receive, for instance, detailed information on specific POIs of a route, for example on relevant car-sharing vehicles or parking facilities.

The DORA Open Protocols (Service API and Application API) developed within the project will enable easy integration of additional City Nodes into the DORA system and of DORA services into third-party applications. They will provide a state of the art open data exchange format for mobility services and applications.

2.1   Outdoor Module

Mobility outdoors is mainly handled by two Central Service components: (i) Intermodal Landsite Router for the intermodal landside part and (ii) Flight Routing Service for the flight part. Multimodality is probably the most relevant and challenging feature for the outdoor part of a trip, as there are many different ways (e.g. public or private transport) to get from one intermediate place to another. However, at the same time it is also a driven factor for potential business cases.

The mobility options of a city are included in the landside routing features covering all available transport modes, such as Car, Car sharing, Public Transportation, Walking and Bike. Regarding data for the road network, the entire routing system in general and the specific local modal routers in particular, are provided with intended and real time traffic situation as well as planned events and construction sites. This is realized in both DORA test sites and no manual data handling was necessary for adapting them to the Door-to-Door Routing. In addition, the local modal routers will use unforeseen accidents and other not plannable real time events as well. That means all plannable and unforeseen real time events are covered in DORA. With regard to the public transport network, the same granularity has been used for Berlin and Palma de Mallorca. With regard to the modern, flexible mobility options, listed below:

- Station based bike sharing service
- Free-floating vehicle sharing service
- Free-floating other sharing service.

The real departures and arrivals of the flights in combination with actual terminal and gate information are available just 48 h (Palma airport) and 24 h (Berlin airports) in advance. The Flight Routing Service uses the data provided by the local Departure and Arrival Services from the airports in both test sites. The situation looks different if the Flight Routing Service is requested earlier in advance than mentioned. In that case, the accompanying information is completely unavailable for check in, luggage drop off or gate information at the departure airport as well as luggage belt information at the arrival airport. Therefore, default average values have been collected. In the entire routing planning system, default values and scheduled time plans require different types of data and services in comparison to real time requests or trip plan updates during the current trip.

Figure 3 depicts a web (desktop) interface where the traveller can schedule in advance the trip considering different mobility options. The look-and-feel is similar to the mobile app, which is mostly used in real time situations.

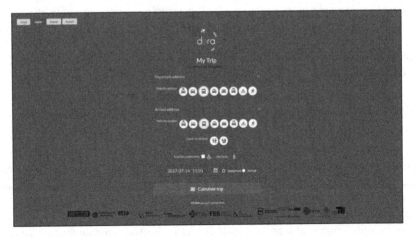

Fig. 3. Trip planning - mobility options in DORA web GUI

2.2 Indoor Module

The indoor part of DORA involves all services that may assist the traveller during the trip inside the airport. From the user perspective, it mainly relates to indoor location and navigation, but there are other services to be considered:

- Indoor maps: indoor maps are an essential part to present a friendly User Interface (UI) during indoor location and navigation modes. In DORA, there has been a conversion process from the initial design (CAD) maps into the resulting vectorial web representation (SHP) that can be offered via a standard OGC WMS (Open Geospatial Consortium Web Maps Service).

- Indoor Data: Indoor data covers all POIs (Points of Interest) available in airports. It includes not only the location of such POIs but also additional information (name, category, business hours, etc.). A key aspect of this service is that it is not static and may change according to changes in airports.
- Monitored data: Some mechanical POIs (elevators, travellators and escalators) and incidents need to be continuously monitored in order not to guide the traveller through a POI that may be out of service. Additionally, waiting times at baggage check-ins and security checkpoints, if available, need to be integrated in order to provide the fastest route to the traveller.
- Trip monitoring: this is an overall service (outdoor, indoor) that permanently monitors whether the traveller will be able to fulfil the trip in time alerting the user in case of incidents that may affect its initial travel plan.

The indoor location service is able to provide an acceptable accurate position inside the airport. DORA utilizes a Commercial Off-The-Shelf (COTS) scheme using available wireless infrastructure as well as mobile phones. An increasing number of airports are equipped with Wi-Fi infrastructure along with BLE (Bluetooth Low Energy) beacons. The indoor location service merges both technologies (readily available in modern mobile phones and tablets) in order to provide a better estimation of the traveller's position. Furthermore, in special areas that have weak or no wireless signals, there is also the possibility to deploy DORA Wi-Fi beacons, a small device easy to install without interfering with other Wi-Fi networks, and provides a stable signal strength. Initial results (with BLE technology and Wi-Fi combined) have shown superior performance compared to the estimation of the internal geolocation plugins available in mobile devices, as depicted in Fig. 4.

Fig. 4. Positioning estimations in different places at TXL airport

The indoor router service provides a path from an origin node (typically the current position of a user) to a destination node according to certain settings. Such settings allow travellers to search for the shortest path in terms of duration or distance. All implied nodes in the path (origin, destination and transitional ones) are georeferenced, and can be displayed in an indoor map. The usage of transitional nodes allows setting up intermediate points along the path that correspond to certain events (e.g. check-in, baggage belt, car rental) a traveller has or wants to perform in the airport.

In order to provide real time navigation, the indoor navigation graph (a set of nodes and weighted edges) is constantly updated according to the obtained real time monitored data. This may cause unavailability of certain nodes during a certain time (e.g. due to dynamic incidents) or that the time to pass a security checkpoint may increase the overall travel time.

The indoor router service provides a complete 'mobility' response considering the transition across different terminals, the use of different POIs, such as mechanical POIs (e.g. travelators) and transitional POIs (e.g. baggage belts and rental car services), as depicted in Fig. 5. Furthermore, the indoor service provides turn-by-turn indications as guiding points in order to guide travellers on their way within airport terminals.

Besides real time navigation, the indoor service also offers scheduled navigation by the time the traveller is planning the trip beforehand (few days in advance). In this case, mechanical POIs are not considered, but predictive waiting time values are used as well as scheduled incidents if they fall under the same timeframe.

The integration of outdoor and indoor router is performed by means of sharing a set of transitional nodes for each airport in order to provide a seamless mobility transition for the traveller. In fact, internal routes within the airport (e.g. shuttles to nearby parking sites) are also covered by the indoor router service.

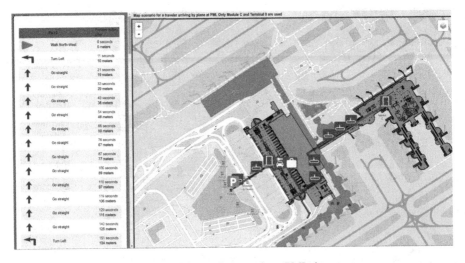

Fig. 5. Routing path example at PMI airport

2.3 Door-to-Door Journey Planner

The core service in the DORA system will be a seamless and integrated Door-to-Door Journey Planner, which integrates existing transport mode specific real-time information services in one single intermodal routing platform for air- and landside transport. This service provides the DORA user with the optimal door-to-door route to a given cost function. For the calculation of the overall route, the Door-to-Door Journey Planner integrates the three DORA routing services for the landside, the terminal and the flight part of the trip. It combines the results of these three routing services to suitable door-to-door route suggestions. The route calculation also takes into account personal mobility preferences so that individual requirements of passengers and specific user groups, for instance, mobility impaired people, travelling families or business travellers, can be met. The Door-to-Door Journey Planner finally provides the route suggestions to the DORA frontends (see Fig. 6).

The route chosen by the user is monitored by the Trip Monitoring Service. In case of disruptions in the public transport network or if there are gate changes or flight delays, the user will be informed about these issues and provided with alternative route suggestions if possible.

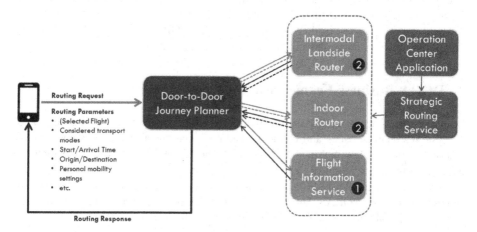

Fig. 6. Door-to-Door Journey Planner

3 DORA Platform Testing Overview

The airports of Berlin (SXF, TXL) and Palma de Mallorca (PMI), respective regional public transports, and passengers (real time end users) are selected for the testing of the DORA platform in realistic environments. The test duration is of one year starting from September 2017 and aimed to recruit at least 500 passengers. These two cities together handled more than 50 million air passengers in 2015 that is roughly equal to 13% of intra-EU flights [4, 8, 9]. There are approximately 12 flights on average per day between both cities, and more than 700,000 passengers in 2015 travelled between these two destinations (Fig. 7).

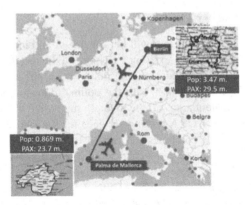

Fig. 7. DORA test locations

A free smartphone application of DORA will be available for android and iOS. This application will be evaluated based on the feedback from user questionnaires, performance of DORA web GUI, and evaluation of Operation Center Application. These tests will help in evaluating the user-friendliness, user interfaces, app performance on different operating systems and devices, functionalities, and improvement ideas. The gathered information will further used to improve the DORA platform and highlighting the results to actors interested in this platform for exploitation.

4 DORA Business Framework

DORA business framework consists of the business model, decisions connected to ecosystem's characteristics and elements, and decisions pertaining to sustained cooperation and innovation within the ecosystem. The framework considers the requirements of a business, mobility trends, and value proposition to each core stakeholder.

A business model illustrates the approaches of an organization to create, deliver and capture value [10]. DORA's business model is founded on the sustainable value creation and fair value distribution among actors with idiosyncratic requirements as well as the competitive strengths of the DORA solution. This basis led to the creation of a three-stage progressive business model, starting from technology licensing through mobility information services to third parties and eventually to an ecosystem management and coordination system. The DORA platform utilizes a modular suite of technologies, which potentially have multiple applications or usability. Licensing of such technological modules and their developments may provide a stream of revenue. The second model based on mobility information services utilizes standardised DORA platform and technologies to offer individual or bundled services to third party app developers through an API. The final model utilizes principles of a business ecosystem to capture, manage, and deliver value using mobility information to several customer segments. A business ecosystem signifies the cooperation and competition among group of organizations, which pooled their capabilities and resources to develop specific solutions for the market [11].

In addition to the business model of the hub firm managing the DORA ecosystem, decisions need to be taken and anticipated that account for the ecosystem development. These decisions will be touching the aspects of ecosystem design, governance and health. Therefore, it is safe to conclude that the framework extends beyond considering the needs of only the hub firm in isolation [12].

The framework also considers the longevity and sustainability of the solution and the ecosystem that supports it by explicitly considering the requirements for continued collaborative innovation at the ecosystem level as well as its components. This requires coordination efforts from the hub firm (Fig. 8).

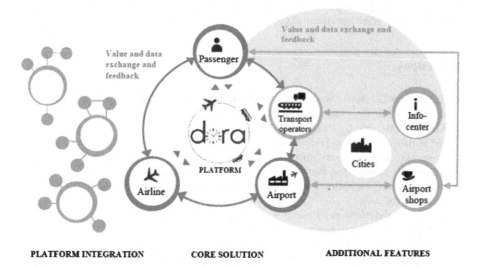

Fig. 8. DORA ecosystem and value flow [13]

DORA business framework consists of core (passengers, airline, airport, and transport operators) and potential extended stakeholders (cities, airports shops, information centre, businesses in shared economy, and technology platforms). The DORA business model offers value creation in multiple ways and distributes value among all the involved stakeholders, which cooperate to manage costs in lieu of information and revenue.

5 Conclusion

The emerging trends and preferences in mobility services driven by technological developments (ICTs, Internet of Things, etc.) and societal requirements (environmental sustainability, sharing economy) demands new solutions and services. The DORA mobility platform integrates on a scalable system various information sources from different mobility operators in order to provide the best multimodal trip recommendation according to user preferences. The management of the trip encompasses both outdoor and indoor parts of a journey and considering the flight between European cities (Berlin and Palma de Mallorca).

The architecture of the DORA system is modular and can be easily transferred, extended or adjusted to meet not only the mobility requirements of any smart city but also the requirements of potential collaborators operating within the city. This open architecture enables a framework encompassing principles of business models and ecosystems that empower the value chain of mobility trends such as Mobility as a Service (MaaS).

Acknowledgements. This research paper was written as a part of the "DORA" project. This project has received funding from the European Union's Horizon 2020 research and innovation programme under grant agreement n° 635885.

References

1. Hollands, R.G.: Will the real smart city please stand up? Intelligent, progressive or entrepreneurial? City **12**(3), 303–320 (2008)
2. Albino, V., Berardi, U., Dangelico, R.M.: Smart cities: definitions, dimensions, performance, and initiatives. J. Urban Technol. **22**(1), 3–21 (2015)
3. Lyons, G.: Getting smart about urban mobility–aligning the paradigms of smart and sustainable. Transp. Res. Part A: Policy Pract. **115**, 4–14 (2016)
4. Air transport statistics. http://ec.europa.eu/eurostat/statistics-explained/index.php/Air_transport_statistics
5. Innovation and Networks Executive Agency, INEA. https://ec.europa.eu/inea/en/horizon-2020/projects/h2020-transport/dora
6. DORA. https://dora-project.eu
7. EC CORDIS: DORA. http://cordis.europa.eu/project/rcn/193356_en.html
8. Record number of passengers at Palma in 2015. https://majorcadailybulletin.com/news/local/2016/01/12/42572/record-number-passengers-palma-2015.html
9. Record year 2015: More than 29.5 million passengers at SXF and TXL. http://www.berlin-airport.de/en/press/press-releases/2016/2016-01-08-verkehrsbericht-rekordjahr-2015/index.php
10. Osterwalder, A., Pigneur, Y.: Business Model Generation: A Handbook for Visionaries, Game Changers, and Challengers. Wiley, Hoboken (2010)
11. Adner, R., Kapoor, R.: Value creation in innovation ecosystems: how the structure of technological interdependence affects firm performance in new technology generations. Strateg. Manag. J. **31**(3), 306–333 (2010)
12. Tura, N., Kutvonen, A., Ritala, P.: Platform design framework: conceptualisation and application. Technol. Anal. Strateg. Manag. (2017). https://doi.org/10.1080/09537325.2017.1390220
13. Tura, N., Kutvonen, A.: Value creation and capture in sustaining platform-based business. In: ISPIM Conference Proceedings. The International Society for Professional Innovation Management, p. 1 (2016)

Author Index

Printed in the United States
By Bookmasters